MW01168413

Sex and the Single Beer Can

Critical Praise

"Walter Brasch is the most informed, opinionated, witty, and delightful commentator on the media scene today."
—John Noonan, *Aspen Media Review*

"Brasch illuminates the dark, and often absurd, sides of society and the media with a style that invites laughter and encourages the reader to look beyond reality to the truth."
—Nancy Baumgartner, *Williamsport Sun-Gazette*

"Brasch keeps the readers entertained not just through his poignant satire, but with his ability to tell a good story first. He always displays a solid point and makes it a fun ride getting there."
—Bill Kohler, *Standard-Journal* newspapers

"A dynamic journalist in the tradition of Andy Rooney."
—Gil Bratcher, WYSP-FM, Philadelphia

"Wonderfully wacked."
—Bob Batz, *Pittsburgh Post-Gazette*

"Entertaining, informative, and fun for everyone."
—Rob Ervin, producer, "The Gary Burbank Show," WLW-AM, Cincinnati

"Walter Brasch has a wonderful way of cutting through the media hype to clarify the 'real' culture and media in a manner that can be understood by all."
—Jack Holcomb, WEEU-AM, Reading, Pa.

"Skewers the American media [in a] satiric romp [that is] hilariously funny and deadly serious. You will never read a newspaper or magazine, listen to the radio, or watch a movie or TV in the same way again."
—Sally Mattero, Koen Books

"A pleasant respite from the overly academic dissections of media events that allows the reader to learn through laughter. A great book of readings for students who are trying to learn how to tell it like it is."
—Dr. Pat Heilman, chair, Department of Journalism, Indiana University of Pennsylvania

"In *Sex and the Single Beer Can,* Walt Brasch is both refreshingly irreverent and irreverently fresh. Little escapes his attention. This is a book about the media, politics, government, war, political incorrectness, religion, the injustice system, the health industry and other corporations, Miss America and, yes, sex and beer. He ties these subjects together under a double-barreled heading of the foibles and strengths of American society. His approach is both biting criticism and healthy respect, both creative imagination and deep understanding. Most of all, *Sex and the Single Beer Can* is a plea for a better media and a better place in which to live.

Because it is broad in its scope, it's also suitable for a variety of journalism/mass communication classes either as a primary or secondary text. It could add important perspectives to classes in ethics, media management, media economics, media and society, media criticism and a variety of other subjects of journalistic interest."

—Dr. Ralph Izard, former associate dean, Manship School of Journalism,
Louisiana State University; professor emeritus and former director,
Scripps School of Journalism, The Ohio University.

"Effective and powerful. In Dave Barryesque fashion, Brasch weaves sights, sounds, feelings, and attitudes into clever, playful, entertaining essays. Brasch provides an excellent guide for students trying to learn the art of writing. For a teacher, this collection offers models of tone, dialogue, description, narrative voice, and point of view."

—Dr. Beverley Pitts, provost and professor of journalism,
Ball State University

"Insightful, readable and tightly written."

—R. Thomas Berner, professor emeritus and
former head, journalism program, Pennsylvania State University

"Outrageous and irreverent, but always on target. Better than most of what passes as commentary in the daily press."

—Dr. Donald Bird, chair, Department of Journalism,
Long Island University

ALSO BY WALTER M. BRASCH

*A Comprehensive Annotated Bibliography
of American Black English*
(with Ila Wales)

*A ZIM Self-Portrait:
The Autobiography of Eugene Zimmerman*

*America's Unpatriotic Acts:
The Federal Government's Violation of
Constitutional and Civil Rights*

Betrayed: Death of an American Newspaper

Black English and the Mass Media

*Brer Rabbit, Uncle Remus, and the 'Cornfield Journalist':
The Tale of Joel Chandler Harris*

Cartoon Monickers: An Insight Into the Animation Industry

Columbia County Place Names

Enquiring Minds and Space Aliens

*Forerunners of Revolution:
Muckrakers and the American Social Conscience*

Sinking the Ship of State: The Presidency of George W. Bush

The Joy of Sax: America During the Bill Clinton Era

*The Press and the State:
Sociohistorical and Contemporary Issues*
(with Dana R. Ulloth)

'Unacceptable": The Federal Response to Hurricane Katrina

With Just Cause: Unionization of the American Journalist

SEX AND THE SINGLE BEER CAN

Probing the Media and American Culture

THIRD EDITION

by Walter M. Brasch

Marqette Books
Spokane, Washington

Cataloging-in-Publication Data
Brasch, Walter M., 1945–
Sex and the single beer can: probing the media and
American culture / Walter M. Brasch -- 3rd ed.
p. cm
ISBN 978-0-922993-98-7 (library binding : alk. paper)

1. Mass media and culture--United States. I. Title
P94.65.U6B73 2009
302.23′0973--dc22

LCCN 2009929770

Marquette Books
5915 S. Regal St., suite 118B
Spokane, Wash. 99223-6970
509-443-7057
www.marquettebooks.com

This book is printed on acid-free paper

PRINTED IN THE UNITED STATES OF AMERICA

Dedication . . .

. . . This book is dedicated to Rosemary Renn Brasch who provided inspiration for many of the columns, and encouragement for all of them. Her ideas and suggestions are always good, her social conscience a model for others to emulate.

. . . And, as always, to my parents—Milton and Helen Haskin Brasch—who provided the inspiration to challenge injustice and stupidity while still being part of the greater community of mankind.

Contents

Information and Society

General Recreation

Persuasion

Acknowledgments

One of the most important influences in American journalism and society is an editor I never met, yet he helped shape my thought process more than any professor or editor. Horace Greeley (1811–1872), editor/publisher of the *New York Tribune* and one of the most influential people in the history of our country, showed just how good journalism can be when it's done well. He believed in integrity, followed a strict code of ethics, and was unafraid to take forceful stands on many unpopular issues. He threw the power of his editorial voice to force the nation to become morally repelled that any person should be held in slavery, eventually convincing Abraham Lincoln to issue the Emancipation Proclamation; by his arguments that all citizens should be allowed to vote, he helped set the base for the nation's 15th Amendment (1870) that gave Blacks the right to vote, and the 19th Amendment (1920) that finally gave women the right to vote. He vigorously supported American agriculture and the working class, even to the point of establishing the first newspaper union and giving shares of his company to the workers. In 1872, Greeley was nominated by both the Liberal Republican and Democratic parties for president, losing to the popular U.S. Grant whose first term was marked by corruption within his staff and cabinet but apparently hadn't touched the President.

During the past two decades, I have worked with dozens of editors who have provided valuable advice and friendship. I am especially pleased to recognize and thank editors Nancy Acitelli, Lorri Auer, Jerry "Politex" Barrett, Wayne Bauer, Peter Becker, Jacob Betz, Chuck Brown, Jim Burchik, Rita Cellucci, Alice Cherbonnier, Carl Christopher, Alexander Cockburn, Bev Conover, Scarlett Corbin, Jeff Cox, Shawnee Culbertson, Jim Curtis, Vivian Daily, Walter Ebmeyer, Robert Fursiewicz, Jim Gallagher, Joe Gandelman, David Gilmartin, Jill Golden, Bekki Guilyard, Andy Heintzelman, Regina Huelman, John Huckaby, Rob Kall, Mark Karlin, Richard Kastelein, Clark Kee, Bill Kohler, Pamela Leavey, Jason Leopold, Rich Lewis, Tom Lowe, Scott Makufka, Leland B. Mather, Holly Matthews, Marie McCandless, Wiley McKellar, John Michaels, Dave Monaghan, John L. Moore, John Morgan, James Oliver, Mitchell Olszak, Jamie Phipps, Harold Prentiss,

Susan Prior, Terri Pyer, Michael Regan, Adam Roufberg, Ray Saul, Charles Schenk, Ed Schreppel, Troy Sellers, Linda Seligson, Sunil Sharma, Joseph P. Shaw, Joe Shea, Jeff St. Clair, Alastair Thompson, Barb Thompson, Jeff Tiedrich, Lynn Vanderberg, Nadeen Walauat, James Wilson, Eileen Winter, and Jack Yoset.

Among journalism professors who helped me not only improve my skills but challenged my intellectual curiosity and understanding of critical social issues were Drs. Earl Conn, Hugh Culbertson, Norman Dohn, Louis Inglehart, Ralph Izard, Lil Junas, John Merrill, Karlen Mooradian, Byron Scott, Chuck Scott, and James Scotton.

Persons who read the manuscript and made valuable suggestions were journalism professors Donald Bird, Pat Heilman, Ralph Izard, and Beverley Pitts.

There aren't many of us who still write satire. Among my contemporaries are Art Buchwald, Joe Glazer, Tom Lehrer, Jim Murray, Michael Moore, Tom Paxton, Mark Russell, the Capitol Steps, Stephen Colbert, and Jon Stewart and the staff of "The Daily Show." They follow in the tradition of master satirists Horace, Juvenal, Rabelais, Cervantes, Moliere, Swift, Addison, Twain, William Gilbert, Sinclair Lewis, and James Thurber. They prove just how powerful humor and satire can be in making people better understand their lives and their society.

Assisting in innumerable ways were Frank Cunniff, Jonathan Gass, and Christine Varner, all of whom provided assistance and intelligent conversation. Special assistance was provided by Ashley Thomas and Alyssa Wernham. MaryJayne Reibsome is not only a good graphics designer, but a *magna cum laude* graduate in journalism who understands the necessity of design as a complement to content, not as its dictator. Her ability to work under intense pressure—and with journalists—is always a most delightful experience.

Librarians Michael Coffta, Bill Frost, and Nancy Weyant helped track facts and numbers that may have led to only a half-sentence here and there but were, nevertheless, important to the stories themselves.

Dr. David Demers founded Marquette Books upon altruistic principles. May his company continue to publish works of substance, and may it prosper.

—WALTER M. BRASCH

Introduction

Hardly anyone admits reading the supermarket tabloids, but someone—other than movie star publicists who "leak" information to the tabloids to create controversy—must be reading them because the combined weekly circulation for the five major weekly newspapers is more than five million.

I read the tabloids.

Usually, I read *The National Enquirer* and, occasionally, one of the other tabs. I seldom read the *Weekly World News* because in the *USA Today* world of splashy color and flashy graphics, the black-and-white *Weekly World News* front page just didn't measure up.

Nevertheless, it was a hot August afternoon when I went into the local air-conditioned supermarket to cool down and, perhaps, to find a few of the 30,000 advertised items that could translate into dinner for six, including two German Shepherds. (The pot-bellied pig and "pound puppies" mix came later.) Apparently, I wasn't the only one that afternoon who figured out how to get free air conditioning. The checkout lines were longer than a politician's lies, so there was only one thing to do.

I guessed I'd be able to read most of the 15 magazines and six newspapers in the "you-got to-buy-this" point-of-purchase racks by the time it was my turn. I also figured that my two sons would have graduated from college, moved out of the house, although still needing weekly "loans," and had children of their own by the time I finished checking out.

Thus, it was in the checkout line that I learned from the *Weekly World News* that a space alien had come to earth in 1992 to advise presidential candidate Bill Clinton. The alien had already advised President George Bush and Reform Party candidate Ross Perot early in the Summer, but had to wait until after the Democratic convention to find out which of the donkeys was going to run.

Being the alert reporter I am, I was upset that a competitor had scooped me on what could have been the most important news of the week. Just a couple of weeks earlier, I had covered the first Clinton–Gore bus tour of America, and no one mentioned anything about an alien. Obviously, the Secret Service had covered it up once again.

That evening, Rick Renn, my nephew from Georgia, called. He had just read the space alien article, and knew I would be interested. The evidence was overwhelming. There were now at least two people who recognized good journalism. It was time to act.

For a few years, usually when I had too much time and not enough sense, I thought about writing a weekly newspaper column. It would be a great catharsis of what I proudly knew to be a warped mind, fertilized now and then by my wife. With only 23,000 other columnists trying to pitch their own catharses, I figured there was room for another 700–800 words a week, especially since newspapers appeared to be desperate for features. How else could anyone explain why they publish gossip columns and capsule summaries of soap operas?

Thus was born "Wanderings," a column that probes a small particle of society. Sometimes it's humor or satire; sometimes it's a wistful essay or a hard-hitting investigative report. Sometimes it looks into politics, the environment, health care, recreation, or whatever needs to be probed that week. About one-fourth of the columns have a media focus. Occasionally, the media are the central focus, sometimes a supporting player, often an extra. But the media are always there; lurking; sometimes playful, sometimes annoying; but most important, informing, persuading, and entertaining.

The skeleton for *Sex and the Single Beer Can* is some of those media-related columns. Most of the columns have been significantly revised for book publication, and new articles have been added. After all, each medium has its own language, structure, and parameters. Besides, newspaper columns stay around a couple of days, while books remain on the shelves, unread, for decades.

No one book—nor for that matter *all* the books currently in print—can explain everything a reader needs to know about the mass media. However, these unique mini-case "slices-of-life" studies that comprise *Sex and the Single Beer Can* do present an understanding not just *of* the media, but of people *in* the media and others affected *by* the media. By understanding the broad perspective presented in *Sex and the Single Beer Can*, it's

3

possible to better understand the nature of mass media. More important, the book should generate discussion and debate, as each reader learns from and then responds to the viewpoints presented.

For more than 30 years I have been proud to be a journalist. I believe in the American media and in the people I am pleased to call my colleagues and friends. For the number of obstacles business, government, and public institutions put into their paths, the media overall do a splendid job. But, like any institution, the media have their problems, some inherent within their own structures. As a media critic and satirist, I have a responsibility to examine the media, hoping that by bringing the excesses and problems to light—something every journalist should strive to do—the media will do an even better job of helping Americans better understand their own lives and issues that affect them.

Read the columns. A few now; a few later. No one will rat you out you if you read them out of order or if you fall asleep while reading the one column that has the secrets of the universe.

Many may wonder where the sex and beer are that the title promises. Like tabloid headlines, book titles are meant to grab readers; more than half of all paperback books are sold on the basis of the title and cover design. In this case, the title is meant to grab two readers—my sons, Jeffrey and Matthew Gerber, wonderful children who enjoy my columns, usually don't read my books, but are fond of what the book title promises. Let them search this book, reading every column until they find what the title promises. For the rest of my readers, there really is a column about sex and beer; more important, it is a key discussion about one part of the media and of the American people.

While reading this book, I hope you find yourself not only informed, entertained, and persuaded, but also mentally stimulated and ready to act against stupidity and injustice. The strength of our society shall always be in the foundation that allows many views to be heard.

"The basis of our governments being the opinion of the people, the very first object should be to keep that right; and were it left to me to decide whether we should have a government without newspapers or newspapers without a government, I should not hesitate a moment to prefer the latter." —Thomas Jefferson, 1787

"I write for the great mass of intelligent, observant, reflecting farmers and mechanics; and, if I succeed in making my positions clearly understood, I do not fear that they will be condemned or rejected."   —Horace Greeley, 1870

The First Amendment

Congress shall make no law respecting an establishment of religion, or prohibiting the free exercise thereof; or abridging the freedom of speech, or of the press, or the right of the people peaceably to assemble, and to petition the Government for a redress of grievances.

~~~~~~~~~~

Only 14% of Americans—and only 57% of journalists—can name freedom of the press as a right in the First Amendment.

43% of Americans believe the press has too much freedom.

22% of Americans believe government should be able to censor the news.

—Survey conducted by the Department of Public Policy, University of Connecticut; May 16, 2005

INFORMATION AND SOCIETY

THE FIRST AMENDMENT

Make Mine Media Rare

People of all political views who become annoyed with the media often demand that reporters be licensed. When challenged that the First Amendment and America's libertarian philosophy forbid governmental bodies to determine who can and can't report the truth as they see it, these critics become even more upset. If reporters wish to be treated as professionals and be taken seriously, they whine, then they should meet certain educational, ethical, and professional standards, like lawyers, teachers, and beauty shop operators, all of whom must be licensed.

And so it was that Sam Frattlebaum, a journalist for 25 years, was the first to be brought before the Court of Ultimate Decisions of the State Board of Journalistic Licensing.

The chairman of the three-member court looked down upon Frattlebaum, and solemnly asked him how he pled to charges of malfeasance, gross negligence, and reckless disregard of the truth.

"Not guilty," came the whimpered response.

"How *dare* you!" thundered the chair. "We wouldn't bring you here unless we were sure you were guilty! Now, stop wasting this court's time, and admit your guilt."

Once again, a frazzled Frattlebaum pleaded not guilty, forcing the chair to present the case.

"By 8 a.m. the day after the murders of Nicole Brown Simpson and that other guy, 3,000 reporters were all over L.A. Where were you?"

"I was in Rwanda covering the massacre of the Tutsis," said Frattlebaum.

"No excuse," snapped the chair. "A half-million dead people in Africa aren't as important as one American football player. Where were you during the preliminary hearings?"

"I had to return to Bosnia to report about a new wave of Serbian ethnic torture."

"Don't you think O.J. is tortured by these charges? During six months of preliminary motions, you again deserted your country."

"Your Honor, I was in Japan to report about the earthquake that killed more than 5,000."

"Did you find any of Judge Ito's relatives? Maybe dig up some sex scandal?" Frattlebaum hung his head. "The record also shows you weren't even in L.A. when the most important trial of the millennium began. A trial that half of all Americans watched breathlessly on television."

"No, sir, I was in West Virginia to interview some hill people for a series about hunger in America."

"Don't you think O.J. gets hungry? What about the prosecutor's favorite foods? What are the judge's eating habits? What's the Defense team's favorite restaurant? Since ice cream is such an important part of the trial, didn't you want to find out its flavor? Was it ice milk or frozen yogurt? How many ounces? What time did it melt? You could have interviewed Ben and Jerry for a feature profile."

"I didn't think that—"

"It's obvious you didn't think," snapped the chair, continuing his inquisition. "You also didn't think about bribing lab techs to reveal the DNA results or badger some cop down in Homicide." He checked his notes, and then smiled. "Ah, I see you did try to meet your responsibilities, and finally made it to Los Angeles."

"Yes, sir, I went there to report about the people left homeless by the floods."

The judge sighed deeply. "I suppose you didn't have the insight to realize that a flood could damage orange trees, lead to higher prices for orange juice, and affect the public's perception of O.J."

"No, Your Honor, but I did get a story about gang killings. Do you know that last week in L.A., 65 people were murdered, 12 of them children?"

8

"I don't care if the whole voter registration list was snuffed. None of them were TV sports commentators and former pro football stars."

"I did try to get to the trial one day," said a sweating Frattlebaum, "but I tripped over TV cables and had to go to the ER."

"Yeah yeah," said the chairman throwing newspapers in the air. "While in the hospital, you didn't steal O.J.'s medical file. When they let you out, did you at least try to interview a juror? Sneak into the O.J. compound for exclusive photos? Plant a hidden microphone in the judge's chambers? Find out if the judge wears briefs or boxers. The public has a right to know!"

"I'm sorry," said Frattlebaum, "but I had to leave to cover the story of a family who were being evicted after they exposed the worst case of corruption in Housing Authority history."

"I suppose you don't even have any insights into the lives, loves, scandals, and homes of Britney Spears, Lindsay Lohan, and Nicole Richey."

"I don't even know who they are!"

"Wait a few years, and you will."

The chair sadly looked at Frattlebaum. "Your failure to report the important stories is killing our credibility. By your own words, you haven't lived up to the standards set by your peers." And with that, he slammed down his gavel, and suspended Frattlebaum's license for one year. "Maybe in that time," said the chair, "you might develop a sense of what's expected of our profession."

Stealing the First Amendment

"Got a match?"

I didn't know where he came from, but there he was, right behind me—as usual. "You know I don't smoke," I told Marshbaum. "Come to think of it, you don't either. What's up?"

"Not much. Planning to roast some marshmallows and hotdogs. Burn some books."

"Marshbaum," I commanded. "You can't burn books."

"Sure I can. All I need is a match. See, first you—"

"Burning books is against everything this country stands for."

"Not when the books are evil."

"Didn't you ever read anything Jefferson wrote? Our country was founded upon the principle that all views must be heard."

"My view is that we're going to burn some books to keep them from causing any more trouble." I could have given Marshbaum a 10-minute lecture about how we no longer have a history of the pre-Columbian Aztec civilization because Spanish conquistadors in the 16th century destroyed the writings of one of the world's greatest civilizations. I could easily have discussed Milton's arguments that those who seek to destroy books destroy reason itself, and that mankind is best served when there is a "free and open encounter" of all ideas. Or, maybe, a few words from philosopher John Stuart Mill who stated, "We can never be sure that the opinion we are endeavoring to stifle is a false opinion, and if we were sure, stifling it would be an evil still." Maybe a little bit of wisdom from Supreme Court Justice Oliver Wendell Holmes who told us that democracy is best served in a "marketplace of ideas." But, I knew Marshbaum was in no mood to hear philosophy. So, all I said was a sarcastic, "I assume you plan to burn everything you think is evil."

"Just Romances. Historical. Contemporary. Anything with a female byline and a cover of a woman with lust in her eyes and a torn dress on her body."

"Why Romances?" I asked.

"Because Romances lead to crime."

"Most Romance novels may be a crime against good writing," I said, "but that's still no reason to burn them."

"It's a case of numbers," said Marshbaum. "The major publishers put out more than 120 Romances a month, three times more than 14 years ago. And, the average romance reader spends about $1,200 a year on the books." He smugly told me he got that information from the Association of American Publishers.

"Wasting money on syrupy nonsense still isn't enough of a reason to burn books," I said.

"Get away from your computer and see what's been happening to America," said Marshbaum. "In the past 14 years, the crime rate has also tripled. It's a direct relationship. Where do you think those bored housewives get all that money to buy Romances? You can't read just one Romance. Once you're hooked, you need 10, 20. You become addicted. You need more and more until one day your whole life is nothing but a long print-enhanced haze of bodice-rippers and sap. Eliminate Romances, and you'll walk safer in Central Park at night."

"That's the most convoluted piece of logic I've ever heard."

"The *Washington Post* says it's OK to burn books," said a smug Marshbaum.

"I doubt the *Post* believes in burning books," I said eruditely. I was eruditely wrong.

"Maybe not books, but newspapers." At more than three dozen college campuses a year, according to the Student Press Law Center, students who disagree with something in the student newspapers steal them from distribution racks, and throw them into dumpsters or burn them. The culprits were often persons who thought of themselves as liberals but whose actions certainly suggest they spent more time in parties than in classes that discussed the founding principles of the nation.

"So, how does all this tie into the *Post*?" I asked.

Marshbaum pulled an editorial from his pocket. "Read this!" he commanded. According to the *Post*, "scooping up copies of publications—whether to send a message or to protest one—may in itself be a form of free speech." It argued that proposed legislation in Maryland to ban the theft of newspapers is "neither a good idea [nor] a worthy pursuit" by the legislature. It was a shocking philosophy from a newspaper that screeches a national emergency almost anytime a governmental agency doesn't yield all its secrets.

"Obviously someone kidnapped all the reporters and editors," I said.

"Obviously the *Post* has divine guidance to determine what is truth," said Marshbaum. "Maybe they have a match I can borrow."

[Against the Post's *advice, the Maryland legislature in 1994 became the first state in the nation to declare it illegal to steal newspapers with the intent to prevent others from reading them.]*

Suspending the First Amendment

The principal of a Bucks County, Pa., high school suspended five students in April 2001 for committing an act that radicals Ben Franklin, Sam Adams, and the Sons of Liberty would have encouraged.

The students didn't threaten anyone, unsheathe any weapons, steal anything, destroy property, openly defy authority, get drunk, or take illicit drugs, all of which were committed by the nation's revolutionaries. What the students did was to create a newspaper.

On four letter-size pages, typeset into three columns a page

11

and sprinkled with shock words, the *Laundromat Liberator* made fun of students, teachers, and administrators at Council Rock High School, Newtown, Pennsylvania. One of the editors said they were trying to emulate the sharp humor and biting satire of *The Onion*, an internet newspaper.

Although the articles fell far short of journalistic excellence, and may have been unnecessarily crude and cruel in the guise of humor, they had an underlining of truth. If no one objected, the newspaper would have been little more than an attempt to be cute, drawing giggles and, hopefully, discussion from the students, while sucking outrage from parents, teachers, and administrators. After a few issues, either the stories would have become sharper, the issues better defined, or the novelty would have worn away, and the editors would have looked at other ways to tap their curious and creative minds.

But, the principal, not unlike most school administrators, confiscated the 100 or so copies of the newspaper, and then suspended the students for five days because of the "emotional impact" that teasing has upon students. He said he was sensitive to what had recently happened in Santee, Calif., when a 15-year-old student, possibly upset by being the brunt of random high school teasing, killed two fellow students and wounded 13 others. The case for suspension, said the principal, was merely "a safety issue." The district superintendent claimed the seizure and suspension was "a disciplinary matter."

Student reaction, according to one of the editors, was "they thought our paper was hilarious. Teacher reaction was, 'you guys did a very bad thing. Do you have any left that I can see?'"

Reacting to questions about the seizure and subsequent suspension, the principal lashed out that media coverage was "a disservice to kids." He argued, "Anger builds [and] you are going to create more interest in what was in it, and what was in it was hurtful."

To further the assault upon the rights of free speech, or a public school's morbid fear of controversy, the local chapter of the National Honor Society began an investigation "to get information and references" that could have led to the expulsion of four of the five editors who were Society members. Two of the students were at the top of their 902-student senior class; a third was ranked in the top 5 percent; one was in the top 20 percent. Fortunately for the school, which would have faced even more media coverage had it expelled students from an honor society, the investigation fizzled. The sanctioned student newspaper, *The Indianite*, never published anything about the alternative newspaper, the students, or the Honor Society investigation.

Those who believe the right way to stop commentary, even "hurtful" commentary, is to silence it and punish the editors have misunderstood their own civics lessons.

The nation's Founding Fathers were well aware of John Milton's somewhat "radical" arguments in Parliament in 1644 that those who seek to destroy writing destroy reason itself, and that mankind is best served when there is a "free and open encounter" of all ideas—even "hurtful" ones. They were also aware of Lord Blackstone's strong arguments against prior restraint of free speech by the government. Influenced by the views of Milton, Blackstone, and others, Thomas Jefferson pushed for the First Amendment to assure freedom of religion, speech, the press, and the right of the people not only to peacefully assemble and raise whatever issues they wished, but also to petition the government for a "redress of grievances."

Ben Franklin, working on his brother's newspaper, snuck articles into Boston's *New England Courant*. Later, under his own name and a series of aliases, in his own paper, *The Pennsylvania Gazette*, published less than 25 miles from what became the site of Council Rock High School, he vigorously challenged conventional authority and the British government. Many of Franklin's articles were vicious attacks upon individuals and the government. Franklin would later write, "Without Freedom of Thought, there can be no such Thing as Wisdom; and no such Thing as publick Liberty, without Freedom of Speech." Sam Adams, Benjamin Edes, John Gill, and other Radicals, a minority in the Colonies even in 1776, used newspapers to unify the people and push for the Revolution. Their words were often hurtful and untrue. Even after the Revolution, newspapers backing Thomas Jefferson and the Anti-Federalists maliciously attacked Washington, Adams, Hamilton, and Madison—and papers backing the Federalists were equally vicious in attacks upon Jefferson. But, as much as each of the Founding Fathers felt the sting of criticism, even if unfairly, they understood why there had to be a free press.

During the mid-nineteenth century, philosopher John Stuart Mill stated, "We can never be sure that the opinion we are endeavoring to stifle is a false opinion, and if we were sure, sti-

13

fling it would be an evil still." Supreme Court Justice Oliver Wendell Holmes told us democracy is best served in a "marketplace of ideas." Justice Charles Evans Hughes in 1925 argued, "When we lose the right to be different, we lose the privilege to be free." Justice William O. Douglas argued, "Restriction of free thought and free speech is the most dangerous of all subversions. It is the one un-American act that could most easily defeat us."

First Amendment freedoms, said Supreme Court Justice Anthony M. Kennedy, "are most in danger when the government seeks to control thought or to justify its laws for that impermissible end. The right to think is the beginning of freedom, and speech must be protected from the government because speech is the beginning of thought."

At the time the *Laundromat Liberator* was being suppressed, the school administration should have known of a ruling by Judge Lowell A. Reed Jr., of the U.S. District Court for the Eastern District of Pennsylvania. In the 1998 case of the *ACLU v. Reno*, Judge Reed suggested, "perhaps we do the minors of this country harm if First Amendment protections, which they will with age inherit fully, are chipped away in the name of their protection."

Individuals have recourse against malicious falsehood through libel laws, the community through ever-tightening standards of obscenity and pornography laws. And, all of the courts, interpreting the intent of those who created our Constitution, agree that the recourse to views and writings we disagree with is through more free speech, not less.

Perhaps, instead of thinking the Constitution doesn't apply to public high schools, school administrators could have brought in writers and journalists to discuss satire, the vital role that alternative and underground newspapers play in America, and how to better craft publications to achieve the impact student writer–editors might desire while respecting the rights of their readers. But, a thick-headed administration, no matter how "humane" it thought its reasons were, saw free speech and an

~~~~~~~~

"If large numbers of people believe in freedom of speech, there will be freedom of speech, even if the law forbids it. But if public opinion is sluggish, inconvenient minorities will be persecuted, even if laws exist to protect them."—George Orwell, 1945 unfettered press not as a right, but as an evil.

Perhaps, more than two centuries after the Revolution, school administrators may soon understand why our Founding Fathers made sure we were a republic founded upon a base of ideas and public discussion, not a kingdom of fear and tyranny.

Conservative Group Is Right: Free Speech Is Not a Political Issue

The Sunbird Conservatives, a student group, put out some pro-McCain campaign literature at a recruiting table at Fresno Pacific University in September 2008.

Seemed innocent enough. The conservatives weren't harassing anyone, nor were they blocking any sidewalks.

But, administrators at this Christian-based college didn't like it. A dean told the students to either remove the McCain literature or to agree to what he said was university policy to present both sides. The dean correctly noted that the First Amendment applies only to government intrusion. A private university, unlike a public university, may curtail any free speech it wants.

The students still argued "free speech rights." Enter the provost, head of academic affairs at the university. She reaffirmed the dean's demands. One of the members shouted: "free speech" at her. They challenged her, arguing that for a political organization to present both views would defy common sense. The provost's response, according to the conservative Leadership Institute, was "Shut up! I'm the provost. That is disrespectful."

The students were warned if they didn't comply with the administrators' demands, they would be restricted in future activities on campus.

The Founding Fathers wanted all views to be heard. Channeling the revolutionary political philosophy of poet John Milton and judge Lord Blackstone, they believed that mankind is rational, and if all the facts were available, mankind would find the truth. That became the basis of the First Amendment.

Now, the twist is that the Fresno Pacific administrators were wrong. Their own university actually believes that all views should be allowed, as long as there is the opportunity for opposing views. It does not require one organization to put out all views.

15

But, the Fresno Pacific administrators are also right. A private university can do what it wants to do. It can encourage or restrict free speech. Except in California.

California is the only state that extends the First Amendment to private colleges, which should encourage, not restrict, freedom of expression.

This means that the wishes of the Founding Fathers have been extended into California. Disregard the fact that both conservatives and liberals actively try to restrict free speech rights of others. Disregard the reality that conservatives who want to keep government out of our lives used both the Constitution and state law to underscore their right to distribute political literature.

It's time for all states to enact legislation to assure that the principles of the nation, and especially the rights of free expression, are extended to all sectors, both public *and* private.

Throwing Out the First Amendment

The American revolution was built upon a libertarian foundation that all views, even ones that may be blatantly stupid or racist, must be heard. In *The Areopagitica* (1644), which Thomas Jefferson freely quoted from, John Milton had written that truth and falsehood must be allowed to compete in a free and open encounter, and that truth will eventually be known. Two centuries later, John Stuart Mill in *On Liberty* (1859) reaffirmed the libertarian philosophy when he pointed out, "We can never be sure that the opinion we are endeavoring to stifle is a false opinion; and if we were sure, stifling it would be an evil still." A few years after that, Supreme Court Justice Oliver Wendell Holmes told us that democracy is best served in a "marketplace of ideas." Even outrageous ones. Even racist and stupid ones. But, for most of us, the First Amendment is little more than words we barely recognize.

On the morning of June 12, 1996, a three-judge federal panel in Philadelphia issued a 175-page decision that declared the Communications Decency Act unconstitutional. That Act would have imposed severe restrictions upon Internet content. "The strength of our liberty depends upon the chaos and cacophony of the unfettered speech the First Amendment protects," wrote Judge Stephen Dalzell.

That afternoon, the owners of Major League Baseball,

apparently having not read the First Amendment, declared the opinions of Cincinnati Reds owner Marge Schott was an embarrassment, and ordered her suspended from day-to-day operations for two and one-half years. The sanction came three years after they had fined her $25,000 and banned her for a year following remarks that most people would label as anti-Semitic and racist. In an ESPN interview, she defended Hitler as someone who at the beginning of his career helped the people and accomplished much, although she did say he later "went too far." In a *Sports Illustrated* interview she insulted Asians, working women, and others. On opening day of the season, after umpire John McSherry died at the plate and the game was postponed, Schott told the *Cincinnati Enquirer,* "I feel cheated. This stuff isn't supposed to happen to us here."

Schott's latest suspension, baseball commissioner Bud Selig told the media, was the "result of a succession of events," including her tight-fisted financial control and her nauseous beliefs that "quite frankly were not in anyone's best interest."

Four years later, Major League Baseball was still suppressing free speech. John Rocker, a 6-foot-4, 225 pound Atlanta Braves pitcher, said he didn't like foreigners, minorities, gays, and just about anyone who doesn't look, act, or think like he does.

He called a Black teammate a "fat monkey," and said Asian women are bad drivers. He said he would quit baseball before he would allow himself to be traded to a New York team because he didn't want to take the subway to work, "looking like you're [riding through] Beirut next to some kid with purple hair next to some queer with AIDS right next to some dude who just got out of jail for the fourth time right next to some 20-year-old mom with four kids."

His views, brewed in a cauldron of ignorance and stupidity, aren't any different from those of millions of Americans. He said them before, to friends, fans, teammates and, maybe, even a few sports writers. Unfortunately, this time John Rocker said them to a reporter for *Sports Illustrated* who included it in a four-page spread at the back of the 3.3 million-circulation magazine.

"I'm not a racist or prejudiced person," Rocker claimed, "but certain people bother me." One of those people was baseball commissioner Bud Selig.

"Mr. Rocker's recent remarks [are] reprehensible and completely inexcusable," said Selig who in January 2000 ordered Rocker to undergo psychological tests.

17

Punishment for Rocker's opinions were warranted, chimed in Atlanta Braves president Stan Kasten. The Players Association, with one-fifth of its members foreign-born and about 40 percent Black or Hispanic, didn't object.

Under pressure from Management, Rocker apologized. But, Major League Baseball suspended him for having views it didn't consider to be acceptable—at least in public.

This, of course, is the same sport that banned Blacks and Hispanics from its fields for more than a half-century, which didn't allow a Black to be a manager for another three decades, which still bans women, and for which the owners were at least half the reason why there was a strike in 1994. But, baseball officials think they, like private enterprise, can dictate what their employees think and say.

"Purists" rightfully claim that the First Amendment applies only to governmental infringement, and that private enterprise, such as Major League Baseball, can do what it wants. However, Major League Baseball enjoys a special status—cities float municipal bonds for stadiums and then issue eminent domain orders to tear away houses and lots; and the federal government has waived anti-trust action against a sport that reeks of blatant disregard of the nation's laws against monopolies. Because baseball willingly accepts extensive government assistance, it should be compelled to adhere to the tenets of the First Amendment.

In 1927, Supreme Court Justice Louis Brandeis, in *Whitney v. California*, wrote that "the remedy to be applied [to evil and falsehood] is more [free] speech, not enforced silence."

Perhaps Rocker and Schott, as well as those justifiably outraged by their opinions, will one day sit down to listen to each other, and realize that education not gags should be the solution for ignorance. Major League Baseball once silenced those who spoke out for integration. It was wrong then. It is wrong now.

Killing Reason Itself:
The Argument Against Book Banning

America's two most popular authors of the late nineteenth century could never imagine their most famous works would be among the nation's most banned books.

Throughout the country, school districts and libraries, intimidated by vocal minorities of parents and special interest groups, many of whom haven't even read the books they are protesting, have banned Mark Twain's *The Adventures of Huckleberry Finn* and Joel Chandler Harris's Uncle Remus/Brer Rabbit tales as racist. *Huckleberry Finn,* after decades as the most banned book in America because of the ideas Twain presented, is now the fifth most banned book of the past decade, according to the American Library Association (ALA).

The book-banners succeeded with Harris. Today, few Americans know about the folktales; even fewer know Harris's name, making him so irrelevant that the ALA's current book-banning list doesn't even include any of his works.

Mark Twain, a fierce abolitionist and political gadfly who freely challenged authority, would have been amused that conservatives challenge the book for not-so-subtly showing that it is acceptable not only to hold certain American institutions up to ridicule but to challenge rules and regulations, both written and unwritten—and that liberal organizations attack the book for what they believe is the use of racist language and stereotypes. Disregarding that *Huckleberry Finn* is regarded by most literary critics as the greatest American novel, and that the Uncle Remus/Brer Rabbit tales were the most accurate literary representation of Black folklore and language of the Antebellum and Reconstruction eras, the critics of the past three decades mistakenly cite the use of the word "nigger" and the American Black English dialogue as "proof" the books are racist. But, these critics overlook the reality that Twain was a vocal abolitionist who forcefully attacked racism and miscegenation laws. Twain, in fact, used the term "nigger" to show just how racist it was, calling Huck's friend Nigger Jim, which Twain made clear was a name given by Whites.

During the latter two decades of the 19th century, Harris was the nation's second most popular writer, just behind Twain. Even two decades after Harris's death in 1908, a survey of high school and college literature teachers ranked the Uncle Remus/Brer Rabbit tales fifth among American literature.

Attacks on Uncle Remus:

By the second half of the 20th century, the critics attacked Harris for what they believed were racist portrayals in his books that featured Uncle Remus telling African folktales to the plantation owner's son. These critics undoubtedly weren't aware that Harris, associate editor and chief editorial writer of the *Atlanta Constitution* for almost 25 years, was one of the nation's most important voices to speak out for human rights and reconciliation during the Reconstruction and post-Reconstruction eras. They also don't understand that Remus, a teacher, is actually one of literature's strongest portrayals of a complex character, a slave only by a law which couldn't imprison his mind. More importantly, they don't understand that the trickster Brer Rabbit, the apparently weaker character who uses cunning and mental agility to overcome stupidity and undaunted strength positioned against him, is really an allegorical depiction of the American Black.

Some well-meaning critics also believe the Black English in both Twain's and Harris's works is blatantly racist, an "inferior" language spoken by "darkies," minstrels, and the ignorant. But, linguists have long recognized that the literary depiction of Black English in both Twain's and Harris's works are accurate representations of the syntax, phonology, and lexicon of the Niger–Congo West African language family brought to America during the two centuries that slavery was legal.

In *Nights With Uncle Remus* (1883), Harris correctly noted that the tales and language were so intertwined that to present them any other way would "rob them of everything that gives them vitality."

The arguments against the works of Twain and Harris are nothing short of "political correctness" gone wrong and stomping upon historical accuracy.

Much of the attack upon Harris probably originated with Walt Disney's *Song of the South* (1946), a syrupy animation and live-action portrayal of the plantation era. Within a decade, at the beginning of the Civil Rights era, Harris and his works would be attacked, usually by persons who hadn't read his tales and knew almost nothing about their author but had seen the Disney film.

In one of the greatest slaps to Harris's memory, the board of trustees of the Atlantic Public Library in 1982 ordered the name of the Uncle Remus Branch to be changed to the West End Branch. Four years later, the Savannah–Chatham County School District banned a theatrical production of *Br'er Rabbit's Big Secret*. The acclaimed Savannah Theatre Company had scheduled the play, with Black actors in lead roles, for second graders; district administrators, objecting to the "inappropriate dialect," banned it after the first of its scheduled 10 performances. The director said school officials told him the tar-baby scene "might be seen as a racial slur."

Alice Walker—winner of the Pulitzer Prize for fiction in 1983 for *The Color Purple*—is one of Harris's most vocal critics. Walker, born in Harris's birthplace of Eatonton, Ga., grew up hearing the Brer Rabbit stories. Harris, said Walker, "stole a good part of my heritage [by making me] feel ashamed" of it. Ironically, *The Color Purple* is on the American Library Association's list as the 17th most challenged book of the past decade. More than 8,500 challenges to various books between 1990 and 2005 were reported to the ALA; as the nation's primary organization for librarians frequently points out, the actual number is likely to be significantly higher than that.

Of the ALA list of the 100 most challenged books of the first decade of the 21st century, eight of the top ten banned books were books written for children. J. K. Rowling's *Harry Potter* series, which consistently led the best-sellers lists, was also the most banned book since 1999. Innumerable individuals and school boards believe that the series is satanic literature, and that "witchcraft" and magic are evil, that neither are acceptable to the "established," more "mainstream" Christian religions. Rowling shouldn't feel ostracized by those who believe there is only one true religion—during the past two centuries, people have also suggested banning the stories of Rapunzel, Sleeping Beauty, Hansel and Gretel, and the Wizard of Oz series, all of which have witches.

Other children's books that lead the ALA list of banned books are Phyllis Reynolds Naylor's *Alice* series (no. 2), Robert Cormier's *The Chocolate War* (No. 3), Alvin Schwartz's *Scary Stories* series (no. 6), Walter Dean Myers' *Fallen Angels* (no. 7), Robie Harris' *It's Perfectly Normal* (no. 8), Justin Richardson and Peter Parnell's *And Tango Makes Three* (no. 9), and Dav Pilkey's *Captain Underpants* (no. 10). More than three-fourths of the banned books on the ALA list were written for children, with books about social issues leading the list. Among the more popular books banned were five critically-acclaimed books for young adults written by Judy Blume.

Among literary classics that have been challenged and banned are John Steinbeck's *Of Mice and Men* (no. 4), Maya Angelou's *I Know Why the Caged Bird Sings* (no. 5), Mark Twain's The Adventures of Huckleberry Finn (no. 11), Alice Walker's *The Color Purple* (no. 14), J.D. Salinger's *The Catcher in the Rye* (no. 19), Harper Lee's *To Kill a Mockingbird* (no. 23), Toni Morrison's *Beloved* (no. 24), Aldous Huxley's *Brave New World* (no. 37), Kurt Vonnegut's *Slaughterhouse Five* (no.

45), Ken Kesey's *One Flew Ouwer the Cuckoo's Nest* (no. 63), Ray Bradbury's *Fahrenheir 451* (no. 72), and Toni Morrison's *Song of Solomon* (no. 76). Daniel Keyes' *Flowers for Algernon*, which was the 47th most banned book in the 1990s, and which became the hit movie, *Charley,* did not make the current list; neither did William Golding's *Lord of the Flies* (no. 70), and Richard Wright's *Native Son* (no. 71).

The list of banned books of the past decade is nowhere near the list of books banned during the past two centuries. The primary antagonist has been the U.S. government itself. During the antebellum era, beginning in the 1830s with the Andrew Jackson administration, the Post Office forbid abolitionist publications from being mailed into the South; the fact that Jackson was from Tennessee was not lost upon the abolitionists who made numerous attempts to sneak their publications into the South. In the late 19th century, the Post Office employed Anthony Comstock to determine which publications should be suppressed. For about a decade after World War I, the Post Office seized copies of the James Joyce classic, *Ulysses.* Among others prohibited during the past century have been Aristophanes' *Lysistrata* and Chaucer's *Canterbury Tales.*

Although there are dozens of excuses to ban a book, the most "popular" reasons seem to be what some critics claim to be for obscene language or sexual content—the Tarzan series was frequently banned during the 1920s because some morally-indignant pure-bloods believed it was a sin for Tarzan and Jane to have sex without marriage. However, the one reason that threads its way through most book banning, even when other reasons are claimed, is that the book challenges authority, or features a character who is perceived as "different," who may even give readers ideas that many see as "dangerous." Both Huck Finn and Uncle Remus, in their own way, challenged authority. One of the most dangerous ideas was proposed in Charles Darwin's *Origin of Species* (1859) which opposed the creationist theory. The mere thought that there could be something known as evolution was so repulsive and heretical that Tennessee, as well as numerous other governmental jurisdictions, banned the book. The issue of censorship, as well as creationism vs. evolution, erupted in the Scopes Trial in 1925 that drew national attention—and international condemnation. *Inherit the Wind*, a 1955 play by Jerome Lawrence and Robert Edwin Lee, became the basis of a 1960 film, and three subsequent made-for-TV films.

In 1644, John Milton, speaking before Parliament to eliminate the licensing of books, declared, "As good almost kill a man as kill a good book; who kills a man kills a reasonable creature [in] God's image; but he who destroys a good book kills reason itself."

Milton's words became a vital part of the base for the libertarian revolution that led to the formation of the United States and the First Amendment to its Constitution. *Should not be*

Bottom line: books are speech, reason, opinion, etc.
taken from us.

Stupid Decisions:
Self-Censorship in America

The author and the publisher could agree upon only one thing—neither of them wanted 50,000 copies of the author's book to be in a 146,000 square foot warehouse in Williamsport, Pennsylvania.

Michael Moore, the author, wanted the publisher to start distributing *Stupid White Men and Other Excuses for the State of the Nation*. ReganBooks, the publisher, wanted to pulp them.

What ReganBooks tried to do to Moore's book may be typical of what has happened to the industry that has often been accused of sacrificing much of its editorial integrity to the business and marketing sides, and continues to publish "safe" books that don't attack establishment values.

Copies of *Stupid White Men* were ready for distribution when terrorists struck America on Sept. 11, 2001. Moore, an anti-establishment social issues and media critic who is adept at using the media to promote his views, had first earned a reputation with his playful film, *Roger and Me*, which looked at corporate greed. He followed that up with a best-seller *Downsize This!* (1996); a brief television series, *TV Nation*; and subsequent "reveal-all" about that series, *Adventures in a TV Nation* (1998). In October 2002, he released *Bowling for Columbine*, a two hour documentary about America's gun culture.

But now, in the days after the terrorist attacks of 9/11, ReganBooks thought Moore's criticism of the Bush–Cheney Administration was not only irreverent but also inappropriate and unpatriotic. In one of publishing's much-too-common intertangling alliances, ReganBooks is an imprint of megapublisher HarperCollins, which less than two years before stopping distribution of *Stupid White Men* had published George W. Bush's political memoir, *A Charge to Keep*. HarperCollins itself is a part of News America, a major division of Rupert Murdoch's News Corporation conglomerate which also owns the FOX TV network. Roger Ailes, FOX's news chair, was a senior advisor to former President George H. W. Bush. On Election Night 2000, John Ellis, first cousin of George W. Bush and Florida Gov. "Jeb" Bush, was a FOX news consultant and on-air political analyst; in addition to analyzing the election, Ellis relayed information in several private telephone conversations to his cousins.

Perhaps none of the alliances entered into ReganBook's decisions about *Stupid White Men*. But, Moore later told *Publishers Weekly* the company had wanted him to rewrite up to half of the book, and change the title and cover art. ReganBooks refuses to discuss what it said to Moore, or to answer numerous questions about why it.didn't want to release the book. Moore says he agreed to a title change and a revision of the cover design. He didn't agree to lose his journalistic integrity. *Self Censorship*

In the book, Moore opened with an attack upon how George W. Bush had become president at the beginning of 2001, although Al Gore received over a half-million more votes in the popular election. He called Bush a "crook" and a "Thief-in-Chief" for having stolen the election by the Supreme Court's 5–4 vote along political lines to uphold the official, but highly controversial, election results in problem-plagued Florida, a state in which Bush's younger brother was governor and the secretary of state were co-chairs of the Bush for President committee. The Supreme Court decision several weeks after the election had given Bush just enough electoral votes for the victory. "We are now finally no better than a backwater banana republic," Moore declared. In other chapters, Moore attacked racism, corporate business practices, those who presided over the recent economic, technological, and environmental decline, the media obsession with sex scandals, and even Bill Clinton, a Democrat whom he called one of the best Republican presidents the country ever had.

After a couple of months of discussions, Moore said that ReganBooks told him it had decided to pulp the warehoused copies; the publisher would allow rights to revert to him after a year. As Moore knew, a year's delay would have killed the essence of the book. He proposed to buy the 50,000 copies, and then sell them himself; the publisher, said Moore, refused. ReganBooks refused to say why it wouldn't allow the author to

24

buy the copies, or why it had planned to kill it.

"We had considered a number of options," said corporate spokesperson Lisa Herling; she refused to say what those options were. Whatever they were, apparently the only viable one the publisher was comfortable with was a rewrite. The book was almost dead.

The day after discussions apparently ended in early December, Moore spoke to the New Jersey Citizen Action Coalition, a friendly audience. What he hadn't counted on was support from a source that is vigorous in First Amendment issues.

"This was all about a publisher censoring itself on a book because it may have been politically intimidated," said Ann Sparanese of the Englewood (New Jersey) Public Library; she had been at the Coalition's meeting as the delegate from the Bergen County Central Trade and Labor Council. Two days later, she e-mailed letters to members of the Social Responsibilities Roundtable of the American Library Association (ALA) and to the Progressive Librarians Guild. "My colleagues apparently picked up the ball and ran with it," said Sparanese. The librarians began writing each other and the publisher. And, they did even more—they placed orders.

Within days, as Moore later told *Publishers Weekly*, Regan Books was receiving "hundreds of letters a day from angry librarians. . . . That's one group you don't want to mess with." The publisher had already sacrificed its editorial integrity when it thought dissent wasn't "appropriate"—and that it would be subject to attacks for releasing the title, and would probably lose sales not only for *Stupid White Men* but possibly other titles as well. But, now there were those letters of support—and all those book orders. Now, *that* was something to reconsider!

About the same time the librarians were mounting their campaign, Jane Friedman, chief executive officer of Harper Collins, asked a question. Moore believes Friedman "was probably a bit of a hero in all this, saying 'Why are we distancing ourselves from something we approved of and worked on?'"

In mid-December 2001, ReganBooks agreed to release *Stupid White Men* without changes. ReganBooks claims the librarians had minimal impact. "We did not receive a lot of comment from librarians, not a lot of feedback from outside," Herling claimed. She said the decision to publish was "made by a team of people"—she refused to identify who was on that team—"and certainly not because of feedback from outside." Was Jane Friedman part of that team? "The team made the decision," said the corporate spokesperson firmly.

In February 2002, Moore began a 12-city author tour, coupled with several appearances on national TV shows to promote the title. The controversy helped assure exposure and eventual sales. Within weeks, HarperCollins even featured *Stupid White Men* on its website home page. Speaking to the ALA annual meeting in June 2002, Moore again forcefully noted that the librarians' campaign was a major reason ReganBooks decided to release *Stupid White Men,* and directly stated that librarians are "the most important public servant in a democracy." Within six months of distribution, there were more than 500,000 sales, making the book a surprise run-away best-seller.

What ReganBooks did to *Stupid White Men* isn't censorship since the First Amendment applies only to governmental interference not to what private companies do. But, the government doesn't need to worry about interfering when so many private companies, especially media conglomerates, seem willing to self-censor themselves out of greed or fear. "Americans are apt to quickly spot and automatically distrust government efforts to impose prior restraint," wrote media analyst Norman Solomon in March 2000, "but what about the implicit constraints imposed by the hierarchies of enormous media corporations— and internalized by employees before overt conflicts develop?"

Self-censorship is the "most corrosive and insidious form of censorship," said Aidan White, general secretary of the International Federation of Journalists. He attributed much of self-censorship to journalists "living and working in conditions of fear, poverty or employment insecurity."

Self-censorship begins when writers submit articles, book manuscripts, and scripts to editors and producers who reject them or demand modifications. Often, there are good reasons. In the print media, it's known as editing; in television and film, it's known as "notes," which could come from any of several dozen places, including executives whose only creative thought may have been to add non-dairy creamer to their cappuccino. Many times, rejection is based upon personal beliefs and news values of the editors, disguised by such comments as "We regret that your manuscript doesn't meet our needs at the present time" or "This area doesn't seem to work." Whatever the reasons agents, editors, and producers have, after enough rejections or requests to delete or modify portions of a manuscript, writers learn what is and isn't acceptable. Soon, writers become

26

socialized to the system, adapting to the wishes of editors.

Self-censorship extends to lunches and dinner receptions, gyms and golf courses, where writers, agents, editors, and owners mix to discuss everything from other writers, agents, editors, and owners to the world economy. Those who travel in the "power circles" of their sources learn and internalize the norms, no matter how independent they believe they are; those who maintain their independence, or can't afford to be a part of a power Felite, are forever knocking on doors that never open.

Self-censorship for editors and producers is the next level of self-restraint. Often, they impose standards they think their own editors, publishers, vice-presidents, and owners might impose, even if nothing was ever said. Vice-presidents and publishers don't need to say anything—their subordinates figure it out. An author who proposes a book attacking book publishing conglomerates probably won't get a warm response from either conglomerates or independents, some of whom may need conglomerates for distribution. Nor is it likely authors will investigate and report about perfidious publishers or supercilious book reviewers, all of whom could be useful to an author who sheds what dignity and integrity he or she may have left in order to become published and, thus, little more than a pawn in the industry.

One leading agent told an author one of the main reasons she couldn't represent his next manuscript was because he wrote about some "dirty little secrets" in the publishing industry— among those "secrets" was a minor sub-plot about a leading character who didn't want to go on author promotion tours, the backbone of many front-list titles. However, greed trumps publisher principles—if John Grisham, Stephen King, or Nora Roberts wrote about a "secret," publishers would undoubtedly defer to the anticipated income rather than any principles they may or may not have.

A reporter for a large Iowa newspaper says he was given permission and a budget to research repair practices among auto dealers and service stations, but his article was spiked when the publisher declared the two-part series wasn't objective since he didn't go to all of the repair shops in town; when the reporter said he could do that, the publisher then decided there wasn't enough money in the budget for the investigation of shady repair practices among some of the advertisers. The experiences of the book author and the newspaper reporter aren't unique.

Fear and cowardice, sometimes sprinkled with a dose of familiarity with the source, often keep even good writers from investigating and reporting about America's institutions—or even about supercilious book reviewers and perfidious publishers.

About one-third of journalists say that stories are avoided because of possible conflicts with the business interests of their employers or advertisers, according to a poll conducted in 2000 by the Pew Research Center and the *Columbia Journalism Review*. About one-third of local newspaper journalists also reported they "softened the tone" of a story to meet what they believed was the interest of their employer. Even if a medium is vigorous in pursuing the truth, even allowing freedom for "in-your-face" reporters and writers, a web of unwritten edicts restricts writing and publishing media analysis and commentary; it may be acceptable to attack others but don't look inside our own houses, many editors and news directors silently tell their staffs.

For every Michael Moore book that gets accepted by a publisher, hundreds are rejected, often for reasons no writer ever hears but are whispered in the silence of corporate offices.

"[I]t's not just the books under fire now that worry me," said best-selling author Judy Blume whose books are often among those that are most challenged by self-proclaimed moralist-censors, "it is the books that will never be written. The books that will never be read. And all due to the fear of censorship."

Michael Moore, still believing he is an independent journalist, is now under contract to the media conglomerate AOL Time Warner which, *Publishers Weekly* reports, paid $3 million for the rights to his next two books. ReganBooks, said Herling, "declined to review" Moore's forthcoming manuscripts.

In a final irony to the story of *Stupid White Men*, the distribution center for HarperCollins in Williamsport, Pa., is less than a half-mile from Brodart, one of the nation's largest suppliers to libraries.

The Fiction Behind National Security: America's Unpatriotic Act

Between a diner and an empty store that once housed a shoe store, video store, and tanning salon, in a small strip mall in Bloomsburg, Pa., was Friends-in-Mind, an independent bookstore that closed in 2008.

On the first floor were more than 10,000 books on more than 1,200 running feet of shelves that created aisles only about three feet wide. On top of the shelves were stacks of 10, 15, even 20 more books. On the floor were hundreds more, stacked spine out three- or four-feet high. There were books in metal racks, drawers, and on counters. It's was almost impossible to walk through the aisles without bumping into a pile in the 1,000-square foot store. In the basement, in reserve, were 2,000 more books.

"Sometimes I ordered four or five copies of a title, but often I only ordered one copy, but I wanted to have whatever my customers wanted," says owner Arline Johnson who founded the store in 1976 after working almost two decades as a clinical psychologist and teacher. Unlike the chain stores with magazine and newspaper racks, wide aisles, track lighting, and even a coffee shop, Friends-in-Mind had only books and some greeting cards. Also unlike the chain stores with large budgets for space and promotion to attract hundreds of customers a day, Johnson said she saw "on a real good day" maybe 25 or 30 people; often she saw fewer than a dozen.

In September 1984, she saw someone she didn't want to see. A week after the Naval Institute Press shipped three copies of Tom Clancy's cold war thriller, *The Hunt for Red October*, the FBI showed up. The FBI, which apparently got the information from the publisher, "wanted to know where the books were and who purchased them," says Johnson. She says she told the two men that she couldn't remember to whom she sold two of the copies, but acknowledged she sent one copy to her cousin, who had served aboard a nuclear submarine, "and had all kinds of clearances." Johnson says she wasn't pleased about the interrogation—"and my cousin certainly wasn't happy about anyone checking on what he was reading."

The FBI never returned, but occasionally residents in this rural conservative community complained about what was in the store. She was challenged for selling books about Karl Marx, gay rights, and even dinosaurs. Johnson says she told the "book police" that "it's important that people learn and read about everything, whether they believe it or not." She also stocked copies of the Constitution and the Federalist Papers. Left-wing. Right-wing. Business. Labor. Anti-establishment. Everything was available in her store. "It's not the government's job to tell me or anyone what they can read," she says.

But the government had decided that under the cloak of

"national security" it could abridge the rights of the citizen. The base is the Foreign Intelligence Surveillance Act (FISA). Under that Act's provisions, the government may conduct covert surveillance of individuals after seeking an order from a special government-created secret court. However, that Court rejected only four of the government's 19,000 requests. In state actions, individuals have the right to ask local and state courts to quash subpoenas for records. If denied, they may appeal all the way to state supreme courts. There is no such protection under FISA. Not only can't individuals and businesses be represented in that secret court, they're bound by a federal gag order prohibiting any disclosure that such an order was even issued. There is no recourse. No appeal.

Throughout American history, all levels of government, under all political philosophies, have in varying degrees tried to suppress the citizens' First Amendment rights. The most recent series of intrusions upon civil liberties began in 1998 when special prosecutor Ken Starr demanded a book store to release records of what Presidential playmate Monica Lewinsky had purchased. It was a sweeping allegation that had no reasonable basis of establishing any groundwork in Starr's attacks upon President Clinton. Since then, there have been several cases in which police, operating with warrants issued in state courts, have demanded a bookstore's records.

And then came the USA PATRIOT Act, which expanded FISA. Six weeks after 9/11, about 85 percent of the House of Representatives and all but one Senator voted for the Act. Formally known as the Uniting and Strengthening America by Providing Appropriate Tools Required to Intercept and Obstruct Terrorism Act but referred to by its cutesy acronym, this legislation was developed in secret by the Department of Justice, and pushed upon a shell-shocked Congress, most of whom had less than a day to read any of the 342-page document; most didn't read any of it. Prior to its passage, a few members of Congress spoke out against the Act, charging that it was developed in haste, and there were Constitutional issues that were swept aside by the Bush–Cheney Administration and its Department of Justice; Attorney General John Ashcroft had publicly declared that anyone voting against the Act was aiding terrorism. But most of Congress voted for it because they wanted America to be free—and the President was flexing his political muscle following the murders of almost 3,000 Americans. Most Americans, with almost no information to the contrary from talk shows or the news media, believed the PATRIOT Act was necessary and vital to securing their nation's freedom. President Bush enthusiastically signed the bill, Oct. 26, 2001.

Among its almost innumerable provisions, the Act reduces judicial oversight of telephone and internet surveillance and grants the FBI almost unlimited, and unchecked, access to business records without requiring it to show even minimal evidence of a crime. By using National Security Letters (NSLs) issued by the Attorney General, the FBI doesn't even need any court's approval, nor does it need to give the individual time to call an attorney. Failure to immediately comply could result in that person's immediate detainment.

Section 215, one of the most controversial sections of one of America's most controversial laws, permits federal law enforcement, without going through the common judicial system, to grab "any tangible thing" in any investigation. This could include taking the sales records from bookstores, grocery stores, and drug stores; rental records from video stores; and all circulation records from libraries to learn who checked out which book. Under authority of Section 215, the FBI can even require internet service providers to release e-mails not just from suspects but from all persons the suspects contacted, thus dragging thousands of innocent persons into the FBI web. A "gag" order prohibits anyone from disclosing that the FBI even asked for the information. The effect of the USA PATRIOT Act upon businesses that loan, rent, or sell books, videos, magazines, and music CDs is not to find and incarcerate terrorists—there are far more ways to investigate threats to the nation than to check on a terrorist's reading and listening habits—but to put a sweeping chilling effect upon Constitutional freedoms. Book publishers, fearful of what the federal government might do, will take even fewer chances on publishing works that, like *The Hunt for Red October*, "might" result in the government investigation; bookstore owners may not buy as many different titles; and the people, fearing that whatever they read might be subject to Big Brother's scrutiny, may not buy controversial books or check books out of the library. Even worse, writers may not create the works that a free nation should read..

The PATRIOT Act also allows "sneak-and-peek" searches (Section 213) without notifying the citizen, to allow a search of the premises while the subjects are away, and not tell the individual of the government's intrusion upon home or office—or upon an innocent second party who may have been a friend of the store manager of a second cousin of the suspect. The search can be not just for investigation of potential terrorism cases but also for "any criminal investigation." That "criminal investigation" doesn't have to be terrorist-related; it can be for any activity, from murder to running a red light. Under Section 806, the government can seize an individual's property without notifying that person.

The PATRIOT Act further gives the government authority to indefinitely imprison legal immigrants and noncitizens without showing any court probable cause that they are terrorists or suspected of aiding others who are terrorists, and doesn't give the accused the right to challenge the government's assertions (Section 412); and expands the definition of terrorism to allow labeling dissenters as terrorists (Sections 411 and 802).

What many once saw as necessary is now seen as violating six Constitutional amendments:

—the First Amendment (freedom of religion, speech, press, and assembly, and the right to petition the government for a redress of grievances.)

—the Fourth Amendment (freedom from unreasonable searches; the so-called "right to privacy" amendment.)

—the Fifth Amendment (right against self-incrimination and due process.)

—the Sixth Amendment (due process, the right to counsel, a speedy trial, and the right to a fair and public trial by an impartial jury.)

—the Eighth Amendment; (reasonable bail and freedom from cruel and unusual punishment.)

—the Fourteenth Amendment; (equal protection guarantee for both citizens and non-citizens.)

The PATRIOT Act also violates Article I, Section 9 of the Constitution which guarantees the right to petition the courts to issue a *writ of habeas corpus* to require the government to produce a prisoner or suspect in order to determine the legality of the detention. Only Congress may order a suspension of the right of the writ, and then only in "Cases of Rebellion or Invasion." Congress did not act to suspend this right; nothing during or subsequent to the 9/11 attack indicated either a rebellion or invasion under terms of the Constitution. During the Civil War, Abraham Lincoln suspended the *writ of habeas corpus*, but was scolded by Roger Taney, chief justice of the United States. Lincoln was so infuriated at Taney's attack that he ordered federal marshals to arrest him; none did.

Several federal courts and two major Supreme Court decisions have dealt blows to the Administration's persistence in defending the PATRIOT Act. More challenges are working their way through the judicial system.

Among organizations opposed to the PATRIOT Act are the American Civil Liberties Union (ACLU), American Baptist Churches USA, American Bar Association, American Book-sellers Association, American Library Association, Association of American Physicians and Surgeons, Association of American Publishers, Bill of Rights Defense Committee, Center for Constitutional Rights, Electronic Frontier Foundation, the Electronic Privacy Information Center, Free Expression Policy Project, the National Association for the Advancement of Colored People (NAACP), and People for the American Way. Among conservative organizations that oppose the PATRIOT Act are the American Conservative Union, Free Congress Foundation, and the Second Amendment Foundation. Among individuals who have been most vocal in opposition are liberals Noam Chomsky, distinguished professor of linguistics at MIT; Chris Finan, president of the American Booksellers Foundation for Free Expression; Nancy Kranich, former president of the American Library Association; Paul Krassner, founding editor of *The Realist*; Judith Krug, of the Office of Intellectual Freedom of the American Library Association; Nancy Talanian, founding director of the Bill of Rights Defense Committee; Sens. Dick Durbin (D-Ill.) and Russ Feingold (D-Wisc.), and Reps. John Conyers (D-Mich.), William Delahunt (D-Mass.), Dennis Kucinich (D-Ohio), and Anthony Weiner (D-N.Y.). Among conservatives opposed to the Act are Newt Gingrich, former House Speaker who engineered the mid-term Republican victory in 1994; former House Majority Leader Dick Armey (R-Texas), and Rep. James Sensenbrenner (R-Wisc.), chair of the House Judiciary committee.

Bob Barr, a former U.S. Attorney, who was later elected to Congress where he became one of Bill Clinton's harshest critics in impeachment hearings, has been especially outraged by the excesses of the PATRIOT Act. "More than any foreign terrorist group," Barr tells his audiences, "provisions of the PATRIOT Act are the greatest threat to America and to American citizens." Barr created Patriots to Restore Checks and Balances to energize the public against the PATRIOT Act and the Bush–Cheney Administration's misguided belief that it is possible to sacrifice civil liberties to guarantee national security.

Several attempts were made in Congress to modify the PATRIOT Act; most failed. In July 2003, the House passed legislation, 309–118, to cut off funding for Section 213, the "sneak-and-peak" section that allows the government to raid a business or home, without the owner present, and to delay for months before even notifying them that materials were seized. The legislation was proposed by Rep. C.L. "Butch" Otter (R-Idaho), one of the House's more conservative members. The vote never moved forward in the Senate.

In March 2003, Rep. Bernie Sanders (I-Vt.) introduced the Freedom to Read Protection Act (H.R. 1157) that would have minimized or repealed Section 215; within a year it had more than 140 co-sponsors, extraordinarily high for any proposed legislation. "One of the cornerstones of our democracy is our right of Americans to criticize their government and to read printed materials without fear of government monitoring and intrusion," Sanders said at the time he submitted his bill. More than three dozen of the nation's largest organizations of librarians, booksellers, journalists, and publishers filed a joint statement that declared their support for the proposed bill.

When it became obvious the House leadership was deliberately stalling action on the bill, a bipartisan group consisting of Sanders and Reps. Jerry Nadler (D-N.Y.), John Conyers Jr. (D-Mich.), Otter, and Ron Paul (R-Texas) tried another way to limit the PATRIOT Act. To the Commerce, Justice, State Appropriations Bill of 2005, they proposed an amendment to cut off funding to the Department of Justice for searches conducted under Section 215. The amendment didn't diminish the government's capacity to investigate possible terrorism. It could still obtain records, as long as it went into a court of law and showed there was "probable cause" to request such records.

A day before the vote, President Bush's budget office sent a memo to House members warning them if they passed anything to weaken the PATRIOT Act, the President would veto the $39.8 billion Appropriations bill. It would be the first veto in the

President's term. By the end of the 15-minute voting period, even with the President's assurances of a veto, the amendment had 219 votes for passage, 201 against. But, the Republican leadership at that point held the voting open for an additional 23 minutes while House Majority Leader Tom DeLay (R-Texas) and his aides bullied Republicans into changing their votes. Among the tactics on the Section 215 amendment, the leadership suddenly produced a letter written by the Department of Justice that claimed a member of a terrorist group tied to al-Qaeda used the Internet at a public library. There were no specifics. Since the Department of Justice continually claimed it had "no interest" in going to libraries, how it learned of computer use at a library leads one to question if the Department lied to the people or if it lied to the Congress. The final vote, a 210–210 tie, doomed the amendment.

Rep. Jerry Nadler (D-N.Y.), whose district includes the area where the World Trade Center once stood, called the Republican leadership "shameful," their tactics "corrupt." In public statements, members of Congress expressed the same outrage as Nadler. "You win some, some get stolen," Otter said. Rep. Nancy Pelosi (D-Calif.) the House minority leader, lashed out at "Republican leaders [who] once again undermined democracy," and declared them to be "thoroughly un-American." Sanders called the vote "an outrage" and "an insult to democracy."

However, there was still the "sunset clause." Although ramming through the PATRIOT Act in the fear after 9/11, the House and Senate leaders understood the necessity to protect Constitutional rights. Into the bill, they inserted a "sunset clause," calling for 16 of the 150 sections of the Act to terminate on Dec. 31, 2005. Those 16 sections were among the more controversial and odious sections, ones that tread dangerously close to, and occasionally exceed, Constitutional rights.

About two years before the sunset clause would terminate those sections, the Bush–Cheney Administration began a massive political campaign not only to keep those sections, but to expand the PATRIOT Act as well. While the President falsely claimed the entire PATRIOT Act itself would cease at the end of the year—and, thus, make a nation believe that the terrorists would win—and while most of the nation's mass media failed to point out the President was wrong, the American people were beginning to realize that the government's use of the PATRIOT Act didn't result in capturing terrorists as much as it did upon violating Constitutional rights of the innocent.

Without a vote by Congress to suspend the sunset clause, the sunset sections would expire; with a vote, they would be kept in place a few months until a permanent vote was taken. If there was to be a vote, the President declared, it must be to extend the complete Act another four years. He said he wouldn't accept anything less. The House acquiesced, but there was a battle in the Senate.

Fifty-two of the 100 senators, including eight Republicans, wrote a letter to the Senate leadership calling for a three month extension, later raised to six months, to allow a calming period and a time to build into the four-year-old Act new citizen safeguards.

"This obstruction is inexcusable," a furious President Bush lashed out after learning of the letter, and demanded the Senate follow the wishes of the House. The President raged that the "senators obstructing the PATRIOT Act need to understand that the expiration of this vital law will endanger America and will leave us in a weaker position in the fight against brutal killers."

To emphasize their determination to keep the most controversial parts of the Act from being permanent, Sens. Feingold and Larry Craig (R-Idaho), representing near-extreme ends of the liberal–conservative continuum, declared they would filibuster the renewal. The Senate voted 52–47 to end that filibuster, but needed 60 votes.

White House Press Secretary Scott McClellan said the Senate Democrats and the turncoat Republican allies were the front for special interest groups, and were trying to "appease" the ACLU "because they want to weaken and undermine the PATRIOT Act." President Bush said the defeat in Congress was because of "partisan reasons." He told the nation, "the enemy has not gone away; they're still here, and I expect Congress to understand that we're still at war and they've got to give us the

~~~~~~~~~

"Experience should teach us to be most on our guard to protect liberty when the government's purposes are beneficent. Men born to freedom are naturally alert to repel invasion of their liberty by evil-minded rulers. The greatest dangers to liberty lurk in insidious encroachment by men of zeal, well-meaning but without understanding."
—U.S. Supreme Court Justice Louis D. Brandeis, 1928

tools necessary to win this war."

In March 2006, both houses of Congress, in what they believed was a "compromise" with the White House, made permanent 14 of the 16 controversial sections of the PATRIOT Act and extended the other two sections by four years. The odious Section 215, which allows federal agents to secretly probe anyone's private life, including reading habits, now allows the recipient of an NSL to challenge in court the issuance of that order. Although the "gag" order remains prohibiting that person or anyone associated with the order from speaking about it to anyone—relatives, friends, or the public—a "compromise" allows persons to speak out one year after the NSL is issued, but only with the permission of a federal court order, and only if the government says the issuance of the NSL doesn't relate to national security or diplomacy. The "compromise" also allows suspects to contact lawyers without having to notify the federal government they did so, or to identify whom they contacted.

By the time Congress extended the Act, 398 cities (including Atlanta, Baltimore, Denver, Detroit, Minneapolis, New York City, Philadelphia, San Francisco, Seattle, and Washington, D.C.) and eight states (Alaska, California, Colorado, Hawaii, Idaho, Maine, Montana, and Vermont) had passed resolutions opposing the PATRIOT Act while affirming their beliefs that the Constitution and Bill of Rights must take precedence over any federal law.

Arline Johnson at Friends-in-Mind says she never kept computer records, accepted credit cards, or even had a store newsletter, all of which could compromise the Constitutional protections of her customers. "I once visited Bulgaria after teaching in Egypt," says Johnson, "and was taking tourist pictures in Sofia when I was stopped, accused of being a spy, and ordered to sign papers." She says she refused to sign "anything in a language I didn't understand." For the rest of her trip, she says she was closely followed by Bulgarian state police. "I don't like totalitarian regimes," she says defiantly. It makes no difference if it's a Balkan dictatorship or one created out of fear in a democracy.

Benjamin Franklin told us, "They that can give up essential liberty to obtain a little temporary safety deserve neither liberty nor safety." The words of one of America's most distinguished radicals, in an era of greater terror than would exist at any time in the nation's history, were true more than 250 years ago; they're also true today.

The Highest Form of Patriotism

As Texas governor, George W. Bush had ordered peaceful protestors away from the governor's mansion. As president, he directed there be zones as much as a half-mile from any Presidential cavalcade or speech for anyone protesting his policies. It made no difference if the protestor was a Quaker or anyone else opposed to violence, the rules were all the same—all protestors must not be anywhere near the President. For those who refused to enter into these remote and generally obscure "free-speech zones," local police arrested them for disorderly conduct, and then detained them until the President or Vice-President was out of the area and the media left. When challenged, law enforcement officials claimed the separation was for security reasons. Persons carrying pro-administration signs were allowed to be in the visual range of the President and Vice-President. Obviously, anyone wishing to harm the President needed only to carry a sign praising the President or not to carry one at all.

By creating a protest zone hundreds of yards away, the Bush–Cheney Administration's actions were designed not so much to protect the President as to give the political illusion of the President's "popularity." The media, especially the television media, focused upon the President and crowds that were carefully selected and deftly manipulated to show enthusiastic support. Because the media believe the "story" is with the President, they usually ignore dissenters; it makes no difference if it's a Democrat or Republican, liberal or conservative.

However, according to a ruling by the federal district court in Philadelphia, all persons, no matter what their personal or political views, must have equal access to the President under the First Amendment guarantees of free speech and the right of assembly.

The Bush–Cheney Administration wasn't the only one to have tried to reduce the presence of dissenters. Throughout American history, persons not in elected office rise up to protest the policies of those in elected office. Persons in political power, at all levels, seem to have developed mystical auras that wash their political souls, leaving them to believe the people don't have all of the facts—why else would they protest?—and it is they, those in power, who are working so hard "on behalf of the people," who know what's best to govern the city, county, state, or country. That political philosophy also applies not just in government, but business and educational institutions as well. For some, such as Bill Clinton and Barack Obama who enjoy political debate, that aura of "divine invincibility" is only the thinest of coatings; for others, opposition to dissent is worn like the heaviest cloak.

At every Bush or Cheney appearance, official or political, persons were pre-screened before being issued tickets, and then were allowed into the rallies only if they weren't critics of any of the Administration's policies. Thousands were forced to sign loyalty oaths. In Albuquerque, Michael Ortiz y Pino, a Vietnam combat veteran, told the Associated Press he was also asked by the organizers to identify if he was with any groups that were associated with veterans, pro-life/pro-choice, gun rights, or teachers. In Tucson, the Republicans demanded to know the race of some photojournalists before issuing them credentials. Those who questioned the necessity of providing personal data and social security numbers were told the Secret Service required it. "We don't require that information," Tom Mazur, Secret Service spokesman, said. Heather Layman, spokesperson for the Republican National Committee, said the purpose of the screenings was because, "We just want to assure a positive experience for those attending."

In November 2002, seven persons, each with a ticket, went to a University of South Florida (USF) rally attended by President Bush and Gov. "Jeb" Bush. However, Republican event organizers refused admission to the men because each was wearing a campaign button for Gov. Bush's opponent in the forthcoming election. The individuals said they hadn't planned to protest, were at a public university, and just wanted to hear the President.

At that same rally were three other men who went specifically to protest the protest zones. Documentary film producers Adam Elend and Jeff Marks, and nightclub owner Joe Redner raised protest signs, and handed out literature with information about free speech issues decided by federal courts. The three men were about 150 feet outside the entrances to the stadium where the President would speak; all three were peaceful.

University of South Florida (USF) police and Hillsborough County sheriff's deputies, who claimed to be under Secret Service orders, directed the three men to move almost a half mile away.

When the men refused, they were charged with obstructing without violence, disorderly conduct, and violation of "trespass after warning." The Republicans incorrectly had claimed the President's visit was a "private event" at a public university.

In Tampa, Fla., two grandmothers and a gay rights activist were arrested for peacefully holding protest signs. In Columbia, S.C., a 54-year-old man was arrested at a campaign rally for carrying a sign, "No More War for Oil." In Evansville, Ind., a photographer who had won the Pulitzer Prize, was charged with disorderly conduct and resisting arrest for holding a 30-inch by 40-inch sign, "CHENEY—19th Century Energy Man."

In March 2001, a Western Michigan University police captain arrested student Antoine Jennings for trespass and disturbing the peace when he refused to go to a "free-speech zone" about 200 yards from the President's supporters, and behind a building. The reason Jennings presented such a security risk was that he was carrying a sign, "Welcome to Western, Governor Bush," a reference to the disputed 2000 election. In a subsequent trial, he was fined $100 for trespassing. In Saginaw, Mich., a woman was thrown out of a Bush appearance because she had a rolled-up pro-choice T-shirt. Barbara Miller says she was told, "We don't accept any pro-choice non-Republican paraphernalia at this event."

On Independence Day 2004 at an official presidential appearance at the state capitol in Charleston, W.Va., all of it paid by taxpayers, Nicole and Jeffrey Rank were arrested when they refused to turn their T-shirts inside out so an anti-Bush message didn't appear. Nicole Rank, an environmental scientist with FEMA, was later fired after receiving consistent ratings of "excellent."

In Scranton, Pa., a woman was ordered to remove a small metal peace button from her lapel. "I was told it was an unauthorized symbol," says Jean Golomb, who bought it at a Hallmark store. About 40 miles south of Pittsburgh, on Neville Island in the Ohio River, Allegheny County police arrested Bill Neel, a 65-year-old retired steelworker, on Labor Day when he refused to leave a rally for President Bush and go to a "free speech zone." His offense was carrying an anti-Bush sign. Neel, who had served six years in the Army, says he was "off the street and out of everyone's way." At the same time, pro-Bush supporters carrying signs were allowed into the speech. "I thought everywhere in America was a free speech zone," Neel later told the media.

Both major political parties have used exclusionary zones, most often at national conventions. The Department of Justice and the City of Boston planned to establish a "protest zone" far enough away from the July 2004 Democratic convention as to be unseen by the delegates as they walked into the convention hall. The site, after negotiations, was moved closer to the convention hall, but still established a confined atmosphere for protest. That site, beneath an abandoned elevated train line, was bound by chain-link fences covered by mesh, nets, and razor wire. "One cannot conceive of what other elements you would put in place to make a space more of an affront to the idea of free expression than the designated demonstration zone," stated Judge Douglas P. Woodlock. However, because of arguments from law enforcement and the Department of Justice, represented by three assistant United States attorneys, apparently unchallenged by the Democratic National Committee, he allowed the protest zone. However, in opposition to the Department of Justice and the City of Boston, the judge allowed a two-hour protest parade on Sunday before the convention. All of the protests, even illegal ones outside the zone, were peaceful. Police made only a half-dozen arrests.

In contrast, at the Republican convention in New York City in September 2004, which was deliberately planned to invoke memories of 9/11, staff, police, and Secret Service constantly harassed reporters, especially those from smaller circulation newspapers and magazines. Police claimed they were acting under orders of the Secret Service or requests of the Republican campaign.

By placing the convention in New York City, the Republicans had to deal with the largest protests in several decades. A federal judge had to intervene to keep New York City and the Republican National Committee from creating an even more restrictive set of conditions than what existed at the Democratic National Convention. U.S. District Court Judge Robert Sweet ruled that the city could not create interlocking metal "pens" for protestors without assuring that citizens had the right to enter and leave at their choosing, that police needed to have a reasonable suspicion and probable cause to do general searches of all bags of protestors, and that the city, which planned to close several streets near Madison Square Garden, site of the convention, had to inform the public about other ways to get to planned protest sites.

Outside the site of the Republican National Convention, police arrested more than 1,800 persons, almost all of them non-violent, who posed no physical threat to delegates or speakers. Most of the charges were for parading without a permit and disorderly conduct, violations in the same category as unpaid parking fines. All of the protestors were handcuffed, often so tight it caused bleeding and swelling, left for as many as three hours on the streets, and then taken to an abandoned bus terminal at Pier 57, where they were placed into a holding area of chain-link cages with razor wire on top. The concrete floor was oily from years of diesel fuel and antifreeze spillage, washed over by massive amounts of Clorox. Many of those detained later complained of rashes. There were few benches inside the cages, each of which held 30–100 individuals, forcing most of those arrested to take turns sitting on the benches and to sit or sleep on the floor; blankets were not provided. Food was usually corn flakes, warm and sour milk, rotting apples, and near-stale cheese or bologna sandwiches; persons had to share them with each other and, sometimes, the roaches in their cells. There were no trash bins, and portable restroom facilities were filthy.

Among those incarcerated was a 16-year-old student at Malverne (N.Y.) High School. Benjamin Traslavina, editor of the *Malverne Mule,* and a credentialed reporter to the convention, was arrested when he tried to photograph a protest on the floor of the convention. The Secret Service detained him, turned him over to the New York police, who then handcuffed him, confiscated his credentials, destroyed his film, and charged him with inciting to riot, assault, and disorderly conduct. He was finally released, with charges still against him, after about 30 hours. Most protestors were held for up to 60 hours until the end of the convention. In contrast, petty criminals were usually processed and released on bail within 24 hours. The city's delays in complying with the judicial orders to process the protestors quickly, said Judge John Cataldo, was "willful and intentional."

In Clive, Iowa, one month after the Republican political convention, a student wearing an anti-Bush button was ordered to remove it, and was ordered by a party official to explain why he was at the rally. John Sachs replied he was there to ask questions about the impending war in Iraq and about health care coverage. According to the *Des Moines Register*, the campaign worker then told the student, "If you protest, it won't be me taking you out. It will be a sniper." In Central Point, Ore., three peaceful women were thrown out of a campaign rally, and then threatened with arrests. Their offense? They wore T-shirts that said, "Protect Our Civil Liberties." Their cases are just a few of thousands throughout the country.

Democrat–Republican Thomas Jefferson said that dissent is the highest form of patriotism. During World War I, reiterating statements he had made for several years, Republican Theodore Roosevelt wrote, "To announce that there must be no criticism of the president, or that we are to stand by the president, right or wrong, is not only unpatriotic and servile, but is morally treasonable to the American public." Their views, explaining the reason for the First Amendment, should be the ones that matter.

Tearing Down the Marketplace of Ideas

Katharine Nyden was a 14-year-old high school student who wanted to see the President of the United States when he visited Charleston, W.Va., However, she didn't get a chance to see or hear much of what the President said.

She and her brother, Christopher, 11, were wearing T-shirts that offended the Republican organizers and the police. On the front of the T-shirts was a silk-screen of the Edward Munch painting, "Scream," with the words "Bush Again?" On the back was a cowboy hat with a slash through it.

Either in ignorance or in defiance of the federal court order in Philadelphia in September 2003 that forbid exclusionary zones for dissenters, the local political committee decided that a "free-speech zone" across the street from where the President was to speak was necessary to separate those who didn't agree with the Bush–Cheney Administration policies.

Well before the President's speech, one of the event workers told Nyden and her brother, who were walking with their parents, they would have to take off any anti-Bush pins and turn their shirts inside out. The family walked on, but Katharine recalls she saw "many people staring at us with utter disgust." Another campaign worker then told them they had to remove their pins and get rid of the shirts because the President's visit wasn't a political campaign trip. Nyden remembers telling this woman, "What about the people wearing Bush T-shirts? And how is your hat not political?" The woman then told Nyden that if she didn't turn the shirt inside out, "I will have to ask you to leave. It's the law." The feisty Nyden asked "What law would that be?" only to be told, "Young lady, it is not my job to understand the law!" But Nyden wasn't done with her questions. "You work for a congresswoman and it's not your job to understand the law?" she asked.

When that campaign worker couldn't make Nyden and her brother comply with the non-existent law, the campaign brought in state troopers, one of whom told the family, "One of our event coordinators told us that you were causing problems and we'd like you to leave." He explained, says Nyden, that because the Presidential appearance was an invitation-only event, "we can make you leave whenever we want."

The Nyden family, defying authority, refused to leave, and were threatened with being arrested. At that point, Sarah Sheets, the mother, sharply asked if they were now in a police state. Still defiant, Katharine Nyden asked to see the law "that permits you to just arrest us for no reason?" She recalls that the state trooper replied, "Ma'am, I don't have to show you anything. I'm not a man that lies. I don't have to tell you why I'm arresting you!" Nyden says she "couldn't believe what I was hearing," and so she again asked to see the law "but he only raised his voice and said he didn't have to show me anything."

Paul Nyden—Sarah's husband, Katharine and Christopher's father—deliberately stayed out of the confrontation to protect his role as an investigative reporter for the *Charleston Gazette*. But, at one point he could no longer resist. "I had been amazed at the arrogance of some of the younger people working for Bush that day," says Paul Nyden, who told two of them there was "a good document" they might read. He pulled a copy of the Constitution from his pocket, but says "it seemed to have little impact."

Katharine Nyden recalls she "found it a bit ironic that as the trooper was telling us to leave, Bush was talking about freedom of speech." Within moments, about a dozen state troopers surrounded the family but eventually backed off, apparently figuring that a 14-year-old girl and an 11-year-old boy, armed only with T-shirts, violated no law nor did they pose any threat.

The Nyden family was threatened and harassed, but none were arrested. Nicole and Jeffery Rank were.

Nicole Rank, an environmental scientist working as a reservist with the Federal Emergency Management Agency (FEMA), had come to Charleston a little more than a month earlier following heavy flooding; her husband was an oceanographer who had accompanied her, but wasn't working with FEMA.

On their own time, they decided to attend the rally. They had tickets, and were quietly standing with the rest of the crowd of about 6,500. On their T-shirts were the words, "Love America, Hate Bush." When the Ranks refused to turn their T-shirts inside out or to move to the "free-speech zone" as directed, they were handcuffed, taken from the rally, arrested, fingerprinted, and had mug shots taken. A White House official told the *Charleston Gazette* that persons are discouraged from bringing any campaign items, no matter what their message, to official presidential visits, and that the White House did not have any role in asking for or ordering the arrests.

Charleston Mayor Danny Jones told the *Gazette* that his city police were acting under direct orders of the Secret Service when they arrested the Ranks. The Secret Service disagreed. "We work with the local law enforcement, but they do not work under the direction of the Secret Service," said Tom Mazur, spokesperson for the Secret Service. Then, in an incredible twist of logic, Jones claimed, "The officers, quite frankly, feared for the safety of the Ranks." Mark Rutherford, the Democratic candidate for sheriff, told the police, "You can't arrest them for this." A state police officer bluntly replied, "I don't have to tell you." FEMA terminated Nicole Rank's assignment and cut off her pay, although her supervisor had given rated her "excellent" for her work in Charleston.

Rather than returning home to Corpus Christi, Texas, the Ranks stayed in Charleston, living in a motel, to fight the charges. "It was difficult for us financially," Jeff Rank told the *Gazette*. Less than two weeks later, the Ranks, represented by the ACLU, went to court. In minutes, it was over. Municipal Court Judge Carole Bloom quickly dismissed all charges.

"We're going to get on with our lives and go back to Texas and get jobs," Jeff Rank said, noting he and his wife "will continue to exercise our right to free expression when we see fit [but] we're not professional protesters."

A day after the court dismissed the case, Sen. John Kerry came to Charleston for a political rally. "The only reason you would be asked to leave," said Amy Shuler Goodwin, Kerry's spokesman for West Virginia, "is if you were disrupting the event or causing harm to someone." In contrast, Reed Dickens, a Bush campaign official, told the *Gazette* that persons "interested in supporting the President's message" are welcome at Republican campaign events, and erroneously claimed that even on public land, "campaign events are private events, and therefore, by their nature, it's up to the discretion of each campaign who comes in." Bush–Cheney '04 and Victory '04, the two major umbrella campaign organizations for the Republicans, also claimed that political rallies are "private" and, thus, not subject to any Constitutional restraints. But, the visit to Charleston wasn't a private event. Because the President's speech was billed as a Presidential address, the Republicans didn't have to pay the $53,000 cost the budget-strapped state had to cover for local security, nor any federal costs associated with transportation, security, staffing, and promotion.

The rally that the Nydens and the Ranks attended on the grounds of the West Virginia state capitol on public land was July 4, 2004, the 228th birthday of a revolution founded in dissent and the libertarian belief that for a democracy to succeed, all views have a right to be heard in a "marketplace of ideas."

'Always There':
The Voice of a Gold Star Mother

Laura Bush, surrounded by a cadre of Secret Service agents, went to Hamilton, N. J., in September 2004—and Sue Niederer, surrounded by the Secret Service, local police, and some very angry Republican volunteers, was arrested.

Bush was at a township firehouse, telling about 700 pre-selected ticket-holding Bush faithful why they needed to vote for her husband. Niederer also had a ticket, but she had a mission.

The First Lady discussed her husband's accomplishments, frequently invoking the memory of 9/11. At the back of the hall stood Niederer. And then Laura Bush told the crowd why the nation needed to support the war in Iraq. "It's for our country, it's for our children and our grandchildren, that we do the hard work of confronting terror and promoting democracy,' said the First Lady.

That's when Niederer, a 55-year-old teacher and Realtor, just couldn't take it any more. "If the Iraq war is so necessary," she called out, "why don't your children serve?" That's also when the Secret Service came over to her, when Republican volunteers pushed and shoved her, and raised Bush campaign signs around her to block her from talking and the media from turning their cameras to her, and the partisan crowd to again chant, "Four More Years! Four more years!"—just in case Niederer had anything else to say the crowd thought might be high treason.

Until she spoke out, exercising what she believed were her First Amendment rights of freedom of speech and to petition the government for a redress of grievances, most had not seen her shirt. She had taken off an outer shirt to reveal a T-shirt with a picture of her 24-year-old son, and the words, "President Bush, You Killed My Son." Her son was 2nd Lt. Seth Dvorin, of the Army's 10th Mountain Division. On Feb. 3, 2004, he was killed in Iraq by an Improvised Explosive Device (IED), sometimes known as booby-traps and land mines. Dvorin wasn't trained in bomb disposal, says his mother. His unit had been sent to locate IEDs along roads. "It was a suicide mission," says Niederer.

After their son was killed, Niederer and her ex-husband, Richard Dvorin, Seth's father, both sent letters to the President; the only response was a form letter asking for campaign contributions. She spoke out a number of times since then. But now, with Laura Bush in town, this grieving mother wanted to make sure that another mother heard her anguish.

The Secret Service and Hamilton police forcibly removed Niederer from the hall. "They told me this is a private party," she recalls. She showed authorities her ticket; they confiscated it. Outside the hall, she was handcuffed; she demanded to know what she was being charged with, but was never told. Police put her into a police van, drove her around for more than a half-hour, probably to keep her from the media, and then took her to the police station where she was charged with defiant trespass. The next day, the Mercer County prosecutor refused to pursue the police charge.

Only a few local newspapers picked up the story; the national media ignored it. But, videotapes of her arrest were shown to her son's troops in Iraq. The intent, she says, was to say, "Look at how unpatriotic she is; look at what she did."

Throughout the Bush–Cheney era, Niederer protested the war. At schools, she told students there were options other than volunteering for the military. "I'm not against the military," says Niederer, "I just wanted students to make an informed decision."

Her son was pursued by recruiters since high school. "I told them that Seth was going to go to college," she says, "but they kept going after him." He had majored in criminal justice at Rutgers University, hoping to become an FBI agent. The Army, says Niederer, "convinced him that they would train him for the FBI, that he'd never see the front lines." His three month Officer Candidate School training "was a total positive experience," she says.

Shortly after completing OCS, he was sent to Iraq, a few days after being married. The Army first claimed Dvorin was killed while disarming a bomb, and then changed the official reason for his death to having been killed by the IED while on patrol. The Army ordered an autopsy for the devout Jew, something the religion doesn't permit and which, says Niederer, the Army knew. "There was no necessity for it," says Niederer, "but his widow gave permission." The Army claims a rabbi was present at the autopsy. The Army also promoted Dvorin to first lieutenant, and then rescinded that promotion because he didn't have enough time in rank.

Greg Niederer, her Republican husband, supported her anti-war campaigns. "He didn't at first," she says, noting, "he didn't quite understand what I was doing and why." And then they went to the premiere of Michael Moore's *Fahrenheit 9/11*. After seeing that film, he turned to his wife and apologized for not supporting her more strongly. "Everything you've been yelling about," she remembers him telling her, "it's right there." He began attending more rallies with her.

She went to schools and universities, to small and large rallies, always drawing the media. "I may stay behind the scenes at times," she says, "but I was always there," just as the death of her son is always with her.

~~~~~~~~~

"Our ability to disagree and our inherent right to question our leaders and criticize their actions define who we are. To allow those rights to be taken away out of fear, to punish people for their beliefs, to limit access in the news media to differing opinions is to acknowledge our democracy's defeat."

—Tim Robbins, April 2003

'I Don't Need to Tell You':
A Personal Account of an Encounter
With the Bush–Cheney Campaign

by Rosemary R. Brasch

I'm not sure what turned me into a one woman menace to the Vice-President of the United States. Perhaps it was the pad and pen instead of a flag. Maybe it was that I was dressed in pink as opposed to red, white, and blue. Or, it could have been my status as the wife of a social issues journalist who just five minutes earlier had been told he wasn't allowed into the rally and would be taken into custody, arrested, and removed from the premises if he didn't go willingly.

The rally for Dick Cheney, one week before the Republican National Convention, took place at Bloomsburg University, a state-owned facility in northeastern Pennsylvania. As a registered Republican, I had received a semi-personal pre-taped telephone invitation that I could pick up tickets for this rally, the only time either the President or Vice-President would be in our home town.

In addition to having two spectator passes, as journalists we had also received press authorization from national headquarters of Bush/Cheney '04. No one at the local level knew this.

About 90 minutes before the Vice-President was to be in the area, we went to the press table on the university lawn where my husband received his official press pass, issued by a university PR person who claimed she was a "volunteer" for the campaign. There were many other state employees who had also "volunteered." The university later claimed these "volunteers" had taken personal time during that afternoon. However, none of the state employees had to "make up" the time they spent as "volunteers" for the Bush–Cheney campaign. Although Bloomsburg University claimed the event was private, it never charged rental fees to Bush–Cheney '04, and asked only for reimbursement of expenses, including 2,000 bottles of water and labor costs of non-professional staff.

Within moments of receiving his press credential, my husband was promptly confronted by an "event coordinator" who told him he wasn't welcome and must leave at once or else be escorted out by security. I later learned that the junior event coordinator had brought out a senior event coordinator who reinforced Junior's demands to leave. When my husband demanded reasons, he was told where the "protest zone" was, and he was more than welcome to go there, a mile from the speech. When my husband again explained that he was a reporter, had not only been credentialed to this event, but had covered every Presidential administration for more than 30 years, never with any problems from the campaign or the White House, and was not at this event to protest, the Bush–Cheney campaign worker brusquely replied, "You're protesting now!" and reinforced his demands to leave.

While my husband was, as he recalled, "politely discussing the campaign's disregard of the Constitution," I had quickly left, avoiding asking for my own press credential, and went to the end of the "common person line" and worked my way to the table at the entrance of a gymnasium where two women were check-ing lists. We had no intention of going into the gymnasium to hear the Vice-President speak. The national press rides on char-tered campaign buses, talk with each other and then get off the buses, to be herded into a designated press area shortly before the candidate enters the venue; they listen to the speech, stay a few moments afterwards, and then again board the buses.

Isolated from the people, they report what the candidate wants them to hear, and may interview a few pre-selected mem-bers of the audience to get a "hometown flavor." It works for the national press; it doesn't work for us; we had other stories to cover, and the Vice-President was only an incidental part of our coverage. But, here I was in line, trying to get into the gymna-sium and now working another story from an angle we hadn't anticipated.

I was once on the list to be admitted into the gymnasium; now I wasn't. But, a sweet local volunteer told me sweetly that it wouldn't be a problem since I had a ticket and just had to show a driver's license. Enter the paid-staff event coordinator one more time. He had been otherwise occupied with my hus-band. He brusquely explained I also was not allowed into the gymnasium, and had to leave the premises.

"Why is that?" I challenged. "I have my ticket, have been a clerk at the election polls, and have been a Republican longer than our state senator who jumped parties a couple of years ago." I didn't tell him I was also a liberal who has disagreed with the direction the Republican party and its leaders have chosen over the past few years. No need to further infuriate him, especially since he probably wouldn't believe a liberal would be allowed to register as a Republican.

"I repeat, you are *not* allowed in." He continued to refuse to explain *why* I wasn't allowed into the gymnasium.

Another try—"*Who* decided I can't attend? By whose authority are you forcing me to leave? *What* is the precise reason?"

"I don't need to tell you that—I already told your husband and he can tell you. I don't have time for this."

"Excuse me, but not only am I a registered Republican with a ticket, I'm also a separate entity from my husband. I wasn't there when you were explaining to him, Therefore, you need to tell *me* why I am being denied access."

"I said," he huffed, "I told your husband and I'm not repeating myself." As I soon learned from my husband, the event coordinator and his assistant also refused to identify themselves or to answer any of his questions.

A couple of minutes after I was thrown out of line, I was with my husband near the press table. Now, hired goons beget hired goons, and while this officious functionary was "I can't"-ing and "I don't have to"-ing us, silently approaching were two men who wore suits, had ear pieces, looked silently official, and wore a mysterious one-inch cardboard sticker on their lapels. Everything about them suggested Secret Service. As I later learned, that was the image they wished to portray.

"If you don't leave the premises right now, we will be forced to take you into custody," one of them officially stated. We were told we had two choices—leave the premises or be escorted off the grounds. When they refused to identify themselves or which agency they were with, I knew they were only pretend law enforcement.

But, it wasn't the pretend law enforcement or the Secret Service that enforced whatever rules they thought they could enforce, it was the state university police director who knew us, knew we posed no physical threats to anyone, and knew that we knew we were standing upon public land at the time. The university's director of police told us if we didn't leave the area voluntarily, he would arrest and incarcerate us. In response to a question, he refused to indicate what the charges would be. But, he did state that one of the main reasons he was asking us to leave was that our car was parked in the wrong area. Avoiding

51

laughing in his face, we could easily have moved the car—except that we were parked in the same place as the TV satellite trucks and other logo-covered press cars.

Into the area now came other campaign staff, perhaps some civilian-clothed police, and someone with a German Shepherd. As expected, none identified themselves. We could have stayed and been arrested—we had the phone numbers for the ACLU and the Reporters Committee for Freedom of the Press—but we left the area to continue our reporting.

We also observed that neither of the professors in charge of the Young Republicans who knew us protested our exclusion—nor had any reporter; after all, they had their own pedestrian stories to file.

The Center for Public Integrity later reported that Dick Cheney unilaterally declared himself exempt from travel disclosure laws that govern all travel by the President, his staff, and all persons in the executive branch. According to the Center, when private funds are spent, "federal law requires that officials report where they went, how much it cost, and who paid." The Vice-President's counsel, however, said that the Vice-President never took private funds for travel; thus, all travel, more than 275 times between January 20, 2001, and November 16, 2005, were paid for by public funds; therefore, all speeches would have to be considered to be public not private speeches, and all persons not violating state or federal laws allowed to attend. (For the eight years he was Bill Clinton's vice-president, Al Gore routinely filed travel reports for the public record.)

The university later claimed it was acting under authority of the Secret Service. The Secret Service denied the university's claim. The university, which didn't permit persons to display non-Bush/Cheney signs, allowed the campaign committee to decide who was allowed to be at the rally; it didn't challenge the campaign workers who demanded that the two non-protesting reporters not be allowed on the premises; it allowed a clause into its Facilities Use Agreement that it "reserves the right to eject any objectionable person or persons from University premises at all times" without defining "objectionable." Yet, that university had trumpeted in a news release two days before the Vice-President's visit, "As a university, it is our duty to provide a forum for the exchange of ideas. . . . We are pleased to welcome Vice President Cheney to our university and to have this opportunity to participate in the American Democratic [*sic*] process."

Free Speech on Death Row

Usually, a five-minute radio commentary about fatherhood wouldn't be controversial. But Temple University decided that anything a death row inmate has to say shouldn't be broadcast on WRTI-FM, its 50,000-watt noncommercial radio station that has a range of more than 100 miles.

Not only did Temple cancel the series of 13 commentaries in February 1997, it also cancelled the one-hour daily "Democracy Now" program—a magazine-format show that includes news, features, and commentaries—and all of the Pacifica Network News programs.

George Ingram, Temple's associate vice president for university relations who ordered the programs cancelled midway through its $6,000 contract, said the decision had been "under consideration for some time," but acknowledged that the abrupt termination was "accelerated" by the commentaries. None of the station's executive staff had input into the decision.

The new programming, said Ingram, reflected more classical jazz and gave the university the opportunity "to provide audiences with a window into the academic excellence and enormous educational resources that Temple University offers." Since the radio station is under control of the university's PR office, the university apparently believed airing diverse views wasn't the proper image for an urban university, but that using a radio station as a PR vehicle is.

Although Temple cancelled "An Alternative View" in 1997, apparently listeners of the 24 stations that didn't cancel the programs, including those in New York, Los Angeles, and Washington, D.C., had no problem with the commentaries. Coughlin said the response had been "8 to 1" in favor of the commentaries.

Steve Geimann, at that time president of the 14,000-member Society of Professional Journalists (SPJ), called Temple's action "censorship." In response, George Ingram emphatically stated, "we can program what we want to program." Many legal purists agree with Ingram, claiming censorship exists only when the government tries to stop publication or broadcast. However, if the news and programming divisions of a station had no voice in the cancellation, as Ingram stated, and if Temple University, which received almost $150 million of its $565 million budget from the Pennsylvania state government in 1996–1997, made a decision while concerned about public funding issues and outside pressures, then no word other than "censorship" could apply.

At the center of the controversy was award-winning journalist Mumia Abu-Jamal, convicted in June 1982 of killing a Philadelphia police officer. He is on "death row" at the state's Greene County prison, still maintaining his innocence. According to undisputed facts, about 3:50 a.m., December 9, 1981, Philadelphia police officer Daniel Faulkner stopped William Cook for driving the wrong way on a one-way street. Shortly after that, Abu-Jamal, moonlighting as a taxi driver, drove past, saw his brother being beaten by a police officer and stopped. Not long after that, Abu-Jamal was in critical condition at a nearby hospital, having been shot by Faulkner; Faulkner, shot four or five times, was dead. It took police about 45 minutes to get Abu-Jamal to a nearby hospital. "They beat me on the street. They beat me in the paddy wagon," said Abu-Jamal.

At the time of his arrest, Abu-Jamal, who had that year won a Peabody award, the most prestigious award in broadcast journalism, was a Philadelphia radio journalist with no criminal convictions, nor any history of violence. In fact, he had been under both FBI and local police surveillance since he was almost 15 years old, the result of having been a member of the Black Panther party, a connection that the prosecution illegally and repeatedly used to discredit him. But, the prosecution couldn't find anyone who claimed Abu-Jamal was anything other than a gentle and caring individual who uses words not physical violence to make his points.

In contrast, the Philadelphia police at that time had a reputation for violence, something Abu-Jamal had frequently reported, and for which Abu-Jamal's attorneys say is why he was singled out for police revenge. Three years before the killing, the U.S. Department of the Justice sued the city and police for violating due process of the suspects. Not only did the federal government prove that the police used unreasonable force against suspects, it also brought out evidence that the Philadelphia police planted evidence and lied under oath. One of the six officers convicted of lying and planting evidence was part of the investigating team at the scene where Faulkner was murdered. The police never ran standard tests to determine if Abu-Jamal had recently fired a gun, nor did they run ballistics tests on his own licensed gun.

Abu-Jamal's "confession" is equally suspect. Gary Bell, Faulkner's partner, claimed he heard Abu-Jamal, lying semi-conscious on a hospital gurney following surgery, shout, "I shot the motherfucker and I hope he dies." But Bell didn't report the "confession" until two months later, and only after there were questions about police brutality the night of the murder. A corroborating witness who said she heard the same confession denied knowing Faulkner, until it was pointed out she had coffee with him several times.

Even a cursory review of trial evidence reveals significant problems with the judicial system. The prosecution used 11 of its 15 peremptory challenges to exclude Blacks from the jury pool solely because of their race, leaving a jury of 10 Whites and two Blacks in a city that is 40 percent Black. Some prosecution "eye witnesses" may never have even been at the scene; those witnesses who were at the scene identified a heavy-set man with an Afro who stood over the officer's body; Abu-Jamal is thin and wore dreadlocks. Information favorable to Abu-Jamal's case was never given to his defense attorneys by the prosecution, a violation of court rules. Witnesses later claimed that police and prosecutors harassed and intimidated them, threatening to arrest them if they testified for Abu-Jamal, but would overlook their felonies if they testified for the Commonwealth.

Further, the judge who assigned Abu-Jamal an inexperienced attorney who constantly asked to be removed from the case, refused sufficient time to adequately prepare a defense, allowed only $150 expenses for investigations, quashed subpoenas for essential defense witnesses, kept a White juror who had said he couldn't be fair to both sides, violated acceptable trial procedures, suppressed conflicting reports, allowed improper cross-examination of defense witnesses, refused to grant a continuance so the defense could bring to court a police officer who was on vacation at the time of the trial, and gave faulty instructions to the jury. He also answered questions intended for witnesses, injected his own opinions during testimony, and badgered defense attorneys. In an appeals hearing in October 1996, the judge, the same one who presided over the trial, declared that Abu-Jamal's brother would be arrested on outstanding warrants if he testified, and then allowed New Jersey police to enter his courtroom to arrest another defense witness on a charge of having passed a bad check.

That judge was Albert F. Sabo, who had been undersheriff of Philadelphia County and a life member of the Fraternal Order of Police before he was elected to the Court of Common Pleas. In his judicial career, he was "distinguished" only for having handed down more death sentences than any other active judge in the nation; of the 31 persons he condemned to death between 1976 and 1991, 29 were Black. Appellate and supreme courts reversed 11 of those cases.

"Sabo has long since abandoned any pretense of fairness. He's openly hostile to the defense and lavishly liberal with the prosecution," wrote Jill Porter, a Philadelphia *Daily News* columnist. Although she has written against Abu-Jamal's conviction being reversed, she says, "Defense attorneys barely get to voice their objections to testimony before Sabo overrules them with a snarl and threatens to throw them out if they continue to object." Terri Maurer-Carter, a court stenographer, in a sworn statement, later declared she had heard Sabo state outside the courtroom that he was "going to help 'em fry the nigger!" Incredibly, a common pleas court judge later ruled that if Sabo was racist, it had no relevance. Sabo, who died in 2002, never answered defense questions about the racist comments he was alleged to have made.

Leonard Weinglass, a nationally-known attorney who became Abu-Jamal's chief counsel in 1995, argued in a 182-page memorandum of law that there were 19 critical Constitutional violations during the original trial. Both the state's appellate and supreme courts have rejected Abu-Jamal's appeals. Of the four justices who accepted the lower court rulings, even with their inconsistencies, was one justice who had earlier had a personal confrontation with Abu-Jamal, but didn't excuse himself from the proceedings. Two other justices refused to participate in the decision. The state Supreme Court's "Keystone Kops" reputation had kept it in headlines on numerous other cases before one justice was eventually impeached. In May 2002, the defense filed a petition to compel Pennsylvania Supreme Court Justice Ronald D. Castille to testify under oath about a significant conflict of interest. Castille was one of the justices who had ruled against Abu-Jamal's claims that the jury was not representative of the community since the prosecution had deliberately made every effort to exclude Blacks. However, the Defense legal team claimed that Castille, while Philadelphia district attorney, had produced a training video for the DA staff on how to exclude Blacks from juries. The video may have been produced not long after the Supreme Court of the United States ruled in *Batson v. Kentucky* (1986) that such tactics violate provisions of the 14th Amendment.

Because of innumerable trial inconsistencies, and evidence that Abu-Jamal may have been framed by police who wanted to avenge the death of a comrade by blaming a Black militant who spoke out against police abuse, thousands of Americans during the past two decades have rallied to Abu-Jamal's support.

The Rev. Jesse Jackson called the original trial "a charade, prejudicially carried out by the state for the pursuit of vengeance in the name of justice."

Amnesty International argued that "adverse inferences to [his] past political beliefs and affiliations was . . . used by the prosecution to persuade the jury to impose the death penalty." Citing human rights violations and myriad inconsistencies of evidence, several countries, churches, organizations, and several hundred thousands of individuals have formally petitioned first Gov. Robert Casey, and then Govs. Tom Ridge, Mark Schweiker, and Ed Rendell to commute Abu-Jamal's sentence. Petitions were signed in Italy by 100,000 citizens, and in France by 40,000 citizens. Among other petitioners were South African president Nelson Mandela, the NAACP, Southern Christian Leadership Conference, the United Church of Christ, the Episcopal Church of the United States, the National Association of Black Journalists, the National Lawyers Guild, the Association of Black Police Officers; former U.S. attorney general Ramsey Clark; former New York City mayor David Dinkins; critically-acclaimed best-selling writers Maya Angelou, Angela Davis, E. L. Doctorow, Roger Ebert, Molly Ivans, Maya Lin, Gloria Steinem, William Styron, Alice Walker, and John Edgar Wideman; and actors Ed Asner, Alec Baldwin, Ossie Davis, Mike Farrell, Danny Glover, Whoopie Goldberg, Paul Newman, Tim Robbins, Susan Sarandon, Peter Sellers, and Joanne Woodward. The response of the Fraternal Order of Police was to recommend a boycott against films starring Asner, Farrell, and Goldberg.

Numerous national and international unions—including the 1.8 million member California AFL-CIO, the American Federation of State, County, and Municipal Employees, International

Longshoremen and Warehouse Union, and the National Writers Union—came to Abu-Jamal's defense. Both San Francisco and Detroit passed resolutions in support of Abu-Jamal. In October 2003, the city of Paris declared Abu-Jamal an "honorary citizen," the first time it awarded that distinction since 1971 when it honored Pablo Picasso. France now requires all school children to study the Abu-Jamal case to better understand issues involving free speech, international criminal justice, and the use of the death penalty. In April 2006, the city of Saint-Denis, a Paris suburb, renamed a street in honor of Abu-Jamal, prompting two Pennsylvania members of Congress to introduce a House resolution demanding sanctions against the French city if it didn't reverse its decision. The media frenzy, however, was overwhelming in support of those who wished to execute Abu-Jamal.

In December 2001, following several years of legal appeals and maneuvering, the U.S. District Court for Eastern Pennsylvania—specifically refusing to look at what the Defense tried to show as new evidence—ruled that Judge Sabo in the trial gave faulty jury instructions. Judge William Yohn, in a 272-page opinion, ordered the Commonwealth to set a new sentencing hearing within 180 days; if it failed to do so, Yohn said he would order the death penalty set aside and sentence Abu-Jamal to life in prison without possibility of parole. However, Lynn Abraham, the Philadelphia district attorney, claimed the federal court didn't have jurisdiction. Both the defense and prosecution filed appeals with the 3rd Circuit of Yohn's ruling, Abu-Jamal's attorneys seeking to overthrow the original verdict, the DA seeking to assure the death penalty. A later ruling by the Third Circuit rejected the appeal for a new trial, but noted there were faulty directions to the jury by Judge Sabo; the death penalty was set aside. The Supreme Court in April 2009 refused to hear an appeal for a new trial based upon the exclusion of Blacks in the jury pool.

During more than a quarter of a century in prison, Abu-Jamal has continued to write newspaper columns, radio commentaries, and books, usually while being intimidated and harassed by prison officials. The courts have ruled that prisons may discipline disruptive inmates, but they have also ruled that Abu-Jamal was not disruptive, and most restrictions placed upon him were the result of him speaking out about a variety of social issues unrelated to his own case.

In May 1994, National Public Radio (NPR)—which prior to Abu-Jamal's arrest 13 years earlier had broadcast his news reports and commentaries about police community relations in Philadelphia—abruptly cancelled his commentaries after succumbing to pressure from a gaggle of conservative radio talk show hosts, a handful of conservative congressmen, and Philadelphia's Fraternal Order of Police (FOP). At the time, NPR claimed it cancelled the commentaries because it had "serious misgivings about the appropriateness of using as a commentator a convicted murderer seeking a new trial, particularly since we had not arranged for other commentaries or coverage on the subject of crime, violence, and punishment that provided context or contrasting points of view."

The day after NPR cancelled the commentaries, Senate majority leader Robert Dole (R-Kansas) said he was "pleased that the program was cancelled," and demanded a "closer oversight by the Congress" of the budget for the Corporation for Public Broadcasting which funds NPR.

NPR, says Abu-Jamal, never told him it cancelled his commentaries. Fifteen months later, NPR's Scott Simon hosted a 30 minute discussion of the case, with comments by Abu-Jamal and several persons associated with the case, but barely mentioned significant trial discrepancies although there was widespread commentary elsewhere. Temple's George Ingram cited the NPR cancellation three years previously as one of the reasons why the university also cancelled Abu-Jamal's commentaries. "If that position [to cancel the commentaries] was good enough for NPR," said Ingram, "it was good enough for me." Pacifica, however, had offered the slain officer's family and the FOP air time for their views. They declined.

In February 1995, prison officials suspended Abu-Jamal's family and social visitation rights for 30 days, and barred all media access to him for 90 days for "engaging in the profession of journalism." A five page disciplinary report, issued June 6, 1995, four days after "law and order" Gov. Tom Ridge signed the death warrant, appeared to be retaliation for Abu-Jamal writing *Live from Death Row*, an eloquent series of essays that condemn the law enforcement, judicial, and prison systems for significant civil rights violations. Many of the essays had been scheduled to be broadcast on NPR a year earlier. Among his conclusions were that Latinos and Blacks were victims in 97 percent of all beatings by police officers, and that 93 percent of all police officers in such incidents were White. The book included an afterward by attorney Leonard Weinglass who pointed out innumerable judicial "outrages" at the original trial. Hours after publication, a plane trailing a banner—"Addison Wesley Supports Cop Killer," hired by Faulkner's widow, flew over the publisher's Massachusetts offices. The American Booksellers Association named *Race for Justice*, by Weinglass, as Best Book on Politics for that year. Subsequent books written by Abu-Jamal were *Death Blossoms* (1996), *Live From Death Row* (1996), *All Things Censored* (2000), *Death Blossoms: Reflections from a Prisoner of Conscience* (2003), *Faith of Our Fathers: An Examination of the Spiritual Life of African and African-American People (2003)*, *We Want Freedom: A Life in the Black Panther Party (2004)*, and *Jailhouse Lawyers: Prisoners Defending Prisoners Vs. the U.S.*, with Angela Y. Davis (2009).

The day after he was disciplined for committing journalism, about two months before he was scheduled to be executed, Abu-Jamal wrote, "They want me to die alone—silently. So much do they fear my words that they want me muzzled as they prepare to garrote me."

In a "friend of the court" brief, six national journalism organizations, led by the Society of Professional Journalists, and including the American Society of Newspaper Editors, argued, "Despite incarceration, inmates maintain many of the constitutional rights afforded law abiding citizens including the First Amendment right of freedom of expression." The organizations took no stand on Abu-Jamal's guilt or innocence. In September 1996, a U.S. district judge, after reviewing a recommendation by a federal magistrate, ruled that prison officials violated not only Abu-Jamal's First Amendment rights but his civil rights as well when they opened, photocopied, and widely distributed mail sent to him by his attorneys.

In October 1996, and with the assistance of the Prison Radio Project, Abu-Jamal—shackled and forced to read his scripts that were posted on the other side of a thick Plexiglas window recorded 13 three- to five-minute segments on a wide range of topics, including Mad Cow Disease, rap music, corporate influence upon the media, the use of tobacco as a drug, racism, and prison reform, but never discussed his own case. Less than two weeks later, the state's Department of Corrections created new rules that forbid journalists from bringing cameras and audio and video equipment into the interview, required them to register as part of a prisoner's 40 person maximum "social list," (not as journalists), and forbid them from being on more than one prisoner's social list. Further, if a journalist wished to talk with a prisoner, the prisoner's allotted time with family and friends was reduced.

David Mendoza, executive director of the National Campaign for Freedom of Expression, said the ban "clearly is intended to silence Abu-Jamal." Six other states have also severely limited prisoner access to the media. California's Department of Corrections in 1996 issued rules that forbid all face-to-face interviews with prisoners, and excluded reporters from bringing even pencils and notepads into the prison.

The Supreme Court of the United States, affirming First Amendment freedoms, has ruled that "reasonable and effective means of communication [from and to inmates must] remain open, and no discrimination in terms of content be involved." Pennsylvania's Department of Corrections appears to have violated that Supreme Court ruling.

"We went ahead with the commentaries," says Dan Coughlin, "Democracy Now" producer, "because we wanted to take a stand against growing restrictions on media access to prisoners, and to affirm the right of prisoners to talk with the media and to the public." But there was a third reason—"they were just good commentaries."

The PEN American Center, an organization of writers and editors, pointed out that Abu-Jamal's work "and that of other inmates like him . . . has had enormous value, both in its own right as literature, and insofar as it has alerted audiences to conditions prevailing in our country's jails. Were this means of communication to be broken, prisons would become even more than they are already, an opaque and forgotten part of our society, a place where living conditions would deteriorate still further without provoking any public concern."

In a related case, a federal magistrate revoked the one-year probation for C. Clark Kissinger and sentenced him to 90 days in the federal Metropolitan Detention Center in Brooklyn, beginning in December 2000. Kissinger's crime was that he also committed journalism. An activist and journalist, Kissinger had written and spoken out against the court system, and had previously been convicted for failure to obey a lawful order during a protest for Abu-Jamal in Philadelphia. Among terms of his conviction, he was to get court permission for any public speeches and to stay away from the City of Brotherly Love. In August 2000, while still on probation, Kissinger returned to Philadelphia to cover the Republican National Convention and to give a speech to several thousand protestors, where he was arrested and subsequently sentenced for a violation of probation terms. In revoking Kissinger's probation, the federal magistrate declared, "Past behavior shows that his speech ends in civil disobedience." Similar language had been used three decades before in the South to imprison civil rights workers.

Abu-Jamal was the June 2000 graduation speaker, and again at the center of controversy, at Evergreen (Washington) State College. The students had selected him as their speaker, a decision backed up by the administration. President Jane L. Jervis pointed out that Abu-Jamal had a right to be heard because of his social activism as a journalist "to galvanize an international conversation about the death penalty, the disproportionate number of blacks on death row, the relationship between poverty and the criminal justice system." Rep. Tom DeLay (R-Texas)—at that time House majority whip before becoming majority leader and then indicted on federal charges that included money laundering—called the invitation "socially irresponsible." Gov. Gary Locke was also a scheduled speaker, but since he was running for re-election he cancelled. Abu-Jamal's 13-minute pre-recorded audiotape graduation speech was met by cheers and hostility throughout the state. Abu-Jamal—who had earned both B.A. and M.A. degrees in prison—also gave graduation speeches at Antioch College, Occidental College, and the University of California at Santa Cruz.

Reflecting the views of Thomas Jefferson, author of the Declaration of Independence, and James Madison, principal author of the Constitution, SPJ president Steve Geimann argued in 1996, "In our American democracy, broadcasters and news organizations seek to offer numerous points of view. Our democracy is strong because we protect everyone's right of free speech, even those whose views we may find objectionable or discomforting."

At Temple University, the departments of journalism, broadcasting, history, philosophy, political science, and religion all teach about the First Amendment and the necessity for all views, even controversial ones spoken by controversial individuals, to be heard. Students learn that denying freedom of speech to others often means we are afraid to face the truth. The university administration has demonstrated to its students, and to the world, that it is uncomfortable with the philosophy that shaped our democracy.

REPORTING PRACTICES

Enquiring Minds
and Space Aliens

When I don't believe I'm getting all the news from the nation's 1,408 daily newspapers, 6,250 community weeklies, 30,000 radio and TV stations, 20,000 magazines, or 170,000 books published every year, I turn to the supermarket tabloids for the truth. After all, it was the 3.1 million circulation *Star* which first revealed the existence of Genifer Flowers, Bill Clinton's alleged pre-presidential extramarital playmate.

Since most of the tabloid reporters have journalism degrees, worked on major daily newspapers, and are earning $60,000–$100,000 in their new assignments, I place great credibility in what is being reported in the five major tabloids, all of them published in Boca Raton or Lantana, Fla., and which have a combined circulation of about five million.

From the tabloids, I can monitor where Elvis is this week, learn first about who is seen with whom, and which TV series is planning to replace which megastar, and more than anyone ever needs to know about soap stars, none of this reported by our usually vigilant local press. I also know everything there is to know about Jennifer Aniston, Britney Spears, the British royal family, Big Foot, and why taking coffee bean baths can perk you up. I have also learned about monkey-faced boys, dog-faced girls, human-faced pigs, an 8-year-old who gave birth to twins, a woman who gave birth to a litter of 12 children, a 28-year-old grandmother, a man who was pregnant, and a tribe in South America that found a cure for cancer.

From the 350,000-circulation *Sun*, in one week alone, I learned that a survivor of the Titanic spent 20 years on an iceberg, that there really is a flying elephant with jumbo ears who lives in Zaire, that a woman is turning into Marilyn Monroe, that scientists in Jerusalem found Goliath's mummified head, and that miracles occur near a Florida tree that has the face of Christ. The establishment media also don't report much about house hauntings, psychic revelations, reincarnations, and extraterrestrials. However, all are conscientiously reported by the tabloids, and all for a buck or so a week.

In just one issue of the 722,000-circulation *Weekly World News*, in August 1992, I learned that condoms cause breast cancer, that a 7,000-year-old gargantuan shark patrols Lake Superior, that Hitler was really a woman who survived World War II and died in 1992 in Buenos Aires at the age of 103, and that a spaceship (with 14 perfectly preserved extraterrestrial corpses) was found in the Gobi Desert.

More importantly, I learned that a friendly space alien, not too unlike E. T., declared his (her? its?) support for Bill Clinton. A photo on page 1 showed the smooth-skinned, large-headed, long-fingered, unclothed alien shaking hands with the Democratic Presidential nominee after a 40-minute super-secret visit in Madison Square Garden during the Democratic National Convention.

It wasn't the first scoop for the *News*. In May, the newspaper had reported that the alien visited President George H.W. Bush at Camp David; in July, it reported the alien stopped by Dallas for a chat with Ross Perot who, apparently taking the alien's advice, soon dropped out of the race. Pictures also accompanied these articles, thus proving the alien's existence.

We learned that the alien—who came from the most success-ful planet in the universe—gave Gov. Clinton advice on health and environmental issues as well as how to turn the economy around. The alien's mission—other than to evaluate and rec-ommend a candidate for the confused American masses, most of whom would vote for the alien over any of the Presidential can-didates—was to seek "trade concessions that would benefit his home planet," according to reliable sources who talked with the *Weekly World News*.

A few of my more cynical journalist colleagues, obviously jeal-ous they were scooped on the biggest news story of the decade, called the story a hoax. To get to the truth, I made a few phone calls. A member of the White House staff said she believed that the President made several light-hearted comments about the visit of the alien, but referred me to another office for confirma-tion. An official spokesman for President Bush at first indicat-ed he didn't know what I was talking about when I asked about the space alien. After informing him of this late-breaking news, he said he didn't think the President made any comments about "that alleged meeting." He then informed me that "as far as we're concerned," there was no meeting, thus confirming my belief that if the White House says it didn't occur, it probably did occur.

On to Bill Clinton's team. The Governor had previously acknowledged that he discussed certain issues with an alien, and was pleased to receive the alien's support, an indicator that the Clinton-Gore team was broadening its base. At least that's what a few media reported.

Being the hard-hitting investigative journalist that I am, I had to get actual confirmation, if not from the Governor, certainly from an official spokesperson. Did you ever try to find an official spokesperson when you need one? After three days of phone calls, all I had was a lot of conversations with a pack of confused but obviously arrogant campaign officials who couldn't or wouldn't confirm or deny anything. Obviously, the Clinton team was more impressed with themselves, and the possibility they may one day be able to walk into the White House without a tourist pass, than in revealing the truth.

To clear up the confusion, I finally contacted Eddie Clontz, editor of the *Weekly World News*. Eddie was a pleasant fellow and an excellent journalist who worked for the AP, then for several years as a wire editor of the *St. Petersburg Evening Independent*.

"We had been working the story for a year," said Eddie who revealed that the newspaper received the tip from "some of our people in the military." He said that credible sources "often don't call regular newspapers because the dailies take it as a joke or will treat it as such," thus confirming my suspicions that daily newspaper reporters are more concerned with trivial things like crime and city council meetings than they are with news of interplanetary consequence. The photos, Eddie said, were submitted by one of the newspaper's sources. A true journalist, he wouldn't reveal a confidence. He did confirm that the newspaper plans to follow the alien's travels through the country, but probably won't be tracking either George Bush or Bill Clinton.

"We don't get into political coverage unless it has to do with a space alien," the newspaper's editor slyly said. Now, for the big question. Does Eddie Clontz, editor of a newspaper with larger circulation than all but the top five American dailies, believe in the alien? "I really don't think so," he said, noting that although "the photographs look real to me, as a skeptic I'd say it's not true." Actually, he also called the existence of the alien "preposterous."

In every political campaign, there is always something to break the tension, something to lighten up a campaign that tires out candidates, staff, reporters, and voters. In 1992, it was the alien's visit with the candidates. Sometime, it might be that the alien returned to the U.S. to declare his own candidacy.

Escalating an American Paranoia

Worried that a gang of thieves will break into your house, and that your dinky 9-mm. won't have enough firepower to stop them from taking your family's jewels? What if an alien nation launched an invasion, and your .357 Magnum liquified in your hands? How about those tank-sized rats in the basement who frightened your pet lion—or the moles who are building a city in your backyard and are planning to vote you out of office?

Fortunately, there's a solution. Get Rhino-Ammo, the "defensive" hyper-destructive hollow-nose bullets that fragment into hundreds of razor-like pieces within the body. "The beauty behind it is that it makes an incredible wound," David Keen, owner of the Florida-based Signature Products, told the media the last week of 1994. "They're going to die," he said. "There's no way to stop the bleeding. I don't care where it hits. They're going down for good." The package for Rhino-Ammo proclaimed, "the wound channel is catastrophic . . . Death is nearly instantaneous."

A second bullet, the Black Rhino, even more destructive, was designed to penetrate body armor, the kind police officers and some criminals wear. To allay Americans' fears, Keen promised that the Black Rhino would be sold "only to the right people," the 400,000 law enforcement officers and the 275,000 federally licensed gun dealers. If the wrong people get the bullets, it's only because the "right" people gave it to them, Keen said.

In a nation in which 1.1 million violent crimes were committed with a gun the year Rhino bullets were developed, and there were only 80,000 instances of the use of guns for self-defense, according to the Department of Justice, it's reassuring that only the "good guys" will get the bullets.

Federal laws prohibit the manufacture of "cop killer bullets," made of special metals, plastics, or coated with Teflon. However, these bullets don't fall under these regulations because Keen says they're not made of the prohibited materials.

The story of the Black Rhino began when Keen first fed it to his hometown newspaper, the *Huntsville* (Ala.) *Times*. After several other publications, including the *National Enquirer*, turned it down, Keen sent samples and test data to *Newsweek* when it expressed an interest in the story. The news brief in the December 19, 1994, issue opened with a description of what the bullets were likely to do, based on Keen's claims on the package, then quoted an unnamed federal narcotics agent—"they'll be used against the good guys."

The Associated Press quickly picked up the story, leading its December 27 coverage with an ominous message—"Two bullets more deadly than those used in the Long Island Rail Road massacre last year are about to be sold, despite fierce opposition from gun control advocates and police."

Within hours, most of the news media reported the latest "advance" in firepower, causing panic among the public, angry charges against Keen by the nation's police forces, and proposed federal legislation to ban "cop-killer" bullets, all of it reported by the national media.

The next day, Keen was on NBC-TV's "Today Show" to declare he was temporarily suspending production of the Black Rhino, but was continuing with plans to distribute the "less deadly" Rhino ammo.

And then ABC's "Nightline" checked out Keen's claims, and determined that the Rhinos it tested were no more devastating than an average hollow-nose bullet; it was devastating enough but ABC could not confirm that such an armor-piercing bullet even existed.

The news media now turned to claim the bullets were really a hoax. Keen's response was that the bullet "Nightline" had was a "work-up" load Rhino, and not the actual bullets.

In its February 1995 issue, the *American Journalism Review* had reported that Keen was "shooting blanks," and that the bullets were "too bad to be true." Keen says the *AJR* review was based solely on other articles and not on an analysis of the facts. "They slammed us," he said, bitterly claiming, "Nobody [in the media] lied to us more than *AJR*" in getting the story.

But, Keen faced attacks from an even deadlier foe. The National Rifle Association (NRA), knowing the public was irritable at widespread violence in America, had claimed, almost from the day of the Rhino's nationwide disclosure, that the bullets were a hoax, certainly no more devastating than anything else on the market. Furthermore, the NRA also put the word out that Keen was a member—or at least a plant—of Handgun Control, Inc., whose purpose, they believed, was to stir public fears about guns so they would support handgun registration.

"The only friendship I'm going to have is the NRA," Keen said, "and I've made an enemy that's very dangerous." Keen also claimed, "I am more frightened by the NRA than the death threats I have received." Three months after the controversy began, Keen simply said, "It's been a very bizarre three months in my life." But it wasn't yet over.

That spring, *Handgun* magazine conducted tests revealing that the .45 Rhino, now renamed the Razor, left a wound channel 5 inches wide and 7-1/2 inches long in a test against ordnance jelly. Jan Libourel, editor of the 180,000-circulation magazine, said the bullets, although not as catastrophic as what Keen claimed, were nevertheless more deadly than almost all other bullets on the market. However, critics pointed out that ordnance jelly, while often used to simulate humans, still is not human, and that not only was the magazine the "lapdog of the manufacturers," the magazine's "political agenda" was suspect.

Then in August, eight months after its first report of the catastrophic effect of the Rhinos, the AP distributed an article that tended to confirm the *Handgun* report. The AP had contracted with the H.P. White Laboratory to test the Razor against three other high-tech 9-mm. bullets. Both the Razor and Glaser bullets, each of them composed of lead pellets within a plastic-filled shell, left almost identical wounds when fired into ordnance jelly. All four bullets—Razor, Glaser, MagSafe, and Federal— were deadlier than whatever else was available to civilians, but none could penetrate body armor. However, the laboratory cautioned that because the Razor and Glaser bullets require high gun pressures, the risk "is that it could damage your gun or cause it to blow up."

In order to get a story, says Keen, the media "pit one group against the other," with the controversy partially stirred by "information merchants eager for sensational headlines," but who didn't check out the truth.

Maybe Keen's original claims were all hype by a company that was trying to switch in a post-Cold War era from making protective coatings for the Stealth aircraft to a consumer-based industry. Maybe Keen really did have a secret bullet—that Black Rhino he took out of production at the end of 1994—that was more devastating than anything else on the market.

Whatever the truth is, the Rhino stirred America's fears, and the media were right there to tell us the bullet existed—or didn't exist—or that it may exist. Either way, the story played well in headlines and the evening news for about two weeks, and then died while other claims or hoaxes moved to the media's short attention span.

War in the Gulf:
Lessons of an Obsession

In October 1990, two months after Iraqi troops invaded Kuwait, a 15-year-old girl testified before a Congressional committee that she was a hospital volunteer who saw Iraqi soldiers enter a Kuwaiti hospital and "take the babies out of the incubators, and left the children to die on the cold floor." Her unchallenged testimony was reported by most of the major American media. Several members of Congress said her testimony helped them decide to support what became Operation Desert Storm less than three months later.

With flags flying, Buck Rogers technology, and an allied army of 500,000 from a loose and temporary coalition of more than two dozen countries, led by a charismatic teddy bear general, we sounded forth the trumpets, declared we believed in democracy, and systematically decimated Iraqi forces in a one-month air and artillery barrage, then Hail Mary-ed them in a four day ground assault.

When it was over, and 20,000 people lay dead, about 2,300 of them civilian, almost 200 of them Americans, and another 150,000–200,000 injured, the Bush Administration proudly declared we defeated not only the "Butcher of Baghdad," but dictatorships and territorial aggression as well. A Memorandum of Understanding between Iraq and the UN ended the war.

Seventeen reporters had gone to Saudi Arabia in August 1990 at the beginning of Operation Desert Shield. By the end of the month-long Operation Desert Storm at the beginning of the next year, almost 2,000 reporters were crawling all over themselves to be first on the air or in print with the latest in war news.

In a month of saturation bombing, Americans were subjected to saturation media coverage. CNN and the BBC usually had the latest and most comprehensive coverage; most of the others, with few exceptions, had rumors.

The military told us, and the media reported, that Iraq had, and was likely to use, chemical, biological, and possibly nuclear warfare. In contrast, the American military piously proclaimed that we, noble warriors all, would never use those weapons. But, the media either didn't know, or they didn't report, that during the war the coalition had limited nuclear weapons in Saudi Arabia, driven as much as 500 miles from the ports to the front by American Marines.

From the war, we learned that our military intelligence wasn't as precise as we needed. While the media parroted almost daily official statements that precision bombing by the coalition had destroyed all of Iraq's SCUD missile bases, the SCUDs somehow kept popping up, often against Israeli targets. We also learned that the highly-touted U.S.-built Patriot anti-missile missiles were about one-third effective. Later, we reported that even after the largest air assault in history, Iraq still had numerous bases, missiles, and possibly the foundations for making nuclear weapons. We learned that Saddam, as part of that "Memorandum of Understanding," would allow UN inspection trips, but we didn't know he would block the inspections long enough so Iraq could hide much of whatever nuclear capability it had.

We learned that the military bunker in Baghdad we bombed really did hold hundreds of frightened women and children. Our military and press claimed Saddam had deliberately put them there as hostages. Saddam declared, with some justification, that they were in a heavily defended bunker to be safe from American attacks. The baby milk plant we destroyed, which the media dutifully reported to be a front for weapons manufacturing, really produced baby milk.

Fortunately, this was a short, easily managed war, unlike the seven years the United States was bogged down in Vietnam's rice paddies and jungles. In the Vietnam War, the American government realized too late that it needed to win the "hearts and minds" of the enemy. In the Gulf War, the American government realized it had to win the "hearts and minds" of Americans, especially since this war, unlike any other, could be reported live.

The Pentagon quickly and efficiently established two Joint Information Bureaus in Saudi Arabia, and set up two briefings a day to provide as much information as most reporters could handle—and possibly, to make sure that the reporters would be so bogged down in certain information that they wouldn't have time to find anything else. For their part, most of the reporters didn't have a clue of how to cover a war, asked dumber questions than freshmen after an all-night beer party, and allowed themselves to be manipulated by an efficient public relations operation. Meanwhile, the reporters thought they were courageously giving the American people their "right-to-know."

The Pentagon didn't want pictures of body bags being prepared at Dover Air Force Base, Del.; there weren't pictures of body bags. The Pentagon didn't want reporters to talk with the military, private through general, or Arab civilians unless an "escort officer" was present; the media didn't do 1-on-1 interviews.

To assure the media didn't overstep their boundaries and jeopardize the security of the troops, the Pentagon established media pools, selecting a few reporters, mostly from what it identified as the major organizations, to accompany the troops and to provide coverage that all the media could take and disseminate. "Pools rub reporters the wrong way, but there is simply no way for us to open up a rapidly moving front to reporters who roam the battlefield," said Pete Williams, assistant secretary of defense for public affairs. He claimed the use of the pools got "reporters out to see the action, [and] allows the military to accommodate a reasonable number of journalists without overwhelming the units that are fighting the enemy." It also assures that there would be fewer stories, and that only acceptable viewpoints of "establishment" media would be heard. Working under extreme pressures and deadlines, the "pool" did report the facts; often, they overlooked not only stories they were surreptitiously kept away from, but the truth behind the facts.

Nevertheless, said Williams, "Our goal is to get as much information to the American people about their military without jeopardizing the lives of the troops or the success of the operation." It was a different military philosophy than the one in Grenada, which Williams readily acknowledged as "a journalistic disaster." As a result of complaints against the military's refusal to allow media coverage of its mini-invasion of a Caribbean island in October through December 1983, apparently to make the world safe for American medical students, but truly a cover for the U.S. to try to destroy a Marxist regime allied with Cuba, the Pentagon created a quick-strike media pool which, said Williams, "could be called upon on short notice to cover the early stages of military missions."

At the end of the Gulf War, we reported we destroyed the Iraqi military, and then were surprised when Saddam, apparently with little opposition, launched attacks upon Shi'ite and Kurdish populations within Iraqi borders.

What we didn't report is more of an indication of how impotent or culpable the media were. Although thousands of combat troops, even five years after the war, were reporting health problems that didn't occur before the war, the media accepted official Pentagon explanations that the illnesses were not the result of combat activities. The media had reported that because of the danger from chemical and biological weapons, Americans were getting all kinds of vaccinations. Fortunately, Iraq did not launch nerve, chemical, or biological weapons. But, it took five years for the establishment media to finally report that the Pentagon required soldiers to take experimental drugs to reduce the effects of possible nerve gas attacks and that the evidence was becoming substantial that the Americans and allied troops became ill from the drugs.

It wasn't until five years after the war that we reported that 5,000 troops may have been exposed to sarin nerve gas when they destroyed a weapons depot. We reported that we used strong pesticides to rid the desert of insects, but didn't report that the pesticides we used were probably more dangerous than the life we sought to eliminate.

Coalition attempts to protect Kuwaiti-owned oil, which may have been the primary reason we went to war, failed when Iraq near the end of the one-month war destroyed the Kuwaiti oil wells. They reported that Americans were exposed to the Kuwaiti oil fires that blackened the sky, but didn't report that thousands of soldiers and Marines were complaining of health problems that were probably related to the fall-out from burning oil from the 751 wells.

Shortly after the Iraqi invasion, many Kuwaitis, including most of the royal family, fled to Cairo, London, and other capital cities where they took their wealth, complained about Iraqi atrocities, partied, and waited for the Coalition to hand them back their country. There is little question that Iraq committed atrocities, not only against its own minorities, but also against Kuwaitis. The Department of State for several years reported that Iraq's human rights record is "atrocious."

But, the Kuwaitis weren't exactly saints. A Human Rights Report issued by the U.S. Department of State pointed out there were "continuing reports of torture and of arbitrary arrest, as well as limitations on the freedoms of assembly and association." The report also condemned Kuwait for seldom releasing prisoners with severe medical problems, and stated that "sanitary conditions are such that a communicable disease would spread easily throughout the entire prison."

Four years before the Iraqi invasion, Kuwait's royal family had dissolved Parliament. Under American pressure, the al-Sabah royal family, safely in exile and promising anything to the Coalition, promised that once the war was over it would permit elections. In October 1992, the Amir restored a 50-man parliament, but political parties were still banned. The "democracy" we fought to preserve is for the 90,000 or so voting citizens of Kuwait. More than 550,000 Kuwaitis—including women, servants, and laborers—have no voting rights. Only males older than 21 who can trace their ancestors to having lived in Kuwait prior to 1920 may vote.

The Kuwaiti Constitution, suspended in 1962, still has not been restored. Freedom of the press was curtailed in 1985, and then barely restored after the war. Although prior restraint upon the media has been abandoned, the media and people still face severe restrictions. A Department of Censorship exists. The people and the media may not criticize the Amir, the Kuwaiti government, or the Islamic religion.

We have also learned a lot about PR and media manipulation. Within months of the end of the war, we learned that the 15-year-old who talked about atrocities in Kuwaiti hospitals was not a volunteer but really the daughter of the Kuwaiti ambassador to the United States, and that there may not have been an atrocity at all. We learned that her testimony was orchestrated by the New York PR firm of Hill & Knowlton which received a large chunk of more than $20 million which Kuwait paid to establish two American-led front groups whose missions were to convince the American government—and, of course, American business—that there was overwhelming support by the American people for war against Iraq to preserve what we thought was "democracy," but was probably more of America's obsession with oil for energy that fueled this war.

For that, we sent in hundreds of thousands of Americans to kill, and to be killed, by hundreds of thousands of Iraqis, and to

73

pretend we were fighting to preserve a democracy that never did and probably never will exist.

[Twelve years after the liberation of Kuwait, the U.S. and England, with a force of 300,000, invaded Iraq. In five weeks of attacks, and with minimal resistance by a nation with few war-making resources, the "Coalition" overthrew the Hussein regime. But, the war continued; in more than five years, more than 4,300 Amerian soldiers were killed, more than 30,000 wounded, by insurgents.]

All the News That Fits—
In 500 words or a Graphic

The editors of *USA Today*, as they do every day, had to decide what to make its "Cover Story."

The death toll from the cyclone in Myanmar was approaching 25,000, with about almost a million homeless, and the ruling military junta was still refusing to accept foreign assistance.

A Pentagon report revealed that about 43,000 medically unfit troops were sent into combat.

In Philadelphia, six police officers were under investigation for beating suspects. And, in Russia a new president was inaugurated.

What the editors chose to dominate the front page was a three-column head photo of presidential daughter Jenna Bush and a story about her forthcoming non-public private wedding. The only reason *USA Today* didn't run the story on its front pages Saturday and Sunday was because it doesn't publish on weekends. But, just about every other news medium gave the wedding heavy play.

When *USA Today* debuted in 1982, it was a glitzy full color alternative to the average gray newspaper. Focused upon an audience of travelers, and primarily available at airports and hotels, the five day a week newspaper, then as now, had short, quick looks at the news. "Across the USA" is a series of one paragraph stories from every state, plus the territories, something to let the lonely traveler know his home state still exists. A color weather map informs travelers what to expect when they arrive at an airport a dozen states away. Extensive business stories target middle- and upper-management workers who don't have the time to read that day's *Wall Street Journal*.

With an emphasis on polls, *USA Today* tells us what we think. And what we think is divided into four equal parts—News, Lifestyle, Sports, and Money. Thus, news is one-fourth of the newspaper.

Ridiculed as McPaper, but read by about two million people a day, most of whom get their daily dose from vendor boxes that look like a TV on a stand, *USA Today* has set the agenda for almost every newspaper in the country. Following the *USA Today* model, local newspapers have splashed color and graphics on its pages. The stories are shorter, but not necessarily tighter. And, in an era of downsizing, there are fewer reporters, fewer in-depth stories, fewer and narrower pages, and a greater reliance upon wire service stories. But, celebrity-based stories and increased fluff—what editors wrongly believe the readers want—have taken over the front pages.

USA Today was never designed to replace the local newspaper, nor should it be a model for local newspapers, which are struggling to find ways to survive both bad business decisions and a national recession. *USA Today* has a niche, and serves that niche well. But, local newspapers have become *USA Today* clones. That's why if *USA Today* places a celebrity wedding as its most important issue of the day, then it's reasonable to believe that the clones also believe that 25,000 deaths can be relegated to the inside pages.

Fewer Words, Less Filling

It was a delightful show. All 37 Shakespearean plays, cleverly and humorously abridged to just two hours by the Reduced Shakespeare Co. Short of having a set of *Cliff's Notes*, source of innumerable student essays for more than a half-century, or a collection of Classic Comics, it was the least painful way to "learn" Shakespeare.

The condensation of the media probably began in 1922 with the founding of *Reader's Digest*, the pocket-sized magazine that keeps its 12.5 million U.S. subscribers happy by mulching articles from hundreds of other magazines. Books also aren't safe, as the *Reader's Digest* editors grind four books into the space of one, and call it a "condensed book." The company entered the World Wide Web in 1996, doing what it does best. Reader's Digest World, a navigation system to search millions of home pages and documents, seizes relevant materials so anyone with a computer can download slices of knowledge.

Reader's Digest edits literature to allow readers more time to participate in society's more meaningful activities, such as doing sit-ups with Richard Simmons, watching the adventures of Luke and Laura on "General Hospital," or swapping useless lies with the folks at the country club. However, most media condense life solely to save money and improve corporate profits.

Once, for a buck, you could spend the entire afternoon at the movies, watching an "A" film, a "B"-quality second film, two or three six-minute cartoons, and a couple of "trailers" promoting upcoming films. Inflation now dictates a $6–$10 admission, for which you get three or four trailers and only one film. Even the films themselves have been downsized. Once, "A" films ran at least two hours. Now, with few exceptions, they tend to be about 100–110 minutes, long enough to fit into comfortable two hour cycles that allow theater owners 10–20 minutes to rewind the film and clear a theater before showing the same film again.

Once, television was divided into four 13-week blocks a year. Three of the blocks were for original programming; the fourth block was for summer reruns, pilots, and specials. However, network executives figured that even with reduced advertising rates and union-mandated requirements to pay residual fees to numerous creative personnel each time the same episode is aired, it would be less expensive to schedule re-runs than to order new programs. The result is that the networks have reduced original programming to 22 shows a year.

In radio and television news, the seven-second sound bite is now standard, forcing news sources to become terse, witty, and superficial. News stories themselves average about 30 seconds, topping out at 90 seconds, down considerably from the era when journalists, not talking heads and image consultants, were responsible for what appeared on air.

The print media during the past 30 years have downsized not only the quality of paper, but the size as well. Page sizes of 8-1/2 by 11 inches are still the most common magazine size, but several hundred major national magazines are now 8- by 10-1/2 inches, a 10 percent reduction.

Book publishers demand shorter manuscripts, and then to save even more costs squeeze more type onto a page, sometimes photographically compressing type to save a few bucks. The book publishers, which have been swallowing up each other for the past two decades, have even figured out how to do a *Reader's Digest* number for people who don't like to read, or who pretend they don't have the time. The publishers have now placed more than 60,000 books onto CDs, allowing the driver to digest words while simultaneously talking on his cell phone and weaving among traffic jams.

Newspaper page width has dropped to 13-1/2 inches, from almost 15-1/2 inches during the 1950s; many Sunday color comic sections are now being printed in 12-1/2 inch widths.

USA Today, the *Reader's Digest* of newspapers, condenses the world into four sections. Publishers of community newspapers, citing both *USA Today's* format and nebulous research about reader attention span, impose artificial limits on stories—15 inches is a common measure for most stories—while throwing color and graphs at the readers.

Editing the 12 Commandments

The downsizing of news content isn't a new problem for writers. God and Moses faced the same problem 3,000 years ago. Fortunately, a reporter was present at that meeting on Mt. Sinai. Unfortunately, he could hear only Moses' side of the conversation. . . .

Now, Yahweh, I really have to talk to you about those commandments. We have an economic crisis at the moment. You see, the price of stone tablets has gone sky high. That means we have to cut back on some of the commandments in order to save money . . . Yes, I know you think 12 commandments are necessary, but it'll cost us more to use three tablets. . . . Yes, I guess you can just make more rocks.

But, Yahweh, there's this other matter. You see, your people have too many things to do than read all those commandments. Right now, they're in the desert partying and watching a real cool comedy routine from Maimonides Seinfeld. . . . No, I don't think there's going to be a problem with the Jews acting like they were life members of a college fraternity since my brother Aaron is taking care of the people when I'm gone. . . .

Now, Yahweh, because your people don't have much of an attention span, we'll add color charts and pictures, and float them into one killer page design on the tablets. Of course, it means we'll have to cut some of the text. A few words here. A

77

couple of paragraphs there. . . . I realize that the words are the most important thing, but work with me on this.

For starters, you have given me seven paragraphs just about you. Don't you think that's a bit egotistical? . . . . WO! Hey, Yahweh, could you lighten up with those lightning bolts? I'm just looking out for your own interest. I mean, Yahweh, you say you're the boss-man. The Big Kahuna. We all know that. But then you go ahead and say all that stuff about graven images and jealousy and vengeance and swearing. How about we just tighten it up a little. How's this sound?—"I'm in charge and don't you forget it." . . . Well, we can work on it.

Now, the next three paragraphs all have to do with taking a day off. That's good. Shows the people that you believe in the labor movement. But, *three* paragraphs? Why not just, "Don't overwork yourselves and others so you have time for reflection?" The people just don't have time to read too much these days.

Now, of the next six, isn't there any you could do without? . . . Oh, I see, it's commandments that the Jews can't do without. Well, what about dumping the "don't kill" commandment? I mean, there's going to be a lot of killing in this world. What about a few exceptions? . . . I see. It's your world and you don't want people killing anything. No exceptions. Well, then, *you* deal with the NRA.

Now, the commandment against that adultery thing could get a bit tricky. After all, a lot of your chosen people have chosen to go into the entertainment industry. . . . OK, so the commandment stands as you wrote it.

Maybe we could combine the commandments about not stealing and coveting? Seems a bit redundant. . . . Well, that's true. I guess some Philadelphia lawyer could claim that lusting for things isn't the same as stealing them, and some D.A. in the name of justice could tack two charges upon some thief so there's something to work with in a plea bargain. Maybe we dump the false witness thing. . . . I see, you're saying that it's needed because of something known as an O.J., which won't occur for three millennia? Well, if you say so.

I suppose the clause about honoring mothers and fathers stays? . . . Well, sure, if you have this covenant with Hallmark Cards, I'm not going to tell you to renege.

But, Yahweh, we still have to cut you back by half. . . . *Six Snappy Secrets to Success* is a better book title than your *The Daily Dozen.* . . Yes, I know you have final right of edit. OK, here's the deal. Dump just two of the commandments, let me tighten up the writing on the rest, and I may even be able to get you a film deal; maybe even a big-name star. Add in some special effects, and we'll call it *Firestorms of Desire.* . . . O.K., have it your way, but I'm telling you, *The Ten Commandments* just isn't sexy enough.

A Righteous Indignation

There was enough blame passed around as to who or what caused Princess Diana's death in 1997, and those of her companion and chauffeur. But no one took the responsibility. Not the paparazzi who incessantly chased her for 17 years, nor the media which paid several million dollars to the freelance photographers, nor the world-wide public whose insatiable demands for fuzzy pictures taken from 1,000 yards away drove the media to sell their editorial souls for circulation revenue.

Some of the righteous claimed the fault was the driver's, that had he not been running 60–100 m.p.h. before losing control, three people would still be alive. They said if he had slowed down, so would have the pursuers. But, fear is one of the most basic of all human emotions, and when a gang of seven people on motorcycles and scooters are pursuing you, it's not possible to know if they plan to shoot you with a Leica or a Lugar.

Two days after the crash, the Parisian prosecutor stated that the chauffeur's blood alcohol level was at least twice that of the legal limit. Even if the driver was drunk, it's still the paparazzi who are at fault, wailed millions of righteous folks who never sold a photo in their lives. If the paparazzi hadn't intruded upon the privacy of others, if they hadn't been so aggressive, if they hadn't pursued the princess to her death, if they hadn't been so greedy, none of this would have happened, they moaned.

It's the tabloids who pay the outrageous prices for celebrity photos, shrieked millions of those same righteous folk who bought at least 10 million tabloid newspapers every week in America alone and gave TV tabloid shows high enough ratings to justify paying thousands of dollars for "exclusive" and intrusive video clips of celebrities.

Without question, it's definitely those evil tabloids, sanctimoniously preached righteous editors from the nation's "establishment" press. "We never buy [photos] from the paparazzi," Janice

Min, senior editor of *People* magazine, told a CNN audience the morning after Princess Diana's death. "We compete against them all the time [for pictures]," retorted Stephen Coz, senior editor of *The National Enquirer*. The publication rights are so important for a newspaper's perceived "reputation" and, thus, sales, that the going rate is now about $1,000–$2,000 for pictures of movie stars with new lovers, to more than $10,000 for exclusives of celebrities who are in legal trouble. London's *Sunday Mirror* even is reported to have paid £250,000 in summer 1997 for first rights for 16 paparazzi shots taken from several hundred yards away of Diana and her fiancé. Tipsters, family, friends, and employees all get paid by the paparazzi to make sure there are no secrets left among celebrities. Ironically, the *Daily Mirror* four months before the Princess's death stopped buying and publishing those fuzzy long-lens "candids," a staple of the tabloid press.

People published 43 cover photos, as well as hundreds of inside candid photos and innumerable gossip stories of Diana since she first became a celebrity. Eventually, the magazine featured Diana on more than 50 covers. *People's* August 25, 1997, eight-page spread about the new romance of Di and Dodi even included thumbnail pictures of British tabloid front pages.

Almost every daily newspaper, general circulation magazine, and network news show has run stories and pictures not only of Princess Diana but most superstar celebrities, often republishing the same information while sanctimoniously saying how bad the tabloid press is.

Katherine Graham, former publisher of the *Washington Post*, who occasionally played tennis with the princess, told investigative reporter Mike Wallace on a special edition of CBS-TV's "60 Minutes" how wonderful Diana was—and that the *Post* wouldn't ever stoop to the level of the tabloids. But the *Post*, the haughty but sainted *New York Times*, and more than 1,000 daily newspapers, with the behind-the-scenes assistance of hundreds of publicists, publish gossip columns that clue in their subscribers to which celebrity is doing what with whom and where it's being done.

While in denial over their role in publishing or broadcasting celebrity gossip and paparazzi photos, and claiming they would never buy photos taken by the paparazzi at the death scene, the media have published and broadcast innumerable pictures of the car. This is also the same media, which give scanners, two-way radio communications, cell phones, and pagers to their staff photographers to make sure they get the first pictures from fires, traffic accidents, and crime scenes.

As the first rumors spread about the deaths, TV stations canceled programming to broadcast network-created tributes. Community newspapers, which boasted how little national and world news they publish, opened up two to three full pages to stories about the princess, including interviews with local residents whose only knowledge of the royal family came from the media themselves. These were the same media which published only a few inches or broadcast not more than a couple of minutes of news about the 100,000 who were evacuated in floods in North Dakota, the thousands killed in Algeria, or the suffering of millions of starving Africans.

In less than a year—two months in some cases—dozens of book publishers churned out Princess Di books, loaded with photos, rumors, innuendos and, maybe, some facts. Their marketing and promotion departments designed extraordinary ways to place their products onto best-sellers lists. For their parts, the bookstores bought more copies of Princess Di books than anything about the contemporary social and consumer issues.

And that leaves the righteous public which condemn paparazzi and the media. But, the American culture is obsessed by celebrities. Unable to be a part of their lifestyle, they live fairytale lives by fixating upon the media's reporting of every intimate fact, factoid, or ridiculous rumor. The media response, when not hog-tying themselves in righteous contradictions, is "The public has a right to know," "It's in the public interest," and "We're only giving the public what it wants."

Charles Spencer, in mourning for his sister, told a news conference that he had long ago said, "The press will kill her in the end. Every editor has blood on his hands." Perhaps he might have added, "and so does every person who read or watched gossip stories about any celebrity."

An Unbalanced Media

The death of oceanographer/filmmaker Jacques Cousteau in 1997 rated a mug shot and a few sketchy lines. So did the deaths of writer/musician John Denver, and actors Jimmy Stewart and

Robert Mitchum.

Mother Teresa rated a larger mug shot.

TV Journalist Charles Kuralt, best-selling authors Harold Robbins and James Michener, comedian Red Skelton, golfer Ben Hogan, and Supreme Court justice William Brennan didn't even rate a mug shot.

Princess Diana got the cover and 10 inside color pages.

It wasn't the *National Enquirer*, or even *People*. The Diana splash was the centerpiece of *Newsweek*'s "Pictures of the Year" wrap-up, and its way of saying what it considered to be important in 1997.

"But we were doing a year in pictures," *Newsweek* editors probably believed. "It was an international tragedy, and there were more dramatic pictures of the Princess than of anyone else."

That's one of the problems. The media—almost all of which pretend they don't use paparazzi—opened their pages to an almost unlimited collection of photos and in-depth stories, liberally sprinkled by speculation, rumor, innuendo, and hearsay. It's hard to believe that the *Newsweek* editors didn't have in their own files photos of Michener and Kuralt, or that they couldn't easily acquire those pictures. There might not have been as many pictures of Brennan, one of the First Amendment's staunchest defenders, as there were of Diana, but there were pictures. They could easily have been more dramatic, more insightful than any of the Diana pictures. For almost two decades the media placed a higher value on the life of a storybook princess than for those who have committed their lives to helping society better understand and improve itself.

"But the people want the Diana pictures," the editors wailed in the delusion they were giving the people what they wanted, thus abrogating their responsibility of reporting about all issues that affect the people to give them a balanced version of what they need.

"Balance" is the other major problem in the "year-end" wrap-ups. *Newsweek* picked and chose what it thought was the "best." Among the photos in the "living" section, *Newsweek* designed two-page spreads of boxer Evander Holyfield's chewed ear (from a bite by Mike Tyson), George H. W. Bush skydiving, three Buddhist nuns testifying before Congress, the reconstruction of the TWA 747 that crashed off Long Island in Summer 1996, and one-page photos of dead 6-year-old JonBenet Ramsey who had been abducted.

Newsweek did publish a two-page landscape of a flooded and burned out section of Grand Forks, N.D., But it could have published a couple of pictures showing people helping each other, or perhaps even one of the staff of the local newspaper working against flood and deadlines to publish every day. Those pictures would be more representative of what happened than a portrait of water and buildings.

Newsweek ran only one photo of Bill Clinton. Of the photos that were shot of the President, of which *Newsweek* photographers shot thousands, the editors chose a picture of the President hobbled by a ripped knee tendon, and supported by members of his staff. It was a dramatic photo. But, there were other dramatic photos.

Most media, like *Newsweek*, focus on the unusual, the different. Guess what picture the media will publish should a football player who gains 200 yards in a game slips on the sidelines. Guess what picture will be used should one politician stifle just one yawn in all of his days in office. Guess what picture the media will choose between a scientist in a lab who won the Nobel Prize and the latest celebrity spotting of Jessica Simpson or anyone whom the media so anoint as a celebrity.

The media need to balance their reporting to make sure the public gets enough information that it can better understand our society and all of its contributors, not just the deeds of criminals, the weird, the unusual, and pop celebrities.

The Tired Media

Howard Kurtz, media reporter/editor for the *Washington Post,* said on CNN's "Reliable Sources" that the reason he sent two reporters home from the floods in North Dakota in May 1997—which forced about 100,000 people to be evacuated and caused over $1.5 billion in damage, including wiping out a major farm industry—was because "after a week of flood coverage, people get tired." He said "they need to go home to their families." Barbara Cochran, president of the Radio and Television News Directors Association, chimed in that with television, "you're making a decision about dozens of people. It's very expensive to keep the satellite trucks and the edit packs and the camera crews and everyone out there and they get tired . . . So there is a reason to pull them out."

About 12,000 reporters and crews were accredited to cover the three weeks of the 1996 Olympics. About 4,000 reporters and crews camped out next to the courthouse for the first marathon O.J. trial. The "All-O.J.-All-the-Time" TV networks ran 30-minute, one-hour, and all-evening "specials" on top of nightly news stories about O.J., something they never did during the floods. There was media saturation of the rape trial of basketball superstar Kobe Bryant and King of Pop Michael Jackson, both of whom were found not guilty.

Apparently, the media are allowed to be "tired" only when celebrities aren't involved.

Flip-Flop Flap

The media have an insatiable appetite to gobble up even the most superficial minutia and spit it out as hard news.

During the first few months of 2005, spread across every daily newspaper, tabloid, and pop culture magazine, discussed endlessly on afternoon talk radio, aired on myriad news and feature TV shows, was the Brad Pitt–Jennifer Aniston break-up. So well known had the media made the TV and film stars that just referring to them as Brad and Jen was enough. Media coverage went into overdrive when Brad and Angelina Jolie starred in *Mr. and Mrs. Smith*, giving the media enough fodder to scream that not only were these two stars dating but that Angelina might have been the cause of the Brad–Jen break-up. Enquiring minds wanted to know. Soon the media merged them into Bragelina.

For a couple of years, the media gorged on the dating habits and engagement of Ben Affleck and Jennifer Lopez, whom they dubbed Bennifer. This being a Hollywood romance, there was the break-up, followed by the sequel. Bennifer II starred the engagement, pregnancy, and marriage of Ben and Jennifer Garner, who had become America's "cute couple of the moment."

Still searching for critical news, the media dished out the secrets of Jude Law cheating on Sienna Miller, Britney Spears' pregnancy, and the latest Jessica Simpson brain cramp. For more "enlightened" audiences, the media were all over Tom Cruise jumping onto Oprah's couch to proclaim his love for Katie Holmes, and his "Today" show dissing of post-partum depression and psychiatry.

In crime stories, the media had feasted upon pretty young White girls who were abducted, the Laci Peterson and Bonnie Lee Blakely murders, and Michael Jackson's trial on child molesting charges. Media pundits proclaimed Jackson was guilty, especially since late night comics were talking about the King of Pop more than they were spewing politics and dirty jokes. But the Justice system betrayed the media and acquitted Jackson of all 10 charges. Stung by the verdict, the 3,000 on-site reporters, assistants, and camera crews that had camped out in Santa Maria, Calif., during a mild Winter by the ocean, haughtily packed up and left.

During the 2004 Presidential campaign, Bush–Cheney supporters drew media coverage when they showed up at John Kerry rallies and waved flip-flops to suggest, often correctly, that the Democratic nominee flip-flopped on his answers to critical questions. But, it was flip-flops in the White House that got the media salivating onto their keyboards.

About a week after the nation's 229th Independence Day celebration the media again got the story it needed, unwittingly provided by the national champion Northwestern University women's lacrosse team. Beneath a headline that quoted the lawyer-brother of one of the players—"You Wore Flip-Flops to the White House?!"—was a well-crafted front-page story in the *Chicago Tribune* about the team's meeting with President Bush. In a routine group picture provided by the White House, four of the nine women in the first row were shown wearing flip-flops; the others wore open-toe sandals. About half of the other members in the other three rows also wore flip-flops. "Don't even ask me about the flip-flops. It mortified me!" the mother of one player told the Associated Press.

President Bush, partially in response to the casualness of the Clinton presidency, had established an edict that there would be a more professional dress standard in the White House. The President, who often wears cowboy boots, was dressed in a blue suit, blue tie, and dress shoes to meet the lacrosse players, but didn't seem to think the casual footwear of his guests was a problem; after all, his own 19-year-old daughter, Jenna, had worn black flip-flops to court in 2001 to plead "no contest" to a charge of underage possession of alcohol. Confronting pedicured toes, few in the White House or the media noticed that the University of Michigan softball team wore khaki shorts, polo tops, and sneakers in its meeting with the President.

Reporters, columnists, fashion mavens, and just about anyone with access to a writing implement, or who could dial their
favorite talk show, all spoke. Hundreds of local newspapers
localized the story by asking residents their opinion, and business executives their policies. In-depth investigations bared the
facts that flip-flops are comfortable, ubiquitous, and are manufactured in styles from plain $3 rubber beach wear to $500
Gucci leather-strap and sequined fashion statements. The shoes
the Northwestern women wore into the East Wing and flip-
flopped onto the South lawn were neither.

Next for the media might be investigative features about why
hospital gowns have slits down the back and the medical risks
of the Secretary of State wearing high heels.

Perhaps they could report about what shoes to wear while
pumping $3 gallons of gas, or what suitcases are appropriate
when the President packs for frequent vacations in Crawford,
Texas. Maybe the media could discuss if presidential advisor
Karl Rove should wear a toupee to impress the Grand Jury if he
is subpoenaed for his role in possibly leaking the name of a CIA
agent in retaliation for her husband's attack upon the
President's credibility.

Whatever the next story arc is, it will be designed to play into
the public's lust for all the news that's fit to scandalize.

Ooops, She Did It Again

Ever vigilant, the mass media dug into a critical social issue
and rooted out the information in their never-ending quest to
guarantee the people's right to know.

The people's right to know, they determined, was that 16-
year-old Jamie Lynn Spears, star of Nickelodeon's "Zoey 101,"
was pregnant. Jamie Lynn is the younger sister of Britney
Spears, the former Mouseketeer who has combined a chart-top-
ping career as a singer/dancer with being America's Celebrity
Super-Skank.

The *National Enquirer* first broke the story about Jamie
Lynn in its July 28, 2007, issue. Unfortunately, Jamie Lynn
wasn't pregnant at the time. This prompted her horde of
lawyers to notify the nation's largest newspaper that their
client is "a devout Christian with a spotless reputation, who
lives in accordance with the highest moral and ethical stan-

dards in accordance with her faith." They demanded a retrac-
tion, pending an all-out legal assault to defend Jamie Lynn's
good name.

Shortly after the *Enquirer*'s story appeared, and thousands of
bloggers became sexually active, Jamie Lynn's "good name"
became semen-stained when she became pregnant, probably in
September. The father was 19-year-old Casey Aldridge, who
lived with Jamie Lynn and her mother in an L.A. condo, and followed the teen mini-star to the "Zoey 101" set almost every day.

True to the ethics and business practices of tween celebs,
Jamie Lynn hid the news until she could find a price high
enough. High enough to run the story was *OK!* magazine, which
put Jamie Lynn and a mega-hype teaser on its cover, and trumpeted the six-page in-depth investigation as a "world exclusive."
The magazine's hyperventilating publicist told the media and
the public if they wanted to get all the details of this breaking
news interview with Jamie Lynn and her mother, they needed
to "pick up the new issue of OK!—on newsstands everywhere."
In true media tradition, the "news" was released a day before
the magazine appeared on the shelves, Dec. 19, two weeks
before its cover date. Circulation was expected to rise faster
than a pubescent boy's hormones.

Naturally, the rest of the messed-up mainstream and alternative media also had to jump onto the story. *OK!*'s not-so-hard
news interview led off the news segments of the network morning shows, was discussed thoroughly by the mid-morning and
afternoon talk shows, and was featured by CNN, MSNBC, and
FOX News—which paused just long enough to report about a
fire in the Eisenhower Executive Office Building adjacent to the
White House; a chemical plant explosion in Jacksonville, Fla.,
that killed three and injured 14; and the President signing an
Energy Bill. Radio, the Blogosphere, and internet-based newspapers wasted no time polluting the airwaves and the world's
bandwidths; print newspapers were caught in the wrong news
cycle and had to publish "day after" not-so-investigative stories.
Underreported, or not reported by most of the media, was that
in four separate instances in Iraq, seven civilians were killed
and 27 wounded. Nevertheless, enquiring American minds
wanted to know all there was about Jamie Lynn; within a day,
Google recorded more than 150,000 separate stories and blog-
ger comments.

Jamie Lynn said she would raise her child in Louisiana, "so

it can have a normal family life." What she really meant was that those danged Hollywood people, infused by pregnancy-causing smog and ocean air, was what led to her pregnancy. If she stayed in Southern California, she feared she could again become impregnated before she graduated from Home-School High School.

Since the Spears family are devout Christians, they believe in abstinence-only sex education; older sister Britney even rode the reputation as a chaste and oh-so-moral virgin, telling her fans and the media she was saving her hymen until marriage— until she was so overwhelmed by California air and pop singer Justin Timberlake, as well as several others, before her two-year marriage to model/rapper Kevin Federline.

Devout and once-abstinent Jamie Lynn's condition, combined with whatever condition sister Britney was in, also led to collateral damage. Mother Lynne Spears was the author of a book about parenting, scheduled for publication during the Spring 2008 season. Thomas Nelson, America's sixth largest trade publisher and the top publisher of Bibles and Christian and inspirational books, delayed the how-to/memoir. That "exclusive" information was revealed by *People* magazine, which undoubtedly believed it, not *OK!*, should have gotten the Jamie Lynn world exclusive. In Fall, Thomas Nelson published *Through the Storm*, which Lynne Spears said was "the story of one simple Southern woman whose family got caught in a tornado called fame, and who is still trying to sort through the debris scattered all over her life in the aftermath. It's who I am, warts and all, with some true confessions that took a long time to get up the nerve to discuss."

Sex, Violence, and Media Credibility: Celebrity Journalism in America

The abrupt end of "Days of Our O.J." in October 1995 caught Americans by surprise, leaving them confused and whining that three hours were long enough for a football game but not acceptable for a jury's deliberation.

Simpson, the former NFL all-Pro running back, sports commentator, movie actor, and TV ad huckster, was accused of murdering his ex-wife and an employee of the restaurant in which she worked. A slow-speed two-hour 60 mile chase on the L.A.

freeways in June 1994 was watched by thousands from the edge of the freeways and by more than 95 million Americans who watched it on television. For awhile, the arrest and subsequent trial—with Simpson's "million dollar defense team," an interracial prosecution team, made-for-TV celebrity witnesses, a respected judge who couldn't control the media or his court room, and an underlying tension of race relations—all covered live by the media over almost eight months—was often the highest rated show on daytime TV. More than 1,000 reporters, cramped into the parking lot known as Camp O.J., were credentialed to cover the trial. Thousands more had some part in O.J. coverage; CNN alone devoted more than 600 hours to the story; the other networks devoted more time to the case than any other story, including the Oklahoma bombing, floods in the Southeast, and ethnic slaughter in Bosnia.

Two years after the slo-mo Bronco ride, FOX and MSNBC developed 24-hour newscasts that needed to be constantly fed, and would exploit any celebrity sighting or trial that came along. By the end of the decade, several cable networks opened time for a steady diet of celebrity sightings, as nutritious to the soul as junk food is to the stomach. Newspaper editors, who blamed the "newsprint crisis" for increased subscription costs and fewer newspaper pages, laid off reporters the previous year but always made sure there was sufficient room in the paper for O.J. coverage. And then the trial ended, and America went into withdrawal.

Unable to quit cold turkey, the media desperately milked the story of The Juice. Within minutes of the verdict, it seemed as if every reporter in L.A. bought ladders so they could peer into O.J.'s Brentwood yard and continue to give the people their daily dose of O.J. in the form of all the gossip that's fit to be smeared.

The jury said that O.J. was not guilty. The media needed more than a jury's opinion, so they published summaries of every hour of testimony, and devoted interminable sidebar opinions of everyone who ever watched a football game and, therefore, absolutely knew whether or not O.J. was guilty. But, the story wasn't over. A subsequent civil suit by the families of the murdered ex-wife and the waiter provided even more opportunities to fill space. This time, O.J. was found guilty by a "preponderance of evidence" rather than the standard of "beyond a reasonable doubt" necessary in a criminal trial.

Those who defended the coverage claimed it was news—and

that it did bring about a national debate about race, celebrity, and the American judicial system. Others just claimed the trial titillated America's fascination with celebrities and had only minimal news value, compared to all other possible stories.

With Camp O.J. over, and with the public believing that the media hounded Princess Diana to her death, the press corps created Monica Beach. As at most beaches, the reporters lied around, watched the scenery, and salivated over every inch of skin they could find, whether it was sexual acquaintance Paula Jones's nose job, big-mouth Linda Tripp's appearance, or presidential playmate Monica Lewinsky's weight and semen-stained blue dress, all of it detailed in the conservative Internet blog, *The Drudge Report* that became the opinion leader for the establishment press.

The day Monica and her four-limousine entourage arrived at the federal courthouse to testify about her relationship with Bill Clinton, the media bumbled into each other to get "exclusives." While waiting for her to say nothing after her testimony, they constantly replayed the same scene and chatted about what she was wearing—and why. They "interviewed" onlookers to get the "man on the street" opinion and lied to the public by calling it "hard news." Their teammates, instead of questioning and investigating, staked out the White House, waiting for news to happen.

For several months, the Monica story led off the evening news, and was blocked for as much as five or ten minutes of our dinner time, while other stories got 90 seconds at the most, if they made it on air at all. The news magazines devoted pages to the scandal, while other stories got little more than "news brief summaries"; newspapers ran front-page banner headlines, while avoiding in-depth coverage of the economy, corporate downsizing and out-sourcing to "maximize profits," and problems of poverty and the health care industry.

Reporters, like inquisitors and politicians, believed they could leech onto a president and get their own 15 minutes of fame. However, former *Washington Post* investigative reporter Carl Bernstein who, with Bob Woodward, helped bring about the end of the Richard Nixon administration, repeatedly said that Bill Clinton's affair and probable cover-up weren't even close to what Nixon and some of his senior staff had done in the Watergate scandal.

Sen. Orrin Hatch, Utah's oh-so-moral Republican senator,

sounded forth the trumpet of moral righteousness, planning to step over a lame duck Democrat while on the path to a Republican White House in two years. The Press, of course, gave Hatch almost unlimited air time to spout his invective, failing to challenge his statements, while lapping up everything he said like the puppy dogs they had become.

House Speaker Newt Gingrich, second in line to the presidency behind Vice-President Al Gore, cautioned his fellow Republicans to reduce the invective and gesturing until the independent counsel's investigative report was sent to Congress. It was a smart move since the Speaker may have committed adultery while his first wife had cancer. The Press was also relatively silent about former Senate Majority Leader Bob Dole, the Republicans' moral-bearer in the previous presidential election, about an affair he might have had while married to his first wife, whom he left for a younger woman. Like Congress, the Press sanctimoniously pontificates about morals, while network anchors have pasts that include adultery. Larry Flynt, *Hustler* publisher, posted a million dollar reward for persons turning in adulterers in the same Congress that was outraged at the President's actions. Among those Flynt's net caught was Rep. Bob Livingston who had been recently elected Speaker of the House. In resigning, he declared Flynt to be a "bottom feeder." Flynt agreed, saying, "but look what I found on the bottom."

People are interested in the lives of celebrities. They will read about the fairytale world of high-priced clothes, cars, and houses; they will dream about a world they would like to be a part of, but know they never will, and so are content with following the lives of their favorite celebrities; perhaps, on a rare occasion, they may even glimpse one in a public area, maybe even get a word or two and an autograph. When celebrities get into trouble, the people will follow that part of their lives just as intently as they follow their much-reported love lives.

Sex, violence, and celebrity formed the base for extensive media coverage in the murder trial of Harry K. Thaw of Pittsburgh (1871–1947), 35-year-old multimillion dollar playboy heir to a coal and railroad fortune. In a New York nightclub/restaurant, Thaw shot 53-year-old Stanford White (1853–1906), one of the nation's most prominent architects, to avenge the "deflowering" of Thaw's 21-year-old wife, Evelyn Nesbit (1885–1966).

Nesbit, also from Pittsburgh, five years earlier had become a New York model and show girl. White, married and the host of innumerable parties with young women, seduced her, and she became his willing mistress. About the same time, Thaw also decided he wanted Nesbit, and pursued her for almost three years until she agreed to go to Europe with him in 1904. In Europe, Thaw, who had a violent temper and often hit the young show girl, demanded to know the details of Nesbit's affair. Vowing vengeance, Thaw, who married Nesbit the following year, stalked then murdered White. The New York newspapers, engaged in the "yellow journalism" circulation wars, interviewed dozens of "witnesses" to the murder and to the parties, printing an assortment of lies, innuendoes and, occasionally, even the truth. Irvin S. Cobb of Joseph Pulitzer's *New York World*, a respectable journalist working for a respected publisher, wrote more than a half-million words spread over dozens of articles. From what editors knew sold papers, the scandal of orgies at White's apartment was more salable than Thaw's temper and wife-beating. At Thaw's second trial in 1907—the first one ended in a hung jury, thus giving the media more opportunities to exploit the scandal—the jury found Thaw guilty by reason of insanity. It was, according to the media, the "crime of the century"—and the century was only seven years old. For decades, hundreds of newspaper and magazine articles, dozens of books, and the film, *The Girl on the Red Velvet Swing* (1955), retold the story; E. L. Doctorow used the murder in his best-selling novel, *Ragtime* (1974), which became a film (1981) and Broadway musical (1998).

Dozens of scandals and 14 years after the "trial of the century," the media latched onto the life of Roscoe "Fatty" Arbuckle (1887–1931), a million dollar a year film comedian, second only to Charlie Chaplain in popularity. His physical comedy of pratfalls and somersaults, combined with nimble dancing routines, belied his appearance. Arbuckle, known to work hard and party even harder, was arrested in San Francisco following the rape and subsequent death of a woman known to be a party girl. All of the lascivious elements for public interest and media coverage were present, but this time it became the first major mass media scandal. Because of the national distribution of films, the entire nation knew who Arbuckle was, and the nation's powerful newspaper chains and newly-emerging radio networks were able to send the story across the country. But, it was the Hearst empire, with the *San Francisco Examiner* leading the way, that kept the story in its headlines, forcing other newspapers to continually play "catch-up." William Randolph Hearst—whose *New York Journal* had been one of the leaders in publishing stories about the salacious Stanford White, the "virginal" Evelyn Nesbit, and the "heroic" Harry K. Thaw—by the early 1920s was at his peak as the nation's most powerful media baron. The media saw the scandal as another way to increase circulation, publishing innumerable stories fueled by half-truths, distortions, and doctored photographs. Even *The New York Times*, which once promoted itself as the newspaper that "does not soil the breakfast cloth" to emphasize it wasn't a part of the Yellow Journalism sensationalism at the end of the nineteenth century, had long before abandoned its moralistic editorial philosophy and was not only pushing for Arbuckle's conviction, but gleefully recounting the sins of the entertainment industry, even if it had no evidence. However, Hearst also saw the scandal as a way to punish the film community for its well-publicized excesses. Although Hearst owned a movie studio and was also known for his own licentiousness, he also had a long-time hatred for the film industry for settling in Southern California rather than in Northern California, his home. After three sensational trials, with prostitutes, show girls, actors, and publicity-seeking coroner, prosecutor, and witnesses, this jury, unlike the first two that were deadlocked, found Arbuckle not guilty. In an extraordinary action, the jury, following 31 days of testimony, not only rendered its verdict in only six minutes but also gave the judge a statement that it felt "a great injustice has been done to [Arbuckle.] There was not the slightest proof adduced to connect him in any way with the commission of a crime. . . . [T]he evidence shows [he] was in no way responsible."

The film industry banned him for almost a year, but reluctantly lifted the ban when it received bags of mail from fans who wanted Arbuckle to again star in full-length comedies. It wouldn't happen. The ban may have been lifted, but the industry didn't want to risk offending anyone, especially Hearst and the sensationalist press. The comedian spent most of the remaining decade of his life directing low-budget films under an alias.

The next "crime of the century" was the kidnapping and murder of the 19-month-old son of Charles and Anne Morrow Lindbergh. Eventually, the media barage, including significant violations of privacy, forced the Lindberghs to flee America and live in Europe from 1935 to 1939.

It wasn't unusual for the Press, once onto a celebrity case, to use whatever means possible to secure information, even if some reporters had to violate the law to get to it. Reporters, sometimes with police deliberately looking the other way, often broke into crime scenes, stole evidence, interviewed witnesses, published the names and addresses of the jury pool, and slanted news coverage to meet their editorial beliefs, all in the mistaken belief it was the "public's right to know." It was no different when the state of Ohio charged Sam Sheppard in 1954 with the bludgeoning murder of his wife. For the media, this was a circulation-building case of the highest magnitude. Sheppard was a 30-year-old neurosurgeon from a prominent Cleveland family of physicians; his beautiful wife was pregnant. When the media tracked down facts of Sheppard's adultery, they knew they had a sensational case. During the Thaw–Nesbit–White triangle sex-and-scandal case of 1906–1907, the media were newspapers and some magazines. With the Arbuckle case, radio was added. Now, with the Sheppard case, television, combined with the other media, would bring the story throughout the country. The public would be able to see Sheppard live, not in newsreels. TV cameras were allowed to intrude in the coroner's inquest, where Sheppard was grilled for five hours without an attorney present; it was allowed to interview witnesses and jurors. With heavy coverage by the city's newspapers, the media had already poisoned the jury pool with innumerable stories all pushing for the physician's conviction. Eleven of the jurors acknowledged they had followed the case in the media not only prior to the trial but during the trial as well. On the first day of trial, the judge even told nationally-syndicated columnist Dorothy Kilgallen that Sheppard was guilty.

For the past seven decades, millions of Americans have wondered how it was possible for the Holocaust to have occurred. We need to look no further than America's reading habits for the answer. In 1993, the worst-selling single issues for *TIME* and *Newsweek* were cover stories about the war in Bosnia. For *U.S. News & World Report*, the worst-selling cover story was about the war in Somalia. The best-selling issues? Cover stories about radio talk host Rush Limbaugh and lesbianism.

In 1966, ten years after Sheppard was first imprisoned, the Supreme Court remanded the case to the lower court, ordering a new trial. In a scathing opinion, written by Justice Tom Clark, the Supreme Court ruled:

> Bedlam reigned at the courthouse during the trial and newsmen took over practically the entire courtroom, hounding most of the participants in the trial. . . . The movement of the reporters in and out of the courtroom caused frequent confusion and disruption of the trial. . . .
> As the trial progressed, the newspapers summarized and interpreted the evidence, devoting particular attention to the material that incriminated Sheppard, and often drew unwarranted inferences from testimony. . . .
> From the cases coming here we note that unfair and prejudicial news comment on pending trials has become increasingly prevalent. Due process requires that the accused receive a fair trial by an impartial jury free from outside influences.

However, the Supreme Court, delicately avoiding a First Amendment issue and staying with Sixth Amendment (fair trial) issues, reserved its strongest comments for the conduct of the trial:

> The judge lost his ability to supervise the environment. . . . The court should have made some effort to control the release of leads, information, and gossip to the press by police officers, witnesses, and the counsel for both sides. Much of the information thus disclosed was inaccurate, leading to groundless rumors and confusion.
> Given the pervasiveness of modern communications and the difficulty of effacing prejudicial publicity from the minds of jurors, the trial courts must take strong measures to ensure that the balance is never weighed against the accused.

In a subsequent trial, Sheppard was found to be not guilty, but was never able to overcome public opinion and his 10 years imprisonment. The former neurosurgeon became an alcoholic and a professional wrestler, dying at the age of 46. Subsequent DNA evidence showed that the probable killer wasn't Sheppard but was the "bushy-haired stranger" Sheppard had repeatedly said he saw leaving the house. The Sheppard case became the basis for the TV series, "The Fugitive" (1963–1967 and 2000–2001), and a film (1993). More important, the case established rules for the conduct of a trial by the presiding judge, while also allowing a freedom of the press.

By the beginning of 2004—thousands of scandals after the first of several dozen "trials of the century"—celebrity news puffs and trials had pushed from the front pages and magazine covers the wars in Afghanistan and Iraq, the nation's health care crisis, the declining economy, and increased unemployment, environmental destruction, and corporate white-collar crime. During 2003 alone, a high-water mark in celebrity scandals, the press and the public feasted on murders, rapes, drug charges, thefts, abductions, and child molestation, splashed onto front-page headlines, magazine covers, TV news, and the ubiquitous TV "infotainment" shows where journalists and pretend-journalists pretend to present news and "exclusive features" that are disguised to attract ratings. Among those involved in murder investigations were Robert Blake, who starred in the TV series "Baretta," and who was accused of killing his con-artist gold-digging wife outside an L.A. restaurant; Phil Specter, legendary music producer, accused of killing a B-movie actress; and Scott Peterson who, of all the people accused of murder that year, the media made into a celebrity. Peterson, a 30-year-old fertilizer salesman in Modesto, Calif., was accused of murdering his pregnant wife. As the media gleefully trumpeted, Peterson had committed several acts of adultery, and his primary liaison was fair game for interviews. Peterson was eventually convicted and sentenced to death.

In other circulation-building "crime-of-the-century" celebrity scandals, NBA all-star Kobe Bryant was accused of raping a 19-year-old, whom the media, based upon leaks and unnamed sources, quickly identified as being a mentally ill "party girl." Roman Polanski, who won that year's Academy Award for directing *The Pianist*, was in Romania and couldn't accept the award; he had fled the United States in 1978, after being charged with statutory rape of a willing but still under-aged 13-year-old. Several other celebrities were arrested for hitting people. Martha Stewart, a media favorite, was hit by the Securities Exchange Commission for insider trading, although the evidence to convict her seemed to be flimsy. Singers Glen Campbell and Wynona Judd were arrested for drunk driving. Actor-Comedian Tommy Chong was sentenced to nine months and fined $20,000 for distributing drug paraphernalia; drug charges were also filed against singers Courtney Love, Lil Kim, and dozens of others. No charges were filed against talk show host Rush Limbaugh who was addicted to prescription pain killers, which he obtained illegally. The trial of two-time Academy Award nominee Winona Ryder, who pleaded guilty in 2002 to taking more than $5,000 in merchandise from an upscale Beverly Hills department store, was long over, but still in headlines and on talk show monologues.

Of almost 60,000 children abducted by non-family members in 2003, about 60 percent of them minorities, the media focused upon one—Elizabeth Smart, a 14-year-old in Utah who was abducted in June 2002. It wasn't an unusual selection; when the media extends coverage to an abducted individual, they focus upon abducted White, good looking girls or young women from upper middle class or upper class families who have the resources to reach and convince the public and the media to raise that one abduction beyond all others. Nine months after she was abducted, Elizabeth Smart was found; by then, the media had run thousands of stories about her; there would be thousands more as the public tried to learn about what happened during her kidnapping and why she either didn't or refused to escape.

And then in November 2003, the Santa Barbara Sheriff's Department issued an arrest warrant for pop superstar Michael Jackson on charges of child molestation. All media hype during the all previous celebrity trials, including O.J.'s, would pale by comparison. First, the media spread the rumors that Jackson would be arrested, followed by a five hour watch for Jackson's plane to land in Santa Barbara, Calif., the District Attorney's jovial press conference, self-serving stories from the police and the prosecutor's office, and dozens of quotes from neighbors, friends, and strangers. It didn't take long for the media to discover the identities of the divorced parents of the alleged victim, and to run innumerable conflicting stories. In June 2005, with much of the media salivating at the "probability" of Jackson's conviction, the jurors ruled him not guilty on all counts. Instead of just tearing up their prepared scripts, many commentators re-emphasized the charges and, in opposition to the nation's system, of justice, declared that Jackson should have been convicted.

Pretending they are covering "news" by watching who was

going in and out of courtrooms, or flooding Sunset Blvd., or reporting the latest buying habits of media-made movie stars, the Press pretends to be pundits and analysts, projecting oh-so-wonderfully witty opinions. With the glare of TV lights, reporters even become equals to the personality-drenched celebrities they are covering.

One of the primary roles of the journalist is to uncover the truth—not just what people say is the truth—and to help people better understand their lives and the critical issues that affect them. But it's easier to hype celebrity lives and to create a feeding frenzy based upon leaks, innuendo, gossip, rumor, myriad unnamed news sources, and occasional facts than to meticulously look into the social fabric of a nation. The media's sex-and-scandal pandering and personality-drenched news make the supermarket tabloids look respectable.

The mass media and celebrities have been almost intertwined since the dawn of printing, with both using the other. The same mass media which are the vehicles for persons to become celebrities and elected politicians then report, exaggerate, and magnify their lives, often from "leaks" provided by the celebrities' publicists, are the same media which will exaggerate the importance of their scandals, rightly figuring that the public will want every lurid detail about a celebrity's life. But, with each article, the mass media raises even the insignificant to match and possibly exceed previous levels to keep reader interest. Celebrity news coverage in news magazine more than doubled since 1980; about one-third of all Americans have "celebrity worship syndrome," according to a study conducted by *New Scientist* magazine in 2007.

By inflating minor scandals—a shoplifting arrest of a celebrity, for example—or the personal and romance lives of every A-list celebrity—and not reporting on more significant issues affecting non-celebrities—the media have lost the ability to discern what is vital and what is truly insignificant and not worthy of extensive coverage. More important, they have abrogated their responsibility of helping readers to place news events into context.

Instead of giving saturation coverage to celebrities, inflating the stories out of proportion to their place in the day's news, the media could do extensive reports about prosecutors who must plea bargain justice in order to clear the overburdened court calendars, or judges who are giving lighter sentences because prisons are overcrowded. They might report that most defendants, unlike the celebrities, can't afford "dream team" legal representation, and are given public defenders who are only a couple of years out of law school and whose budgets barely cover legal pads. They could report more on the social reasons why many in the underclass turn to crime or those of that economic class who are affected by crime. They could also do far more about why the justice system, with only a few exceptions for celebrity thieves, seems to focus upon petty thieves who steal from a few people rather than upon the upper class white-collar criminals whose actions affect thousands.

Perhaps, the media might look into doing extended coverage of the issues of spousal abuse, the homeless, the health care crisis, the burgeoning right-wing survivalist and militia movements, teenage alcohol and drug abuse, the economy, and the consequences of catastrophic fires, floods, and hurricanes. The media might give as much coverage to the lives of volunteers for the nation's social service agencies as they do for the exploits of $500 an hour lawyers or for stories about which shoes the latest starlet wore to Spago's Restaurant. In response, the media titans say they are giving the people what they want, that they are merely feeding the public's frenzy for the sensational, that it's not the media but the public that wants the salacious and lascivious, that the public loves seeing the fall of the rich and famous. Besides, it's much easier to report, and for the masses to understand, a trial with clearly-defined protagonists and antagonists than to do in-depth coverage of greater social issues.

But by devoting the top five minutes of the 6:30 p.m. newscast to O.J., Kobe, Martha, and Michael (they no longer need last names in our celebrity-obsessed society), and less than 90 seconds to issues of poverty, the health care crisis, and natural disasters, the media already told us what they think is important—or what they think the public thinks is important—and we believe them because it's easier for them—and us—to ignore the greater issues. Since they don't hear the people complaining, the media assume that's what the people want.

Historians a century from now, using the mass media as their primary research documents, might believe that Americans were enshrouded by sensationalism and voyeurism. They might conclude that Americans were concerned about diets, appearance, sexual intimacy, ways to build both relationships and investment portfolios—and celebrities, including their crimes, clothes, and current love interests.

The American public may have lost their sense of what is news, but until the media quit lying to us with their pandering—and pretending it's "the public's right to know," we have little reason to believe the media aren't relying upon less than professional standards in coverage of the other news. It makes no difference if it's a city council meeting, the pre-story of a high school football game, or the investigation of a president.

Fantasy Week at Walt's

Some people think columnists spend all morning lying around on the couch, surrounded by beautiful women while contemplating outrageous things to write. In the afternoon, in an opulent office funded by outrageous royalties, they write the column.

All of that is true, of course, but that still leaves the evening when we're expected to incessantly grill our sources until they admit to having shot the Easter Bunny so we can justify writing our 700-word pack of lies. The result of all that writing is that I have tendonitis in my shoulder.

First stop, my family physician who said if I'd lose a ton I'd feel much better. Of course, he also believes that being hit by a truck is good for you since you can lose weight in the hospital by drinking dinner through an IV.

Next stop, an orthopedist with tendonitis. He said he couldn't prove I became lame because of writing, but that he got his injury at Baseball Fantasy Camp.

For $3,500–$5,000, depending upon the team, you can spend a week in Arizona or Florida training with major league ballplayers, and even get to play in a game with the veterans. It's an opportunity for social workers, speech pathologists, fire fighters, cancer researchers, and others to actually do something with their lives instead of wasting it away helping humanity. By hitting a home run and possibly getting that $3 million contract and $10 million in endorsement fees next year, they qualify for front-page news coverage and the right to do 30-second TV commercials that tell us how important Nikes and Cokes are in our lives.

While on the Columnists Injured List, taking drugs and lifting weights like all athletes, I decided to go into coaching. For $4,000 each, I'll let a couple of readers follow me around all week. I'll even bring in a strength conditioning coach; after all, you have to make sure those fingers and eyelids are in top shape. Here's the deal . . .

You would stay in a 110-square foot spare bedroom in my house in a quiet rural working class neighborhood. During work breaks, you'll have a chance to talk with Nuggette, a wide-bodied newspaper-delivering Golden Retriever; Kashatten, a wise, noble, protective german shepherd; and Sherkka, a majestic and overtly friendly German Shepherd. You can play with Sheba, a bouncing bundle of laundry-stealing mixed breed joy; Cabot, a playful but intellectually devious shepherd/husky; and Pig Floyd, a miniature pot-bellied PWA—Pig With Attitude. Among the trees and bushes of the backyard are bunnies, squirrels, chipmunks, birds, and dozens of other wildlife, all of them capable of making you better understand mankind's integration into their world, all of them capable of distracting you from your deadlines.

For meals, you'll have a choice of raiding the refrigerator or dining out at any of the exclusive Route 11 fast food restaurants. After a hard day's thinking, you could experience part of the columnist's fast-lane entertainment lifestyle by watching TV and falling asleep in the recliner or chatting with any of my neighbors, all of whom know I'm a journalist, yet still talk to me.

At the end of the week, just as in Baseball Fantasy Camp, you'll get a chance to write a column. As deadline approaches, you'll get exclusive tips on how nationally-syndicated columnists check e-mail and play games on the computer to avoid writing. Sunday night, hours before the deadline, you'll panic and ask my wife for an idea. Since she's a labor relations specialist, she'll even advise you on contracts and how to earn that $3 million a year as a star advice columnist.

Monday morning, with a 10 a.m. deadline, you'll get up at 7 a.m., and dash off 700 words that you swear is the best lexical effort since Noah Webster walked the earth, but for which some readers can prove their letters to Aunt Matilda are better written and more thought-provoking.

Now, before you rush off to your bank and take out that $4,000 in small unmarked bills, it's only fair to warn you that you'll have to read a half-dozen newspapers, watch two or three TV newscasts, and listen to the radio and CD player a couple of hours every day, as well as read a half-dozen magazines during the week to find not only the news, but how the media cover the news. This much exposure to the media could result in a mental meltdown.

But, it's all worth it since writing a weekly column isn't much harder than getting a major league hit. As for that opulent office with the dancing girls—you'll have to sign-up for Advanced Columnists Week. It's only $8,000, and I'll guarantee you'll have a better batting average than the Phillies.

ACCURACY

The Press Meets the Afo-a-Kom

The return of a ritualized and functional royal throne figure of African heritage from a New York City art dealer to the Kom people of Cameroon was widely but poorly reported by the world's media in late 1973. Not much has changed since then in either the worlds of art or journalism.

The Kom story was part of the budgets of virtually all American and several overseas wire services. News and feature articles appeared in most of the world's media, including *The New York Times, Washington Post, National Geographic, Die Bunde Illustrierte, Ebony,* and *Esquire,* as well as the three major American television networks. The Afo-a-Kom even became the answers to questions on a number of television quiz shows, including "Jeopardy." The story was hot, and the media knew it.

Depending on what was read at the time, the Afo-a-Kom, a 100-year-old statue, was either a god . . . a phallic symbol . . . an icon . . . or a symbol of tradition, unity, and harmony. It was either "as sacred as" two other Kom statues . . . or the most sacred of all. It was either a national shrine of the Cameroon . . . or a part of the Kom people. It was 5- or 5-1/2-feet tall, or 62-, 62-1/2-, or 64 inches tall. It was made of ebony . . . wood . . . iroko. It was covered either by red beads . . . or reddish-brown and blue beads . . . or brown and blue beads. The beads were coral . . . plastic . . . semi-precious stones.

It was stolen from the people of Kom in 1966 . . . or 1967. It was taken from a storage hut that was loosely guarded . . . or not guarded at all. The original thief—there were many—was the son. . . or the nephew . . . of Fon (King) Law-Aw . . . or Al-Aw

. . . who died shortly thereafter . . . or who died before the theft. The thief was ostracized . . . punished . . . not convicted. The Fon himself was powerful . . . or not-so-powerful . . . or had no power.

Aaron Furman, a New York City art dealer who had either an unblemished reputation. . . or was a scoundrel . . . purchased the Afo-A-Kom in Cameroon . . . or Paris . . . or somewhere else . . . in 1967 . . . or 1968. . . . It was brought to the United States, with Furman apparently believing that it was legitimately purchased . . . or knowing it was stolen. It was valued, by American standards, at $30,000 . . . $51,000 . . . $60,000 . . . $65,000 . . . $80,000. Furman eventually sold the statue for "his expenses" . . . or "a substantial sum". . . or $25,000.

According to the media, Kom is a series of villages . . . a tribal enclave . . . Shangri-La. But, no matter what it is, Kom is located, according to the popular media, in West Cameroon . . . or East Cameroon; in the Federal Republic of Cameroon . . . or the United Republic of Cameroon. As for the people of Kom, that remote Cameroonian kingdom, they number 30,000 . . . 35,000 . . . 40,000 . . . 81,000 . . . or 92,000. No one was really certain. The Kom, stated the media, are also primitives . . . savages . . . or trapped by modern civilization.

The first story about the Afo-a-Kom broke in the October 25, 1973, issue of *The New York Times*, after one of its correspondents had learned from two Peace Corps workers of the Afo-a-Kom's theft. Within hours, the other national media jumped onto the story and became overzealous, rewriting and compounding errors. Even the *Times*, which published 15 stories (about 700 column inches) over a two-month period, committed numerous errors of fact and interpretation.

When the media weren't bungling the facts, they were locked in a trap of ethnocentrism. The majority of articles that came from the American media showed a basic lack of understanding of cross-cultural communication, as well as a lack of understanding of the people whose beliefs, world views, languages, and cultures are not those of certain Americans.

Not untypical of the views were those of a writer for *Esquire* who apparently overdosed on *Tarzan* movies. Armed with an experience of less than a half-day in Kom, a place she never knew existed prior to her desire to suddenly write a "definitive" study of the Kom people. She claimed she had been "to the edge of the earth." She admitted, reflecting the views of many reporters, "I wanted to go to Kom. I wanted to see the

Fon's 50 wives and half-naked slaves and all the pomp and panoply of great African kingdoms, where the people would receive us white bwanas, bowing low or maybe even casting themselves to the ground and throwing dust on their heads. I've heard of things like that. Also I wanted to see the Fon ride out on his legendary pure white horse to greet us, followed by ten servants carrying calabashes of palm wine and his umbrella and his chair." She worried whether the salad was safe to eat, called the flora of Cameroon "strange plumy vegetation," and called Kom's history "bloody murder, war, witchcraft, fire, famine, and flood," without recognizing that a part of the history of the Kom is no different than the history of any people, including the Americans.

The *Times*, with numerous reporters parroting its reporting, inaccurately claimed, "The women of Kom are completely subordinate to their men. They are expected to work hard, bear many children and not complain. The women do all the farming, cooking, cleaning, child raising, and most of the market selling . . . Many women say they like polygamy because it lessens the very heavy work burden." The Kom, however, are a matrilineal society, and there are clear cut distinctions in Kom society between sexual, biological, and sociological wives.

In contrast, some of the media, especially the BBC and the *National Geographic*, were relatively accurate, taking the time to verify facts and evaluate the sources of information.

Why the major media gave the story such heavy play probably is a reflection of Americans' fascination with "exotic" lands, crime, and conflict, and by what we thought was a work of art that carried a price tag. Johnson Ndimbie, at that time cultural affairs officer at the Cameroon Embassy to the United States and Canada, believed the story received the coverage it did because not only were the media trying to find stories about Africa, but because they are "more concerned, or more capable, of covering the bizarre and sensational. They seemed to be more interested in coups and conflicts because it makes good reading."

In contrast to the exploitation of the story by the larger media, the smaller papers usually spiked the wire service copy. Most newspapers argued, "Well, you know that there's a newsprint shortage and we really don't have the room. Also, no one is interested in things happening in Africa. It's just too far away."

And that's the problem, but it isn't solely one caused by the media; they merely mirror society.

Creating Historical Fiction

A few years ago, I tried to tell my younger son that some passages in his 9th grade history book were incorrect. He refused to believe me. After all, there it was, written in print and paraphrased in lecture by his teacher. Even if he believed me, he knew he'd lose points on the next test if he didn't answer the way his teacher and textbook expected.

Even in the most meticulously-researched and written text, errors are inevitable. However, because many public school social science texts are little more than well-designed cut-and-paste jobs from other texts, written to please the masses rather than to tell the truth, and often put together by committee, the errors in one are often compounded in the next.

Nevertheless, errors of *commission*—a wrong date, the wrong name, an interpretation not based upon facts—can usually be fixed either by an addendum, circular to teachers, or in the next edition.

Errors of *omission*, however, are more serious because they can't be verified as easily, and may have been caused by author, editor, or publisher bias, ethnocentrism, or just plain lack of knowledge of an area or, more seriously, a failure to challenge authority or to question politicians and corporations that are better able to spin the truth than reporters are able to uncover it. It's these errors that skew the understanding and interpretation of history.

Most media-perpetuated errors of omission hoaxes aren't the result of deliberate lies by the media, but sloppy reporting and a failure to adequately investigate sources and data. One day the media report that oat bran is the "be all, cure all" of all life's problems; a few days later, they report there may be no effect of oat bran in the diet. One day, Vitamin C is the cure for cancer; the next day, it's Selenium. Sometimes, it's a new cancer killing drug; the next, it's an admission that the drug still needs to be tested. If you believe the supermarket tabloids, it's a cancer killing drug made of oat bran that was brought to earth by space aliens who plan to marry Madonna in a group ceremony in Fresno. In spite of their image as cynical, reporters often buy official statements dished out by official sources. Local reporters often buy statements by well dressed truth-spinning executives over the statements of the impoverished, unemployed, or the "whistleblower."

Majority cultures write the histories, and their texts often reflect their biases and political agenda. During the latter twentieth century, Japanese texts overlooked the slaughter of thousands of Chinese civilians; Soviet texts failed to mention America's massive economic and humanitarian assistance to that country; and the texts of all countries reported little about the Holocaust. Publishers in America, trying to reap the widest possible financial benefit by not offending anyone, often force authors to overlook significant historical and social trends. For more than a century, books which targeted buyers in the North consistently overlooked or minimized Southern views about the Civil War; for at least a century, other books which targeted a Southern readership discussed the War of Northern Aggression or the War Between the States. And, almost all newspapers, magazines, and books overlooked significant issues about slavery or of the genocide against Native Americans.

There have been dozens of reporters—among them George Seldes, I.F. Stone, and Sarah McClendon—who asked the tough questions and refused to accept official versions. However, most are from the "alternative" press or are consciously separated from the "establishment" media. Even Helen Thomas, who spent most of her 60-year career with UPI and was known as the "dean of White House correspondents," was often viewed as an "outsider."

White House correspondents, and most of the country's news media, bought President Richard Nixon's version of what became the Watergate conspiracy, even attacking the reporting of *Washington Post* reporters Bob Woodward and Carl Bernstein, until the evidence became overwhelming.

During the 1960s, innumerable newspapers, including *The New York Times*, passively accepted government doctrine, and ran stories that exaggerated the "threats" posed by Black militants during the Civil Rights battles and by anti-war demonstrators protesting the nation's involvement in Vietnam. In the daily "5 O'Clock Follies" during the war, military officers discussed that day's operations, as well as the body count. The reporters, having an official source and apparently thinking that body counts were a good way of quantifying the war, much like scores quantify athletic contests, included the numbers in their daily stories. By the end of the war, if readers believed the media, they would have learned that every North Vietnamese and Viet Cong civilian and soldier was killed at least twice.

During the first Gulf War in 1991, reporters blamed the military for not giving them more information, but seldom challenged Pentagon claims of how many Iraqi SCUD missiles were destroyed or how effective the American Patriot anti-missile missiles were.

During the second Gulf War in 2003, the media became "embedded" with the troops, giving Americans "first-hand" information. By focusing upon the individuals and smaller units, the media often overlooked the greater issues that defined the war. And, as with reporting during the Vietnam War and the previous Gulf War, what the media didn't do was to adequately report the massive anti-war protests. The mass media essentially left unchallenged the President's claims that the U.S. needed to go to war against Iraq because it not only harbored terrorist camps allied with al-Qaeda, responsible for the 9/11 murders, but also possessed significant weapons of mass destruction. By the time the U.S. did go to war, more than three-fourths of Americans believed the Administration's claims, with about half of all Americans believing that Saddam Hussein was behind the 9/11 murders, according to a CBS News–*New York Times* poll in April 2003, a month after the U.S.-led invasion of Iraq. Numerous non-American media challenged these claims; Americans who protested were declared to be unpatriotic or traitors. Following the war, the CIA and other intelligence agencies acknowledged that the Administration's desire to go to war may have been an exaggeration of what was truth. Both the *New York Times* and *Washington Post* publicly apologized for running stories that never challenged the President's statements, nor questioned the truth of the claims about reasons to go to war.

The "super-patriotism" by Clear Channel, a 1,200-station radio network headquartered in San Antonio, Texas, by the FOX news network, and some other major media, combined with the failure to adequately investigate and report the war, led to questions about American media objectivity and reporting skills. Both conglomerates say there was no correlation between their unabashed acceptance and promotion of the Bush Administration plans and pending FCC regulation that would have further loosened restrictions upon electronic media ownership. Even if there was no correlation, there were substantial concerns. "I was shocked . . . by how unquestioning the broadcast news media was during this war," charged Greg Dyke, director general of the British Broadcasting Corp. (BBC), regarded by journalists, the public, and most heads of state for its probing but objective reporting. In a speech at the University of London in April 2003, Dyke charged, "If Iraq proved anything, it was that the BBC cannot afford to mix patriotism and journalism. This is happening in the United States and if it continues, will undermine the credibility of the U.S. electronic news media." In contrast, al-Jazeera, an Arab wire service, received high praise from the international community, as well as from most American journalists, for its objective and in-depth coverage of the war and related issues. Because of its attempt to counter-balance U.S. policy, al-Jazeera came under attack by the Bush–Cheney Administration. Shortly after the U.S. launched a massive military campaign in Falujah during April 2004, as part of the war in Iraq, al-Jazeera broadcast the story that more than 600 Iraqi civilians, including many women and children identified by the U.S. as "collateral damage," had been killed. Secretary of Defense Donald Rumsfeld was furious, telling the nation, April 15, "What al-Jazeera is doing is vicious, inaccurate, and inexcusable . . . It's disgraceful what that station is doing." The next day, according to reporting by London's *Daily Mirror*, President Bush proposed bombing al-Jazeera's headquarters. The response by the White House was that the President was only joking. However, those familiar with a classified five-page memo of a meeting between President George W. Bush and British Prime Minister Tony Blair said that Bush was serious about destroying al-Jazeera headquaretrs, but was strongly talked out of the action by Blair. In August 2004, the Iraqi government, apparently encouraged by the United States, closed al-Jazeera's Baghdad bureau for 30 days. Interim Prime Minister Ayad Allawi said the reason for closing the bureau was because, "They have been showing a lot of crimes and criminals on TV, and they transfer a bad picture about Iraq and about Iraqis and encourage criminals to increase their activities."

The American media also bought the official versions of what happened at Wounded Knee, Ruby Ridge, and the Branch Davidian compound, all scenes of what many later claimed was FBI "overkill."

To establish standards for the study of history in the public schools and to correct some of the nation's textbook wrongs, the National Endowment for the Humanities, under Congressional mandate, gave $1.75 million to UCLA's National Center for

History in the Schools to bring together a wide range of academics to study the problems and to recommend a model text that would present history as it was, rather than what we hoped it was. The concept was good; the execution was abysmal.

The Center rightly determined that texts were "sugar-coating" and distorting American history, that there was an over emphasis upon a recitation of facts and in recounting the deeds of a few people, mostly white males, but far too little discussion about major trends and social issues that defined the American republic. But, in its recommendations, the Center did exactly what it condemned. With a political and social ideological agenda, the new standards, presented in a 271-page document at the end of 1994, discounted the Western European influence in the formation of the United States, and presented a distorted overview that the formation of the country was a convergence of Islamic, African, and European influence. It claimed that the nation's history is little more than struggle, conflict, and the abuse of the rights of people. It barely discussed the historic role of a free press and of free speech, mentioned the Gettysburg Address only briefly, and relegated the complexities of the "cold war" as merely a "quarrel" among imperialistic nations. The Committee's proposed guidelines, although rightly adding many civil rights leaders, left out Eli Whitney, Thomas Edison, and the Wright Brothers among many other scientists; it overlooked Daniel Webster and other major diplomats and politicians; and it gave few lines to innumerable creative artists. However, the emperor of an ancient African civilization was praised, as were numerous individuals, often female or of minority cultures, who were merely footnotes in America's 300-year history.

About 55 percent of Americans believe that news media stories are often inaccurate, according to a 2007 study by the Project for Excellence in Journalism. More frightening is that about 63 percent believe the media try to cover up their errors. This may be accurate, or it may reflect incorrect perceptions. But, perception often becomes the reality.

In historiography, as in journalism, the better writers not only research the facts, but also analyze and interpret them to help the people better understand the critical issues that affect them. It is not acceptable for the writers of public school social science and history texts to distort the reporting of history by creating fiction.

Only a Part of the World

She quietly walked into the classroom from the front and stood there, just inside the door, against a wall.

The professor continued his lecture, unaware of her presence until his students' eyes began focusing upon her rather than him. "Yes?" he asked. Just "yes." Nothing more.

"You shouldn't have done it," she said peacefully. He was confused. So she said it again, this time with a little venom.

"Ma'am," he began, but she cut him off. He tried to defuse the situation, but couldn't reason with her. She pulled a gun from her purse and shot him, then quickly left. He recovered immediately. It took less than a minute.

The scene was another exercise in the professor's newswriting class, this one unannounced but highly planned. His assignment was for the students to quickly write down everything they could about the incident. What happened. What was said. What she looked like. What she was wearing. Just the facts. Nothing more.

Everyone got some of the information right, but no one got all the facts, even the ones they were absolutely positively sure they saw or heard correctly. And, most interestingly, the "gun" the visitor used and which the students either couldn't identify or misidentified was in reality a . . . banana; a painted black banana, but a banana nevertheless. The actual gun shot was on tape on a hidden recorder activated by the professor.

It was a lesson in observation and truth. Witnesses often get the facts wrong, unable to distinguish events happening on top of each other. Sometimes they even want to "help" the reporter and say what they think the reporter wants to hear.

Reporters are society's witnesses who record history by interviewing other witnesses, and they all make mistakes, not because they want to, but because everyone's life experiences and perceptions fog reality. Put 10 reporters into a PTA meeting, court trial, or a Congressional hearing. No matter how well reporters pay attention to the proceedings, there will be 10 different stories.

Of the infinite number of facts and observations that occur during a meeting, reporters must select a few. Which few they select, which thousands they deliberately don't select—and, more important—which parts of a meeting or of society itself

110

they don't even know exist—all make up a news story, usually written under deadline pressure. Thus, it isn't unusual for readers to wonder how reporters could have been in the same meeting as they were since the published stories didn't seem to reflect the reality of the meeting.

The New York Times arrogantly proclaims itself to be the "newspaper of record," that it publishes "all the news that's fit to print." CBS News, however, is more honest. At the end of the newscast, we learn that we have seen just "a part" of today's world.

ETHICS

Long Island Lolita Meets the Journalistic Lowlife

It was 6 a.m., Monday, when the phone rang, so I knew it was Marshbaum eager to involve me in his latest scam. I wasn't disappointed.

"Got any extra money?" he whispered.

"Not since I became a humor columnist," I replied.

"Too bad," said Marshbaum. "I'll take it elsewhere."

"Take *what* elsewhere?" I asked sleepily.

"Revelations about my life with Amy Fisher."

"*You* had a life with the Long Island Lolita? The teen who shot the wife of her lover?"

"Actually, I once bought some fabric at the sewing store her parents own, but I figure what they told me about their daughter is worth a few thousand on the journalistic market."

"What'd they tell you?" I asked.

"Not so fast. It'll cost you. You been looking at the tabloids lately? They pay real good for my kind of news."

"The papers I write my column for are ethical. Usually. They won't pay for revelations."

"Everyone else is!" he snapped. "Three hundred thousand to the woman who got shot and her husband who either was or wasn't Amy's pizza-eating pimp. Fifty thou to some boyfriend. A bundle to a trigger-man. Quarter million to some hack to write a paperback about all this. Thousands to just about anyone who ever lived in the same country she did. Millions to produce the Amy Fisher Film Festival on TV. Add in a half-dozen tabloid TV shows, a few talk shows, and all the local news, and you have a billion dollar Amy Industry."

"But, that's schlock entertainment," I said. "Newspapers are more into news."

"Yeah," he said sarcastically, "like the New York papers that have photographers staking out everyone's houses? Or, the battalion of reporters who invaded her upper class hometown to talk to all the neighbors? What about the newspaper reporters who are being paid by the entertainment industry to be 'consultants'?"

"I have no desire to write about sex-crazed teenagers on the prowl for body-shop repairmen," I said. "Besides, every hour they take to report on this teenage prostitute with a Fatal Attraction complex is one hour less they can investigate corruption. Every inch they use in every paper is one inch less than can be devoted to stories about the economy and health care crises."

"What about a scoop on bodyshop repairmen who lure teenage girls into lives of crime?" he asked. "I can sell that one a little cheaper."

"He may have been a sleaze," I said, "but there's no evidence he asked his alleged lover to kill his wife."

"Precisely," said Marshbaum. "There's no evidence of any of this, but already TV has devoted more air time to it than they did the Gulf War and the Presidential campaign. Besides, you're the only one who hasn't written about it. Aren't your editors concerned that you're not giving them the latest news? Sin sells papers. Makes money for publishers. Publishers reward sinners by increasing their salaries. Frankly, you're well behind at the moment."

"OK, Marshbaum, what choice piece of trivia did you learn that'll save my career and get me the Pulitzer Prize for Sensational Journalism?"

"Like I said, I'm no fool. This stuff's too hot to entrust to someone not willing to pay."

"I said I had ethics."

"Ethics don't pay the bill at Victoria's Secret," he said. "Besides, it's relatively simple. You get the scoop on why Amy's parents never thought it was unusual that their 16-year-old daughter not only had a pager, but a nearly-new usually bent-up Dodge Daytona with an automatic pilot to guide it into the body shop owned by her lover. You put it into your column. Some low-life publisher or producer with a wad of bills calls you up, pays you ·even more. Everyone makes out."

"Everyone but the readers," I said.

"It's the readers who want this stuff," he reminded me. "They'll read scandal before they'll read about poverty and the health care crisis."

"That may be true," I said, "but I'll pass on this one. My readers will just have to remain ignorant of the life of an obsessed teen and her sleazy adulterer."

"Don't come crying to me when 'Hard Copy' scoops you, and your editors replace you with someone known as 'a highly reliable source.'" I said I'd have to risk it. "By the way," Marshbaum said shortly before hanging up, "I'm sure you'll get a column out of this somehow. I'll send you a bill in the morning."

For Sale: Justice—O.J. Style

"Get your O. J. T-shirts, mugs, and witnesses here! All shapes, sizes, and colors! Get 'em while they're hot!"

Behind a stainless steel vendor cart on Manhattan's Avenue of the Americas was—who else?—Marshbaum, who was doing a brisk business.

"Marshbaum!" I shouted, "what are you doing selling witnesses in New York!"

"Because L.A. doesn't allow vendor carts on Sunset."

"That's not the point," I said. "You shouldn't be selling witnesses anywhere."

"I'm just their agent. I put witnesses together with attorneys and editors, and get a 15 percent commission."

"We got two forensic pathologists available! Bargain basement price. Only two thousand a day plus expenses. They will go either way." Two attorneys opened their wallets and walked away with the discounted docs.

"Marshbaum, I don't know what scam you're working, but I think it's illegal."

"Hardly," he said snickering. "It's good old-fashioned American capitalism, and supported by the Constitution."

"The Constitution allows this?" I asked skeptically.

"Sixth Amendment," said Marshbaum smugly. "The right to capitalize on crime."

"Got a psychiatrist here. A little crazy, but does well on the stand.

Take her at only three hundred an hour, minimum of four hours."

Almost before he finished his spiel, another attorney opened a large briefcase, gave Marshbaum $1,200 in unmarked bills, and bought the psychiatrist.

"You can't be selling justice like this," I said shocked.

"Who said it's justice?" he said. "I'm selling expertise to the lawyers, and information to the news media."

"But only the seedy media believe in checkbook journalism," I said smugly. "The establishment media would never pay a source."

"Got someone here who says he used to deliver diapers to the Simpson home. Only three thousand, and you get 30 minutes with him." A buyer who demanded anonymity put a brown paper bag with low denomination bills on the counter, grabbed the owner of Tidy Didy Diapers, and was last seen darting between traffic on her way back to Times Square.

"The *Times* bought a source?" I asked shocked.

"Can't tell you," said Marshbaum. "But this week alone, I've seen editors from 30 papers. The *Post* bought an exclusive to a witness who said she could prove aliens soaked up O.J.'s spirit and are using it to cure cancer."

"How long you been doing this?" I asked.

"A month. And if I don't keep hustling, the other agents will grab what's available."

"There's *other* agents doing this?"

"Of course there's other agents. Why do you think O.J.'s friend A. C. Cowlings turned down a million bucks to drop the dime on his friend? Why did house guest Kato turn down a hundred grand? It wasn't because they're Boy Scouts. They got some smart agent on the West Coast holding out."

"O.K, folks, this one's a little tainted, but it'll wear just as well on TV. She says just before she was arrested for robbery and assault with a deadly weapon, she saw O.J. buy rubber gloves from the store she hit." Three editors tore each other apart trying to get the highest bid. When they were through, an ambulance carried them away, but Marshbaum had $15,000—15 percent of it his commission—for the thief's guarantee that she'd tell the truth.

"That's terrible!" I said, still shocked by the display before me.

"You think *that's* bad," said Marshbaum, "two days ago, I had to have the cops clear the sidewalk when the staffs from 'Inside Edition' and 'Extra' began fighting over a witness who says not only did he sell O.J. the white Bronco, but heard him say it's a killer machine."

"Jurors! Live jurors! Get the exclusive story of what went on in deliberations! Only five thou apiece! Available only to the news media!"

"That's ridiculous," I said. "They didn't even pick the jury pool yet. How can you be selling jurors?"

"They choose jurors from the voting lists," said Marshbaum. "In the past month, I signed exclusive letters of intent with every voter in L.A. County. Hundreds have registered every day. It's only a matter of time until the lawyers choose who they want on the panel."

"Is there anyone you don't represent?" I asked.

"Yeah. I don't represent lawyers. Even agents have ethics."

Cockroach Hormones
and Biblical Giants

Michael Born just wanted to be involved with the television industry—and make several hundred thousand dollars. The TV industry just wanted some exclusive video footage; it didn't care of what, as long as it was exclusive "bring-home-the-ratings" footage.

Among the 32 videotapes Born sold to the German networks were footage of a Ku Klux Klan rally, some men shooting a cat, and drug dealers sneaking into Germany. The only problem was that Born staged the events. A German court called it fraud and sentenced him at the end of 1996 to four years in prison.

Journalists pietously proclaimed that people who commit fraud should be jailed. Born claimed the networks salivated all over his videotape, didn't check out the stories, and may have even known some of the stories were false.

A few months earlier, Britain's Independent Television Network broadcast an 80-second video allegedly showing sex scenes of Princess Diana and a riding instructor known to have been her lover at one time. The *Sun* took still photos from the video, recast them into blurry black and white images, and splashed them across five tabloid pages. The only problem, other than a massive invasion of privacy and a medium's voyeuristic quest for ratings, was that the scene was a hoax; the "princess" and the "riding instructor" were look-alike actors. A mysterious

"American lawyer," acting on behalf of an equally mysterious man known only as "the Sergeant," had sold the tape to the *Sun*, which slobbered all over the offer before parting with a few thousand British pounds.

Hoaxes in journalism aren't new. In 1835, Americans believed life existed on the moon because a reporter for the *New York Sun* reported that astronomers with a powerful telescope saw winged creatures and vegetation. The modern tabloids have the aliens on earth, usually breeding with vestal virgins.

An Iowa farmer in 1868, upset about his pastor's constant proclamation about Biblical giants, arranged for a block of granite to be carved into an exact likeness of a 10-foot man, then buried it in his field. When the "fossilized" man was accidentally discovered, the media jumped all over the story, quoting innumerable "experts" who declared the man was real. In Minnesota 30 years later, the Kensington Stone, with purported Viking writing and the date of 1362, titillated the American public and media. In 1908, the skull of what became known as the Pilt-down Man, believed to be the 250,000-year-old "missing link," was discovered in England. Although cynics doubted the authenticity, the media spent five decades quoting innumerable sources who had placed the skull in archeological history. In 1955, the newly-developed Carbon-14 dating method placed the skull at 700 years old. But, C-14 wasn't even necessary—additional studies proved that the jawbone was that of an orangutan.

In 1983, a Biblical scholar and archeologist led the media into a trap to show the public how gullible the media were when he arranged for an actor to feign discovery of a piece of pine wood from Noah's Ark. Sun International created a two-hour film, sold it to CBS-TV, which hyped it and ran it as a prime-time special. The print news media, without investigating, devoted large chunks of their "news hole" to perpetuate the fraud. It took only a simple C-14 test to prove the wood was recently dipped in chemicals, but the media didn't ask. C-14 dating in 1990 also put an end to thousands of media stories that the Shroud of Turin had been on the body of Jesus.

In 1981, the media first reported that crop circles and designs in England's fields may have had an extraterrestrial origin. For the next decade, new circles and headlines appeared each growing season, baffling scientists and giving "proof" that UFOs existed. Finally, in 1991, two artist/farmers gleefully admitted they created the circles and for more than a decade watched the media reactions.

Prankster and media satirist Joey Skaggs has proven how easy it is to fool the media. Disguising himself as innumerable scientists, Skaggs titillates the media first by news releases, then by elaborate follow-ups. The media fell for the claim that cockroach hormones are the basis of super vitamins, that there really was a "Solomon Project" that developed a voice-stress computer test which proved O.J. Simpson was guilty of murder, and that there is a celebrity sperm bank. Among media that reported his innumerable pranks as truth, victims of their failure to fact-check their sources, were *The New York Times*, the *Washington Post*, the *Philadelphia Inquirer*, *USA Today*, and the three major TV networks.

The Hollowed Halls of Ethics

The nation's journalists were surprised, shocked, and outraged. Jayson Blair, a 27-year-old *New York Times* national correspondent, had lied and cheated his way through a four-year career at the paper that not only claims to have the highest journalistic standards but also believes it's the national record.

At the time he resigned under pressure at the end of April 2003, Blair had not only left a trail of innumerable factual errors, but had fabricated quotes, "covered" stories in other states while not leaving New York City, and plagiarized from metropolitan newspapers. The *Times* found 36 separate instances of plagiarism or fraud.

Several persons, according to the *L.A. Times*, didn't report Blair's errors because they "shrugged off his mistakes as more examples of sloppy, melodramatic reporting." Only about one-fifth of all Americans even believe "all or most" of the stories in their newspapers, according to a survey by the Pew Center in 2002. A separate poll revealed that almost half of all Americans thought news stories "are often inaccurate." The *L.A. Times*, *Newsweek*, and dozens of other publications reported that even when some sources tried to report errors, they were met by an arrogance in which editors didn't return phone calls—a common problem among all major media, not just the *Times*. The *Times* senior editors apparently also didn't listen to reporters who questioned Blair's accuracy, or to metropolitan editor Jon

Landman who a year earlier had written them a terse memo calling for Blair's termination.

The story itself was kept alive, and even fueled not by the establishment media but by Internet bloggers (most of them conservative) who saw an opportunity to attack what they believed was the mightiest newspaper in the country, one that represented all they believed was wrong with the "liberal East Coast establishment press"; it was a David v. Goliath attack, assisted by leaks by *Times* staffers who saw an opportunity to challenge the leadership of senior editors. Under a relentless attack from blogs and alternative media for condoning Blair's work for so long, and for establishing a workplace that discouraged full discussions of editorial decisions, both the executive editor and managing editor eventually resigned.

In an unprecedented 14,000 words of explanation and apology almost two weeks after Blair's forced resignation, the *Times* excoriated the chain-smoking, scotch-drinking, cocaine-using Blair for having "committed frequent acts of journalistic fraud," wailed that it was the worst "black-eye" in the newspaper's 152-year history, and promised to take steps not to allow it to occur again. But, it will occur again, just as it had occurred for decades, not just at the *Times* but in all the media.

During the nineteenth century, in their quest for political power and circulation, newspapers not only exaggerated and fabricated, they also played innumerable hoaxes upon their readers. In the twentieth century, "jazz journalism" replaced "yellow journalism," but reporters still looked for ways to meet their publishers' needs to sell papers. Journalists have come a long ways since then. But, as in any profession, there are still significant holes of ethics.

TV shows sponsored by Ford in the 1960s and 1970s either shot away from New York City's Chrysler Building or electronically eliminated it. The *National Geographic* digitally altered the pyramids for "aesthetic" reasons for one of its covers. Janet Cooke, who won a Pulitzer Prize for a feature about an eight-year-old boy who was addicted to cocaine while in his mother's womb, was stripped of her prize and fired from the *Washington Post* in 1981 when the story proved to be as much fiction as her résumé.

NBC-TV broadcast a story about fish that were supposedly killed on government land, but it was footage of a different forest—and the fish weren't dead. NBC also came under a fire-

118

storm of protest when the public learned that to enhance a story about truck safety, the network's "Dateline" staff rigged a GM truck with an explosive to illustrate how easily those trucks burst into flame. FOX-TV obliterated the distinction between news and hucksterism when it "interrupted" its coverage of the 1997 Super Bowl to air a "special report" by news anchor Catherine Crier. The breaking news? The Blues Brothers "escaped" and were about to headline the half-time show.

Both Ruth Shalit and Stephen Glass fabricated stories at *The New Republic* in the 1990s. Associated Press correspondent Christopher Newton invented quotes and sources in 40 stories. In 1998, the *Boston Globe* fired columnist Patricia Smith, and then two months later allowed long-time columnist Mike Barnicle to resign after they acknowledged they made up sources and quotes. Ironically, *Globe* editors had been warned by some reporters that Jayson Blair, who was an intern for two summers and freelanced after that for several months, had a credibility problem. Only one month after the scandal at *The New York Times*, the *New York Post* acknowledged that it published an article by freelancer Robin Gregg that was plagiarized from *The National Enquirer*. The deceit doesn't end with the stories reporters file. A few American reporters, embedded with troops in the second Gulf War, apparently assumed they could plunder Iraq of national treasures, including art, antiquities, and weapons.

Author Clifford Irving, armed with forged letters, got a $750,000 advance in 1969 to write the official biography of reclusive billionaire Howard Hughes. Konrad Kajau in the early 1980s forged diaries of Adolph Hitler and fooled *Newsweek*, the *London Sunday Times*, and Germany's *Stern*.

Monique De Wael hoaxed the nation with her book, *Misha: A Memoir of the Holocaust Years* (1997). De Wawel, writing under the name Misha Defonseca, claimed to have spent a part of World War II walking throughout Europe with a pack of wolves to find her Jewish parents. Finally, in 2008, more than a decade after publication of what became a literary best-seller, and with several geneologists and readers questioning the authenticity, De Wael finally revealed the truth—she wasn't Jewish but Catholic; her father died of natural causes after being a collaborator with the Gestapo.

James Frey managed to hoax megastar Oprah Winfrey and the American public with his alleged memoir, *A Million Little*

119

Pieces (2003), the story of his addiction to alcohol and crack cocaine, and how he overcame the obstacles. Largely on the basis of laudatory reviews in numerous national newspapers and magazines, and an appearance on Oprah's talk show, the book stayed as no. 1 on the *New York Times* best-sellers list for 44 weeks. More than 4.5 million copies in both hardcover and paperback were sold.

Shortly after the book's publication, the *Minneapolis Star-Tribune* questioned the accuracy, but the story was buried by a nation and literary community that refused to believe the truth. Finally, in January 2006, a website, Smoking Gun, not the establishment media, uncovered the truth. Part of that truth was that Frey had been unable to sell the manuscript, which he had written as fiction, so he made it into a "non-fiction memoir," and sold it to Doubleday, a major publisher. Neither his literary agent nor the publisher ever verified any part of the manuscript. After the controversy had begun, Oprah eventually agreed with numerous exposes that there were just too many inconsistencies in his tale. She again had Frey on her show, and said she felt "betrayed" by him. Frey's notoriety and deliberate manipulation of the wall between fiction and non-fiction apparently didn't have a lasting effect upon the publishing industry. In mid-2007, mega-publishing conglomerate HarperCollins signed Frey to a three book seven-figure deal. The first of the books, published in Spring 2008, also became a best-seller.

Not reaching the top of best-sellers charts, but doing well financially, was *How Opal Mehta Got Kissed, Got Wild, and Got a Life*, by Kaavya Viswanathan, a sophomore at Harvard when her Young Adult novel was published in April 2006. Shortly after its publication, the *Harvard Crimson*, the university's student-produced newspaper, revealed that *Opal* included several major passages similar or identical to two books by Megan McCafferty, *Sloppy Firsts* and *Second Helpings*.

Within a month, publisher Little, Brown (part of the Time Warner Book Group) announced it was pulling all copies of the book, and wouldn't be issuing a revised edition. In a statement to the media, after first denying she was influenced by any

~~~~~~~~~

"I hope I shall possess firmness and virtue enough to maintain what I consider the most enviable of all titles, the character of an honest man." —George Washington other work, Viswanathan tried to explain how the plagiarism occurred:

> When I was in high school, I read and loved two wonderful novels by Megan McCafferty, *Sloppy Firsts* and *Second Helpings*, which spoke to me in a way few other books did. Recently, I was very surprised and upset to learn that there are similarities between some passages in my novel . . . and passages in these books.
>
> While the central stories of my book and hers are completely different, I wasn't aware of how much I may have internalized Ms. McCafferty's words. I am a huge fan of her work and can honestly say that any phrasing similarities between her works and mine were completely unintentional and unconscious.

Subsequent discoveries revealed that Viswanathan had passages in *Opal* that were variations of passages from *Haroun and the Sea of Stories* (1990), by Salman Rushdie; *The Princess Diaries* (2000), by Meg Cabot; *Born Confused* (2002), by Tanuja Desai Hidier; and *Can You Keep a Secret?* (2004) by Sophie Kinsella. Viswanathan graduated with honors from Harvard and entered Georgetown University law school.

Assisting Viswanathan was Alloy Entertainment, one of dozens of major book packagers, which work with publishers, finds writers, assign plots, and even has its own staff writers ghost much of a work to meet publishers' marketing desires. Some-times the byline is even a phony; other times, it reflects only that the writer may have contributed anywhere from some writing to most of the writing. Alloy, distancing itself from Viswanathan, said the author did all of the writing. Nevertheless, Alloy split about $500,000 on a two book deal with its now-disgraced author. If Alloy had merely acted as an agent for Viswanathan, it would have received only 10–15 percent, not half, of the royalties.

As much as journalists may want to believe these are only isolated examples, they aren't. As much as the public wants to believe that the problem occurs only in journalism, it doesn't. A survey conducted by the editors of *Who's Who Among American High School Students* in 1998 revealed that 84 percent of high school students believe cheating was common. About 60 percent of high school students admitted to plagiarism, according to a survey conducted in 2005 by Don McCabe, a Rutgers University professor, for the Center for Academic Integrity (CAI). McCabe's survey also revealed that about 70 percent of college students admit to cheating, that about 15 percent of all students say they bought research papers, and almost half admit to having copied passages, without attribution, from published sources.

More important, students don't see that cheating, lying, or plagiarizing are necessarily immoral or unethical. Almost half of high school students, according to the Josephson Institute of Ethics, believe "a person has to lie or cheat sometimes in order to succeed." College graduates pad their resumes and lie in their recommendations. Psychologist Robert Feldman of the University of Massachusetts found that among 11–16 year old students, there was a high correlation between lying and popularity. "Politicians have known for a very long time that telling people what they want to hear is a very good social tactic," Feldman told the Associated Press. Politicians and CEOs, aided by hordes of PR professionals, also know they can spin the truth because the media, often faced by increased work loads and diminished resources, have largely abrogated their roles of cynical watchdogs.

Americans lie on their income tax returns, on claims to insurance companies, and about the condition of their used car which they're about to unload. They lie about productivity to their bosses, and use "sick days" to play golf. And when it comes to managers and executives, Enron, Adelphia, Halliburton, Worldcom, most of the major Wall Street investment and stock brokerage firms and dozens of others may not be exceptions to how many corporations do business.

The nation's journalists shouldn't be shocked, surprised, or outraged about Jayson Blair's theft of honesty; they, like most Americans, are all part of the problem.

The Write Stuff

It was close to deadline, and I was hurriedly flipping through newspapers and magazines, trying to find a news hook upon which to hang this week's column. I didn't have time to read the *Congressional Quarterly*, source of innumerable columns, and every two-bit humor "wannabe" was mining the Bar Association for cheap lawyer jokes.

Dejectedly, I thumbed the classified ads—maybe there'd be a

job for a washed-up columnist. My mind wandered over to the "literary services" section. In *Harper's*, one of the nation's most respected magazines, was my salvation. Among ads from vanity publishing companies promising to turn my drivel into bestseller status if I paid for everything was exactly what I needed. Three companies said they'd write this week's column.

The first ad promised, "We write everything. Reports, papers, company books." The ad even claimed the company was "professional." Alas, it had only a mailing address, and I needed something in less than a day. Next was a Los Angeles company with a "toll-free hotline." John, a polite young·man eager to help, told me most of the previously written term papers in the company's catalog were 6–20 pages, and the cost was only $7.50 per page. The company was even so concerned about its clients' finances that it never charged for more than 17 pages, and threw in the footnotes and bibliography for free.

"I'm on a deadline," I told him.

"No problem," he helpfully said, "we can fax it to you or send it by overnight mail."

I told him I really didn't need any of the advertised 19,278 term papers, but thought maybe there could be some "special" assistance he could provide. There was no problem there either. For only $20–$25 per page, the company would custom make an "undergraduate level" report to my specific needs. For $25 to $45 per page, I could get a graduate or professional level report. It could be six pages; it could be 400 pages. My choice. "Of course," he said, "we expect you to put in some of your own opinions." Of course.

In exchange for this "fully written report"—with my own opinions—I'd have to sign a statement guaranteeing, "I understand this report is to be used for research purposes only." Right.

I opted for the professional level report, and was told to call another number and to talk with a Dr. Something-or-the-Other who was in charge of the researchers. Not wanting to lower the quality of my column, I first asked her about qualifications, and was told "every one" of the staff has at least a master's. I didn't have time to verify writing ability, subject knowledge, or even if the M.A.s were from the schools that advertise in the classifieds of supermarket tabloids. Alas, she said the company doesn't do fiction. "Try a grad student at a university," she suggested. "Someone in English might be able to help you."

A grad student? In English! Obviously, this woman had the artistic sensitivity of a drainpipe.

Time for my last contact. A kindly voice answered, "Research Services."

"Can you do a custom report?" I asked.

"Everything we do is custom made," he replied. He charged $12.50 per page, with a special rate of $200 for the first 15 pages. I'd have to supply the cover page, but he'd throw in footnotes and bibliography at no cost.

"Can you do satire?" I asked.

No problem, he answered. However, he explained that writing satire "is time consuming because there's no library research, and it involves creative writing." I said I understood.

"I'd like a foil in it if possible. You know, Mike Royko used Slats Grobnik, and this writer in Pennsylvania uses a guy named Márshbaum?" Still no problem. "I need it pretty soon," I begged. No problem there either.

However, if he were to do a good job writing a satire, he might need more time since "if you do it too fast, a good idea may come after it's in the mail." But, for $50 he'd do something relatively quick. Three pages. Even with a foil.

That's when I decided not to hire him. I spend all week perfecting my column. And he wanted only $50? For 800 choice words? It seemed awfully cheap. Besides, by then, I had my column.

Giving the Media a Fix

On "The View," ABC-TV's 11 a.m. dedication to "women of different generations," 30-ish Star Jones presented a tiara on a pillow to 60-ish Barbara Walters who appropriately blushed at the honor of being officially anointed the queen of interviewers.

The presentation came in February 1999, about 12 hours after ABC aired a two-hour prime-time interview with Presidential sleaze-mate Monica Lewinsky. The interview was watched by about 48.5 million Americans, with another 25.5 million persons hyperventilating at least six minutes of the two hour show, according to the Nielsen ratings. The largest segment was women over 50, but about 15 percent of the audience were children 2–11, and 25 percent were teens, all of whom heard details about oral and phone sex. Overall, Barbara and Monica were in about one-third of all homes with TVs.

Not watching was President Bill Clinton who was at a fundraiser in New Jersey which included a group sing of disco-hit, "I

Will Survive." Based upon the ratings, media watchers solemnly declared the syrupy interview to be the most watched news event in the history of television.

News? A hyped-up two hour interview by a woman who lobbed softball questions at a guest who has been prepared for months? News? For the "revelation" that Monica believes the President is "a good kisser" and that he is her "sexual soul-mate"? News? For Monica telling us that the President wasn't her first married man encounter, and that she had an abortion? News? For disclosing she was tormented by the media and others for about a year as they tore away "layer upon layer" of her soul? News? For disclosing that she thinks Bill Clinton lies, and that she once thought about jumping out of a window.

But, the thong-wearing Presidential playmate didn't say anything about her hatred and contempt for special prosecutor Ken Starr. In a blatant violation of Monica's First Amendment rights, he ordered her, as part of an immunity deal, not to comment upon him, his legal team, or any of the witnesses.

The ABC interview couldn't have come at a better time for the media. During the previous year, *TIME* and *Newsweek* had given Monicagate 27 covers, the TV networks had devoted thousands of network minutes to her seduction, with all its intimate details, and newspapers routinely ran 6-column banner headlines over stories that bumped almost everything else to spots somewhere near the classifieds.

Following the acquittal of the President on charges of perjury and obstruction of justice, the media went into cold sweats; they needed a fix. The career-saving interview was taped about two weeks before it was scheduled to air, thus giving the media a chance to speculate on what more Monica could say, drooling all the time over their overheated computers.

For her part, Walters every day promoted the upcoming interview, coyly revealing nothing. The day before the interview aired, she hyped the show; on the morning of the show, she even gave viewers a preview. Buoyed by the media-heavy hype, and America's fascination with sleaze, advertisers lined up to pay $800,000 for a 30-second spot, about five times what they normally paid for the Wednesday night "20/20" show.

Almost every news operation, tabloid, and talk-show in the country had tried to interview Monica who declined them all, even rejecting a $1 million fee for appearing on the morning talk show "Roseanne."

Walters, adamantly and virtuously, stated she and ABC-TV News, being the "principled journalists" they were, got the interview without paying anything to Monica. But, Monica, who needed family connections to get a White House internship and was still unemployed, even with the personal intercession of Presidential consultant Vernon Jordan, wasn't after money; she wanted just one thing—Ken Starr's storm troopers and the accompanying media to stop infringing upon her life.

But, if she were to get a lucrative spotlight job, preferably in the media, it might ease her pain. This, of course, is the same Monica who once whined to White House assistants trying to wean her from the President's libido by finding her a job, "I don't want to have to work for this position, I just want it to be given to me."

Walters, seeing absolutely no ethical or professional conflicts, promised to introduce Monica to the "right" people at the network. Then, almost breathless, Queen Barbara suggested that Monica would be a good possibility to represent the 20s generation on "The View," which was going through a series of young female guest hosts. Naturally, Walters, executive producer of the all-female five-host show, already one 20-ish female short, saw no conflict in interviewing a media-made celebrity, calling it news, and then asking her to be a co-host for "The View." Being as scrupulous as she is, she probably didn't even think about the ratings boost and significantly higher advertising revenue. Within the week, *TV Guide* had an interview with Walters who declared she found Monica to be warm, intelligent, and open; the other media soon began brawling over access, not only to Monica but also to the Queen. For their part, the supermarket tabloids played catch-up to the establishment press.

Walters had nothing to do with the early release of *Monica's Story*, the official authorized 288-page tell-all confessional by Andrew Morton who had spent about three months interviewing Monica, her family, and friends. But, how many authors or their subjects can command a two-hour network prime-time special the day before the release of their book? There were significant questions about the book's accuracy and the author's objectivity, especially since Morton wasn't an independent journalist but Monica's confidante, splitting his $1.6 million advance with her, and deeding her 10 percent of the list price on all sales above the advance. Because of significant advance orders, the book, with a 450,000 copy first print run, became the top-selling book for internet goliath Amazon.com the day of the Walters–Lewinsky interview. Within a week, publisher St. Martin's ordered a 100,000 copy reprint, and the book began riding the top of most other sales charts.

ABC limited the excerpts from Walters' interview so foreign media could have their own exclusives. In England, Channel Four paid Monica about $667,000 for an exclusive one-hour interview, which aired the day of the book's official publication. One of the advertisers that helped pay for the interview was Vanish, the stain remover. London's *The Daily Mirror* paid about $100,000 for an interview and book serialization.

Morton, a British citizen, began making the rounds of the news and talk shows in the United States; Monica went on a two-week tour in Great Britain. The first Monday after publication date, she was at Harrod's. A couple of hours and 1,100 books later, *Monica's Story* had topped all sales records for the central London department store. After England, Scotland, and Wales, Monica crossed into France, Germany, and the Scandanavian countries. Because of her notoriety, she soon had deals with numerous media organizations that brought her well over $4 million—about twice what she needed to pay all legal bills—all because she lifted her skirt and flashed her flesh through a thong bikini to a horny president, because Ken Starr and the Republicans thought they finally found a way to get rid of a popular political nemesis, and because Americans like sleaze more than they appreciate substance.

As for Barbara Walters, "Today Show" co-anchor Katie Couric unintentionally told the truth not only about TV "journalism" but also about Barbara Walters. In an interview with *TV Guide* in November 2002, Couric said that Walters was "the hardest-working woman in showbiz."

Politically Incorrect Weather

A high-pressure front swept across the newsroom of KMJ-AM, Fresno, Calif., with a 100 percent certainty that it would leave a new low in its wake.

Depending upon whom you believe, weatherman Sean Boyd was either fired for being accurate, or program director John Broeske had finally had enough of Boyd's insolence and refusal to be "a team player." Boyd, an independent contractor, had forecast

127

weather as many as 20 times a day for 17 years at the station.

However, for at least the second time in two months, Boyd was politically incorrect, a sin for anyone in our society but especially so for a weatherman whose continued employment may have been based upon being meteorologically inaccurate.

In March 1995, Boyd had determined there was a better than average possibility it would be partly cloudy, breezy, and cool for a station-sponsored golf tournament. Boyd says he remembers his program director suggesting that it would be better if the forecast could say it was partly sunny, not partly cloudy. Actually, why not report it would be mostly sunny with highs in the 70s and "let people make their own decision," Boyd remembers Broeske telling him. Nevertheless, Boyd stuck by his forecast; the weather for the divot swingers that afternoon was, in fact, partly cloudy, breezy, and cool.

Two months later, Boyd again got into trouble. KMJ, which carries the Rush Limbaugh talk-show, sponsored the Second Annual Dittohead Barbecue and Politically Incorrect Picnic, Saturday, April 15. Since it was already politically incorrect, it was apparently no big deal that it was also Easter and Passover weekend.

Why do TV weather people get five minutes to tell us that it may or may not rain tomorrow, explain the history of Arctic clippers, and high and low temperatures from 10 years ago, when there isn't the same time for reporters to explain health care, the economy, or labor issues?

It's the same TV cuture that fills the screen with the latest juicy gossip about a 50-something male actor dating a 20-something starlet, reported by a 50-something male anchor and his 20-something "trophy wife" co-anchor.

Four days before the Dittoheads were to meet, Boyd forecast a chance of showers, based upon reports of the National Weather Service. Broeske possibly didn't think that anyone, including the clouds, had a right to rain upon his plumped-up sizzling raucous barbecued hotdogs. After all, the station, which sends 5,000 screaming watts of conservative thinking into one of the state's biggest media markets, had something of an investment in making sure thousands showed up to celebrate the Biggest Mouth That Roars, even if the Chief Ditto-head himself had no plans to attend.

So, Broeske strongly suggested that Boyd revise the forecast. After all, you never know with California weather. It *could* have been a wonderful day in the neighborhood.

"Do you want me to change all the forecasts?" Boyd asked, and then sarcastically suggested that the program director could just write down what *he* thought the weather should be, "and I'll tell it just the way you have asked." The program director might have thought about the temptation to move a few clouds but declined. Boyd stuck with his weather report. About 3 p.m. that Saturday, rain began falling upon the char-smoked Dittoheads.

Boyd says he and Broeske had "meetings in the past about how he wanted me to do things." The station manager even told him that the program director had once mentioned that dealing with Boyd was "like a Chinese water torture."

Ten days after the Dittohead Debacle, Broeske approached Boyd. The Arctic Clipper cold front came with more warmth. "You can say you resigned because of stress and long hours," Boyd remembers Broeske telling him.

Broeske has a different version of the events. "Everything he's saying is completely untrue," said Broeske. However, he cited "station policy" for reasons why he wouldn't discuss the events further. "No comment" was the extent of Broeske's official version.

Apparently other media and their listeners didn't have a problem with Boyd's personality or forecasts. Since 1988, Boyd had provided weather information throughout the day, including weekends when necessary, for the independently-owned KAAT-AM/KTNS-FM radio stations in Oakhurst.

"Sean has been very responsible to us and to our listeners," said Larry Gamble, station manager and owner of the stations. He noted that Boyd not only "provides the detailed information necessary," but also receives "very positive feedback from our listeners."

At KSEE-TV, an NBC affiliate in Fresno, news director Eric Hulnick also had no question about Boyd's competence. In the eight TV-station metro market, Boyd not only "has the most accurate forecasts in the Valley," said Hulnick, he's quite simply "the best forecaster in Fresno."

However, continued employment in the radio and television industry is often determined not by on-air competence. For that reason, contracts with on-air talent are often issued in renewable 13-week increments, with few anchors and reporters receiving contracts longer than a year. In February 1998, the KSEE-TV management didn't renew the contract of the "best forecaster in Fresno." The reason, according to an official statement, was the nebulous, "because of the changing needs of the station." Five months later, KJEO-TV, a CBS affiliate, signed Boyd. Two years later, Boyd survived an ownership change; in August 2002, the recently-renamed station, now KGPE, didn't renew his contract.

"I received unbelievable support from the public," says Boyd, pointing out that people still remember what happened at KMJ-AM when he was fired for being politically incorrect. And, they also remember that one TV station didn't renew his contract after 10 years of accurate and comprehensive on-air reporting, while another chose to go in a new direction after four years. After more than two decades as a weather forecaster in the Fresno market, the "best forecaster in Fresno," whose audience was now reduced to radio station listeners in two smaller towns in the Valley, became a new car salesman.

The Intruder

He came to the front door late one Saturday morning in March 1995 and knocked. When there was no answer, he knocked again, and then began yelling "Hello," hoping someone would answer. When no one answered, he opened the front door, and walked into the house.

"I heard a man shouting 'Hello!'"said Rachel Kerr, a 21-year-old speech pathology major at Bloomsburg University of Pennsylvania, and one of two women in the sorority house at the time, "but I didn't go down because I thought it was for someone else."

He walked up the first flight of stairs. Kerr, in her bedroom at the time, heard him, but didn't know if he was friend, repairman, or burglar.

"Hello!" he again shouted. No answer. So, he walked down to the living room, looked around, left, then returned to the other side of the house and looked around. At the top of the stairwell, alerted by a sorority sister who had just come into the house, was Michelle May, sorority president and a 21-year-old speech communications major.

Before he could identify himself as a reporter for WNEP-TV, Wilkes-Barre/Scranton, May sharply told him, "I know who you are. We have nothing to say to you."

He politely asked if there was anyone he could talk with. "I'm the president," said May sharply, "and we don't want to talk with you."

The reporter probably thought he was being fair, trying to get the other side of the story—or at least a decent 10-second "sound bite." After all, a 19-year-old pledge nearly died from alcohol overdose two days earlier in what was rumored to be a hazing incident.

"Can you at least tell me her name?" he asked. May refused, and then snapped, "You can walk out of this house, just like you walked in." He walked out of the house.

Although reporters expect everyone else to open up their life histories to them, this reporter said his station's policy is that its reporters may not talk to the media. Officially, he had "no comment" about the incident.

The women of Chi Sigma Rho were frightened, upset, and acknowledged they weren't as courteous as they could have been. "We felt violated," said one of the women.

The reporter trespassed on private property, a civil not a criminal action, according to Pennsylvania law; if there was no damage, any charges would probably be dismissed in court. For there to have been a defiant trespass, the reporter had to be in the house after being told to leave. To be charged with burglary or breaking and entering, he had to be in the house with the purpose of committing a crime.

Nevertheless, the reporter's actions, although not criminal, violated the ethics and standards of the journalism profession. There is a universal implied consent for reporters to go onto private property when there is breaking news, such as a fire. Reporters also usually have access to privately-owned quasi- public institutions, such as malls. However, there are ethical limits.

"You just don't enter someone's house without being invited," said Reggie Stuart, assistant news editor for the Knight–Ridder News Service; at the time of the incident he was president of the 13,000-member Society of Professional Journalists. "If you do walk in," he said "you should stay in the living room until you're recognized. You should never, under any circumstance, proceed to go through the house."

David Bartlett, president of the Radio and Television News Directors Association (RTNDA), agreed. "I don't think I would have gone into the house," he said, noting that the reporter probably didn't exercise "very good judgment." Item 3 of the

RTNDA Code of Ethics asks reporters to "Respect the dignity, privacy, and well-being of people with whom they deal." The situation in which a reporter enters a house uninvited, says Bartlett, "might be construed as an invasion of their dignity" even if no damage was done, and the reporter was courteous and respectful.

The SPJ Code of Ethics specifically states that not only must the media "guard against invading a person's right to privacy," but that "Journalists at all times will show respect for the dignity, privacy, rights, and well-being of people encountered in the course of gathering and presenting the news."

During the next three days, the local media ran innumerable stories about the alcohol incident, many of the stories factually inaccurate, some based on the WNEP-TV reporting.

Four days after the media first reported the alcohol incident, a WYOU-TV reporter and his cameraman stood on the sidewalk before the house and, said witnesses, "taunted" sorority members following a university-wide meeting. "This is your chance to tell your side of the story," he said, a perfectly acceptable request, and important in the issue of fairness. But, said witnesses, he also kept taunting the women. "Tell us. Tell us," he kept saying over and over. "You look guilty if you don't say anything. Why don't you talk? This is your chance." He even told the women, "You need to take advantage of the media for your own good."

Three times the women asked the reporter to leave. That night on air, he identified Chi Sigma Rho as "the bad girl sorority," while the station aired footage of the women persistently yelling for the reporter to quit bothering them and to leave.

The public has a love-hate relationship with the media. They want the press to meet their obligations to make sure the public knows what's happening in society. But, they also hate the way the media go about their jobs.

Surveys show media credibility is at one of its lowest levels historically. The public is upset not only with factual, grammatical, and spelling errors, but also with the media's failure to admit mistakes. They are also upset with poor writing and editing, reliance upon unnamed sources, glorification of the criminal and of the bizarre. They don't like the media's failure to report on itself as well as it tries to cover other American institutions, and perceived unfairness, political bias, and conflicts of interest.

But most of all, they don't like "ambush journalism" and the invasion of individual rights and privacies.

"We know we were wrong to allow a minor to drink," said May. But she and her sorority sisters also had every right to be upset with what the media may have done to them and to their own credibility.

A Major Conflict of Interest

Like reporters everywhere, Keith Martin had wanted to be where the action was, and during the first part of 1991 the action was in the Persian Gulf. Unlike the other reporters, Martin was a double agent. In fact, the other reporters at WBRE-TV, an NBC affiliate in Scranton and Wilkes-Barre, Pa., where Martin was senior anchor of the evening news, even proudly acknowledged his conflicting assignments—although they never mentioned the phrase "double agent." They didn't see it as a conflict.

Martin was also in the Pennsylvania National Guard. Not a grunt, but an officer. And not just any officer, but a *public affairs* officer; in 1991, he was commander of the 109th Public Affairs Detachment. The military's very own flack. If it has anything to do with the National Guard or the military and there could be a positive spin, count on Keith Martin to have gotten it air time.

Martin spent a week in February 1991 in the Persian Gulf, reporting about the war and local units from northeastern Pennsylvania. He wasn't activated by the Department of Defense— apparently even the military has its limits on how many PAOs it can tolerate in combat zones. No, he was in the Gulf as a journalist, although the distinction between flack and journalist blurred when on-air promotions and fellow reporters identified him as *Major* Martin. In addition to daily reports, Martin produced a one-hour special in which he interviewed 85 troops from northeastern Pennsylvania.

When the war ended in April 1991, there were still stories to report. So, Maj. Keith Martin went to Fort Drum, N.Y., to report on the encampment of the 109th Infantry. For the 6 p.m. newscast, he reported on the training the unit was getting so it could convert to being an armor unit by the end of the year. For the 11 p.m. newscast, he reported on the "excellent" safety record of the 109th.

Because Maj. Martin was on active duty at the time, a part of his 15-day a year commitment, he fed video and sound to all three stations in the Scranton and Wilkes-Barre market. Not surprisingly, only WBRE-TV aired his report. And, of course, he was identified on air as *Major* Martin. But that wasn't completely necessary since he was dressed in battle fatigues, complete with combat face paint.

The following year, he began producing and hosting a weekly half-hour program, "Veterans' Views." The National Guard later promoted Maj. Martin to lieutenant colonel, and then to colonel, where he commanded the 55th Armored Brigade Combat Team. After almost 34 years of service, he retired in August 2002 and was given the honorary rank of brigadier general. In 2003, he became the first director of the Pennsylvania Department of Homeland Security.

Martin's conflict between news and public relations wasn't his first brush with ethics. Before going to WBRE, he resigned as anchor at WGAL-TV, Lancaster, Pa., after admitting to accepting a $10,000 consulting fee from one of his news sources.

The codes of ethics of the various journalism organizations are fairly clear about conflicts of interest. The Society of Professional Journalists states that journalists "must be free of obligation to any interest other than the public's right to know the truth. . . . Secondary employment . . . should be avoided if it compromises the integrity of journalists and their employers."

The Radio Television News Directors Association code states that "Broadcast journalists shall govern their . . . nonprofessional associations as may impinge on their professional activities in a manner that will protect them from conflict of interest, real or apparent."

The American Society of Newspaper Editors states that journalists "must avoid . . . any conflict of interest or the appearance of conflict."

And the Associated Press Managing Editors code declares that journalists "should make every effort to be free of obligations to news sources and special interests . . . Outside employment that conflicts with news interests should be avoided. Secondary employment by news sources is an obvious conflict."

So, what did Larry Stirewald, WBRE-TV news director, say about all this? Stirewald didn't believe there was a conflict of interest. "We make it very clear that Keith is in the National Guard," said Stirewald. "As long as you're straight forward with the people, it's all right," he said. All journalists have conflicts,

134

he pointed out, and "being a professional means compensating for whatever baggage you're carrying." Then he asks the question, "Why *shouldn't* journalists [be able to] serve their country in the National Guard?"

Journalists, if they choose, should be able to be in the Guard or any of the military reserves. Or even the Rotary Club. They just shouldn't be reporting about them. *unethical*

Compliments of a Thief

He's there by 7 a.m. almost every Sunday except in Winter to make money in one of the largest permanent flea markets in northeastern Pennsylvania. In three-foot long cardboard boxes he has an inventory of hundreds of paperbacks, all of them displayed spine up. Westerns. Romances. Adventures. Whatever you want. Three for a buck; fifty cents each. The books are virtually mint condition, and if you don't mind reading something without a front cover, it's a bargain, especially since paperbacks with the covers, sold at supermarkets, pharmacies, and bookstores, are now going for $5.95–$6.95 each. The only problem is that it's illegal.

The sale of stripped books, says Roger Williams of the Association of American Publishers (AAP), is a "significant and ongoing problem" that involves fraud, possible copyright infringement, and some areas that take the crime into interstate commerce violations. However, police departments and prosecutors often don't have the time, manpower, or resources to investigate and bring to court sellers of stripped books. "It's not the thing prosecutors want to spend time with," said Eric Raymond, an executive at Simon & Schuster, one of the nation's largest publishing houses.

To understand why the sale of stripped books is illegal, it's important to know a little about the nature of book publishing. Although the major book chains usually buy books on the basis of a book's cover and the promotion effort put out by the publisher, no one can predict which books will titillate American reading appetites, even with a $100,000 promotion campaign. So, publishers of the mass market paperbacks—the kind with colorfully-embossed titles superimposed over pirates and scantily-clad women on slick 4-1/4 by 6-3/4 inch covers—order large print quantities to try to saturate American bookstands. They sell these books to distributors for 50–65 percent of the list price, and hope a few titles bring in enough profit to carry the rest of the line.

Unique in the field of retail sales, booksellers can return to publishers for full credit any books they can't sell. However, publishers have no desire to pay shipping costs for books they probably won't redistribute, especially since there are another couple of dozen titles they're trying to push that month. And, neither bookseller nor publisher wants several skids of taxable inventory. So, distributors and publishers sign contracts that allow the bookseller to send only the cover back to the publisher, tack on shipping costs, get credit for the book, and agree to destroy the rest of the book to prevent further sale.

The bookseller usually sends stripped books to a recycler who picks them up at no cost and makes his money by selling recycled pulp. Mass market paperbacks accounted for about $2.3 billion in sales in 2007, but about half of that was credited for returns—most of them supposedly shredded and destroyed—according to the AAP.

However, some booksellers "forget" to send some books to a debindery or recycler, either selling some in their own store or, more likely, selling books for pennies apiece to mini-distributors. But, even if the bookseller (who can be the owner of just about any kind of a business) plays by all the rules—and most major retailers do—and sends the books to a recycler, that doesn't mean the books don't show up again. Some books may be stolen in transit or in storage; and, a few unscrupulous companies may file claims they have shredded 10 tons of what is now literally literary garbage, but have really gotten rid of just nine tons, throwing the coverless books into the streets, like left over food for the cats. The cats, in this case, have pick-ups, pay for the leftovers, and sell them at flea markets.

While the sale of stripped books is clearly illegal, there are other ways to make money off of authors and publishers. The sale of complimentary copies by bookstores and by college professors falls within a "gray" area.

Every publisher sends complimentary copies to booksellers to evaluate for possible purchase and to the media to evaluate for possible reviews. Although publishers will usually send booksellers and the media four or more months prior to publication date "Advance Reading Copies," uncorrected page proofs bound to look like the final production, publishers will also send copies of the finished book close to or after publication date. These books often become part of the inventory for unethical bookstores and journalists.

Bookstores will put the comp copies they receive onto their shelves; thus earning extra income without having to pay for the merchandise. Sometimes, bookstores have to pay for their supply of complimentary copies. That supply comes from book reviewers who sell the books at a fraction of the list price. For a bookstore, which normally pays 40–50 percent of the list price to a publisher or wholesaler, paying reviewers only 5–10 percent assures greater income. "There [is] no law against it," Nick Taylor, Author's Guild president, told his members in Spring 2002, "but it [breaks] the unwritten rules." The problem, of course, as Taylor points out, is "the sales produced no royalties, and displaced new book sales that would. Only the sellers and the store made money."

Nevertheless, until the fourth quarter of 2000, publishers and authors, while complaining about lost income from the sale of complimentary copies, have been a rather tolerable bunch. And then Amazon.com—the nation's largest virtual online book, music, and film vendor, with sales of about $2.8 billion that year and about 20 million separate customer accounts—compounded the problem by allowing its customers to buy "used" books on line. Near the top of the same web page where a customer can buy a just-released copy of a book is a click-through button that allows that customer to buy the book at a "used" price. The inventory is supplied by other customers who set the price for their books. Amazon.com charges a $3 shipping fee—the seller does the shipping; Amazon.com doesn't keep the book in its inventory—and takes a commission of 99 cents plus 15 percent of the sales price; the seller gets the rest.

For most books, "used" means just that—"used"—some damaged, many out of print. The seller benefits; the customer benefits; Amazon.com benefits. Amazon's first profit after its founding in July 1995 finally came in the fourth quarter of 2001, with about 15 percent of its sales the result of the sale of used books. Not profiting, of course, are the author and publisher. But, both long ago accepted the reality that used books don't bring income to those who create literature.

What they won't accept is that many of the "used" books are really mint condition comp copies, provided by book reviewers. "With the return on sales of used books so rich, Amazon has created a system that compels it to push used copies over new," according to the Guild. The Guild proposed several alternatives, including moving the click-through "used" window and not allowing customers to purchase used books for 6–12 weeks following publication. The Guild also charged that Amazon.com "refused to change anything," and then launched a counter-attack that resulted in more than 6,000 e-mails, many from authors and professors who naively claimed they didn't mind losing royalties—they just wanted their voices heard.

In a strong letter to Jeff Bezos, Amazon's founder and chief executive officer, Nick Taylor argued: "We're not against Amazon's selling used books, or used book sales generally. We're against Amazon's selling 'used' (frequently new copies sent out for review) books on the same page as new ones. Neither authors, who frequently devote years of hard work to their books, nor publishers, who invest faith and money in bringing books to print, receive credit for books sold this way. Only the seller, who often paid nothing in the first place, and of course Amazon, turns a profit."

In 2003, amazon.com added a "search inside the book" program that allowed readers to read several pages from a book, hopefully before buying that title. The Authors Guild was quick to point out that almost entire books could be printed using some rather simple technology. In October 2003, faced by heavy author attacks, amazon.com finally disabled the print function of "Search Inside."

Complementing Amazon's profit-making at the expense of authors and publishers is the American university system. At the end of every semester, book buyers descend upon the college campuses to buy books from the profs. Not the used books that students sell back to the bookstore the day after their finals, but new books. Complimentary ones often sent at the professor's request. The purpose of complimentary copies, sometimes as many as 5,000 per press run, is to entice the professors to adopt the books for a course. No one knows how many of the nation's 1.7 million post-secondary faculty sell comp copies, although good estimates are that of more than 100 million college texts published a year, as many as half of the estimated one million complimentary copies may make it into paid distribution.

As with sales on Amazon.com, almost everyone benefits. The profs make out well since they can sometimes make $300–$400 in undeclared income merely for filling out requests for comp copies, then opening shipping bags a few times a semester and occasionally thumbing through the merchandise.

The agents make out well since they buy $50 books for,

maybe, $5. And the wholesalers and bookstores make out well since they buy books at far less than half the cost of new books.

In 1986, the last time the Book Industry Study Group analyzed hard data, authors were losing $10 million a year in royalties, and publishers were losing $80 million a year in sales to the comp book racket. A few years ago, Karl J. Smith, a math professor at Santa Rosa (Calif.) Junior College, quickly learned how bad the problem was; more than half the students in his class had purchased "used books"—although the book he wrote had just been released three weeks earlier.

Professors, in rebuttal, say that many of the copies are unsolicited, so it's their right to sell them. They say even books they asked for may not after inspection be appropriate for the courses they teach. The publishers suggest sending back the unused books, and often include postage-paid coupons and mailers; they suggest the professor may place the books on department library shelves or even donate the books to charitable agencies. But, the comp copies are still being sold for "spare change."

To stop the sale of complimentary copies, publishers have begun embossing "Complimentary—Not for Sale" on the covers; many are also stamping the same message on the end of the pages. But, wholesalers have placed non-removable "USED" stickers on the covers, and sanded off the message on the pages. Many wholesalers even rebind some titles.

Many colleges have policies that forbid the professors to sell their comp copies. "We strongly suggest that stores don't buy comp copies," says Jerry Buchs of the 3,000-member National Association of College Stores. But, the Association can only recommend since it has no enforcement powers in its code of ethics. Nevertheless, says Buchs, "We keep addressing the issue."

Except for authors and publishers not receiving money for writing and producing books, and some ethical considerations swirling around bookstores and professors making money from books they had no part in creating, students, like flea market buyers and Amazon's customers, wonder what the problem is. After all, they're getting new books at "used" prices. One of the problems is that the sale of complimentary textbooks to agents—not the sale of legitimately purchased used books the students sell back, but which also yield no income to authors and publishers—directly leads to higher list prices for all textbooks as well as a necessity for continuous updates (some with only minor changes) so one edition doesn't stay in print more than two or three years, says James Lichtenberg, vice-president of the Association of American Publishers (AAP).

The greater issue, said Nick Taylor, is one of "intellectual property." In an article in the Spring 2002 issue of the *Authors Guild Bulletin*, Taylor wrote:

> "The people who wrote [the Constitution] recognized that writing and other forms of creativity—intellectual property—were valuable to a free society. So to 'promote the progress of science and the useful arts' they gave writers temporary monopolies in the form of copyrights.
>
> "Churning 'used' books through the new book marketplace defeats the purpose of copyright protection. Royalties aren't just money; they're food for thought and new ideas, the thing the Constitution intends by carving out a special place for writers. Books aren't like other forms of property. They're not useful as objects. It's the ideas they contain that make them useful. Treating books like widgets may be good merchandising, but the framers knew there are things more sacred than the marketplace."

It's rare that a customer doesn't complain about the spiraling cost of books; it's rare that students don't complain about the high price of textbooks. They should be complaining about greedy, unethical recyclers, book dealers, and professors who force publishers to raise list prices to partially compensate for stolen income.

The Jessica Lynch Story: Spinning the War in a Cauldron Devoid of Media Ethics

The relationship between the TV networks, both the news and entertainment divisions, and nation's publicists is incestuous. Most guests on the morning news shows and the late evening talk shows are actors and musicians plugging their latest releases. Some of the guests, however, are writers and editors for mass-market magazines. NBC's "Today Show" often broadcasts stories that first appeared in *People* magazine.

At WFLA-TV, the NBC affiliate in Tampa, Fla., it's possible to buy interview time. For $2,500, "Daytime," which follows the network's "Today Show," will allow almost anyone hawking just about anything to be interviewed for four to six minutes in a journalistic-like format. The station management says that charging guests is acceptable because the entertainment division not the news division produces the show. However, the station places its "News Channel 8" logo at the bottom of the screen.

In October 1999, the distinction between news and advertising was blurred when the *Los Angeles Times* published a special edition of its respected weekend magazine about the newly-opened Staples Center, and split the revenue with Staples. More than 300 *Times* journalists protested what they saw as an issue of lack of integrity; stories in other newspapers condemned the *Times.* Publisher Kathryn M. Downing later apologized for what journalists and much of the public saw as ethically wrong, and said the publication and revenue split was because of her own "fundamental misunderstanding" of journalistic principles.

Then, on April 9, 2009, with the public having forgotten the Staples incident, the *Times,* which had been running front page advertising for two years, published a one-column front page story about the first day of a rookie police officer. Although marked as "Advertisement," and in a different typeface than news type, the story was a well-disguised promotion for the new NBC-TV series, "Southland," and could easily have been read as news not advertising. The ad-story (known in the industry as an "advertorial") appeared adjacent to a five column color ad for "Southland" at the bottom of the page. In response, more than 100 of the newspaper's editorial staff signed a petition opposing the blurring between advertising and news.

"What was great about this ad unit is it gave us [an] 'editorial voice,'" Adam Stotsky, president of entertainment marketing for NBC, told the *New York Times* the day the story ran. He explained to the *New York Times,* "The more relevant you can make your advertising, the more contextualized you can make your advertising, we find the more engagement can be created, and ultimately the more effective your marketing can be." The official *L.A. Times* spin was that "The delivery of news and information is a rapidly changing business and the Los Angeles Times is continuously testing innovative approaches. That includes creating unique marketing opportunities for our advertising partners and today's NBC 'Southland' ad was designed to stretch traditional boundaries."

One of the most serious cross-over between news, entertainment, and advertising occurred when the media began a bidding war to get the "exclusive" Jessica Lynch story, and found themselves in collusion with the government and advertisers. By the time the story had played out, news media credibility and ethical boundaries had been shattered.

The Washington Post first broke the story shortly after Lynch was rescued after nine days in a six-story Iraqi hospital in April 2003. Using unnamed sources, the *Post* reported that Lynch, a 19-year-old supply clerk who was driving a water tanker, "fought fiercely and shot several enemy soldiers after Iraqi forces ambushed [a convoy of] the Army's 507th Ordnance Maintenance Company, firing her weapon until she ran out of ammunition." The unnamed sources also told the *Post* that Lynch "continued firing at the Iraqis even after she sustained multiple gunshot wounds and watched several other soldiers in her unit die around her in fighting. . . . She was fighting to the death . . . She did not want to be taken alive." The *Post* also reported that Lynch "was also stabbed when Iraqi forces closed in on her position."

Other media quickly jumped onto the story and reported not only was she was shot several times by her Iraqi attackers but was also tortured while in the hospital. A daring Navy SEAL/Army Ranger/Air Force rescue effort, against possible hostile fire, freed her after nine days in the Iraqi hospital. Based upon the words of an Iraqi and the Department of Defense, The *Post*, quickly followed by other media, reported that "four guards in civilian clothes stood watch at Lynch's first-floor room armed with Kalashnikov rifles and radios." The rescue came, according to CBS, when special forces "ran through a hail of gunfire." The media gave the story front-page play and top-of-the-news broadcasts for several days.

There was only one problem—most of the story, piped to the media by unnamed sources and the Defense Department, and never verified by the media—was wrong. Lynch wasn't driving a water tanker but was a passenger in a Humvee; she never fired a shot, nor was she shot; her injuries were caused from being trapped by the overturned Humvee; the convoy wasn't ambushed—it had gotten lost, and then was hit by a rocket-propelled grenade from a small group of Iraqi irregulars; she was treated well by Iraqi physicians; she wasn't beaten while held as a prisoner; there was no military opposition to the rescue attempt; the Iraqis even offered to give the Americans a master key to the hospital. Equally important, the Department of Defense had alerted the media a full day before the "rescue" attempt.

Lynch herself later said the military exaggerated what happened in the desert. In an interview on ABC-TV, she said the lies and use of unnamed sources by the media "hurt in a way that people would make up stories that they had no truth about." In April 2007, before a Congressional hearing, Lynch said "[T]he American people are capable of determining their own ideals of heroes and they don't need to be told elaborate lies."

Lynch was quick to praise others who had died in the crash or who fought; one, a young soldier, would eventually receive the silver star for heroism—and almost no media coverage. But, the blonde-girl-fights-off-soldiers-and-survives-torture made a good story. So good that a CBS News senior vice-president, trying to get exclusive rights, wrote a letter to the Army that blurred the distinction between news and entertainment. In that letter, Betsy West wrote: "Attached you will find the outlines of a proposal that includes ideas from CBS News, CBS Entertainment, MTV networks and Simon & Schuster publishers. From the distinguished reporting of CBS News to the youthful reach of MTV, we believe this is a unique combination of projects that will do justice to Jessica's inspiring story."

Writing in the November 2003 issue of *Quill*, the official publication of the Society of Professional Journalists, Peter Y. Sussman pointed out "it would be exceedingly difficult for any of CBS's 'distinguished' journalists to question dispassionately an interviewee whom their boss had wooed with intimations of lucrative deals and the assurance that the network found her story 'inspiring'."

Nevertheless, it was NBC, ABC, and publisher A. A. Knopf that won the first rights. NBC ran a two-hour semi-fictionalized docudrama during Fall 2003, and ABC aired the first "exclusive" interview with her on Nov. 11—the same day a book, based upon interviews with her, was published. "That interview, to be followed in quick order by interviews on other major networks, thus completes the transition from news story to promotional sales campaign, with the 'news media' playing the role of compliant handmaiden," Sussman wrote, pointing out, "It is . . . hard to imagine how any true journalism can emerge from the blizzard of Lynch interviews on news shows that networks

143

fought so hard to secure during the . . . promotional campaign for her book."

Ethical issues have continually clouded the information, entertainment, and persuasion areas of mass communications, dissolving any pretense that there are walls between journalism and advertising. Perhaps, we should just classify the mass media as entertainment and disregard the belief that journalistic integrity is important in the media's quest for circulation, ratings, and higher profits.

The media is so inaccurate

BROADCAST JOURNALISM

TV News 101: Intro to Makeup

It was the first of 114 episodes of the critically acclaimed TV series "Lou Grant" (1977–1982), and I eagerly awaited seeing it again, now in syndicated reruns. The first episode reintroduced Ed Asner to American television as the crotchety, hard driving, but cuddly journalist who once worked on a Detroit newspaper and had just been fired as news director of WJM-TV Minneapolis—you know, the one where Mary Richards (portrayed by Mary Tyler Moore) was a producer, and Murray Slaughter (portrayed by Gavin McCloud before becoming the "Love Boat" captain) wrote copy for the bumbling Ted Baxter (Ted Knight) who was everyone's idea of the typical anchor. Lou was 50 years old and had $280 in the bank. Coming to his rescue was Charlie Hume, a once tough reporter now buried as a corporate-leaning managing editor, who said Lou would be perfect as city editor of the *L.A. Tribune* as long as Mrs. Pynchon, the publisher, agrees. But, just one word of caution, said the editor. When meeting the publisher, avoid mentioning those years on TV—"she hates it."

"Then what do I tell her I've been doing the last 10 years?" Lou asked.

"Tell her you were in jail," said Charlie.

And so it began. The first episode was directed by Gene Reynolds of "M*A*S*H" fame, from a brilliant script by Leon Tokatyan. During its four-season run, some of Hollywood's finest directors and writers worked on the series. In each episode were social and journalistic issues that made the one-hour show the best journalism classroom any student could imagine. But, I always remembered those early throw-away lines of cynicism

144

between Lou and Charlie, that it was better to admit to having been in jail than to having worked in TV news.

The more I watch local TV news, the more I am convinced that even the worst of our local newspapers—and, certainly, the print media seem to have as many problems as there are lines of type—may be better than the average local newscast, most of which seem to be concerned more about appearance than content.

In December 1996, a reporter from WYOU-TV, a CBS affiliate in Wilkes-Barre, Pa., was punched out by a guy who declared, "So you think you're so pretty!" Station management, of course, would have maintained that the reporter, a hunk who sported a great Winter tan, was hired on the basis of his competence not his looks. However, management then told the viewers the hunk was going to continue to report stories, but wouldn't be on air until the cut over his eye looked more presentable. The next time we saw him on air, he was wearing a hat and sunglasses.

The typical TV news room has about as many reporters as a small daily, but at least 10 times the news to cover. To compensate for the lack of reporters, the station leases a helicopter to give it "a presence in the market," hires three meteorologists to tell us the weather in Muscogee, Okla., and two or three washed-up or never-was athletes to pump the latest exploits of the local Wattabago Whales Single-A baseball team. But, the station doesn't give us stories about the environment, health, labor, or the economy. What it does give us is gore.

To lead the news, local stations send camera crews to fires and car crashes to get that "visual" and to shove microphones up someone's nose and ask, "How do you feel now that your house burned down and your only son died in the inferno?" The rush to "quickie news" dominates the local newscasts.

"The locals use any old barn burning or jack-knifed trailer truck, and pass that kind of thing off as news," former CBS anchor Walter Cronkite told *Women's Day* readers in 1995. Station executives, he said, "have probably costed it out and that even maintaining the satellite trucks to run around to crime scenes is cheaper than having enough people on staff who can understand the news and spend time reporting it."

Find good reporters—and TV news does have good reporters—and their station management limits them to about 90 seconds of air time, no more than about three paragraphs in the local newspaper, and then restricts their budget to nothing more than covering the local Miss Petunia Pageant, while

145

encouraging the sports reporters to chase college and pro teams all over the country. But, as TV news viewership has plummeted over the past two decades, consultants have constantly come up with newer ways to hold the viewership, usually by pandering to the lowest tastes.

Unable or unwilling to dig out stories of substance, the typical 30-minute newscast gives us eight minutes of commercials and promos, five minutes of sports, four minutes of weather, a couple of minutes of nauseating happy talk banter broken up into 10-second bites, a minute or two of canned network cast-off news, a minute of teasers and "upcoming at 11" self-promotion, and no more than 10 minutes of local news. That, of course, leaves no time for local editorials, which is fine with management since it believes cordial relations with viewers and advertisers is preferred to journalistic integrity. In fact, the official CBS-TV policy is a very stark, "We do not take advocacy positions on controversial issues."

Desperate for ratings, station managers and news directors turn to consultants. These ubiquitous "consultants" are paid mini-fortunes to tell Management that stories about some starlet "accidentally" losing her bra in the surf is more substance than how the latest Senate hearings on health care reform will impact the local market, and that the station could squeeze another one-tenth of a rating point by lighting the set differently to highlight the anchor's "pool green" eyes. But, the viewers are brighter than consultants, and so they turn away from the news even more. Fortunately, for the consultants, the more the ratings drop, the more that station management demands their services.

It's not as if local television doesn't have any models. "60 Minutes," "Dateline," "20/20," "Nightline," and just about anything on MSNBC and CNN can go one-on-one with the best newspapers and news magazines. But more Americans watch local news than the network news magazines. However, even the major players are noticing problems. Morley Safer, a "60 Minutes" anchor, said in March 1997 there "is generally a lowering of standards about what we see on the air," and Lesley Stahl admitted she occasionally had been asked to report a story she hadn't thoroughly researched. "It's frightening," she said.

"One thing missing from local TV news is reporting," says Paul Stueber, who retired in 2007 after spending four decades as a news producer and news director for award-winning top-rated stations in major markets, including New York City, Detroit, Miami, and Cleveland. Stueber observes that in current news operations, "No one is doing hard digging, and no one is camped outside the mayor's office waiting to ask tough questions. It's easier to shoot the fires and shootings and stabbings and robberies. The audience doesn't seem to notice or care, so it gets 'lowest common denominator' news."

Charles Kuralt (1934–1997), one of the nation's most distinguished network correspondents, once explained what TV news has become: "Urgent electronic music plays, the lights come up, and an earnest young man or woman says to a camera, 'Good evening, here is the news.' This is said very urgently and with the appearance of sincerity most often by an attractive young person who would not know a news story if it jumped up and mussed his coiffure."

Andy Lack, NBC News president, was even harsher. "There's a generation of reporters coming along who are more interested in who their agent is or whether they're 'in play' at Fox than in going after the big stories," he charged. Because many of the reporters aren't willing "to invest in the homework that comes with really developing your skills as a first rate reporter," said Lack, "there's very little emphasis on quality of work and a great deal of emphasis on compensation for it."

CBS anchor Dan Rather simply called much of what passes as TV news "fuzz and wuzz."

However, actor Greg Kinnear best summed up what has happened to TV news. Kinnear said he was unsure of whether to be an actor or broadcast journalist when he entered the University of Arizona in 1981. A year later, his drama teacher told him that only 2 percent of actors made their living as actors. "I thought to myself, 'Geez, that leaves the news,'" Kinnear told the readers of *Parade* magazine in December 1996.

"Let's face it," said Kinnear, targeting what has happened to the profession, "the lines between entertainment and broadcast journalism were blurred way before I came along. . . . It's increasingly difficult for the viewer to discern between what is true and what's a lie. That's incredibly scary."

Maybe if the journalists, both print and broadcast, learned more about their profession by watching what happened at the fictional *L.A. Tribune*, then maybe Lou Grant could have proudly admitted he once worked in TV news, and we wouldn't have thousands of journalism students begging for a chance to be the next million dollar anchor, and preparing for it by checking hair styles instead of courthouse records.

The Only Alternative for KFAD

The news rating of television station KFAD went out to lunch and didn't return. This, of course, caused great concern for the news director who didn't like the possibility of being exiled to a small 500-watt radio station in Hogshead, Iowa.

"What about story length?" the station manager snapped. "Haven't they been getting longer?"

"No, sir! We've never run a story longer than 90 seconds, and most of the stories are 15 to 20 seconds."

"Good. We're still using the local newspapers, right?"

"Oh, yes sir! My reporters know that the only way to get good television news is to rewrite from the local papers. That way we devote our energies to stories of real importance."

"Like that beauty pageant last week," said the station manager enthusiastically. "Real hard-hitting news coverage."

"It just lent itself to news film. I sure hated to miss the Senate investigation, but since they don't allow cameras in the chambers, there wasn't any sense in having a reporter there."

"Well," said the station manager reflectively, "there's nothing wrong with our basic news coverage, so it has to be our on-air personalities. How long has it been since Susie Sweetwater changed her hairstyle?"

"About two months, but I think we should let it stay that way another month or so just to increase viewer identification."

"In another month or so," said the station manager tersely, "we may be fourth in a three-station market. How's Susie handling the slump?"

"Remarkably well. Just yesterday, she had her fingernails manicured, and bought a new dress. I think she looks a lot better than Laura Landfill over at that other station. The technicians certainly have noticed."

"But, hasn't she presented a few special problems to your staff?"

"It's true our news writers are cramped writing scripts with no more than two syllable words, but someone saw Susie actually trying to read a newspaper last week."

"What about Heartthrob? You know the co-anchor is just as important."

"He's been putting on a little weight, so I sent him over to the spa. It'll boost his image immeasurably."

"How's our ethnic balance? You know how the FCC is. Can we get better ratings by adding another ethnic?"

The news director shook his head. "We already have two Chicanos, three Blacks, an Alaskan, an Indian, two Laplanders, and a Southern Baptist on the news team. I don't think we can add any more right now."

"Maybe we can laugh it up more on the set. Maybe expand the Happy News format?"

"We're saturated now, and I don't think the viewers are ready to tolerate Susie giggling through another air disaster."

"What about the weather?"

"As you know, McDonald gave the weather once in a raincoat, and another time in a bikini. And remember the times she brought the chickens into the studio to apologize for laying an egg with the previous forecast? You can't do much more than that to get ratings!"

"Pack your snow shovel," said the station manager. "It looks like you're heading to corn country."

"Give me time," pleaded the news director, "I'll come up with some innovative way to boost the ratings." There was a moment of silence, then the news director blurted out his idea. "A journalist!"

"A what!?"

"A journalist! That could be the radical new way to boost the ratings. We could hire a journalist to give the news!"

The station manager was furious. "Don't be ridiculous! A journalist on TV would be a disaster!"

"No, Boss, I mean it. No one else has a journalist on the air. It could be the novelty that sells the station to the advertisers. Imagine our slogan—'Watch KFAD, the station that has the only journalist on the air.' It could be big!"

"Well," said the station manager thoughtfully, "we did have one journalist who applied for a job a couple of months ago. Claimed to have won something called a Pulitzer. I'm afraid I was rather rude to him. It lowers our image just to have them around."

"We're desperate, Boss, let's give it a try."

The station manager leaned back in his overstuffed chair, pushed away from his eight-foot conference table, lit an over-sized cigar, and thought a moment. "A journalist . . . On TV . . .

149

It's radical enough . . . It's even revolutionary! OK, hire him, but make sure he gets special attention in Hair and Wardrobe."

A Television Snow Job

During the Blizzard of March 2008, with heavy winds, tornadoes, subfreezing temperatures, and more than two feet of snow falling over much of the eastern United States, with 17 deaths, thousands injured, and several hundred thousand left without electricity, local and state officials closed down roads and highways. The only vehicles allowed were for snow removal crews, emergencies, health professionals, and other essential workers. Because TV journalists believed they were essential, let's see what an "essential" broadcast during that four-day storm probably looked like. . . .

"I'm Harry Handsome. Susie Sweetwater just called in. Her car had slid into a ditch about eight miles from the studio. Fortunately, she had her three-speed bike in the car, and is pedaling furiously to get in so she doesn't lose a day's pay. We begin our extended and comprehensive team coverage of the snow emergency with chief meteorologist Flake Sepulveda who's at his command post on the roof."

"From on top of the 85th floor, I can report more accurately than any other weather person that the high was 25 today, with a low of 8. That's well off from the records. The record high, set in 1945, was 68 degrees. But, in L. A. today it was a sun-drenched 87, and those babes in the Sunshine State must be catching some real cool rays. Here's a reminder. If you do get to California this week, always wear a good sunblock. That sunshine can really do some damage. The record low in our area was a bruising minus 11, set way back in 1981. Maybe you old-timers will remember that one. The nation's low today was set in Washington when the Congress and President still couldn't come up with a budget, but that's another story. We're currently tracking a low pressure system that may meet up with a high pressure front just north of Minneapolis and begin to move southeast at 25 miles an hour. However, one of our computers has it starting in San Francisco and cruising east along I-80 at 65 miles an hour. But our third computer says the only storm front at the moment is forming 30 miles west of Death Valley, with snow expected all over the Mojave Desert before coming out here where it may or may not drop anywhere from two inches to seven feet of sleet, snow, or acid rain."

"Flake, can you see what's happening right now?"

"Not with all these rooftop barriers, Harry. Let me fight the bruising wind and go to the edge and take a closer look. From the roof of the KFAD building, it appears . . ."

"We've lost communication with the roof. Let's check traffic with Barry Blades in HeliCam 2."

"It's real white out there. I can't see the road, but it looks like I'm up to my rear rotor in snow. I'm also running out of fuel. Back to you, Harry."

"For a ground-eye view, we go *live* to Polly Prattle."

"I'm standing in the middle of the Interstate. Because the Governor closed the roads, we haven't seen much traffic the past hour. Just a few snowplows which we'll let through as soon as we finish this vital and essential report. As you can see, there's nothing but snow all around me. If my dumb cameraman hadn't broken his leg trying to set up his 50 pounds of equipment, we'd have even better pictures of nothing."

"Thanks Polly. Now to Bob Covina, *live* at the mall."

"Harry, I'm standing *live* in the parking lot at the West Begonia Mall. There aren't any cars in the lot. Except ours, of course. There's a lot of snow and the mall is closed."

"Do you know when it'll open?"

"It's a little past 11 p.m. right now, so I guess it'll probably open tomorrow morning sometime."

"Thanks for that insightful report, Bob. Now, *live* on Second Street is Kiki Vertigo who's been interviewing residents about their response to the snow."

"With me right now, *live* on Second Street, is resident Homer Bigeloo who has a snow shovel. Homer, what are you doing?"

"I'm shoveling snow."

"Have you been shoveling long?"

"Yeah. I don't like snow."

"How long haven't you liked snow?"

"A long time, I guess."

"Thanks, Homer. I'm Kiki Vertigo, *live* on Second Street. Back to you, Harry."

"Another great interview, Kiki. We'll be back with our comprehensive team coverage right after this message from Menodcino Frozen TV Dinners."

Commentaries About TV Journalism

In May 1997, Chicago's WMAQ-TV, owned by NBC, brought in TV talk show host Jerry Springer to do commentary on the 10 p.m. evening news.

Calling Springer "the poster child for the worst television has to offer," and infuriated over what she believed was a deterioration of TV news integrity, Carol Marin resigned after an 18-year career at the station, the last 12 as co-anchor of the evening news.

Springer said what he thought about the subsequent controversy over his hiring and Marin's resignation—"It's only reading a teleprompter," he said about TV anchors. "I mean, they make it seem like journalism."

Marin was right; there has been a deterioration of TV news, much of it brought on by insipid infomercials designed as news, an obsession with police, fire, and celebrity stories, and a hyperactive quest for ratings.

Springer was also right; there is little resemblance between TV news and journalism. However, Springer was an ideal commentator, even if the station hired him not for his mind but because he could bring in ratings. After receiving a B.A. in political science from Tulane and a law degree from Northwestern, Springer became a campaign aide to Sen. Robert F. Kennedy. Subsequently, he was one of the leaders to reduce the voting age from 21 to 18, became a councilman and mayor of Cincinnati, and then a journalist. At Cincinnati's WLWT-TV, he won seven Emmys for commentary during his 11 years at the NBC affiliate, the last nine years as managing editor and anchor.

Certainly, Springer doesn't confuse the entertainment and acting he does on his tabloid TV show with journalism, just as most viewers probably don't confuse the banal happy-talk of many TV newscasts with journalism.

If newspaper reporters—most of whom are justified in their opinion about the lack of journalism in TV news operations—resigned because they didn't want to work for a medium that publishes sleazy advice columns, the horoscope, and pablum features about new shopping carts at the local supermarket, there wouldn't be any editorial staff left on all but a handful of the nation's newspapers.

152

Nevertheless, after just two commentaries, Springer resigned, having been blasted by the nation's journalists, almost all of whom piously proclaimed how bad TV journalism had become, all of whom seldom read their own newspapers.

Anchoring Miss America

Miss America 2009, Katie Stam of Indiana, says she wants to be a TV news anchor. And so do Miss Massachusetts and Miss Virginia.

Miss South Dakota says she just wants to work for a television network. But, if an anchor job opened, she'd probably take it.

Miss Louisiana wants to become either a classical singer or a TV journalist. Miss New Mexico also has a lot of ambition. She wants to create a program to help students prepare for college, an excellent career choice for an image-conscious pageant. But, she'd also like to record a music CD and become the host of a world traveling TV show.

Miss Idaho and Miss Minnesota don't say anything about being a TV anchor; Miss Idaho plans to go into advertising; Miss Minnesota wants to work in public relations or event planning. Perhaps they will team up to represent on-air celebrities and TV anchors. Miss Montana doesn't plan to go into TV journalism. She says she wants to get a Ph.D. and become a professor of communications. She doesn't say if she has any plans to actually work in the field of communications before teaching communications.

Ten of the 52 contestants in the 2009 Pageant wanted to go into the field of mass communications. Five years earlier, 16 of the 52 planned to go into TV; none, neither in 2004 nor in 2009, wanted to become writers or newspaper or magazine reporters.

It won't be all that difficult for the beauties to reach their life ambition. TV journalism has become more fluff than substance, with hair-do's and smiles more important than reporting and writing. Miss Michigan reveals the truth of TV journalism. She says she wants to become a TV anchor in a Top 10 market. To better prepare her, she plans to earn a master's in integrated marketing communication. Should she become a Top 10 news anchor, she will have proven that beauty and PR, rather than reporting and writing, are what's necessary to deliver the news.

The Miss America Organization, claiming a "desire to create

153

exciting television," and pretending to match current TV trends, says its final evening competition "has been providing viewers with high stakes reality television since its broadcast debut in 1954." The CEO, a man—there has never been a woman—says the contest is "the end-product of a year of competition that begins with 12,000 women and culminates with one previously unknown woman who overnight becomes an internationally renowned celebrity. That's real reality TV." In 2007, it finally became one of several dozen "reality TV" series, with a seven-part mini-series, "Finding Miss America." The "fly-on-the-wall" series followed the 52 finalists in September 2006 in Los Angeles during preliminary competitions, with the series airing shortly before the Finals in January 2007.

As much as the organization has tried to pander to current tastes, its TV audience had been diminishing—from about 25 million in 1995 to about 9.8 million in September 2004—leading ABC-TV to relinquish the pageant's demographics to Country Music Television (CMT) in 2005. Art McMaster, the Miss America CEO, trying to put a spin on the break-up with ABC, said, "We needed to find a better partner, one that better understands our values." The "family values" pageant and the "heart of America" cable network moved the next competition from the family-friendly casinos of Atlantic City to the nation's first gambling mecca, which advertises itself with the salacious slogan, "What happens in Las Vegas stays in Las Vegas." By 2007, only about 2.4 million viewers tuned in to see who would become Miss America.

The following year, The Learning Channel broadcast the pageant. Continuing to acknowledge the ratings popularity of Reality TV, the Miss America organization and TLC created its own reality with "Miss America: Countdown to the Crown," in which the contestants went through a set of challenges; four of the 16 finalists were picked by TV viewers. The January 2009 pageant saw a rise in viewers to 3.5 million, according to Nielsen Media Research data. The rise in ratings led to yet another Pageant media spin. "After partnering with TLC for the last two years, we have been able to build our Miss America audience and reach new and younger demographics," said Sam Has-kell III, Miss America's chairman of the board. "We are thrilled with the results," he beamed, "and we have been able to successfully rebrand our Miss America image while continuing to expand the reach of our program." He never mentioned that viewership

154

was only about one-third of what it had been when ABC finally dropped the broadcast.

With the sincerity of a talent agent and a structure that makes the Mafia seem to be nothing more intimidating than Junior Achievement, the Miss America Organization emphasizes it isn't a (*shudder, gasp*) beauty contest, but a "non-profit business and culturally specific brand that transcends just being a beauty pageant" but is an organization that provides "personal and professional opportunities for young women and promote[s] their voices in culture, politics, and the community." The Miss America Organization emphasizes, "Almost all contestants have either received, or are in the process of earning, college or postgraduate degrees and utilize Miss America scholarship grants to further their educations." Apparently, brilliant, talented people who look good in swimsuits and evening gowns but don't go to college aren't wanted.

To get those grants and become "Scholar of the Year," the contestants immerse themselves into a series of mini-competitions that are designed to make us believe that swimsuits and evening wear are merely afterthoughts on the path to more than a thousand speaking engagements a year. Groomed by voice coaches and image consultants who have bathed them with the lessons of "interpersonal communications," or "integrated marketing strategies," the contestants are primed to cover any possible question with variations of the same prepared answer, a talent every female TV news anchor needs.

To de-emphasize the public perception that the pageant is a beauty contest, the Miss America Organization manipulated the swimsuit competition into "Lifestyle and Fitness in a Swimsuit." The Pageant's marketing geniuses tell us the category emphasizes "contestants maintaining a healthful, positive lifestyle [with] drive, energy and charisma." Apparently, the judges are endowed with divine knowledge to determine all that by just watching a woman in a swimsuit strut around a stage. Although "swimsuit" is worth only 15 percent in preliminary judging, it's worth 20 percent in the finals.

Evening wear is worth another 20 percent in both preliminary and final competition; talent is 35 percent in the preliminaries, but drops to 30 percent in the finals. Filling out the percentages is the preliminary rounds are a private interview (25 percent) and an on-stage question (5 percent). The finals competition, with the top 16 contestants, also has a composite score

155

from the preliminaries (30 percent), an on-air question, and a final ballot by the judges, which could transcend all other scores.

For awhile, the Miss America Organization had a "poise, presence and family" category, a way "to remind viewers that the contestants are real people, with real lives." To make sure the viewers knew that Miss America was a family-vaoues organization, it once allowed each contestant to be "escorted on stage by her father, brother, or a special male relative." Until a rules change in 2003, none were escorted by another female, apparently so the TV audience wouldn't believe that mother and daughter were really a lesbian couple.

Because this is a pageant, not a beauty contest, Miss America contestants must present their "platforms." The Miss America mandate encourages "young women to explore the relevant social issues of their times and to excel in arts, science, communications or any area of inquiry that inspires their interest and devotion." The social issues that the contestants say they are interested and devoted to platforming are relatively safe issues of health care, education, or children. After all, how can anyone speak against the platforms of contestants who want more cancer awareness or who think the nation should be more literate?

Miss New Jersey 2006 said she planned to get a master's in public relations and teach at a college; her platform, appropriately, was "the power of positive thinking." Miss Vermont that year, with a broadcast journalism degree, fully understood the harsh demands of on-air journalism—her platform was "Healthy Weight for Life." One year, Miss Wisconsin and Miss Wyoming, possibly because they were at the end of the list and didn't get to choose any of the "way cool diseases" to campaign against, chose to promote sexual abstinence, hopefully only until marriage. However, Pageant officials discourage the topic of abstinence since they believe it's a "turn-off" to judges, the media, and the American people. When Erika Harold, Miss America 2002, later tried to speak out for abstinence, the Miss America organization tried to silence her by invoking "The Contract." The contract, which all contestants sign at the state level, mandates which social issue the contestants will use as their "personal" platforms. As Miss Illinois, Harold had agreed that her "personal platform" would be to speak out against youth violence. After she became Miss America, she discussed sexual abstinence, infuriating Pageant functionaries, the same ones who invoke innumerable clauses about disqualifying contestants for "moral" inappropriateness, which can include having sexual relations before marriage.

While the nation was focused upon sex or the absence of it, they weren't looking at a reality that none of the Miss America candidates have platforms that deal with pro-choice or pro-life issues. None will express themselves about corporations that exploit the work force, or which have laid off most of their labor, and outsourced most of their product in order to gain a higher profit margin for investors and overpaid executives. None will advocate for animal rights, campaign finance reform, preservation of the environment over the lumber and building industries, or take a stand for or against gun control. Although several contestants speak against drug addiction, none discuss gambling addiction, a particularly sensitive subject in both Atlantic City and Las Vegas.

None of the future TV anchors and on-air personalities will use their "talent" to do investigative documentaries about the problems of the homeless of Atlantic City and Las Vegas and the duplicity of local governments that allows poverty to co-exist close to the casinos. When the pageant was in Atlantic City, none of the contestants or the TV cameras walked a block off the Boardwalk and into the low-income neighborhoods, their residents living in contrast to the fairy-tale glitz and glamour that TV, the casinos, and the pageant would like us to believe is the real Atlantic City. Don't expect social workers to make it into the Finals in Las Vegas or any other pageant city, either.

None of the TV anchor-wannabes are prepared to express themselves against the thousands of instances of suppression of free speech and free press rights or violations of the right-to-know and sunshine laws that occur every year. Miss America's squeaky-clean image is of the "girl next door," not the crusading activist. Spiritual descendants of Mother Jones, Emma Goldman, and Rachel Carson need not apply.

For one year, Miss America is a paid employee of a corporation and, says her employer wrapped within the gobbledygook of public relations and marketing, is "a critical member of the Miss America Organization marketing team [who] works to advance the business of scholarship and community service for women." That should dispel any notion that Miss America is selected because she looks good in swimsuits and evening gowns. While on her one-year national tour, she is continually watched over by a chaperon who may be a "mother confidante," event planner, and trouble-shooter, but whose job description requires her to monitor and report to headquarters Miss America's performance, including what she looks like and what she says to the public.

If any Miss America contestant has ambitions to be a broadcast journalist, she already has a long history of selling her body and soul to a corporation, and should have no trouble spewing happy talk.

Dead Air at the Convention

With scripts more complex than $100 million feature films, and about as deep as *Dumb and Dumber*, the quadrennial PR spectacle known as political conventions invaded Denver in the Summer of 2008 before moving to St. Paul.

There were TV and movie stars, rock bands, dozens of corporate-sponsored $300,000–$500,000 parties, and babbling pomposity about compassion, education, defense, and whatever other issues party pollsters determined the people wanted to hear. The politicians, recognizing the pervasive nature of the mass media, raised the art of pandering to a level no call girl could ever achieve.

With both parties having already determined their presidential candidates, the only major surprises at the conventions would have been if the man known as "No Drama Obama" had let out a primal scream or if John McCain, tortured in North Vietnam, had now said that the Bush–Cheney Administration use of torture was comendable and necessary.

Each of the four major TV networks devoted only four hours of live coverage to each convention, plus a few minutes on morning wake-up programs and the evening news for discussions and taped highlights. This is about two hours less than the 1996 convention, and significantly less than the gavel-to-gavel coverage of two dozen conventions. The politicians, tripping over each other to find anyone with a microphone and get a few seconds of air time, were upset about so little TV coverage. They wanted ABC, CBS, NBC, and FOX not CNN, PBS, and MSNBC; they settled for newspaper reporters when no one else was around.

The first televised conventions were in Philadelphia in 1948.

158

Only about 170,000 of the nation's 42.2 million households had televisions. The networks, desperate to fill their government-issued airwaves, begged the nation to believe that television was at the cutting edge of the future. TV needed politicians; politicians weren't so sure they needed TV.

By 1960, more than 46 million of the nation's 58 million households had at least one TV set, and most stations were broadcasting at least 16 hours a day. If anyone doubted the potential and power of television, it was quashed that year during the televised Nixon–Kennedy debates. Persons who heard the debate only on radio gave Nixon the advatage; however, those who watched it on television gave the advantage to Kennedy, a lead he never lost. Eight years later, the cameras recorded the Chicago riots, giving credibility to the antiwar movement and virtually destroying the Democrats' chance to defeat Richard Nixon, even though the liberal Hubert Humphrey deplored the police response and Mayor Richard Daley's iron fist tactics.

The networks cite low ratings and the absence of news as the reasons why they won't waste their time on coverage. Only about four million Americans at any time watched the 1996 conventions. In contrast, the equally quadrennial Olympics in 2008, with 171 hours of TV coverage, attracted a average of 27.7 million viewers at any one time, with about 214 million watching at least one part of the 17-day event.

Even with significant coverage by a half dozen news cable networks, fewer Americans watched the first night of the 2000 Republican convention than heard what comedian Dennis Miller said on his first night as color commentator on ABC's "Monday Night Football." However, ABC-TV, the NFL, and the Republicans apparently worked out some kind of a limited partnership—ABC broadcast the football game a bit earlier; after it was over, the Republicans ushered Gen. Colin Powell onto stage. CBS, NBC, and FOX didn't cover it live.

It was the television media that created the atmosphere that demanded "interesting visuals" and the seven-second sound bite; and now the media are upset that politicians, in their infomercial packaged conventions that play to the camera, have nothing to say.

Ted Koppel, saying there was so little to cover, pulled his ABC-TV "Nightline" crews from the Republican convention in 1996. "People know there's nothing really happening" at the conventions, ABC News vice-president Jeff Grainick told the

Chicago Tribune that year, and then stated that the "meaningfulness of these conventions has declined." NBC-TV executive producer Jeff Zucker said he doubted any network would give much coverage to future conventions, a self-fulfilling prophecy for the next 12 years. It's hard to believe that 16,000 members of the media credentialed to cover each convention couldn't find any news.

For the 2008 conventions, we saw the mass of media think they were covering American politics by giving us the usual slickly-prepared mini-bios of the candidates, innocuous featurettes about souvenirs and local foods, and the obligatory interviews with fawning and self-important delegates. There was also endless semi-erudite commentary that bored viewers more than any politician's hour-long speech.

If the media were to leave their color-coordinated broadcast booths and hospitality suites, and dig beneath the puffery and pageantry, they may find the greater social and political issues that need to be reported, as well as the delightful "slice of life" stories that help us better understand our own lives.

As it is, the writers for Jay Leno, David Letterman, Conan O'Brien, and especially Comedy Central's "The Daily Show with Jon Stewart" and "The Colbert Report" give America better insight than the sound-bite politicians who stand before television cameras, interviewed by personalities who pretend to be journalists.

LANGUAGE AND LITERACY

'Local Reporter Cops Lexicon Story'

If Rudyard Kipling was right that "words are the most powerful drug used by mankind," then a lot of the media are in great pain.

Almost every day, we read or hear about a "spectacular fire" or "spectacular accident" where (pick one) (a) a car, (b) a truck, (c) a fleet of skateboards "careened out of control." Nonsense! Fireworks on the Fourth of July is spectacular. A "fatal fire" (reporters love alliteration) or a traffic accident in which three people are killed are *not* spectacular.

And, where else but in the media can we hear about some psycho with a high-power assault weapon holding "police at

160

bay"? When the battle is over, we are likely to learn that the "perp"—who used to be a criminal before the debut of TV's *Hill Street Blues* (1981–1987)—was "racked by guilt." And, since "racked" is such a popular piece of "journalese," we also learn there are people in our society, maybe even the criminals just before their sentencing, who are also "racked by pain" and "racked by anguish." All this, of course, leaves most readers being "mental racks."

Has anyone else noticed that if a young lady is "brutally murdered" (as if some murders aren't brutal?) she's often identified in the lead as "A pretty 27-year-old woman was killed late last night." Does anyone recall reading about "An ugly 27-year-old was poisoned early this morning"? How about men who are killed? Do we identify them as "A 27-year-old Greek god hunk with rippling muscles was stabbed yesterday afternoon while pumping iron in his West Catcall basement"? So far, the media haven't identified any murder victim as having been "drop dead gorgeous," a term they apply to numerous living actresses and models.

Should there be an "eyewitness," apparently someone more alert than just a plain, ordinary witness, we might learn that the criminal or victim was last seen "exiting the building at approximately 11 p.m." Apparently, "leaving the building about 11 p.m." doesn't sound as menacing.

To pretend we are covering all possible law suits, we drop in "alleged" now and then. Thus, if one "alleged" is good, then several of them apparently protect journalists from suits even more, as in "the alleged burglar was arrested by police who charged him with allegedly committing the alleged crime." One Denver TV reporter claimed "several alleged shots were fired," and a northeast Pennsylvania newspaper, apparently believing that everything must be attributed to someone, splashed a headline: "Stabbing victim dies, police say."

On coverage of labor issues, the media often report that both sides are "eyeball-to-eyeball," a condition that leads either to a "strike-bound condition" or a visit to an optometrist. Nevertheless, following these "tense moments," both sides "come to terms" and are now in the "process of hammering out a contract"—just as soon as they "nail down the clauses."

Sportswriters seem to believe language was invented so they could butcher it. There are no longer any athletes; they're booters and gridders, tankmen, grapplers, and hoopsters. As for the teams themselves, they don't defeat an opponent, they maul, exterminate, pulverize, crush, and annihilate them. Check out the headlines and see "cop" become a verb, as the "locals cop a victory." In baseball, pitchers no longer throw fastballs, they're "flamethrowers" who "toss the pill" or, even worse, "throw with velocity." A sports editor in Anderson, Ind., once wrote about a high school player who, with a few seconds left in the game, brought victory to his team when he "hooped the brown spheroid through the draped iron doughnut."

From the nation's 700,000 professors have come so much incoherent babbling disguised as professional papers, journal articles, and books that a ban on what poses as academic scholarship would help save the rain forests. Unfortunately, much of the bad writing comes from professors of mass communication, few of whom ever worked more than a few months in a newsroom, and who believe that conducting pseudoscientific research will give them respectability, or at least tenure. The following are just *parts* of titles of what passed as scholarship in a recent convention of an association of journalism professors: "symbolic modeling and persuasive efficacy information on self-efficacy beliefs," "heuristic perspectives," "contextualist cultural functionalism," "concept mapping," "conceptions of salience," "systemic methods of measuring free recall," "synchronous and asynchronous forums," "dyadic interaction," "news framing and audience framing," "structural pluralism," "discourse analysis," and "observations on a conundrum."

Indeed, most "mass communicologists" are more comfortable with running statistical analyses with two degrees of freedom, and in jabbering about channeling, cognitive dissonance, and content analysis than they are with leads, transitions, and conclusions. Perhaps, that's why we're still wondering why many recent journalism graduates can't write.

Linguistic Larceny

A government investigation of Chicago's Veterans Administration Hospital (VA) in 1992 revealed that many of the resident physicians were poorly supervised, and that there were substantial instances of crucial diagnostic mistakes and inappropriate surgery. Sometime while all this was going on, six patients died in the operating room, and the VA was forced to make large cash payments to the families of those individuals. According to an official explanation, each of the deaths was a "surgical misadventure." Sort of like the TV show, "Adventures in Paradise," or even *Pee-Wee's Big Adventure*. Maybe the VA thought it was on a campout, and nothing worse occurred than the tent fell during the rain.

But, the VA isn't the only one to use the great linguistic cover-up. A Colorado state legislator proposed a plan to clean up Denver's polluted atmosphere, at that time well within the nation's "Bottom 10." Instead of spending millions to clean up the air, the legislator suggested a little language manipulation would solve the problem. "Hazardous air" would become known as just "poor air." "Dangerous air" would be "acceptable," and "very unhealthful air" would be "fair air." As for just "unhealthful air," it would be "good air," so pure that smoke-puffing industries would just have to bottle it and sell it as distilled. Even the Environmental Protection Agency has helped make American air safer by simply reclassifying acid rain as "wet disposition."

Because truth is the first casualty of war, we willingly accept the great linguistic cover-up. Our Civil War wasn't a revolution, but a "war between the states." World War I, which we obtusely believed was "the war to end all wars," was the "Great War." Fortunately, no one labeled World War II the "Greater War," although NBC-TV news anchor Tom Brokaw did label the era as "The Greatest Generation." At the beginning of the 1950s, we peace-loving Americans learned that a "police action" in Korea looked remarkably like a war and that peace was a "cold war."

A decade later, we were in an "undeclared war" known as the "Vietnam Conflict" where "military advisors" helped direct "preventive air strikes." The use of Agent Orange to defoliate the countryside was merely employing a "resources control program," and we learned that to "exterminate with extreme prejudice" meant that someone was going to be killed. About this time, the Pentagon, feeling its linguistic superiority, tried to slip a "radiation enhancement device," a neutron bomb, past Congress.

During the Vietnam War, Gen. William Westmoreland, commanding about a half-million troops, declared the reason the military wasn't giving the American people the truth was because "without censorship, things could get terribly confused in the public mind." From linguistic manipulation in the Persian Gulf War in early 1991, we learned that "foul ups" that caused injuries and death to our own troops were "accidents as the result of friendly fire." Our soldiers learned that exposure to nerve gas could result not in death but in "immediate permanent incapacitation." Warplanes were really "weapons systems" which were merely "visiting a site." If the pilots succeeded in "cleansing," "neutralizing," or "sanitizing" that site, they could report they "were successful in servicing their intended targets." If they over-bombed or missed entirely, wiping out civilians and their houses, the pilots merely reported a lot of "collateral damage." A missile that went astray was known as an "anomaly."

Of course, we are well aware that many of the Arab Coalition allies believe that sand fleas are more important than women. But, did we really have to accept the Saudi Arabian demands not to include women in combat units and then agree that among the half million coalition troops in Operation Desert Storm about 40,000 were "males with female features"?

When President George W. Bush ordered the military to invade Afghanistan to search out and destroy al-Qaeda and Osama bin Laden, the Pentagon justifiably named the war "Operation Enduring Freedom." Within a year, Bush targeted Iraq, which had nothing to do with 9/11, but which he led Americans to believe had the capability to manufacture nuclear weapons, and named the invasion, "Operation Iraqi Freedom." The previous name, "Operation Desert Freedom," proposed by the Department of Defense, apparently to continue the terminology of the previous war in 1991, was changed by the White House to emphasize what it wanted Americans to believe—that the U.S. was liberating Iraqis from the dictatorship of Saddam Hussein.

Trying to explain what the U.S. did or did not know prior to the invasion, Defense Secretary Donald Rumsfeld in 2002 explained, "Reports that say something hasn't happened are always interesting to me, because as we know there are known knowns; there are things we know we know. . . . We also know there are known unknowns. That is to say we know there are some things we do not know. But there are also unknown unknowns—the ones we don't know we don't know."

Following 9/11, President Bush declared that the U.S. was engaged in the "War on Terror," often mentioning the "War on Terrorism." Later, to make sure that the world didn't think that the U.S. invaded Iraq, which wasn't involved in the 9/11 conspiracy but which became a basis for that invasion, the President delcared we were now involved in a "Global War on Terror." It soon became known as the "Long War." Then, in March 2009, President Barack Obama declared the war over—or at least his linguistics did. The U.S. was now involved in "Overseas Contingency Operations."

"Post Traumatic Stress Disorder"—known as "shell shock" in World War I, and "battle fatigue" in World War II—has become the universal way to explain actions not only of persons traumatized by war but also the actions of spouse abusers and mass murderers as well, even if their only combat was changing printer cartridges in an air-conditioned HQ. Nevertheless, there are serious and significant cases of PTSD that the Veterans 'Administration and innumerable governmental bodies refused to recognize, probably out of a fear that the public would think that wars could be dangerous and that money should be spent elsewhere.

In Bosnia–Herzegovena, the Serbs didn't murder, rape, or pillage, they merely went on a campaign of "ethnic cleansing."

In Somalia, the Sudan, and Mozambique, the starving masses are "nutritionally deprived." In the United States, we are loathe to admit that we also have starving masses or homeless people living on our streets, so we reclassify them as "individuals without permanent structural domiciles." During the Reagan–Bush era, "the Great Communicator" told us about a "revenue enhancement" program that looked suspiciously like we were going to have to dip into an "equity recovery program" or a second mortgage to be able to afford the new taxes. And for reasons probably best left forgotten, when it came to nutritionally-balanced meals, the administration declared that ketchup is a vegetable.

Although some students spend their academic years vegetating, even they have a cover-up. Students who don't get good grades are "socially or culturally disadvantaged," but there are fewer bad grades now than ever. Grade inflation lets students believe they actually learned something when they have a 3.0 average, and that no one will be the wiser when half the class graduates in the top 10 percent. Naturally, if they can find a job, they'll soon learn that an evaluation of "competent" roughly translates as "does the job, but with no great ability."

The 1966 plans for Hampshire College in Amherst, Massachusetts, probably written by a PR person, and undoubtedly edited by a pseudo-intellectual committee, called for the new college's mission to center around "a social structure [that] should be optimally the consonant patterned expression of culture . . . that higher education is enmeshed in a congeries of social and political change . . . that the humanities offers a surfeit of leeching [and] the exquisite preciosities and pretentiousness of contemporary literary criticism. [Further,] a formal curriculum of academic substance and sequence should not be expected to contain mirabilia which will bring all the educative ends of the college to pass."

From a plethora of psychobabble, often originating within the colleges, have come phrases meant to let us believe all of us aren't "at the margin of mental health." So, we merely need "our space" to avoid "feeling so vulnerable," the result of having had an "emotional disturbance" with our "significant other," and forcing us even more into a state of either being "hyperacidic" or "inner directed" when we should all just "mellow out." For those who cause us stress, we just ask them not to "harsh our mellow." To keep our "warm fuzzy" instincts alive, a pharmaceutical chain recently mailed its advertising flyers not to "occupant" or "resident," but to "valued friend." (By the way, you can thank me now for "knowing where you're coming from," "feeling your pain," and for "sharing" that information with you.)

To make sure we all have a "feeling of self-worth," we have changed job titles, but not responsibilities. Mechanics are "service technicians" or "performance maintenance specialists" who often work on "pre-owned vehicles." Trash collectors are "waste management specialists"; movers are "relocation service representatives"; gardeners are "horticultural technicians"; cabbies in the big city are "urban short-run transportation specialists"; telephone operators are "information referral assistants"; e-mail spammers now call themselves "commercial bulk e-mailers," and waiters and waitresses are "beverage delivery consultants" or, in the era of being politically-ambiguous, "waitrons." Sort of like what Buck Rogers might have for a pet.

In business, we look to the "bottom line" to "maximize profit" so we have a better "cash flow" and achieve a "high degree of liquidity." Helping business avoid clear language are the legions of PR people, some of them former journalists, who have invented their own secret language to justify their existence. PR textbooks often inform future "strategic planning analysts" or "consulting image enhancement specialists" how to determine

166

behavioral and attitudinal objectives to better "target" the "multitudinous publics," while taking "proactive" stands. To accomplish their mission, the "practitioner" must be able to anticipate, analyze, and interpret; counsel, research, and evaluate; plan, implement, and organize their multifaceted campaigns in order to provide an "intensification of existing positive behaviors" and a corresponding "reversal of negative behaviors."

If for some reason, business must "reorganize," "shift responsibilities," or even "go back to square 1," we should realize that they are only in "a state of temporary incapacitation," possibly caused by a "negative economic growth." But, if it continues, then business cites the "bottom line" and the need for "maximizing profits" as justifications for "downsizing" and "restructuring" which, naturally, has caused "a realignment of the work force" and subsequent "involuntary severance." That's why Sears "involuntarily severed" 48,000 employees; General Motors "involuntarily severed" 85,000–100,000; and IBM "involuntarily severed" 125,000. (Somewhere in Bangladesh, thousands of 12-year-olds earning $5–$12 a month are making clothes for distribution to Americans who have been involuntarily severed when their companies "restructured" to "maximize profits," and went overseas.) Of course, the only ones who aren't being involuntarily severed by American business are the bosses (pretentiously known as chief executive officers) who caused all the problems to begin with.

Down for the Count

Why do the news media salivate all over their keyboards whenever anyone with a royal moniker does anything more than just wake up in the morning? Even with newspapers in freefall decline in space for news, editors find space to pander to our fascination with royalty.

The typical American doesn't know who England's prime minister is, and if asked to name three Canadian provinces probably comes up with North Michigan, Yuccatan, and Sasspittoon. Ask that same person to name the latest Royal scandal, and you have instant response.

The British royalty of the Middle Ages and Renaissance had far more scandal than today's mentally-challenged blue-bloods. But no one published any of it. Not only did the printers know they could lose their heads for revealing gossip, they also knew there were more important things to report than who Henry VIII was fooling around with.

Americans have always had a fascination with royalty. Although we organized a revolution to overthrow the monarchy's hold, and created a president not a king as head of State, we have spent more than two centuries trying to regain a royal image.

Our fast food restaurants are called Burger King, Dairy Queen, and Pizza King. We have prom queens, homecoming queens, and even a Rose Bowl queen. The media, of course, are part of the royal awe.

Within weeks, *TIME* magazine alliteratively crowned four different singers—Barbra Streisand, Whitney Houston, Debbie Gibson, and Japanese superstar Seiko—as a "pop princess."

Just about any young ice skating star is known as an "ice princess," but the media in 1989 derogatorily dubbed Deborah Norville an "ice princess" when she took over for popular Jane Pauley on NBC-TV's "Today Show."

Princess Cruises may have the "Love Boat," but there was no love lost when Donald Trump sold his 282-foot Trump Princess for about $100 million after he, mistress Marla, and wife Ivana had formed a Ménage a Tabloid.

Among googobs of movie princesses have been Leia who helped Han Solo, Luke Skywalker, and that giant furry thing make the world safe for high-tech special effects; and a Lion King that made the Disney Co. rich enough to devour all other media companies, and take on the corporate shape of Jabba the Hutt.

TV's "Queen for a Day" during the 1950s required contestants to be women who could sob a good story and get a washing machine to help them do the laundry for their 17 handicapped foster children. A spin-off was *The Prince of Tides*, the story of a psychologist and her patient, but which many may have thought was the story of a royal and his soap detergent.

The greatest baron, until he was shot down by Snoopy, was Manfred von Richtofen, the Red Baron. However, for some reason the media prefer to use the title "baron" to refer to evil "kingpins"—as in "drug baron," "robber baron" and, understandably, "media baron."

The music industry abounds with royalty. Bessie Smith was the Empress of the Blues; Roger Miller was King of the Road. Among other kings are those of Ragtime (Scott Joplin), Blues (W.C. Handy) Swing (Benny Goodman), Rock and Roll (Elvis

Presley), Pop (Michael Jackson), and Waltz (composer Richard Strauss or bandleader Wayne King.) One of the best singers was Nat "King" Cole. Among others in the King Family singers are Alan, B.B., Billie Jean, Carole, Don, Larry, Martin Luther, and Stephen.

Aretha Franklin may be the Queen of Soul, but James Brown is the Godfather of Soul; cross him, and you could find a broken treble clef on your pillow in the morning. Rap singer Queen Latifah may think she's royalty, but British rock group Queen truly has a better shot at sitting in Buckingham Palace than she does.

Among singing princes are the Fresh Prince of Bel-Air and Prince, formerly known as the singer-with-the-unpronounceable symbol, who then renamed himself.

The most famous duke is the "Duke, Duke, Duke of Earl, Earl, Earl, Duke of Earl" who proved in the late 1950s that anyone can grow up and write song lyrics. Other less royal dukes have been baseball great Duke Snider and musical genius Duke Ellington who, had he gone to baseball games, would have had to sit in segregated seating in most ball parks.

Upset there are no more "colored" seats, drinking fountains, and rest rooms is David Duke who once cornered the market on pointy white Klan hats and dull-witted Whites.

Babe Ruth was the Sultan of Swat. But no royal monikers were attached to Roger Maris, who broke the one-season record, or to Hank Aaron who broke Ruth's lifetime record and had to put up with numerous racist comments. In other sports, pro-fake wrestling had its Royal Rumble, pro basketball has the Sacramento Kings, and pro baseball has the Kansas City Royals.

Really, the only royalty that matters are the Counts—Tolstoy, Dracula, and Basie. As for the rest, perhaps the media might dump the nomenclature and then dump stories of the British royalty in favor of stories that matter.

'Personages' of the Mind

The Riverside (Calif.) *Press-Enterprise*, a 175,000 circulation daily newspaper, was looking for a "hip, groovy, experienced personage . . . to oversee weekly see and do tab."

The announcement also asked that the "personage should be creative, well-versed in music, movies, TV and have solid assignment desk and copy editing skills."

Not knowing what a "personage" is—I had been a newspaper reporter and editor, but never a personage—I called the _Press-Enterprise._

"What does this 'personage' do?" I asked.

"Oversee a weekend tab," said Sally Ann Maas, assistant managing editor for features and the personage's boss.

"Did you write the ad?"

"Several of us worked on it."

"Including the managing editor?"

"He wrote the final copy."

Obviously, the _Press-Enterprise_ cares about accuracy, especially when several senior personages take time from reporting and editing duties to group-hug each other, feel their pain and suffering, know where each one is coming from, and then share a 58-word ad with the rest of us.

"And this 'personage' has to be hip and groovy?" I asked.

"It was supposed to attract attention," Maas said.

"Could you have used another word than 'personage'?" I asked.

"The ad was meant to be unisex," she said.

"Wouldn't 'editor' have been appropriate?" I asked.

"Maybe it wasn't such a good idea," she reluctantly admitted after a couple of minutes of polite inquisition.

A lot of what passes as "linguistically politically correct" isn't a good idea. A kinder, gentler language often reveals little more than a life based in ambiguity.

In Massachusetts during the mid-1980s, I first saw job ads for "waitrons," which I assumed were emotionless space-age robots designed to take, deliver, and remove food orders from restaurant customers. I now see "waitrons" in many restaurants, all of them emotionless robots.

"Manholes" are now called "sewer hole entrances" or in a few places "personholes." I suppose the artist Edourd Manet, to really be nonsexist, should have changed his name to "Personet," and Thomas Mann might have become Thomas Person.

For many, "herstory" is supposed to be less sexist than "history," and "womyn" is seen as acceptable for "women." Had these "herstorians" done a little linguistic research, they might have learned that the root of "history" is the French "histoire," meaning "story," and that "women" is not "womb from men" as many believe but actually from the Old English "wiffmon," meaning "wife of man." True, there was no equal "monnwif,"

170

but "womyn" is not unique. Since 1200, it has undergone changes, being spelled "wifman," "winman," "wooman," "wymman," "wymmon," and "whoman," as well as "wyman." If the "womyn" truly wanted to have a nonsexist name, they might invent a word that has absolutely no basis in "woman."

Certainly, "poetess" and "authoress," once common appellations, are sexist and unnecessary. And it's good we now have firefighters instead of firemen, and police officers instead of policemen. In many cases, creating a nonsexist lexicon isn't so difficult. But, many have tried to reduce or eliminate sexism by creating lunacy instead of reason.

The reality is that language is fluid. But, in the interest of clearness, let's not have any more personages, waitrons, herstories, and womyn.

Give It Up for Confusion

There's a lot of language today that confuses me. For example, does anyone know why certain people try to get someone's attention by shouting out, "Yo!" And if that doesn't work, they become redundant and shout out "Yo Yo!" That could be very confusing if you work for Duncan Toys or are a classic cellist.

In today's language, everyone is a brother or, if they need to save their voice, "Bro," as in, "Yo, Bro!" When not being siblings, they're "Dudes," as in "Hey, Dude,"not to be confused with "Hey, Jude,"a greeting reserved for hip Jews.

I also don't know, like y'know, what I should, well, like y'know know. From pre-pubescent teens and Hollywood celebrities to, like, other people, it seems that every other word is like, well, y'know. What *is* it I'm supposed to know, and why should I like it? Y'know wha' I'm saying?

Hollywood, whether represented by TV reality series or a variety show at the local Elks, also confuses me. Emcees are enamored with constantly telling us to "Give it up for _____." I have no idea what "it" is. What am I supposed to be giving up? And why should I give it up? Is giving up an "It" deductible as charity expense? Why is it beneficial for the talent to get my "It"? Before someone gets my "It," do they need to first get approval from an insurance clerk in a windowless office half a continent away? Will they, or me, get fully reimbursed for the

171

"It"? Or does "It" carry a large deductible? If I don't have an "It" can I buy it somewhere so I *can* give it up? Should I make sure that I buy only a union-made "It"? Does Walmart sell cheaper non-union "Its" made in China? Do the more upscale stores buy their "Its" from India? During the 1920s, movie star sex goddess Clara Bow was known as the "It Girl." Do my hosts want me to give up sex? Or do they want me to indulge in sex with whom-ever they're introducing, whether singer, dancer, or malleable gymnast?

When not telling us to give it up, emcees ask us to "put your hands together for ____." But, they never tell us how long we should put our hands together? A couple of seconds? A minute? Until the performance is over? And, just how am I supposed to put my hands together? Should I clasp my hands, with fingers interlocked over my head? Behind my neck? On my stomach? If I'm only going to be half-enamored by an act, could I just grasp my left forearm with my right hand, and avoid putting both hands together? If I want the act to succeed, should I put my hands together as if praying? More important, if both my hands are together, how can I give "It" up at the same time?

President Bush confused me. For instance, he told us "When the Iraqis stand up, we'll stand down." That's just not right. If someone is standing, shouldn't we also be standing? That just seems like common courtesy. And if everyone else is sitting, can't we sit, especially if we've been standing so long that we're getting not just knee and back pains but a pain in our ass? Maybe the President wanted us to act like car cylinders that fire in alternating order, and he can play Whack-a-Mole.

When President Obama enters a room, a disembodied voice tells us, "Ladies and Gentlemen, the President of the United States." Everyone sitting then stands up; those who are already standing can continue standing, stand down, or levitate. Perhaps that voice should introduce Mr. Obama with what's more acceptable—"Yo, Dudes and Dudettes, like y'know, put your hands together and give it up for the total package, my Main Man, the Prez!" We could then stand up and give it up. Ya know wha' I'm saying?

~~~~~~~~~

"[E]very man should receive [news]papers and be capable of reading them."   —Thomas Jefferson, 1787

Liner Notes on an American Future

About 4:30 p.m., every other Thursday, Betty Fodness of Millville, Pa., walks into a 24-foot long blue-and-white book-mobile of the Columbia County Traveling Library and checks out five or six books from a traveling collection of about 3,000.

"I'm there right on the button when they get there," Fodness says. By now, the county librarian knows what Fodness likes to read and often has a few books already picked out.

Each month, the bookmobile visits 40 sites in the rural north-eastern Pennsylvania county, stopping about an hour each at pre-schools, day care centers, nursing homes, senior citizen centers, and public schools, as well as relatively isolated communities in the county. In 2009, the library checked out about 35,000 books, almost 200 to Fodness alone.

Millville is an agrarian community of almost 1,000 people. It once had its own library on the third floor of the local bank. But accessibility problems and a general lack of interest by local residents forced the all-volunteer library to close in the mid-1980s. The nearest library now is 10 miles south in Bloomsburg, the 12,000-population seat and geographical center of Columbia County. There are only three public libraries and one general bookstore in the county.

"I used to go into Bloomsburg," Fodness says, "but parking is a problem." Another problem is snow during the Winter, which makes parts of the two-lane Route 42 hazardous.

"When you're a widow, you need a little get-away," says Fodness whose get-away is through literature. She reads a lot—"always have"—but doesn't rent videos or watch much television. "Too much sex and violence," she says.

Although there is sex and violence in books, there isn't much of a chance of a pandemic influence from the printed word. More than half of all adults in 2007 never read a novel that year, according to a survey conducted by the National Endowment for the Arts. Among the key finds of the NEA study, based upon data from the National Center for Education Statistics, Bureau of Labor Statistics, and its own study:

> Americans are reading less—teens and young adults read less often and for shorter amounts of time compared with other age groups and with Americans of previous years.

Less than one-third of 13-year-olds are daily readers, a 14 percent decline from 20 years earlier. Among 17-year-olds, the percentage of non-readers doubled over a 20-year period, from nine percent in 1984 to 19 percent in 2004.

On average, Americans ages 15 to 24 spend almost two hours a day watching TV, and only seven minutes of their daily leisure time on reading.

. . . [R]eading scores continue to worsen, especially among teenagers and young males. By contrast, the average reading score of 9-year-olds has improved.

Reading scores for 12th-grade readers fell significantly from 1992 to 2005, with the sharpest declines among lower-level readers.

2005 reading scores for male 12th-graders are 13 points lower than for female 12th-graders, and that gender gap has widened since 1992.

Reading scores for American adults of almost all education levels have deteriorated, notably among the best-educated groups. From 1992 to 2003, the percentage of adults with graduate school experience who were rated proficient in prose reading dropped by 10 points, a 20 percent rate of decline.

The declines in reading have civic, social, and economic implications—Advanced readers accrue personal, professional, and social advantages. Deficient readers run higher risks of failure in all three areas.

Nearly two-thirds of employers ranked reading comprehension "very important" for high school graduates. Yet 38 percent consider most high school graduates deficient in this basic skill.

American 15-year-olds ranked fifteenth in average reading scores for 31 industrialized nations, behind Poland, Korea, France, and Canada, among others.

Literary readers are more likely than non-readers to engage in positive civic and individual activities—such as volunteering, attending sports or cultural events, and exercising.

U.S. book publishers had net sales of about $24.3 billion in 2008, down about 2.8 percent from 2007, according to data compiled by the Association of American Publishers. Most categories showed significant decreases. Newspaper circulation declined about 14 percent between 1998 and the end of 2008, according to the Newspaper Association of America. With the exception of the *Wall Street Journal,* every newspaper in the top 25 in circulation showed a decrease, most with double-digit decreases. Circulation stability at magazines wasn't better.

Every magazine in the top 25 list, with the exception of *Modern Maturity*, showed a circulation decline in 2008. Among the declines were for *TIME* (-17.50 percent) *Playboy* (-10.04 percent) and *Reader's Digest* (-7.64 percent), according to data compiled by the Audit Bureau of Circulations. Although the Recession contributed to both advertising and circulation declines among print media, the decline had begun long before the Recession. What hasn't declined is non-print media.

Entertainment and information for Millville residents, like those everywhere in the country, tends to be stuffed within pre-recorded DVD and Blu-ray disks, downloads from the Internet, innumerable video games, and television broadcasts. There are about 9,200 public libraries in America, according to the American Library Association. In contrast, Americans can buy pre-recorded disks from more than 120,000 places, including almost 27,000 video stores, according to the *Hollywood Reporter*. Blockbuster alone has about 8,000 stores; Movie Gallery has about 4,500. More than 82 million disks were sold in 2008, according to the Digital Entertainment Group (DEG). Home video sales were about $15.9 billion in 2007, with rentals about $8.2 billion, according to DEG.

The first VCRs for commercial distribution were introduced in the early 1980s. By the end of 2002, about 95 percent of all households had VCR hardware. Digital Versatile Discs (DVDs), was first introduced to the consumer market in 1997. DVDs, with superior picture and six-channel sound, allow viewers to cue and replay virtually any scene with minimal problems. More important, a disk can hold not only the two-hour feature film, but several hours of out-takes, extra scenes that may have had to be left on the cutting room floor, discussions by the actors and director, subtitles in several languages, and even alternative endings and interactive scenes, allowing the viewer to decide which direction the movie should go. DVDs can also present the viewer with trailers of forthcoming films and, of course, ads of all kinds. The one billionth DVD disk was shipped in July 2000. By the end of 2001, video sales had fallen below DVD sales for the first time.

The newest technology is Blu-ray. The Toshiba HD DVDs use infrared rays; Sony's Blu-ray uses the ultraviolet rays at the other end of the spectrum, allowing significant increase in digital storage capacity and picture quality. Sales of Blu-ray disks will probably exceed those of DVDs by 2012, according to the

Entertainment Merchants Association. Paramount's *The Iron Man* generated about 500,000 high-definition (DVD and Blu-Ray) sales its first week. Its record would soon be broken. *The Dark Knight,* a Batman story with a budget of $185 million, premiered in July 2008. On its opening weekend, it generated about $158 million in sales, and was seen on 4,366 screens, extremely high for any film. It would eventually earn $533 million in the U.S., and $1 billion worldwide. Within a week of its release on video, about five months after the theater premiere, *The Dark Knight* generated 1.7 million Blu-ray sales and 13.5 million sales overall worldwide.

Blu-ray sales and rentals are expected to top DVD rentals by the end of 2012. However, online technology may even replace Blu-ray. Online technology, allowing consumers to download TV shows and feature films onto their computers and television screens, accounted for about $2 billion revenue in 2008. By 2012, online video revenue is expected to be about $12 billion, according to IDC, an international market research company. About three-fourths of that revenue will be from sales to consumers; the rest will be advertising revenue. Hulu.com allows individuals to receive streaming video from NBC, ABC/Disney, FOX, and other network and film providers, with advertising paying acquisition costs. Consumers may also receive online video not just from Blockbuster, Amazon.com, and independent producers, but also from Google's YouTube as well. YouTube, known as the medium where anyone can post just about anything in short clips, has negotiated rights to provide feature films and television shows produced or distributed by Sony, Lionsgate Films, and Starz. Consumers will get content at no cost; advertising is expected to give YouTube and the producers the revenue.

In a world now dominated by the visual media, about 80 percent of all film revenue for the major studios comes from revenue not specifically generated by theater receipts. Video rentals, Cable systems, pay-per-view, and digital satellite broadcast systems have given the studios even more opportunities for distribution and the opportunity to show profits. At one time, direct-to-video releases were considered inferior to movies shown in theaters. However, the quality of production has improved significantly, and studios no longer need theater releases to guarantee high video sales. About 95 percent of all videos—from "how-to" tapes to major feature releases—have never been seen in a movie theater. It isn't just smaller studios making money on direct-to-video. Disney's *Aladdin* was released to theaters; its two sequels were released directly on video.

DVD disks of movies made from books make it more efficient to listen and watch than to read. DVD technology now allows a consumer to spend less for the disk with all its features than for the book itself that led to the movie that led to the disk. To make money on books—only about four percent show a profit from print sales—publishers must spin off the print rights to other media, including TV, cable TV, direct-to-video films, and theatrical films.

Publishers have now condensed more than 50,000 books onto CDs that allow almost-readers to shove the book into a car's audio system and do autoaerobics in morning rush hour traffic. Consumers have purchased about $1.1 billion in audio books, with about 10,000 books in CD or digital download formats published each year, according to the Audio Publishers Association.

The introduction of digital video recorders (DVRs) makes it easier for viewers to replay scenes, zap through commercials, and save shows for viewing at any time. Distributed by TiVO, Echostar, and Replay TV, each digital unit is able to capture TV signals and replay them at the consumer's will, allowing viewers to watch shows, take breaks, or to zap through all commercials unwatched, and pick up the show where they left it. It also allows viewers to replay scenes and commercials. TiVO estimates that viewers replayed parts of the 2002 Super Bowl 44 times each, including a PepsiCola commercial featuring Britney Spears.

Music CDs and digital downloads have essentially replaced vinyl records. Unlike records, which have to be played on bulky machines, CDs can be played from small units strapped to a listener's belt; downloads can be heard on a computer's speakers, cell phones, by subscription on a car's internal speakers, Palm Treos and BlackBerries, or or on cigarette pack sized iPods, which have a maximum storage capacity of about 160 gigabytes. Downloads are now replacing the physical media. Total sales of all physical media (CD albums, CD singles, casettes, vinyl albums, music videos, and DVD videos) have dropped from 1.16 billion units in 1999 to 401.8 million units in 2008, according to data provided by the Recording Industry Association of America (RIAA). Digital downloads, according to the RIAA, have increased from 139.4 million in 2004, the first year data was collected, to about one billion in 2008, representing about one-third of the entire market value.

3-D Video games, with the software designers making 13-year-olds think they really are combat fighter pilots, take children from books and magazines, away even from broadcast television, and into hours of maneuvering appropriately-named joysticks before an electronic screen that can throw millions of multi-colored pixels at the human brain.

Contributing to a decline in literaracy is the prevalent use of "thumb shorthand," with everyone from primary school students to professionals text-messaging and e-mailing on a variety of electronic devices.

About 42 million Americans are illiterate; another 50 million can't read at a level greater than that expected of fourth graders, according to a study conducted by the National Right to Read Foundation. Almost half of all American adults are functionally illiterate, reading at the lowest two of five levels, unable to understand the simple directions of how to take an aspirin, according to the National Adult Literacy Survey of the United States Department of Education. A United Nations survey determined that the U.S. literacy rate is 49th of 158 nations. There may be no correlation, but the average time in front of a TV set is about seven hours a day; the average time reading a book is about seven minutes.

Against reading scores from throughout the world, Americans rate somewhere south of Antarctic penguins. At least one-third of all U.S. students lack a basic knowledge of science, the National Assessment Governing Board declared. It's little different for knowledge of geography, history, and current events. Ask the average American about any of their Constitutional rights, and they may know, from watching an excessive amount of TV shows and movies, the Fifth Amendment which allows them not to testify against themselves. Bill Clinton's response to the problems of illiteracy, formulated during the 1996 presidential campaign, and similar to the one Fidel Castro used successfully to significantly raise Cuban literacy rates, was to request a five-year $2.75 billion campaign, staffed by a 30,000-person "Citizen's Army" of reading specialists. The program was never fully developed.

There may be no correlation, but the average American spends about 1,560 hours a year watching television, and only about 165 hours reading newspapers, according to data from Vrdonis Suhler Stevenson Communication; the average American also spends about only about 40 hours a year reading books.

However, CDs, PlayStations, radio, TV, film, pre-recorded VHS tapes and digital disks didn't increase illiteracy. Before the entertainment media technology, Americans who had newspapers, magazines, and books to read had far greater illiteracy levels. However, there is only a finite time in the day; add in the work day and the newer mass communications technology, along with myriad recreational opportunities, and the time spent reading—or learning to read—is significantly reduced. The product is seen in the work of high school and college students whose sentence construction is built upon a base of video games, and whose spelling and knowledge of history, geography, and current social issues is roughly translated not from printed literature but from what they think they hear from the spoken word.

In contrast to all the gloom about literacy, a bright star streaked across the barren literary landscape during the first decade of the twenty-first century. About 60 percent of children surveyed by the Foundation of Children's Book Groups in June 2005 said that the Harry Potter books made them want to read more books. About half of all readers, ages 5–17 years old said they hadn't read books for fun (as opposed to forced reading in classes) before they read the Potter books; about two-thirds said they did better on their schoolwork since reading the series, and about half of all persons who read Harry Potter books said that when the series concluded they would read other books, according to research published in July 2006 by Yankelovich, one of the world's largest analysts of consumer values and lifestyles.

Primary school children will always read Dr. Seuss books and dozens of others that entice and excite them. Young teens will look to Judy Blume, J.K. Rowling, and others. But, at some point, surrounded by myriad stimuli from the electronic and digital media, they lose their enthusiasm for the printed word.

Betty Fodness isn't one of them. She's 86 years old, doesn't have satellite TV, seldom rents videos, but will continue to go to the bookmobile and read 10–15 books a month. Ironically, she now has more books to choose from. In 1995, the Frank Laubach Public Library in Benton, located in the northern part of Columbia County, closed. Its 2,500 books were transferred to the Traveling Library's permanent collection. Laubach, a Benton resident, was the founder of the "each one teach one" literary movement that brought significantly increased literacy throughout America and the world.

In the future, literacy may more appropriately be defined as the ability to read the liner notes on a DVD case.

LANGUAGE AND CULTURAL DIVERSITY

Driven by Ignorance

It's now called Ebonics (ebony + phonetics), after having been called colored speech, Negro English, Black English, Black English Vernacular, and some abomination called Pan-African Communication Behaviors. It's identified as a slang, dialect, or language. But, whatever it is, Ebonics is as controversial today as it was in 1855 when the first major linguistic study was done.

Misinterpretation by reporters has led the masses to believe Black English is "sloppy," "inferior," or "broken English," that certain school administrators want to replace Standard English with Black English, and that the nation's urban areas condone the students' use of slang.

The truth is that these educators, following long-established models for second language teaching, want to understand their students' own language in order to help them learn a different language—in this case, Standard English. A federal court in July 1979, after hearing several days of expert opinion on a civil rights case, had ruled that the Ann Arbor, Mich., school district violated federal civil rights laws by not providing "equal educational opportunity" when it refused to accept Black English as a legitimate language of many of its students. The court ruled "no matter how well-intentioned the teachers are, they are not likely to succeed in overcoming the language barrier caused by their failure to take into account the home language system unless [they] recognize the language system used by the children . . . and to use that knowledge as a way of helping the children to learn to read standard English." In December 1996, the 6,000-member Linguistics Society of America declared that instruction in Black English is an effective way to get many Blacks to learn Standard English.

Nevertheless, innumerable columnists and cartoonists, almost none of whom studied linguistics, have had fun portraying "jivetalking" teachers and their Black students. However, most Blacks don't speak any of the varieties of Black English, nor is

180

Black English restricted to the lower classes. Driven by ignorance and fueled by the media, the public argues that the nation's teachers are "dumbing down" their students by even allowing such "substandard" speech in the classroom. Richard Riley, Bill Clinton's secretary of education, incorrectly stated that "elevating Black English to the status of a language" wasn't acceptable, apparently believing that a dialect can be "elevated" to a language. *Washington Post* columnist William Raspberry, who for almost three decades vigorously opposed Black English instruction, incorrectly claimed in 1996 that "virtually all" adult Blacks know Ebonics and there are no texts for Ebonics instruction. The National Association for the Advancement of Colored People (NAACP) called Ebonics "a cruel joke," 25 years after declaring it was "a cruel hoax."

These well-meaning but largely ignorant critics claim that because of cultural deprivation, Black English speakers have linguistic deficiencies, and that thought is restricted because Black English is a deficient, substandard language. Like all languages, Black English is composed of the lexicon (words), phonology (pronunciation), and syntax (grammar). The public and the media have focused upon the lexicon ("Hey, bro', slap me five!"), and only a couple of syntactic constructions, mocking such phrasing as "he be sick." They do not understand that Black English is based upon African languages, most probably of the Hamitic and Bantu language families. Ship captains and plantation owners separated slaves from the same cultures to prevent them from talking to each other, and possibly planning escapes or overthrows. What the owners never realized was that many of the slaves spoke not only their primary language, but also Wes-Kos, a common trade language, composed of several African languages as well as British English.

In Black English rules, the Zero Copula—"He sick"—indicates that the person is sick at this very time. The invariant be—"He be sick"—indicates that the person is sickly or has a long-term illness. Critics point out that some Black English phonology—for example, pronouncing "desk" as "des"—is sloppy speech, unaware that almost no African languages have consonant clusters in the final position, and that it is Standard English which has *added* such clusters, rather than the African languages *reducing* them. Black English phonology markers (including stress, pitch, timbre, and intonation) are closer to West African languages than to Standard English.

Just as there are many varieties and dialects of Standard English, there are many variations of Black English, including the Gullah spoken off the Sea Islands of Georgia and South Carolina, which few Standard English speakers understand, and the mixture of several dialects of Southern Standard English and Urban American English spoken in Detroit.

During the past three decades, young Blacks searching for their own identities and cultural heritage began using varieties of Urban Black English as their own secret "codes," much like their slave ancestors used language and music, especially hip-hop and rap, as a way of secret communication.

Even if all of this is true, argue the critics, Black English speakers must learn Standard English to survive in America. We arrogantly claim that Standard English is the "right" language for America, naively believing there is one correct language. But, Standard English itself is constantly evolving as millions of immigrants brought their languages to America. The Standard English we use today, with its several hundred dialects, has little resemblance to that spoken by the Puritans.

During the Civil Rights era of the 1960s and 1970s, newspaper editors, most of whom faced all-White newsrooms, hired Blacks. But, Black reporters soon found that being the same color as their news sources wasn't the panacea their editors had hoped to achieve. Those Black reporters who, for the most part acted White and spoke Standard English, found that Black English speakers were just as closed to them as to the White reporters. But, those reporters who were able to code-switch—disguising their knowledge of Black English to their editors while using it within Black communities—found they could get stories others could not.

No one is suggesting that Black English should be the dominant language in education, commerce, or government. Nor is anyone suggesting that Blacks who don't communicate in Standard English can succeed in assimilated American society. Since children usually have an ability to learn new languages, perhaps the school districts could work with 5- and 6-year-old students in kindergarten and the first grade so they develop knowledge of the basics of Standard English, while retaining the rich cultural and linguistic heritage of their own home language.

American White society tried to destroy the slaves' religions, and then kept them from entering White Christian churches; it

182

denied them the right to vote or own property; it kept them out of jobs and neighborhoods; it refused to air Black singers and musicians on radio stations, and then reluctantly embraced White rockers who Anglicized Black music in the early 1950s. Now it wants to destroy the vestiges of Black language, one of the most important indicators of cultural heritage. The failure of teachers and the public to understand the nature of a student's home language—whether Black English, Yiddish, or Pennsylvania Dutch—and then to hold it up to ridicule guarantees not only an inferior education, but also the trivialization of a culture.

Food for Thought

Let's pretend it's dinner time, and you've just developed a sudden craving for Mexican food.

Yesterday, it was Chinese. Tomorrow it may be Italian. But today, it's Mexican.

And, while we're pretending, let's pretend that a four-star Mexican restaurant just opened around the corner.

You walk in, and the red-haired hostess politely greets you in impeccable British Standard English, seats you, and hands you a menu. At the top is a grilled American cheese sandwich. You can order it plain or with tomato (75 cents extra). Below are other specialties of the restaurant—pot roast, chicken pot pie, and fried liver with onions.

Thinking you got the wrong menu, or at least went to the wrong restaurant, you ask the blue-eyed blond-haired waiter to give you the Mexican menu.

"This is it," he says.

"I was hoping for an appetizer of nachos with salsa and guacamole, and a main course of fajitas," you say.

He tells you the restaurant—Matthew's—doesn't have fajitas. Nor does it have tacos, enchiladas, or quesadillas. You can, however, order a mug of Two-X beer, which was once named Dos Equis.

"We used to have 'chili con carne,' which we renamed 'chili with meat,'" says the waiter, "but the Language Police ordered us to take it off the menu because we couldn't translate 'chili' into an American term.

Soon to become "Americanized" will be vodka and caviar;

blintzes, knishes, and latkes; gnocchi, lasagna, fettuccini, and eggplant parmigiana. Most food will have to be renamed, as will the names of most animals and musical instruments. Among 75,000 words of international origin, we'll have to rename candy, coleslaw, dollar, and iceberg (from the Dutch), tomato, hammock, and pow-wow (from American Indians), adobe, coffee, gauze, magazines, soda, and sofa (from Arabic), pistols, polkas, and robots (from the Czech), and banjo, cola, jazz, and zebra (from West African languages). We may even have to rename Santa Claus, which originated as the Dutch *Sintaklaas*. We will no longer sing the "Hallelujah Chorus" at Christmas since "hallelujah" comes from the Hebrew, and "chorus" from the Greek. We'll have to purge hundreds of legal terms in Latin—including, *bona fide*, *habeas corpus*, *in absentia*, and *modus operandi*.

Absurd? Of course it is. But, the truth is even more absurd. During World War I, with Americans despising anything German, and the establishment newspapers fueling flames of patriotic intolerance, "sauerkraut" became "victory cabbage," hamburgers became "liberty sandwiches" and hamburger steak became forever etched into Americans' vocabularies as "Salisbury steak." In March 2003, when France didn't agree with the United States about why the world should invade Iraq, Rep. Robert W. Ney (R-Ohio), chair of the Committee on House Administration, ordered all restaurants in the buildings of the House of Representatives to rename french toast "freedom toast" and french fries "freedom fries." The change was also quickly made at the White House; hundreds of restaurant owners throughout the country followed the Congressional and Presidential will. "French fries" are probably Belgian in origin, but that meant nothing to Americans determined to destroy anything that reminded them of France. Responding to reporters salivating to report upon an international food fight, Nathalie Loisau, a diplomat assigned to the French embassy in Washington, D.C., said, "We are at a very serious moment dealing with very serious issues and we are not focusing on the name you give to potatoes." (Americans didn't have any problems with french horns, french poodles, or french kissing.)

Also absurd are most of the nation's radio talk-show hosts and their ranting gaggle of jingoistic followers who demand the United States be solely an English-speaking country. Hundreds of towns and half of the states, spending millions of taxpayer funds, have created legislation that makes English the official language. It's very simple, they wail, foreigners "gotta learn good English like us Americans." Of course, these good patriotic Americans—wearing T-shirts made in Taiwan, sneakers made in Thailand, and flying Chinese-made American flags from their imported Toyotas, Hondas, and VWs—believe the history of the country began with their own births.

Almost since the beginning of the nation, there have been ethnic and cultural organizations and foreign language newspapers to inform and unite the various nations of immigrants, most of whom felt alienated and isolated from the mainstream American culture that was developed by previous generations of immigrants. The first foreign language newspaper was the *Philadelphische Zeitung,* a German language newspaper published in Germantown, near Philadelphia; its publisher was the ubiquitous Benjamin Franklin who didn't speak German, but knew the settlers needed news. Unfortunately, the newspaper, a few months after it was begun, died in 1732. During the 1790s, the Pennsylvania legislature narrowly defeated a bill that would have made German the state's official language; German language clubs, stores, restaurants, and newspapers thrived as the nation thrived.

In the territory of the Louisiana Purchase, French language newspapers developed to give news to Parisian and Cajun immigrants. In the Southwest and California, it was Spanish language newspapers. In Minnesota, it was Swedish language newspapers. These newspapers, and thousands of others, some of which lasted a few weeks, some many years, gave immigrants the news they both wanted and needed.

Working for these newspapers were reporters who would become some of the nation's leading journalists, tradesmen, professionals, and politicians. Joseph Pulitzer, one of the titans of journalism, came to America speaking only Hungarian and German; his first job in 1868, after service in the Civil War and minor business jobs, was with the *Westliche Post,* a German language newspaper in St. Louis. Pulitzer would later own the *New York World,* at one time the largest circulation newspaper in the United States.

Isaac Bashevis Singer, who won the Nobel Prize in literature, was a reporter and columnist beginning in the 1930s for New York City's *Jewish Daily Forward,* a 275,000 circulation Yiddish language daily.

By 1917, with heavy immigration the previous two decades,

185

there were more than 1,300 foreign language newspapers in America. Today, there are still several hundred foreign language newspapers, from the 1,300 circulation *Macedonia Weekly*, a Bulgarian language newspaper, to *elNueva Herald*, a 90,000 circulation Spanish language paper published by the *Miami Herald*. Reflecting the reality that by 2008 Hispanics were the largest minority culture in the United States, there are dozens of Spanish language radio and TV stations, as well as six major networks. Univision, available on most cable systems, is the fifth largest TV network in the United States; its evening newscast, co-anchored by Jorge Ramos and Maria Elena Salinas, often has higher ratings than any English-language network evening newscast. Telemundo, owned by NBC/Universal, is the second largest Spanish language network. If the rise of Spanish language media, and the popularity of Latino music aren't indications of the presence of the Hispanic population, then a condiment is. In 1991, salsa replaced ketchup as the best-selling condiment in the country, and has been widening the gap ever since.

The languages and cultures that are a part of this nation are what makes this nation unique. By "rephrasing" our linguistic and cultural base to demand an ethnocentric America, we destroy a nation founded upon liberty and developed by immigrants.

DIVERSITY

People. People Who Don't Need *People*

From a pool of about seven billion, those hard-working geniuses at *People* magazine managed to find the 100 most beautiful people in the whole wide world. And—get ready for the surprise—almost all of those beautiful people are rich American celebrities.

Since 1989, *People's* editors believed they were given the divine right to anoint who they believe are the most beautiful people on the planet. The ethnocentric celebrity-fawning *People* editors are so secure in their self-imposed knowledge that they don't even reveal the criteria they used to make their determinations. Not even an "editor's note," common in most magazines.

People etches its version of reality into our minds by attaching cutesy capsulated biographies to full page color pictures of the most beautiful, and drops the 60–80 page section among

186

myriad $254,000 a page full-color ads every May. Advance stories about some of the selections appear in just about every American newspaper and major website, all of which think stories about celebrities are more important than stories about the Recession, thus assuring that the Beautiful People Special will be one of the best-read issues of the year. The reality is the lists are really the "100 most noticed celebrities," but that probably wouldn't get as many sales.

For several years, *People* had the "50 Most Beautiful" list, but apparently had trouble deciding how to reduce those seven billion people to only 50, so the editors doubled the number. But, they still had to squeeze 100 into the space of 50. So, they killed quality writing, and made most of the pictures the size of matchbook covers.

People editors, showing how attuned they are to the young demographic, have given us teenagers and barely-20s TV ensembles. In 2008, the seven member cast of TV's "Gossip Girl" made the list. "Onscreen," *People* told us, "they are gorgeous, scheming, backstabbing high schoolers." Just what America needs—more future business executives and politicians. In 2009, the group was "The Girls of 90210," each of whom was identified by a short quote. One said she collects wigs; one said hair is her "security blanket"; one said she discovered and misused bronzers in the 10th grade; and one said she needs to constantly "pinch my cheeks" because she never flushes.

The first few years, when the editors could find only 50 beautiful people, there was a fairly even split between men and women. The 2009 edition revealed that about three-fourths of all beautiful people are women. One of those beautiful women, given a full page and a minimal quote, was Michelle Obama. Although the editors have become more socially conscious, minority representation in the list is minimal, and certainly not in even close proportion to the reality that one-third of the world's population are Black and another third are Asian. In the United States alone are 45 million Hispanics.

Five years after the first list came out, *People* recognized the elderly. Of course, the elderly were celebrities Paul Newman, Faye Dunaway, and Barbara Babcock. The following year, the "elderly" included 51-year-old Queen Silvia of Sweden and 61-year-old journalist Gloria Steinem who should have been honored for being beautiful, but embarrassed by her inclusion on a list that is distinguished by hyperbole and ethnocentrism. The

2008 and 2009 editions included two page color spreads deep in the magazine for 40 celebrities, 10 in each of the age categories of 20s, 30s, 40s, and 50s. Obviously the editors couldn't find any beautiful 60 year old celebrities like Dolly Parton, Goldie Hawn, Bette Midler, Neil Diamond, or Robert DeNiro; or 70-year-olds, like Bill Cosby, Rita Moreno, Marlo Thomas, Robert Redford, or Quincy Jones; or 80-year-olds, like Tony Curtis, Neil Simon, Burt Bacharach, Tony Bennett, and Sidney Poitier. The editors did find some real oldies for the 2009 edition. They put pictures of historical figures online, and asked readers to evaluate them as "hot" or "not hot." The two "historical hotties" were Nefertiti and Martha Washington.

In 1994, the editors expanded their section to include expanded bodies. Trying to make us believe that *People* thought beauty came in different sizes and shapes, the editors claimed that 5-foot-11 180-pound size 14 model Emme was a beautiful person, representative of the "burgeoning large-size modeling industry." It's hard to explain to these anorexic editors that size 14 isn't fat, and that half of America's women are at least a size 14. Not wanting to set a trend, *People* made sure all of the next year's beauties were modishly thin. As in previous years, the 2009 edition included no large-size beauties, but it does include ads for Jenny Craig and Atkins diets, Medifast appetite suppressants, low-calorie Twinkies and cupcakes, and fat-free Florida grapefruit.

In 1994, after an incestuous five years of casting entertainers at more than three million subscribers, *People* widened its scope of inclusion. For the first time, it "elevated" four professional colleagues to anointed status—former journalist and Vice-President Al Gore, a husband-wife documentary film team, an ABC "Wide World of Sports" interviewer, and an NBC "Today Show" host.

Teachers, social workers, and medical researchers, no matter how beautiful, don't make the final cut. But, they shouldn't worry about it. Neither do Miss America, Miss World, Mr. Universe or, for that matter, Miss Crustacean, Ocean City, New Jersey's, salty tribute to hermit crabs, and a spoof of the beauty contest that once inhabited next-door Atlantic City. Miss USA, however, for the first time in 20 years did make the list, but wasn't a big enough celebrity to rate more than a thumbnail mug shot.

To its credit, *People* editors, probably as an afterthought,

188

Commoners included in Kentucky, and UPS.

Like all people, we in journalism tend to report about, are
attracted to, and understand people and ethnic groups that are
like our own, or of which we are a part. For the most part, we
are White, middle-class, sometimes even upper-class, college
graduates who talk a lot about equality, but look, act, and dress
as if we are part of the establishment we report about. We determine the "newsworthiness" of a story and, equally important,
we decide the standards for media coverage-whether source credibility or beauty. If we see only certain groups of people, we will
report only about those people, leaving everyone else as invisible as the billions of people who weren't even considered. It
takes some ugly and very shallow people to think they can
make up a list of the 100 most beautiful people in the world.

Out of the Closet,
and Into the Living Room

By the end of the 1996–1997 television season, just about the
only ones who didn't know that Ellen Morgan, bookstore worker
on the ABC-TV prime time sitcom "Ellen," or Ellen DeGeneres
who portrays her, were both gay were the trappist monks in the
Media-Free Zone in Lesotho.

Although an *Entertainment Weekly* poll revealed that 72 percent of Americans "would not be personally offended if a lead
character on a TV show were gay," the networks kept gay characters in secondary roles. A half-century after the first TV series
aired, Ellen Morgan became the first lead character on a prime-
time show to be openly gay.

For years, reporters questioned DeGeneres, a stand-up comedian before becoming an actor, about her sexual orientation. For years, she refused to be lured into sensational journalism, her preference hidden beneath a veil of rumor and innuendo. In March 1994, when "These Friends of Mine," later renamed "Ellen," first appeared in prime time, DeGeneres's sexual orientation again surfaced, but it wasn't until three years later, with "Ellen" no longer in the Nielsen "top 10" and headed into the middle of the pack, that rumors began dribbling out that the show would "out" the character—and, maybe, the star. DeGeneres apparently wanted the character to declare her sexual preference, causing innumerable discussions among the show's creative staff, ABC-TV executives, and the Disney conglomerate, which not only owns ABC-TV but also distributed "Ellen."

Shortly after the season's premiere, the *Hollywood Reporter*, quickly followed by *TV Guide*, had suggested the "coming out" plot line. For the next seven months, several hundred stories appeared in the media as the "Ellen" publicity mill fed the media frenzy; *TIME* had stories in four issues; *Newsweek* had stories in two issues.

During the 1996–1997 season, numerous double entendres snuck into the scripts, while innumerable reporters turned into gossip columnists and tried to get DeGeneres to reveal if either she or her title character were gay. DeGeneres herself flirted with the media most of the season, coyly teasing reporters and TV talk show hosts, stating that the character wasn't a lesbian but a Lebanese, telling others that the hoopla is a misunderstanding—the lesbian on the show is really a new character, Les Bian.

The Christian conservatives, and others who piously proclaimed their beliefs in "family values," aligned themselves against the suspected "Ellen" plotline. At the beginning of the season, a rather oblique Pat Robertson of the Christian Coalition had said he found it "hard to believe [DeGeneres was gay] because she's so popular. She's such an attractive actress." The Rev. Jerry Falwell called her "Ellen DeGenerate," and the Rev. Fred Phelps in a hellfire and brimstone speech ranted, "It's a sign we're on the cusp of doom, of Sodom and Gomorrah." Thousands of flaming Internet chatters and morally-outraged newspaper readers declared they would boycott the show and its advertisers if either of the Ellens declared a single-sex orientation.

An internal report from the Leo Burnett advertising agency, which represented McDonald's, an "Ellen" sponsor, strongly recommended against buying time on shows with gay characters. The report stated that McDonald's franchise owners in the Bible Belt could be hurt by such ad placement, especially when confronted by the conservative Christian opposition. McDonald's disregarded the advice, according to *Advertising Age*.

Disney, long identified with "family values," was one of the first major corporations to extend benefits to its single-sex couples. However, the controversy probably backed Disney/ABC into a position that if it didn't approve the "outing," it would be seen as succumbing to hate-mongering and fear.

During the next few months, millions of Americans faced off to fight the battles of fundamental Christianity, morality, and human rights. The Gay and Lesbian Alliance Against Defamation (GLAAD) created a "Come Out With Ellen" campaign that would eventually have parties in seven major cities and 1,500 individual homes the night of the broadcast.

A little more than a month before the broadcast, the religiously fundamental and politically conservative American Family Association and the Christian Family Network, which claimed the outing was "attacking the moral fiber of our nation," jointly created the Ellen Media Watch, "aimed at bringing about changes in advertising practices and ultimately target changes in offensive programming content." However, it was the Internet media campaign, housed within a slickly-designed web page, that led to a massive public e-mail response to the corporations that had previously bought advertising time on "Ellen." Chrysler, JCPenney's, and Wendy's pulled their ads. Microsoft and Intel said they'd remain, no matter what the public said. The other scheduled advertisers at first said they would see what happens, but eventually stayed with the "outing," probably not for any principle other than recognizing that a spike in the ratings, which could make "Ellen" the number 1 show that week, certainly wouldn't hurt their sales.

Recognizing the potential audience for the one-hour episode, ABC raised its advertising rates from an average of $170,000 for a 30-second spot to $335,000, according to *Advertising Age*. But, ABC refused to take ads from the Human Rights Campaign and lesbian-owned Olivia Cruises and Resorts, stating it was network policy to reject "controversial issue advertising." Human Rights Campaign, however, bought spots on 33 local affiliates to alert viewers that 41 states allow employers to fire workers for being gay.

In March, after an entire nation already knew or at least suspected the "coming out" episode was no longer just a rumor, ABC-TV, after six months of internal discussions, finally announced it had approved a revised script, and that Ellen Morgan would be "outed" in a one-hour special, April 30—during ratings-obsessed "sweeps week." Appearing on that episode would be Laura Dern, Oprah Winfrey, Demi Moore, Billy Bob Thornton, and singers k.d. lang and Melissa Etheridge, both of whom are lesbians. In subsequent episodes, Ellen Morgan would tell her parents and her employer she's gay.

Shortly after the episode was filmed, DeGeneres playfully told a media awards dinner sponsored by GLAAD that she spent a lot of time doing "research" for her character. By then, most of the entertainment industry already knew she was gay, some knowing for as long as 20 years. A month later, she said the reality to *TIME*, then to dozens of newspapers, magazines, and TV shows, including an interview on ABC's "20/20," Friday, April 25, after being moved from "Prime Time Live" two days earlier to take advantage of higher ratings and the beginning of the May sweeps.

Two weeks before the coming-out episode aired, *Newsweek* and *TIME* each ran seven pages on "Ellen," Ellen, and gay issues in the American media. Neither ran anything that week about the devastating floods of the upper Midwest that forced the evacuation of more than 100,000 people, and cause about $1 billion damage to homes, farms, and businesses.

The broadcast, possibly the best-written and acted during the show's declining two years, had killer numbers. The show scored a 23.4 rating (the percent of all television homes) and a 37 share (the percent of TV homes that had their sets turned on and were watching TV that time period), and an estimated audience of about 42 million, making it the top-rated show that week. WBMA-TV in Birmington, the largest ABC affiliate in Alabama refused to air the "coming out" episode. The season's average for "Ellen" was a 9.6 rating and a 16 share, placing it 37th of all prime-time television shows during the 1996–1997 season. DeGeneres, who had received Emmy nominations for Best Actress each of the first four seasons, earned an Emmy for Best Writing for the "coming out" episode.

ABC cancelled "Ellen" the following year after its fifth season. After a four year absence from television, Ellen DeGeneres was back, this time on CBS with "The Ellen Show." That one lasted

192

[handwritten marginalia, left margin: Ellen confessed to other media after her episode.]

[handwritten marginalia, left margin: The broadcast had huge numbers, in Alabama refused to air it. WBMA-TV]

[handwritten marginalia, bottom: She returned with "The Ellen Show"]

just four months before being cancelled in January 2002. However, "The Ellen DeGeneres Show," a syndicated daytime talk show, with DeGeneres doing stand-up comedy, debuted in September 2003 to both critical and popular acclaim. During its first six seasons, it received 25 Emmys, including four for Outstanding Talk Show Host.

Several dozen TV series broadcast episodes with gay characters, usually in minor roles, and often in contrived variations of a plotline where a pretty female character has a crush on a handsome athlete whom she later learns is gay.

Possibly the first episode with any gay theme was "The Eleventh Hour," an NBC medical drama which had a secondary story line on one episode in 1963 that centered around an actress and female director. It was four years later that producers were brave enough to again introduce a gay character on prime time television when "N.Y.P.D." debuted on ABC with a one-episode storyline about a group of hoods who blackmailed gays. Four years after that, President Nixon told the nation how disgusted he was that CBS broadcasted a segment of "All in the Family" that showed the bigoted Archie Bunker dealing with a friend he learns is gay.

In 1972, ABC-TV risked viewer and advertiser antagonism when it slid past two socially-restrictive barriers. "The Corner Bar," which included a swishy set designer, was the first American series to include an openly-gay character in a recurring role. That same year, Hal Holbrook and Martin Sheen starred as gay lovers in the ABC-TV film, *That Certain Summer,* a two-hour character study of a gay father who tries to explain his social orientation to his son. The show was probably the first TV movie with a gay theme. "Sidney Shorr," an NBC-TV two-hour movie, starred Tony Randall as an openly gay New York commercial artist. However, NBC-TV refused to allow producers to write Randall's character as gay when the network turned the TV film into a sitcom, "Love, Sydney," for the 1981–1983 seasons.

The 1975 series, "Hotel Baltimore," was the first series to show a gay couple. During the late 1970s, Billy Crystal starred as a gay man in the quirky prime-time series, "Soap."

The basis for the ABC sitcom, "Three's Company" (1977–1984) was that a straight man (portrayed by John Ritter) pretended to be gay in order to fool a prudish landlord and be allowed to share an apartment with two young women. Since

193

Ritter's character was only pretending to be gay in order to advance weekly plots of salacious humor, the nation didn't have many objections.

In 1982, the non-profit PBS network broadcast "Brideshead Revisted," a mini-series based upon Evelyn Waugh's novel. The lead character in the series, set during a two-decade period in post-World War I England, was bisexual.

"Sara" (1985), the story of a law firm with two male and two female lawyers in San Francisco, survived less than a season on NBC. Bronson Pinchot, portraying a gay lawyer, received fourth billing behind Geena Davis, Alfre Woodward, and Bill Maher.

In 1994, "Daddy's Girls," a one-season CBS sitcom about the New York City garment industry, starred Harvey Fierstein as a gay fashion designer. However, Dudley Moore got top billing.

"Northern Exposure" was set in the fictional Cicely, Alaska, founded by lesbian lovers. The city's founding was an almost-invisible underlying theme. Then, in 1994, the CBS series showed the wedding of two men. The following year, "Friends," NBC's ratings smash, had a lesbian wedding.

"Roseanne"—which set new standards in realism before ending its nine-year prime-time run in 1997—had four continuing gay characters, including her boss, mother, a close female friend, and the friend's girlfriend. "Star Trek," which boldly explored social issues other series wouldn't touch, featured a provocative lesbian relationship in a "Deep Space 9" episode aired in 1996. ABC-TV's popular "Spin City" (1996–2002) starred Michael J. Fox as a New York City deputy mayor, surrounded by some of the industry's better comic-actors including Michael Boatman who portrayed the gay Black director of minority affairs

Other series prior to "Ellen" that included gays or lesbians in recurring roles were "The Bob Newhart Show" (1972–1978), "Ball Four" (1976), "The Nancy Walker Show" (1977), "Mary Hartman, Mary Hartman" (1975–1978), "Dynasty" (1981–1989), "St. Elsewhere" (1982–1988), "Hooperman" (1987–1989), "Heartbeat" (1988–1989), "Doctor, Doctor" (1989–1991), "Anything But Love" (1989–1992), "Sisters" (1991–1996), and "My So-Called Life" (1994–1995).

In February 2001, during "sweeps week," Ellen DeGeneres guest-starred as a nun on NBC's "Will and Grace," the story of Will Truman, a gay lawyer, and Grace Adler, a straight interior decorator, who are not only roommates but best friends. A secondary gay character was Jack, a semi-employed actor. By its fourth season, "Will and Grace" was not only one of the 10 best-watched prime time television shows, but fourth in the 18–49 year-old demographic, the TV advertisers' target audience. During the 2001–2002 season, "Will and Grace" was seen by an average of 17 million weekly viewers, and was the eighth most-watched program on network television. However, viewership began declining after that to about eight million in its final season. The NBC-TV hit series—which premiered in 1998 and won an Emmy in its second year for Best Comedy—ended its 196-episode run in May 2006, having been nominated for 49 Emmys and winner of 12, including Emmys for each of its four stars, its director (James Burrows), writers, and the series itself.

"Sex and the City," a quirky HBO megahit about four sexually active single women in New York City, premiered the same year as "Will and Grace," and ran six seasons before becoming a hit in TV syndication. The formula, wrote Garry Maddox in the *Sydney Morning Herald*, "was to write gay male and cast straight female. Its (gay) creator, Darren Star. . . devised one of the gayest hit series featuring straight characters in television history." The series had several continuing gay characters, including Stanford, a close friend of Carrie Bradshaw (portrayed by Sarah Jessica Parker), the series lead, a sex-and-love columnist for a daily newspaper. In his first appearance on the show, he tells Carrie, "The only place you can still find love and romance in New York is the gay community." By the time the first *Sex and the City* movie was distributed in 2008, the audience knew a secret—Cynthia Nixon, who portrayed Miranda Hobbes, was involved in a long-term lesbian relationship.

Three prime-time series with gay characters premiered during the 2003–2004 season. FOX's "Oliver Beene" *(2003–2004)* featured an 11-year-old who we learn, in flash-forward scenes, was gay. Proving that television is repetitive and imitative, two series were based upon a previous series and two real-life examples. "Mr. and Mr. Nash," based upon the television series "Hart to Hart" (1979–1984), which was based upon the popular 1930s/1940s movie series, *The Thin Man*, was the story of two gay interior decorators who solve murders. The show barely appeared in January 2003 before it was cancelled.

Nathan Lane, who, starred as a flamboyant gay in the megahit comedy *The Bird Cage* (1996), was the title character in "Charlie Lawrence," a former actor who becomes a congressman. The Summer 2003 series took liberties in the life of four-term Congressman Fred Grandy (R-Iowa), a straight who was a secondary lead as "Gopher" in the TV series "The Love Boat"; and openly-gay Rep. Barney Frank (D-Mass.), first elected to the House in 1981.

TV soaps have often broken new ground in social issues that primetime series, and network sponsors, wouldn't. In 1992, *All My Children* wove a lesbian into the show's intricate plot lines, but killed her off at the end of the season. In 2000, the series introduced a lesbian teen, although for only a year's run. *As the World Turns*, for the 1988–1989 season, became the first daytime soap to present a major gay character, a fashion designer who died by the end of that season. Through several weeks of the Summer of 1992, the ABC daytime soap, *One Life to Live,* carried a storyline about a 17-year-old high school senior who struggled about his public identity. During the 1995–1997 seasons, ABC allowed story lines that included a gay teacher on the daytime soap, "All My Children." However, the network forbid any on-screen single-sex romance. In 2000, *All My Children* introduced the character of a lesbian teenager.

With more than three dozen reality TV shows on the air by the end of the 2008–2009 season, there was no way that all the non-actors could be straight. In 2000, the CBS reality ratings hit, "Survivor," included openly-gay Richard Hatch, who defied stereotypes and won the first season's $1 million prize for surviving on an isolated island, populated only by 15 other contestants—and several dozen production crew members.

Three years later, CBS-TV proclaimed that one of 12 teams on "The Amazing Race 4" wasn't just gay, but married to each other. The network said there were other gays on the reality TV series, but it was the first time a TV series openly declared a gay couple was married. In response to questions from the media, CBS couldn't identify in which state the couple was married, and deferred to their application indicating they were married.

Hollywood, which once banned gay roles as well as gay actors in any role, now openly flirts with yet another prime-time way to draw sexually-explicit ratings. Media hype surrounded the first lesbian kiss on an episode of "L.A. Law" in 1991, followed by a kiss the following year on "Picket Fences." ABC in 1994 forbid a lesbian kiss on "Roseanne" until Roseanne used her considerable ratings clout to demand the network permit it, justifying it not by ratings potential but by storyline development. Three years later, ABC didn't stop a slobbering lesbian kiss on the drama, "Relativity." In April 2003, ABC aired a same-sex female kiss in an episode of the afternoon Soap, "All My Children." Four months later, pop singers Britney Spears and Madonna exchanged an open mouth kiss at the MTV Video Music Awards, televised live from New York's Radio City Music Hall. Their kiss at the end of a music segment assured the publicity-savvy singer-dancers that their picture would appear in almost every daily newspaper, major magazine, dozens of television news and entertainment programs, and be a topic for discussion for several months.

There are currently more than three dozen gay, lesbian, bisexual, or trans-sexual characters in recurring secondary roles on prime-time television.

Because of smaller, more targeted audiences and the absence of FCC controls, cable networks have the freedom to explore social issues and to air shows with more violence and nudity than permitted on network television. In 1984, the Showtime cable network premiered the continuing sitcom, "Brother," the story of three brothers, one of whom was gay. The series, originally rejected by ABC and NBC, was "one of the first shows on which a major character was gay," according to *The Advocate*, which tracks depiction of gays and lesbians in the media. The Showtime series "Rude Awakenings," featured Rain Pryor as Jackie, a Black lesbian. In the 2001–2002 season, Showtime premiered "Queer as Folk." The original British fictionalized drama series focused upon several gays in day-to-day situations. The American version, set in Pittsburgh, was more sexual, possibly to counter HBO's "Sex in the City." Showtime also premiered "The L Word" in January 2004, a series that portrayed the lives and loves of a cast of lesbians living in West Hollywood.

In Fall 2003, with Reality TV dominating prime time, Bravo premiered "Queer Eye for the Straight Guy." Five gays, each a specialist in food and wine, fashion, interior design, grooming, and culture, took individuals, a few of whom may have been homophobic, and gave them "make-overs."

The first full-time gay cable channel began broadcasting in Canada in August 2001. PrideVision, a subscription channel, owned by the Headline Media Group, had a mix of British and American network and cable shows, as well as an original news-magazine, "Shout." During the 2004–2005 seasons, three cable networks with a predominant theme of gay-oriented shows, debuted. Both Q, owned by Triangle Multi-Media; and Here!, a premium cable channel, debuted with around-the-clock programing at the beginning of the 2004 season; Logo, owned by Viacom, debuted in June 2005 as a basic cable channel, available in urban cities.

However, even with the appearance each year of about two dozen continuing characters on national primetime television series, even with changing social standards in the country, gays on TV is still controversial. Surprisingly, it was an animated character that inflamed American values. During 1997 and 1998, some of the media noted that Tinky Winky of the PBS animated children's series, "Teletubbies," may have been gay. They pointed to the character who dressed in purple, carried a red purse but spoke in a male voice, and had a triangle antenna that could have been the symbol of gay pride. There was minimal reaction until the *National Liberty Journal*, a conservative magazine edited by the Rev. Jerry Falwell, in its February 1999 issue, declared its opposition to the character. Soon, conservative groups rallied around Falwell's accusations, while the nation's talk show hosts and comedians had new material for their acts. As do all media-enhanced controversies, this one eventually died out as most of the nation found it difficult to support the conservative movement's argument that an animated character from a fantasy world was gay.

Although attacking Tinky Winky, America's "family values" conservative base apparently hasn't rallied against the animated character, Waylon Smithers, Mr. Burns' sycophantic executive assistant who remains barely "in the closet" in the FOX mega-hit, "The Simpsons" (1989–).

Nevertheless, national advertisers have had reservations about placement on shows with gay themes, believing they would suffer a backlash from offended viewers. ABC stated it lost about $1 million in advertising when it broadcast a "thirty something" episode in 1989 that showed two gay men in bed. That episode was not included in the re-run schedule. "Ellen," of course, lost advertisers for its "coming out episode," but the networks still were sensitive to the reality that there is a wide swath of intolerance in America.

In December 2004, with gay characters on dozens of TV shows, both CBS and NBC refused 30-second ads from the United Church of Christ, because that church decided to tell America that it doesn't reject persons. The ad shows two men holding hands who are being turned away from attending an unnamed church. The voice-over states that "Jesus didn't turn people away. Neither do we." It then shows a crowd of people of all races and beliefs, including two women, one with her hand on the other's shoulder. The voice-over continues, "No matter who you are or where you are on life's journey, you're welcome here."A CBS official wrote the church the reason for declining to run the ad: "Because this commercial touches on the exclusion of gay couples and other minority groups by other individuals and organizations, and the fact that the Executive Branch [the Bush–Cheney Administration] has recently proposed a constitutional amendment to define marriage as a union between a man and a woman, this spot is unacceptable for broadcast." NBC-TV told the *Boston Globe* that the network rejected the ad produced for the 1.3 million member church because it "violated a long standing policy of NBC, which is that we don't permit commercials to deal with issues of public controversy." Both networks emphasized they don't run "advocacy advertising," a claim that was as phony as their reasons.

Although Americans seem to be more tolerant of alternative lifestyles, a recent *USA Today*/CNN poll revealed that 42 percent of Americans thought there were too many gays and lesbians on television, with significant numbers believing that the representation of gays on TV is well out of proportion to the percent of gays in American culture. The problem isn't that the fictional Ellen Morgan or actress-comedian Ellen DeGeneres are gay, or that prime time series depict gay characters, but of the reluctance of the networks and the news media to deal with controversial issues until they determine what the majority of the viewers, and their advertisers, are willing to support. Then, the networks zealously pursue the "topic of the week," burying the culpable news media under a wall of press releases and hype.

It makes little difference if it's gays, Blacks, Jews, problems of the homeless, unemployed, or of AIDS. Give the publicists for

199

"Ellen" and Ellen DeGeneres hefty raises; they did their jobs well. Give the media a slap upside the head for failing to recognize significant alternative lifestyles, and then for pandering, as well for failing to realize there are other important issues in the world than one's sexual preference.

Laying Off Marshbaum

It was late Friday when I somberly called Marshbaum into my office. There was no way to break it to him gently, so I laid it on the line.

"Marshbaum," I said, "I'm going to have to lay you off."

"What'd I do wrong, Boss?" he asked, wounded.

"It wasn't anything you did," I said reassuringly. "It's what you are."

"I'm your foil," he said. "When you need someone to come up with dumb ideas that have an edge of truth, I'm it."

"That's true, but you're also a white male, and I've used you too much."

"That's my job!" said Marshbaum. "I'm the one who makes you look good."

"You're the one who's going to cause me problems with diversity committees," I replied.

"Because I'm a white male you have to lay me off?"

"I have no choice," I said showing him a study commissioned by the Screen Actors Guild and the American Federation of Television and Radio Artists conducted by a research team at the University of Pennsylvania.

According to the research, of more than 19,000 speaking roles in almost 1,400 shows over 10 seasons, women comprised less than one-third of all speaking parts. The study also said Latinos, Native Americans, the elderly, and disabled, are almost invisible on TV, and lower class persons were represented in only 1.3 percent of major characters in prime time although there are ten times that number in the general population. Even more incriminating, the study reported that almost two-thirds of all on-air TV journalists are men, and that four-fifths of both those cited as authorities and those whom the networks consider as making news, are men.

"But that's TV," said Marshbaum haughtily. "We're *print*."

"Makes no difference," I replied. "If they can target TV, they'll

[margin note: Minorities Latinos, Women, elderly, Native Americans, lower class not on TV]

200

find us next."

"Even if the networks believe the report, they won't do anything about it."

"And what makes you think that?"

"Because TV's *never* done anything socially responsible," said Marshbaum smugly.

"I still have to lay you off," I again told him.

"Sure," Marshbaum said cynically, "then you'll up and move the column to Mexico and take advantage of lax labor laws."

"Don't be ridiculous," I replied. "I have no plans—"

"At the least," he accused, "you'll hire cheaper minorities, and not give them any benefits."

"That may be true," I admitted, "but that's only because you're a white male who has been with the column a long time, so all new hires will be done at entry level salaries and minimal benefits. That's the American way! Besides, it'll only be just long enough so I can get women and other minorities as foils into my column, then I'll lay *them* off."

"What woman is going to be as big a schlemiel as I am?" a tearful Marshbaum asked. "No one can act dumber than me!"

I acknowledged it would be exceedingly difficult to find anyone like him. "You'll get unemployment," I said. "Maybe even food stamps."

"I want a job," he protested. "The one I've held for years. Every time you were stumped for ideas, I did something stupid. Made you look like a genius. Stupidity is my life!"

"Marshbaum," I said, "don't you understand? If I use you much more, I'll probably be caught in some poll that editors conduct when they have nothing better to do with their time."

"But you use women," he said, his voice straining. "What about Susie Sweetwater, your shmuck of a TV news reader? What about—"

"Marshbaum," I said compassionately, "you're a victim of your own ability."

"What about Mike Royko?" Marshbaum protested. "You think he ever laid off Slats Grobnik? What about Art Buchwald? He never gave his foils their notice because they weren't white men?"

"I believe they were grandfathered in," I said.

"Breslin!" Marshbaum thundered. "No one's telling Jimmy Breslin to get rid of Fat Thomas and Marvin the Torch!"

"Marshbaum," I said, "it'll only be a few weeks. A decade or two at the outside."

Reluctantly, he packed up his things and shuffled out the office. The last time I saw Marshbaum, he was reading a Spanish language book about trans-sexual surgery. *He wanted to become a minority*

GOVERNMENT AND POLITICS

This Column Doesn't Exist

Liberals attack the media for failure to adequately question authority, for accepting without much questioning the news releases from government and business, for a conservative bias among publishers and senior editors, and for allowing advertising and corporate issues to breach the traditional wall separating the business and editorial sides of the media.

Conservatives attack the media because they are absolutely, positively convinced that the media are run by liberals, that reporters are Communistic atheistic elites who don't understand the concerns and problems of the "common folk," namely those who identify themselves as God-fearing, traditional values conservatives.

In private, politicians, no matter what their beliefs, complain about the fairness, accuracy, and intent of the mass media. But, in public, they modify their comments, and pretend to buddy-up the reporters, fearing that their adversaries, not competing politicians but the media, will turn on them.

What if there were no media? What if the mass media got together, decided they were tired from being picked apart by politicians, needed a sabbatical, and created a self-imposed moratorium on news, their decision being the last story they published or aired?

The politicians couldn't get together to use the media to complain about how bad the media are. Since there are no media, there would be no one at the infrequent press conferences. There would be no media giving up some of their journalistic integrity to jockey for the best seats on Air Force One or at Washington black-tie parties. How ever would the political parties thrust insipid candidates spouting rickety platforms upon the masses?

There would be no one to accept the myriad pork-barrel press releases from members of Congress who want to show the "folks back home" they care enough about them and their

202

votes, and that's why they successfully got a naval supply house in Haystacks, Kansas, or a museum in the south side of Chicago dedicated to cow tipping.

They wouldn't be able to get national air time because there would be no appearances on "Oprah," the morning semi-news infotainment shows, the evening news, late night talk shows, or even the far more honest and journalistically competent "Daily Show with Jon Stewart" or "The Colbert Report" because they wouldn't even exist.

There wouldn't be any radio to capture their distortions of reality and transmit them to an audience that prefers to hear conservative slobbering talk-mouths and Golden Oldies music from the Bayou.

The politicians could still spew press releases, but without media there would be no one to print or televise them. They could distribute millions of flyers and newsletters, but the Government Printing Office is part of the media and, thus, would also be closed. Paid ads in newspapers, radio, and television would be useless since those media don't exist.

If the Hollywood film industry, which right-wing politicians equate with Satanic verses, went on vacation, the politicians could create their own films and documentaries. But, that won't happen in a media vacuum.

Politicians could still show their "normal" side by jamming with rock, jazz, or accordion bands—except that music is all part of the mass media. Without music, the government could not even blast loud screeches known as "the Top 40" to terrorists to make them cave in.

Politicians could try putting abbreviated epithets of false promise onto billboards but there wouldn't be any billboards because they're also part of the media.

The web? Not a chance. Politicians have been complaining about the web as a source of evil, or at least the repository for both soft-core and hard-core pornography for two decades. The web, the newest mass medium, would already be closed by ethically-challenged and sometimes adulterous politicians who have tried scoring votes by trying to censor Internet sites and messages.

Satellite transmissions would all cease. Politicians could text message their pleas for money or send video clips to the ubiquitous network of cell phones—if cell phones weren't confiscated as part of the mass media.

Without the media, every politician would become useless; they wouldn't matter; they would be irrelevant. People might even start talking with each other, care about each other.

But, that's only a fantasy.

Taking a Dose of Hemlock: The State's Right-to-No Law

by Rosemary and Walter Brasch

All we wanted was to look at some public records from Hemlock Twp., Columbia County, Pa. By the time it was over, we were accused of criminal activity, had a legal bill of more than $3,000, and became front page headlines.

A 115-member citizens group, formed in the late 1990s to investigate inappropriate expenses by the township, learned that in four years the township went from a surplus of $373,000 to having to borrow $117,000 just to pay for road projects. The group had already spent almost $30,000 in legal miscellaneous expenses—and was still blocked at having easy access to public records, even though Judy Snyder, one of its leaders, was an elected auditor for the township. The township supervisors, defending many of their actions to block public access, had spent more than $55,000 of taxpayer funds to fight right-to-know requests and the citizens' attempt to remove the supervisors for malfeasance. One township solicitor even told the press the Hemlock citizens were "unAmerican" for challenging the township authority. Another of the township's attorneys stated during depositions that if the citizen's group didn't cease its efforts he would drag out legal proceedings indefinitely until the township went bankrupt.

Supervisors chairman Joe Harvey, when confronted by a weak state law on the public's right-to-know, told us and our attorney, "I don't care about the Pennsylvania law. This is Hemlock Township." And, he may be correct.

Our case with Hemlock Twp. was typical of citizens dealing with Pennsylvania's anemic law, one of the weakest in the nation. But, it was also typical of what citizens in most municipalities in most states face when trying to find out what their government is doing. Even the strongest laws don't assure compliance.

Although Hemlock Twp. had only 3,000 residents in 1997, it had an assessed value of more than $200 million, with a mall, banks, motels, restaurants, and a major I-80 truck stop. (By 2006, it would have a Super Walmart shopping center, several more major restaurants, and a new Holiday Inn.) Soon after a three-man board of supervisors took office in 1998, residents began to hear about bills and payroll increasing drastically. The supervisors soon laid off half the police force, claiming financial necessity. Asking to see where their tax dollars were being spent, the citizens were defiantly refused access to all records. With no other recourse, a citizens' group of about 100 members hired an attorney and filed a lawsuit seeking access. They needed documentation to determine if excessive pay to the supervisors (who were also the paid road crew) or misappropriation of funds had created the crisis.

In July 1999, we attended a township meeting and formally asked for such records under the state's Right-to-Know law. The chair demanded to know why we wanted public records, and then rebuked us for not living in the township, although the law applies to all citizens of the Commonwealth.

The following day, we contacted the township secretary to review documents and get the necessary copies. She informed us she was going on vacation in a few days, and no one else in the township knew where the records were or could release any information. We would have to pay her overtime and wait indefinitely to get *any* records.

A week later, after several unsuccessful telephone conversations, we went to the township office once again to request the financial information the citizens needed. After 15 minutes we left without seeing the public records or any promise we would ever see those records.

We contacted the Society of Professional Journalists (SPJ) for assistance. Both state and national SPJ leaders sent strong letters to the township. The township's response? Joe Harvey was furious at the "outside interference"—and sent us a bill for $344.99 to be paid before any copies would be made. This included the cost of overtime, staples, paper clips, a toner cartridge, and mileage charges to get the toner and paper clips. (The supervisors also told citizens who were in the offices under a court order to look at certain documents that they would have to pay for air conditioning they used.) Despite the supervisors and their solicitor now being aware of the law that permitted citizen inspection of documents, the township would not allow us to look at the records until we paid the bill. We had no way to know if the time and expenses were legitimate, padded, or a violation of state law. The supervisors also refused to let us see any original documents. There was no way to determine if all requested records were provided, or if some records were deliberately withheld or tampered with. We were also told we could not bring an accountant, lawyer, or other assistance.

Soon after our appearance in the township office, Chairman Harvey ordered "his" remaining police force to investigate us for harassment, disorderly conduct, and wiretapping, although our tape recorder was in plain view. A police officer came to our home and questioned us for two hours. The police officer twice listened to our tape of our visit, and then told us it appeared the township staff were harassing *us*, not the other way around. He reported this to the district attorney who also reviewed the tape. In the end, our 15 minute office visit had triggered a *two month investigation*, which ended when the district attorney finally told the police chief there was no evidence to support any of the supervisors' charges. No one estimated the cost of this investigation, nor if time spent on what were frivolous charges would have been better spent on "other" criminal cases.

After Hemlock Twp. continued to block our attempts to gain public documents, our attorney began legal proceedings. We asked the township to release documents and to establish a formal procedure so other citizens would not undergo the harassment we encountered. Three months and a three-inch thick folder of paperwork produced a form to *request* documents. Not the documents we sought. Not a guarantee that citizens would *get* what they requested. Just a form so citizens could *ask* for what was legally theirs. But the government still could block citizen rights. The office was open on a random basis, and persons couldn't make appointments to get the information from the secretary. (In contrast, Columbia County itself has a strong record of allowing immediate access to public documents.)

In three months, SPJ paid over $2,500 in legal fees—and this was at a significantly reduced per-hour rate. Telephone, fax, and postage costs, incurred by us personally, amounted to more than $500. The average citizen cannot afford legal expenses, doesn't have the knowledge or time to pursue such cases, and has no organization to support their efforts to challenge the government's abuse of power.

Joe Harvey, elected to a six-year term in 1996, chose not to stand for re-election in 2002. The Court of Common Pleas that year fined Harvey and supervisor Ken Martz, elected in 1998, $1,000 and sentenced them to 200 hours of community service for violations of the state's open bidding laws. However, neither was brought to court for violations of the public's right-to-know.

Opposition to improved right-to-know legislation came from members of state legislatures who believed their "open and frank" discussions could better be conducted outside the glare of public scrutiny, from state agencies who believe most of what they do should be "confidential," and from law enforcement and rape crisis centers which use spurious arguments to argue that the public shouldn't have access to certain records. However, most citizens don't want to know all the details of ongoing investigations by the police or the details of a rape case, or who called 911. Just about *any* criminal can—and will—get this information *without* the Right-to-Know laws. The citizens, not the criminals, merely want to see where their tax dollars are going, and how their governments are being run. Fortunately, 37 states now have oversight agencies or specific programs to help citizens get public records from their governments. However, in most states, even with stronger ordinances and laws assuring the public it has access to what the government is doing, penalties are so light—often only $100—and prosecution almost inconsequential, that the public is being denied information that is rightfully theirs. Equally important, every political subdivision can use taxpayer dollars to obstruct public access with little fear of repercussions. And, in most jurisdictions, there is no law to limit the amount of taxpayer dollars a government can spend to block access to public records. A study conducted in 2002 by the Better Government Association and Investigative Reporters and Editors gave Pennsylvania a grade of "F" on Right to Know legislation, rating it 48th in the nation.

That year, with the Pennsylvania Newspaper Association, SPJ, and other media organizations spearheading the effort, and with citizens from Hemlock Twp. testifying before the Legislature, Pennsylvania finally improved its Right-to-Know law, first enacted in 1957. However, even with its "upgrade," the law was still weak and largely unenforceable. And then in 2008, the state legislature, with a push by Gov. Ed Rendell, rewrote much of the law. The major difference was that all governmental documents, with few exceptions, were presumed to be public record and available to any citizen. The law also set reasonable fees for duplications, reduced time for agency response to requests for information, established a searchable database for agencies, and increased penalties for violations. To assist the public, the state established the Office of Open Records to assist citizens to obtain public documents.

Although Pennsylvania realized its responsibility to the people, the problem in Hemlock Twp. was *not* an isolated incident, nor confined just to Pennsylvania. Many public agencies and governments, perhaps from ignorance, exhibit a demeanor which has a chilling effect on the average citizen, most of whom don't understand the amount of information to which they are entitled. Many officials don't want the people to know how government works because they undoubtedly think the people just wouldn't understand, or are blocking access because they're afraid of what the people *will* understand about how their government works.

Killing Americans With Secrecy

The Pennsylvania Department of Health claimed it had a plan to deal with a potential outbreak of H5N1, a lethal strain of the Avian influenza. But it was a secret plan. So secret that local and county health departments didn't know what it was. Nor did physicians and hospital staffs.

"[W]e have to be very careful with how this information is released," a state official told the *Harrisburg Patriot–News* in May 2005, but assured the public that they "can be confident that preparations that we've made can be implemented to the fullest without any difficulties caused by information getting into the wrong hands." In translation, what Troy Thompson said was that the Department was worried terrorists could get the plan, and so the public should just trust government.

The zeal for secrecy has flooded all state and local governments and, in varying degrees, permeates all political parties. It shouldn't take an epidemic, fueled by public ignorance, to prove that secrecy is not what the Founding Fathers demanded of government.

Had George Wisner, editor of the *New York Sun*, trusted government in 1834, thousands might have died from cholera, which

208

had a mortality rate at the time similar to H5N1. Wisner had heard rumors of a death from cholera. The cause could have been in the city's water supply or in tainted food sold in groceries or in restaurants. But, the health department said there was no occurrence. After persistent badgering, Wisner got the health officials to admit there "may" have been a problem. But they said the people would panic and needlessly tie up doctors and hospitals if the *Sun* published the story. The "more responsible" newspapers, said the officials, knew about the potential epidemic, but had kept quiet because it was "in the public's best interest." *Secrecy of the media*

The public's best interest is to know the truth, said Wisner who published the story and suggested the health department was negligent in detecting the disease in the first place. The establishment newspapers, as expected, attacked Wisner for being irresponsible. The public, armed with the truth, neither panicked nor tied up medical resources. An epidemic was averted because the people had the facts.

Claiming the need for secrecy to "protect" America is why the federal government classified the number of rolls of toilet paper it has in stock, a satiric plot against Santa Claus, and what cocktails former Chilean dictator Augusto Pinochet preferred. About 4,000 federal officials have the authority to classify documents. For every dollar spent declassifying documents, executive branch agencies spend about $120 to create and keep documents secret, according to an investigation by OpentheGovernment.org, a coalition of 33 national journalism and consumer organizations. In 2004, the federal government classified 15.6 million documents, about 10 percent more than the previous year, and 4.3 times the number classified in 1995, according to the National Archives.

The Bush–Cheney Administration, charged former Vice-President Al Gore in November 2003, used "unprecedented secrecy and deception in order to avoid accountability to the Congress, the courts, the press and the people. . . . Rather than accepting our traditions of openness and accountability, this Administration has opted to rule by secrecy and unquestioned authority."

The Bush–Cheney Administration had revealed "a pattern of secrecy and dishonesty in the service of secrecy," wrote Walter Cronkite in his syndicated newspaper column in April 2004. Cronkite, a World War II combat correspondent and former CBS-TV anchor who covered 11 presidential administrations,

209

and was once known as the "most trusted man in America," was unrelenting:

> "[T]his administration believes that how it runs the government is its business and no one else's. It is certainly not the business of Congress. And if it's not the business of the people's representatives, it's certainly no business of yours or mine. . . . The tight control of information, as well as the dissemination of misleading information and outright falsehoods, conjures up a disturbing image of a very different kind of society. Democracies are not well-run nor long-preserved with secrecy and lies.

The "zeal for secrecy adds up to a victory for the terrorists," said Bill Moyers, former press secretary to Lyndon Johnson, publisher of *Newsday*, and winner of more than 30 Emmys for television news and documentaries. "Never has there been an administration like the one in power today, so disciplined in secrecy, so precisely in lock-step in keeping the information from the people at large and in defiance of the Constitution from their representatives in Congress," said Moyers in September 2004.

Even John Dean, White House legal counsel for Richard Nixon, whose penchant for secrecy was a defining part of his Administration, found government secrecy under the Bush–Cheney Administration to be excessive. In his best-selling book, *Worse Than Watergate* (2004), Dean wrote that "George W. Bush and Richard B. Cheney have created the most secretive presidency in my lifetime. . . . Not only does this secrecy far exceed anything at the Nixon White House, but much of the Bush–Cheney secrecy deals with activities similar to Nixon's. [It was] a time of unaccountable and imperial presidency."

Patriotism means "not trying to hide from accountability through excessive secrecy and privacy," said Gen. Wesley Clark, former NATO Supreme commander, in January 2004.

Folded within the Bush–Cheney penchant for secrecy were lengthy delays and the highest number of denials in history for release of non-classified public documents requested under the Freedom of Information Act.

In February 2006, the *New York Times* reported that intelligence agencies were secretly removing from the National Archives "thousands of historical documents that were available for years, including some already published by the State Department and others photocopied years ago by private histo-

210

rians." The *Times* noted that about 55,000 previously declassified documents were reclassified. The National Archives reported that about 30 persons a day were at the Archives to read and to reclassify public records.

With the Barack Obama Administration, transparency began to dominate secrecy. The Federal Funding Accountability and Transparency Act—introduced by Sens. Obama (D-Ill.) Tom Coburn (R-Okla.), Tom Carper (D-Del.), and John McCain (R-Ariz.)—had required that beginning in 2007 any group or agency that received federal funds must provide full disclosure by an easily accesible website of how that money was spent.

Throughout his campaign for the Presidency, Obama pledged to increase openness in government. "We're not going to be able to change America unless we challenge this system that isn't working for us and hasn't for a long time," Obama frequently declared.

As president, one of his first acts was to implement his campaign promise. Among his directives was to create a full database available to the public of all lobbying reports, connections between lobbyists and members of Congress, and campaign finance reports. The database would also include all financial data from all cabinet and executive departments.

"My Administration," said President Obama, "is committed to creating an unprecedented level of openness in Government." In an executive memo to the people and his staff, he declared:

> We will work together to ensure the public trust and establish a system of transparency, public participation, and collaboration. Openness will strengthen our democracy and promote efficiency and effectiveness in Government.
>
> *Government should be transparent.* Transparency promotes accountability and provides information for citizens about what their Government is doing. Information maintained by the Federal Government is a national asset. My Administration will take appropriate action, consistent with law and policy, to disclose information rapidly in forms that the public can readily find and use. Executive departments and agencies should harness new technologies to put information about their operations and decisions online and readily available to the public. Executive departments and agencies should also solicit public feedback to identify information of greatest use to the public.
>
> *Government should be participatory.* Public engagement

211

enhances the Government's effectiveness and improves the quality of its decisions. Knowledge is widely dispersed in society, and public officials benefit from having access to that dispersed knowledge. Executive departments and agencies should offer Americans increased opportunities to participate in policymaking and to provide their Government with the benefits of their collective expertise and information. Executive departments and agencies should also solicit public input on how we can increase and improve opportunities for public participation in Government.

Government should be collaborative. Collaboration actively engages Americans in the work of their Government. Executive departments and agencies should use innovative tools, methods, and systems to cooperate among themselves, across all levels of Government, and with nonprofit organizations, businesses, and individuals in the private sector. Executive departments and agencies should solicit public feedback to assess and improve their level of collaboration and to identify new opportunities for cooperation.

The transparency became evident to the public in April 2009, when the federal government quickly mobilized its health resources and gave extensive ifnormation to the people about a flu strain, H1N1, also known as the Swine Flu, believed to have originated in Mexico, and which was rapidly spreading to the U.S. and several other countries. The World Health Organization elevated the threat to Stage 5, one level below pandemic attack. About 100 died from the flu, 10 of them in the U.S.; another 14,000 persons, about half of them Americans, were believed to have contracted the flu. However, largely because of the government's proactive stance and the media's coverage of what could have been a virulent attack, all public health agencies and the public were kept fully informed, and given instructions of how to reduce possibilities of being exposed to the flu.

George Wisner would have been proud.

~~~~~~~~

"Access to public information in a timely and effective manner is a vital piece of our democratic system of checks and balances that promotes accountability and imbues trust. . . . I have devoted a considerable portion of my work in the Senate to improving government oversight, government openness and citizen 'right-to-know' laws to make government work better for the American people, and at times it has been a lonely battle."
—Sen. Patrick Leahy (D-Vt.); Feb. 16, 2005

Responding to the Press

The President of the United States had just concluded a news conference in which he had discussed the federal response to Hurricane Georges, explained that because Congress had violated the legal deadline to pass a new budget he had to sign a "stop-gap" order to keep the country from being shut down, and declared he was proposing major new education legislation.

The first question from the press was, "How do you think the Democrats will do in November?" Had Bill Clinton lingered to hear additional questions, he undoubtedly would have heard reporters ask only about his sex life and the possible impeachment.

Although His Horniness admitted to a slimy affair with an intern, American voters still gave the President a 66 percent approval rating, higher than almost every president since George Washington. Even as important, while such a scandal and the subsequent inquisition would drive most people to irrational acts, the President showed he had more class than his accusers and investigators of the Press. The President had tried to be civil and diplomatic. But, he shouldn't have been.

So, let's rewind this scenario a few minutes, give a little more time to the reporters to ask their critical questions of national importance, and listen to what the President should have said to reporters whose libido-scope is greater than their knowledge and concern of national affairs.

"How do you think the Democrats will do in November?"

"Listen, you simpleton, I just told you there is a major hurricane about to hit Florida. I explained what the federal government is doing to assist the residents. And you demented little piece of mud ask me about elections six weeks from now? Why don't you focus upon the thousands of people who are affected by this storm, who may lose their property and possibly their lives. Publish a few inches of news copy that might be useful to them. You'd still have several thousand inches of space to devote to stories about sex and scandals."

"Mr. President, speaking of storms, what are you doing to weather the upcoming impeachment crisis."

"Did your parents allow you into the gene pool without a lifeguard? Were you speed bumps listening when I said that Congress has violated the law by not passing a new budget and the government stands a good chance of being shut down? Don't you understand anything about economics or how the failure to pass a budget will affect everyone from corporate executives to the unemployed?"

"Mr. President, speaking of unemployment, do you have any plans after you leave office?"

"Listen, Goldilocks, if you were any dumber, you'd be watered three times a week. The students of this country aren't even in the Top 10 when it comes to most standardized tests, the SATs have been dropping, and many students aren't even getting the basics in writing and reading instructions. For six years, I have been pushing to improve our educational system, only to be thwarted by a Congress that is more concerned about stains than brains."

"Mr. President, the special prosecutor is planning to release additional evidence of your sexual life. How do you plan to deal with it?"

"Deal with it?! From what I read in your newspapers and see on your TV stations, your reporting about the critical issues of this country has left a hole in the news coverage as big as the ones in your heads. When I took office, I empowered the First Lady to lead an investigation to determine the facts of the health care crisis, and to come up with recommendations of how to improve the lives of all Americans. But, Congress and dozens of lobbying groups not only killed any possibility of that happening, they mercilessly attacked The First Lady for having courage and intelligence."

"Speaking of Hillary, how's that poor soul taking all this?"

"Speaking for the country, may I suggest what you can do with the slimy tabloid reporting, with its unnamed sources and muddled gossip that you now believe is journalism?"

"Mr. President, are you now attacking our profession?"

"No, Sam, I'm only attacking the people who pretend they're practicing the First Amendment ideals established by Franklin, Jefferson, and Madison, and carried out by Horace Greeley,

~~~~~~~~~~

Does anyone know how Clark Kent gets all that time off to pursue truth, justice, and the American way? Has anyone ever seen Superman attend a city council meeting or interview the guy who grew the county's largest tomato? When was the last time you actually saw him writing a story against a deadline?

Joseph Pulitzer, and thousands of journalists who once believed they were practicing a noble craft."

By a Sneeze, They Shall Be Known

Whenever the President sneezes, 75 reporters file their stories. Because it's the President, and because it's easier to file a Presidential Sneeze story than to root through the causes of the health care crisis, the reporters fall all over themselves trying to beat each other out to get the comprehensive coverage TV-News fans have come to expect.

Anchor: This is Clyde Barrow at the White House. The President sneezed about 2:45 this afternoon. We understand the sneeze lasted about three seconds. We now take you to the emergency room of the Bethesda Naval Hospital. Standing by is Lance Redux.

Lance Redux: The President has just arrived, and we'll be interviewing bystanders, orderlies, and maybe even a nurse or two. Security is extraordinarily tight, and only the 237 accredited reporters have been allowed into the ER at this point. Anticipating a Presidential sneeze, and to give more room to the news media, every area hospital for the past week has been sending patients without health insurance to the Fumigate Center in Arlington. Back to you, Clyde.

Clyde Barrow: With me is Gatekeeper Jones, special assistant to the President for sneezes. Ms. Jones, what does this sneeze mean to the American people?

Ms. Jones: First of all, let me say that the President has made great inroads into understanding and responding to the needs of the American people. This sneeze was not only the result of his tireless efforts on behalf of the people, but also a declaration that he will go to extraordinary lengths to deal with health care issues in this great nation of ours.

Mr. Barrow: Thank you. Now, to Susie Sweetwater with Sen. Porkbelly Pineapple at the Capitol.

Susie Sweetwater: Sen. Pineapple, we just heard that the President's sneeze was in sympathy with the plight of Americans everywhere. Do you agree?

Sen. Pineapple: While all us Americans are concerned about the President's health, this particular sneeze was the result of a President who has disregarded the wishes of the people and of the Congress.

Susie Sweetwater: For an opposing view, we turn to Rep. Horace Sludgepump.

Rep. Sludgepump: While I don't wish to disagree with my esteemed and most distinguished colleague from the other side of the aisle, I should point out that if it wasn't for him and the other cretins from the minority party who filibustered the death of so many of our great and glorious programs which were designed by our party to help the working class, we'd have a chicken in every pot in this glorious country.

Clyde Barrow (interrupting): Excuse me, Susie, but the President's personal physician is about to make an announcement. We now return to Bethesda Naval Hospital.

Dr. Alfred Chiu: After running a series of tests on the President's bodily fluids, examining X-rays of his nasal passages and respiratory system, and checking the results of the MRI scan, we now believe the cause of the sneeze was a pollutant in the air. We have not yet identified that particular contaminant.

Reporter 1: Harry Hotlips, ABC-Action News. Doctor, can you identify that pollutant?

Dr. Chiu: As I mentioned, we haven't yet identified that contaminant.

Reporter 2: Judy Jumpstart, CBS-TV. Just how serious is this pollutant?

Dr. Chiu: We can't determine how serious the contaminant is until we can identify it.

Reporter 3: Darla Dazzling, NBC News. Doctor, just exactly, what kind of pollutant could that have been? Does it have long-term effects?

Dr. Chiu: I don't know, but we will try to find out.

Reporter 4: Sid Serious, CNN. Doctor, what do you believe would be the world consequences of this particular sneeze?

Dr. Chiu: I can't say at this time, but I will ask the Secretary of State to respond as soon as she completes her phone calls to the other world leaders.

Reporter 5: Polly Prattle, FOX News. On behalf of all the gun-loving fiscally-conservative decent Americans, we'd like to know just how long the lyin' liberal politicians that caused this have been polluted?

Clyde Barrow (again interrupting): I regret that we must temporarily interrupt our in-depth team coverage at this point. Right after these important messages from our sponsors, we'll return you to "General Hospital," already in progress.

216

A Dam(n) for the Home Folks

With the arrival of the new TV season, it's only a matter of time until one of the TV networks buys out C-SPAN for the rights to prime-time coverage of "The Congressional Follies."

"Quiet on the set! House of Representatives, Monday session. Take 1."

Speaker: I'm Troy Calhoun, Speaker of the House and your host for Congressional Follies. But first, a message from our sponsors.

Sponsor: Are you tired of people taking advantage of you? Upset that your views aren't heard? At the Ace Lobby Service, we have direct access to some of the people who can improve your life. Whatever your needs, contact Ace Lobby. As always, prices are negotiable.

Speaker: Welcome back. With us today is Rep. Howard Sludgepump of Oklahoma with an earmark to the budget bill.

Sludgepump: Thanks, Troy. And it's certainly good to be here with all you wonderful people. As I tell all my folks back home in Hushaby Holler, Oklahoma—some of the finest people in the world—this is a real honor for me to present their wishes to the Congress of the United States. In fact, just the other day—

Speaker: Forgive me for interrupting, Sludge, but the floor manager just gave me the speed-up sign. Please don't keep us in suspense. What's in your earmark?

Sludgepump: Dams. A billion-dollar dam right in the middle of Hushaby Holler, Oklahoma.

Speaker: Well, let's hear it for Rep. Sludgepump's billion-dollar dam. *(A chorus of cheers).* Now, ladies and gentlemen of the House, are there any questions you would like to ask Rep. Sludgepump? . . . Mr. Popoff.

Popoff: Thank you, Mr. Speaker *("How's my make-up? I hope they get my left front close-up. I look better that way.")* Mr. Sludgepump, according to the records of the Weather Bureau, Hushaby Holler hasn't had rain for 20 years. There are no rivers or lakes. And your district is the wealthiest in the nation because of all the oil you have. Why is that dam necessary?

Sludgepump: That's a very good question. And the folks in your home district of Wattabago, Iowa, can be assured that they've really got a good congressman looking out for their financial interests, especially since you convinced the Congress to open a federally-funded Museum of Corn in your district. Yes, sir, it's hard to find congressmen as concerned about the taxpayers' money as you are. So, all you folks in Wattabago, Iowa, make sure you vote the Popoff ticket in November. Are there any other questions I can answer?

Rep. Hotchkiss: Congressman, isn't a billion dollars a bit much for a dam, espeically during a recession?

Sludgepump: Not really, Mr. Congressman. After all, you who have been doing a fantastic job for the corporations in your district to help them find cheaper labor in Mexico know how important full employment is. You, my esteemed colleague, should be the first to realize that the billion dollars will be used primarily to feed underprivileged construction workers, PR people, and administrators who would be out on streets penniless and starving if we didn't pass this bill. Certainly, a man as courageous as you are in helping the people of your district who will be given preference for work on this dam can see that.

Speaker: Well put, Mr. Congressman. I'm sure Bushneck folks know that Congressman Hotchkiss really cares about them. But, right now, we must break for a public service message from the New York Stock Exchange.

Sponsor: A lot of people say that big corporations are capitalistic conglomerates, bent on making profits at the expense of the people of this country. They say we demand the government stay out of our lives except when we need bailout money. That's not true. We'll also take interest-free loans and property tax rebates. We don't have any great conspiracies, or plans to take over the country. We want to do only what's best for the country. And we want you to know it. Now back to the Speaker of the House.

Speaker: Thanks, Dad. We're ready to vote. All those in favor of the dam bill, signify by taking your sunglasses off. Those opposed, you may leave your sunglasses on, and hit the miniature gong on your desk . . . Well, it appears we'll soon have a billion-dollar dam in Hushaby Holler. This is Troy Calhoun wishing you courage for another tomorrow.

Promises, Promises

Less than a week before the election, Marshbaum was campaigning furiously.

"A chicken in every pot! Free health care for everyone! There's light at the end of the tunnel!"

218

"Marshbaum!" I commanded, "you can't make those kinds of promises."

"You're right. I don't want to offend the health care industry. There's a lot of campaign money there. I'll just make up something else."

"You just can't make up campaign promises."

"Sure I can. It's easy. How about 'Vote for Marshbaum and win a date with Bette Midler?'"

"You don't even *know* Bette Midler."

"I like her movies," he said casually.

"It has nothing to do with her movies," I said.

"Think someone doesn't like her singing? I sure don't want to offend anyone. I could make it a date with Natalie Cole. How about Brad Pitt for the women? The media will report anything I say." .

"Get reasonable!"

He thought a moment. "You're right. Nat and Brad are probably supporting someone else. How about 'Elect Marshbaum and you'll never pay taxes again!'"

"That's ridiculous," I said. "No one will believe you."

"Doesn't matter if they do or don't. As long as they vote for me."

"But you'd be lying to the people," I said.

"It worked for Sen. Packwood," said Marshbaum smugly. Not long after Bob Packwood of Oregon was elected to his fifth six-year term, he admitted he had lied during the campaign when he denied he had made numerous improper sexual advances to members of his staff during the previous 20 years. A group of voters had petitioned the Senate to overturn the election on the basis that Packwood had lied to the people. The Rules Committee thought about issues of the greater public good, remembered their own campaigns, and unanimously declared that lying to the people during a campaign wasn't strong enough grounds to overturn an election.

"There's got to be some law that prevents politicians from lying," I said.

"Even for a journalist, you're dense," said Marshbaum. "The FCC says it's OK to lie.

"The Federal Communications Commission gives its approval?" I asked skeptically.

"Section 315. The FCC says that radio and TV stations can't refuse to run political ads even if the station management knows the ads are outright lies."

"Most people don't believe most of what they see on TV any-how," I sniffed.

"Try the Supreme Court," said Marshbaum.

"The Supremes said lying to the people is acceptable behavior?" I scoffed.

"OK, not the *U.S.* Supreme Court, but *A* Supreme Court."

"Which one? In Tehran?"

"Albany. The New York Supreme Court."

"Not even New York's court could be that incompetent."

"Got it right here," he said, taking a wadded paper from his pocket. Case of *O'Reilly v. Mitchell.* Guy named O'Reilly sued a politician named Mitchell in 1912 and charged him with making promises that weren't kept."

"A promise is a verbal contract," I said. "I'm sure you read it wrong. The Court undoubtedly *upheld* O'Reilly's claims."

"Wrong, Newsprint Breath," said Marshbaum arrogantly. "Court said that politicians lie all the time, that promises in a campaign are just that. Promises. Verdict for the politician. Case closed."

"But that occurred before World War I," I said.

"It's precedent," Marshbaum said. "It's still on the books. How about 'Vote for Marshbaum and he'll wash all your dirty laundry?'"

"You can do whatever you want," I said disgustedly, "but just remember that some politicians actually tell the truth."

"Name one who did and got elected!" he demanded.

"Honest Abe," I replied.

[*The case of* O'Reilly v. Mitchell *is cited as* 85MISC176, 148NYS, 88 SUP,1914. *For those who aren't lawyers, reflect upon Hitler's belief that "the victor will never be asked if he told the truth."]*

Gigolos on the Campaign Trail

The presidential candidates, once promising eternal love to Iowa and New Hampshire voters, deserted their betrothed faster than a gigolo ditching a plain rich girl for a plain richer one.

Together, Iowa and New Hampshire have less than 1.5 percent of the American population, but because the states figured out how to be the first in the race for delegates, and because there isn't a lot to do in January, the candidates and the bus-bound media hordes saturated the two states with their personality-drenched presence.

For three months—as happened four years before that and will happen four years after that—the candidates walked around the non-voting homeless to infiltrate every bar, restaurant, and fire hall, kissing babies, pumping the flesh, and dribbling campaign trinkets of every price category.

In Iowa, the candidates ate corn and pork chops, and talked about the need to help farmers. If pigs could vote—the state has five times as many pigs as people—the candidates would have preached a doctrine of forced vegetarianism. In New Hampshire, they praised granite and talked about why government should stay out of people's lives. The Iowa and New Hampshire voters are so media-savvy that they no longer had to ask what slant the reporters wanted for their stories.

CNN, FOX News, and MSNBC cleared their schedules to give extended coverage to the Iowa and New Hampshire campaigns, significantly more air time than any of the news media gave to the problems of health care, poverty, or unemployment. Both states could have been devastated by fires, submerged by floods, or found out that they were bankrupt, and the media may have sent one "pool" camera crew; everyone else would be working on more important stories—like the cost of Hillary Clinton's pantsuits. Unable to focus upon issues, probably because the Iowa and New Hampshire winters freeze brain cells, the media threw six-column headlines above gossip and conjecture.

After Iowa and New Hampshire, the candidates moved into 17 states for primaries and caucuses in February, and then into 19 states, 11 of them entangled in the "Super Tuesday" primaries in early March. Like they did to their jilted lovers in Iowa and New Hampshire, the candidates whispered sweet-nothings that were overheard and published by the media which, in the movie-script scenarios that have become politics, are cast as lovable klutzes who never get the girl. By the time the candidates waddled into Pennsylvania in April, they were proclaiming that cheese steak hoagies are the perfect food. By June, with the decisions generally made three months earlier, the Alabama, New Jersey, and South Dakota primaries were about as useless as pork rinds at a bar mitzvah.

221

The TV media, with journalists an almost extinct minority among what passes as their news staffs, think the best way to cover the primaries is to display 10 seconds of a candidate's visit to the Rotary Club luncheon, and then shove in another 45 seconds of public comments about the candidate who probably didn't say anything of substance to begin with. Print media reporters spend as much as three minutes with a potential voter, condensing the comments to about 30 words. For variety, the reporters quote each other and the swarm of pollsters who hover like trash-dump flies around political campaigns and the media circus. They eruditely declare that if Candidate X does not do at least so much percent in the vote, then he's finished, and if Candidate Y wins the election but doesn't score at least so many points ahead of the next candidate, he's also toast. But, if Candidate Z does "better than expected," he's "in the race" and "ready for the long haul."

Each of the major Democratic candidates in 2008 campaigned furiously on a two front campaign—against the policies of incumbent Republican President George W. Bush and against each other. The Republicans also campaigned on a two-front platform—not only would they be better at homeland security issues than anyone else, but that although they may have once met President Bush, they don't remember it.

By the November general election, Sens. John McCain and Barack Obama, the two remaining overfed major party candidates, spent more than the human resources and education budgets of a small country, or enough to significantly reduce hunger and poverty in America.

Most presidential candidates are good people caught up in the show that has become politics. On stage, bathed by the media glow, they become "warm and fuzzy," having already compromised their integrity for political expedience. The campaign trail media, however, no matter who is running, will spend more time with each other and the candidates, herded like sheep being rounded up by border collies. However, these border collies are campaign aides whose mission is to keep reporters moving between hotel rooms, planes and buses, and every venue where a politician speaks. This also keeps them from spending too much time with the people. For the reporters, the story is in chasing political rhetoric rather than in discussing social issues.

Rushes and Fixes
in the Political Media

Like heroin addicts, the media need constant fixes. And, like addicts, they often go into hysterical depression when there isn't anything to give them the rush they need, the excitement of being on the edge.

During the late 1990s, there was the Whitewater investigation of Bill and Hillary Clinton, the case of the sleazy presidential intern and the President himself, the double-murder trial of O.J. Simpson, Princess Di's death, and the story of Elian Gonzales, a Cuban boy who had come to Florida with his mother who didn't survive the trip, and was now the subject of an intense fight between his American relatives who were backed by the Cuban–American community and from his father, by all accounts an excellent parent, a Cuban who wanted his son back. And then came the 2000 presidential election.

For more than a year, the media were "pumped," churning stories about the election, usually presenting fact after fact, but never the truth of our process or system. Through the primaries, the media rushed from village to city and back again, chasing the candidates, breathlessly quoting one and then the other, all of them considered by the ubiquitous polls "front-runners" of the two major political parties. During the election, the media primarily quoted George W. Bush and Al Gore, stringing the quotes together with factoids about the candidates' many visits to the "heartland"—of the swing states.

To prove they were where they said they were, and weren't just recycling several forests of press releases and the same speech given five different ways to a hundred different audiences, the media reached out and grabbed "locals," asking them what they thought about the candidates or the visits. It made no difference what the people said, they were there solely as filler.

On Election Night, trying to prove how "with-it" they were, the media spent hours telling us what they thought was happening. And while they were projecting and predicting, they overdosed on their own egotistical charm and hit a wall. They were exhausted, strung-out, ready to crash for a couple of weeks.

Then came the confusing "butterfly ballots" in Florida, "hanging chads," and possible vote fraud. It was the fix the media needed. Their newest drug deal would go down in Florida. There, they could bounce from quote to quote, charge to charge, court decision to court decision. They were high, and enjoying it.

Al Gore had about 500,000 more votes than George W. Bush, but Bush, with a victory in Florida, would have more electoral votes. Bush, whose campaign stressed how he believed in the people and local government, was going to the courts, both state and federal, to assert his claims to the sanctity of voting machines and oppose hand-counting the ballots.

Gore, whose Reinventing Government programs brought the federal government closer to the people and the White House into the Internet Age, argued for hand-counting the Florida ballots because the machines were in error. Bush's response was that hand-counting ballots was subjective and prone to numerous errors, something he never considered when he signed a law in Texas to require hand-counting votes, since he believed it was the most accurate way to resolve discrepancies.

Special interest groups and a horde of lawyers invaded Florida; comedians drew their own stereotypes of Florida and stretched joke after joke, all dutifully reported by the national press. But, the election in Florida, culminating when the Supreme Court of the United States cast a 5–4 ballot to terminate the recount after six weeks, effectively giving Bush a 537 vote margin in Florida and all 25 of the state's electoral votes. The decision left America wondering not about who was elected as much as the underlying fabric of our society, of the sanctity of voting machines, and of the media's failure to report it.

The media should also have questioned the Circle of Manipulation where the media created the polling organization which fed their results to the media, which took it as divine inspiration, which then fed it to the candidates and the people who watched the media and the polls for guidance on how to act or react. It's not unlike monkeys and humans at a zoo watching and imitating each other.

The media should have wondered about how FOX, a major player in the political reporting process, could hire a Bush first cousin as its primary vote projection analyst, and then allow that "reporter" to make frequent calls Election Night to Govs. George W. Bush and "Jeb" Bush, not to mine information for analysis, but just to chat about the election and, for all we know, give confidential information to the Republican candidate.

The media should have questioned why FOX's premature call

for Bush's victory at 2:16 a.m. was immediately followed by almost all other media pouncing upon the same conclusion.

The media should have questioned why the networks scrambled all over themselves to be "first" with results, disregarding Joseph Pulitzer's three rules for journalists—"Accuracy! Accuracy!! Accuracy!!!"

The media should have questioned why they hadn't earlier reported that the co-chair of the Bush campaign in Florida was also that state's chief election official—or how many other states had similar incestuous relationships between elected officials and candidates.

More important, the media should have questioned why they had barely looked into the structure and nature of America's voting system prior to the recount in Florida.

The people, no matter where they lived, should have questioned how many of their own votes may have been thrown out or put against another candidate's name because of machine or human error. They should have questioned how many close races over the past few decades would have been reversed had there been better systems in place and more accurate counts.

The public should have been frightened by the revelation that the only reason they could have fun at Florida's expense was because the media, in their constant rush to a deadline high, didn't take the time to systematically look into the fabric of society and let us know a long time ago that the system, like the media, needs a fix.

Electing the News

Picapole was fighting hard to retain his seat as editor of the *Daily Noise*. Challenging him was Leadshot, a law school graduate who had worked his way up from janitor to president of his father's gun manufacturing company.

The latest polls showed that in the two county area the *Noise* served, Picapole and Leadshot were in a virtual dead heat, with an additional 10 percent of the vote, mostly reporters, aligned against having any editor.

First elected in 1982 as a fresh candidate against trickle-down journalism, Picapole had been comfortably re-elected every two years since. But now with the readers demanding change, Leadshot had charged from 15 points behind, and was on the verge of winning his first election since the 6th grade when he became assistant hall monitor.

"I'll vote for anyone running against Picapole," said a determined Marvin Blunderbuss of Porkbelly, Pa., who admitted he never read the newspaper, but defiantly insisted that anyone who spends more than four years as editor is part of the establishment and must be replaced.

In a slick TV ad campaign, financed primarily by the American Medical Gun Association, Leadshot charged Picapole with being soft on reporters, blasting Picapole for allowing two reporters to leave the *Noise* before their contracts were up. "These scumbags," said Leadshot, "are now writing award-winning stories for the *Morning Blab*, and are killing us with their constant scoops." Picapole acknowledged that it may have been a mistake to allow the reporters to break their contracts, but claimed that in the 18 years he was in office, the *Noise* efficiently picked up its reporters on the streets right after committing a journalism degree, and sentenced them to work slave-like conditions until the end of their terms.

Taking the offensive, Picapole charged that Leadshot himself was soft on reporters. Shaking a sheaf of statistics, Picapole pointed out that for all his histrionic blustering, Leadshot allowed reporters to come away unscathed from interviews 83 percent of the time, and that if he were to be elected there would be "every evidence that he will continue to preach toughness yet be soft on news."

Leadshot countered that at least if he were elected editor, the newspaper would run far more good news stories and fewer stories that "make people cringe whenever they pick up a newspaper and see yet another scandal that has no relevance to their lives." Picapole retorted that the media can't make up hard news when there isn't any.

Picapole then charged that Leadshot not only was a poor businessman, but that the readers shouldn't be swayed by anyone who never worked on a newspaper, never even took a journalism course, and wouldn't know the difference between a hole in newscopy to a hole in his assets. In response, Leadshot scored points when he retorted that the biggest problem with journalism today is that it's being run by journalists.

Not letting up on his attack, Leadshot produced 8-by-10 photos of a press party in which Picapole was seen standing near the editor of *The New York Times*. Picapole responded that although

226

both he and the *Times* editor were members of the same part
they barely knew each other, and would never lower himself ∪∪
ask for an endorsement.

"The economy is in a dumpster," Leadshot charged in a major
speech in Hogswallow, "and Picapole is responsible for it with all
his spending on reporter salaries and expenses." Picapole acknowledged that in the past 10 years he was responsible for increasing
reporter salaries by three percent, bringing them just past the
poverty line, but said he had no choice in the matter of buying
wrist rests and non-glare computer screens since the newspaper
lost a suit when 11 of his nearly-blind reporters with carpal tunnel
syndrome won a class action suit in federal court.

In one of his more popular, yet controversial planks, Leadshot has also proposed that every reporter be required to carry
a gun, a proposal that has split the newsroom's loyalty. "You
never know when your life will be threatened at a school board
meeting," said long-time reporter who asked that for matters of
security he not be identified. However, another reporter who
also asked for anonymity since she feared retribution from the
Leadshot faction, said she would oppose any reporter being
required to carry a gun. "It'll just escalate problems," she said,
then read off a series of statistics that revealed that reporters
who carry guns are five times as likely to be shot by their editors as are unarmed reporters.

Nevertheless, throughout the election the readers have been
puzzled by the lack of substantive debate about issues of news
design over substance, artificial limits on story length, the candidate's response to the lack of resources and personnel to cover
the news, as well as a general lack of health, labor, and environmental reporting. A recent poll shows that 94 percent of voters are making plans in two years to repaginate whoever wins.

CRIME AND VIOLENCE

Jackass: The People

For Halloween week 2002, *Jackass: The Movie* had the highest gross of any film on the nation's 35,000 screens. For several
more weeks, it was in the "top 10" both gross income and fan
reaction.

Based upon the popular MTV series, which aired from 2000

to 2002, the 87-minute *Jackass* was a series of two to three minute grossed-out stunts, many bound by feces and vomit, that appeal to a target audience of pre-pubescent children of all ages. Many of the stunts and practical gags were stupid and benign; some were stupid and dangerous. All were performed by professional stuntmen. Apparently, there were no women dumb enough to attach fireworks to roller skates or to walk across a tightrope over an alligator pit while wearing little more than a piece of raw chicken meat. *Jackass: Volume 2* (2004) was a video collection of the TV series; *Jackass: Number 2* (2006) was the movie sequel. *Jackass 2.5* (2007) was a direct-to-video production.

Dozens of amateur jackasses imitated the stunts. In Denver, three teens decided it would be "fun" to play bumper cars in stolen golf carts. Bruises, strains, and occasional broken bones are usually all that result from such stunts. But, there have been near-fatal and fatal consequences for the copycats.

A 12-year-old boy in New Hampshire suffered third degree burns after lamp oil was ignited on his body. A 15-year-old in Seattle poured alcohol on his shirt, and then set himself on fire while his friends videotaped the stunt that landed him in a hospital. In Albuquerque, a 15-year-old boy, imitating a *Jackass* stunt, jumped from the roof of a car onto the hood, fell to the pavement, and then was run over by the car. And in Seneca County, Ohio, an 18-year-old freshman at Tiffin College, trying to imitate a *Jackass* stunt, rode in the back of a pick-up truck, set a chair on fire, threw it onto the roadway, and then either fell or jumped while being videotaped by his friends. County officials said the youth died from massive head injuries. The official word from MTV/Paramount, obviously reviewed by a horde of lawyers, was that the death "has no connection to any stunts performed" on either the TV show or the movie.

Whether there was any connection, *Jackass* wasn't the first movie to have dumb or violent stunts; it certainly won't be the last. Adults tried horse-riding tricks after seeing stunts in movie and TV westerns. Children tried to fly, sometimes from second floor balconies, after first reading about Superman in comic books, and then seeing the man of steel in movies and television.

A decade before *Jackass*, a five-year-old boy watched moronic TV cartoon characters Beavis and Butt-head, imitated their reckless use of matches, and watched as a fire destroyed his family's trailer and killed his two-year-old sister. The mother (who had left the children alone), the fire department, and most of the community blamed the cartoon. MTV eliminated pyromania scenes from the cartoons.

In Pennsylvania, Texas, New Jersey, and New York, five teenagers, imitating a scene from *The Program*, a 1993 film about excessive football conditioning, lay down on the median lines of highways. Three were killed; two were critically injured. The communities blamed the film; Touchstone Films responded by deleting the scene from all prints. MTV/Paramount didn't eliminate any scenes from *Jackass*.

In California, a 13-year-old boy murdered a friend's father, and then poured salt into the knife wounds. "I just seen it on TV," he confessed. In Kentucky, a 14-year-old boy murdered three teens and wounded five others after seeing a scene from *Basketball Diaries*. In Florida, a 15-year-old boy murdered a neighbor. In Rhode Island, a boy hung himself after watching a magician perform a similar stunt. The parents of both boys sued the TV networks for negligence.

More than 80 percent of all video games contain violence. Among the most popular games are *Mortal Kombat vs. DC Universe*, *Chinatown Wars*, and *Resident Evil*. Some, like the *Grand Theft Auto* series, first released in 1998, encourage player aggression and murder. *GTA: San Andreas*, one of the most popular video games, earned $100 million in sales in its first month of release, October 2004. However, in June 2005, players could install a company-designed patch to make the game a "hot coffee" version that allowed players to engage in a sexual mini-game. That version was soon recalled after political and parental protests. Take-Two, the game's publisher, and Rockstar Games, the developer, agreed to a consent order of June 2006 not to misrepresent content or ratings in any future games. The fourth of the GTA series, *The Lost and the Damned*, just as violent as previous editions, was released in February 2008. The exclusive XBox version, released a year later, was expected to sell more than two million downloads by the end of 2009.

The first studies that tried to correlate a causal relationship between fictionalized TV acts of violence and an increase in American violence were written during the early 1950s as TV began reaching its popular stage. In 1972, Surgeon General

Jesse L. Steinfeld, who based his conclusions upon a panel whose members had been approved by the TV networks, concluded that "the causal relationship between televised violence and antisocial behavior is sufficient to warrant appropriate and immediate remedial action." By 1982, the National Institute of Mental Health, basing its study upon 2,500 other studies, concluded there was a correlation between acts of violence on television and aggressive behavior among children, and that those children who watched the most television were more likely to have more fears than those who didn't. But, the study also suggested that there was no way to predict which individuals would be affected.

About two-thirds of all prime-time television and cable shows contain violent scenes, according to a study conducted by the National Cable Television Association in 1997. *In Violent Television Programming and Its Impact Upon Children* (2007), the FCC concluded that "exposure to violence" could increase aggressive behavior. By they time children become 18, according to the FCC study, they will have watched more than 10,000 hours of television, and have been exposed to about 15,000 simulated murders and 200,000 acts of violence.

There have been more than 5,000 studies about the relationship between violence and the media. Most of the recent studies conclude that Americans believe they live in a violent and unsafe world, that exposure to repeated acts of violence in the media may result in the viewer not only becoming immune to acts of violence, but may identify with the violent characters, may imitate violent acts, and may believe that violence is an acceptable solution to problems. However, it is possible there is a reverse causal effect that most studies don't look at. Persons with violent personalities, whether overt or latent, may be drawn to violent TV, film, and videogames, which release that violence. Thus, studies that conclude that violent acts in the media may lead to violence in society fail to understand the personality who gravitates to violence in the media. Further, there have been comparatively few studies that show that non-violent shows, such as *Sesame Street*, may actually promote a turn from violence.

Innumerable organizations of every political and social persuasion, morally-indignant vote-seeking politicians, and even the federal government often blame the media for the increased levels of violence in the country. With reporters and TV cameras

230

present, they announce that more regulation is needed—unless the industry reduces depiction of violence. It's a no-lose situation since they can put the fear of restrictions into the industry and allow it to make the changes while not having to face that nagging problem about violating anyone's First Amendment rights.

An Associated Press study in 1993 revealed that 82 percent of Americans believed movies were too violent. The following year, a Times–Mirror poll revealed that 72 percent of all Americans thought TV entertainment shows contain too much violence, and 57 percent of all respondents believed TV news devoted too much air time to stories about violent crime. However, a *TIME* magazine poll in March 2005 revealed that only 66 percent of Americans believed there was too much violence on television. The drop wasn't because there were fewer acts of violence, but because Americans have become more desensitized to violence.

But, what people say—and what they actually watch—aren't comparable since the only statistics Hollywood notices are the box office or advertising revenue counts. When the creators of *Jackass* can produce a film for $5 million, rake in more than $60 million in the first month of distribution, and several million more from sale of foreign rights and pre-recorded videotape and DVD sales, it's easy to deflect criticism by counting your money and claiming they're only giving the people what they want.

Nevertheless, if we eliminated all media violence, as demanded by the shrill cries from our moral protectors on all sides of the political spectrum, then we will be forced to eliminate most 32-bit video games, ban TV reruns of the "Three Stooges" and "M*A*S*H," pull the plug on MTV, smash tapes and CDs, stop singing "The Battle Hymn of the Republic," shelve the four-star four-hour film productions of *Gone With the Wind* and *Gettysburg*, stop the reprint publications of *Moby Dick*, *The Red Badge of Courage*, and *Uncle Tom's Cabin*, block publication of *Hansel and Gretel*, *Snow White*, and most of Grimm's fairy tales, rewrite virtually all of Shakespeare's plays, forbid the telling of Aesop's fables, prohibit TV news from appealing to our sense of the morbid by leading newscasts with auto crashes and wars, and order a complete rewrite of the *Bible*, which has more violent acts per page than even a *Dirty Harry* movie. Even if all movies, TV shows, books, magazines, and newspapers become "violence-free," there will still be violence in American society, more than in any other industrialized nation.

Without question, the media influence our behavior and life-style. It's also reasonable to conclude that the media may influence violent or stupid behavior among some, but certainly not most, impressionable minds, and that persons who normally have aggressive behavior patterns or who live in homes where such patterns are present may be more inclined to increase their own aggressive behaviors by watching violent entertainment. But, it's also possible to conclude that those without such personality traits or environmental exposure would not commit acts of violence even if every movie or TV show they watch had excessive levels. Certainly, it would be a leap of faith to believe that Quakers, if shown enough television and movie violence, would buy guns and mug Baptists.

If we honestly wish to reduce violence in American society, we should focus not upon the media but upon the causes for violence. And for those persons who truly are violent, perhaps there should be tougher laws, better prisons, and more responsible rehabilitation programs.

Even more important, maybe we can start taking responsibility for our own actions and stop blaming the media, no matter how irresponsible, inept, or manipulative we think they may be.

Reel Violence

It was yet another stop on the book promotion trail, this time in Philadelphia on a "big time" talk show with a "big name" star. The host was friendly, discussed my background and the book, a history of animated cartoons, but like most hosts she hadn't read any of it.

"Let's get started by finding out what your favorite cartoon show is," she asked. A few years later, I might have added "Pinky and the Brain," "Freakazoid," the "Animaniacs," "SpongeBob Squarepants," and "The Simpsons," excellent cartoons which had helped bring an end of the spiral into mediocrity. But, at the time she asked the question, most TV cartoons were as creative as cold toast. So, I refered to the past.

"I'm partial to the Roadrunner and Coyote series," I said, and then briefly explained how the cartoons, with brilliant writing by Mike Maltese and directing by Chuck Jones, were classic throw-backs to some of the best silent physical comedies of the 1910s and 1920s. I expected an equally soft follow-up question. It came loaded with an explosive not even the Acme Co., the Coyote's supplier, could produce.

"There really is too much violence in cartoons, isn't there?" she rhetorically stated, and then spent two minutes explaining her views.

"Actually," I said calmly when she finally had to breathe, "the physical violence in cartoons is completely different from what you see in live action or even in cartoons with human subjects." I got a couple more sentences in when she came back, expounding the belief that cartoon violence directly leads to violence in real life, and that the studios and networks needed to be more responsible. Perhaps the Industry should establish a commission to review films and cartoons, she suggested.

Keeping my composure, I politely explained that the basis of all literature is conflict, and that most three-year-olds know the difference between cartoon violence and real violence, and if they don't, then parents should learn how to change the channels.

Later, I was able to sneak in my opinion that it was absurd when network television, scared by lobbyists, had temporarily pulled Bugs Bunny cartoons from the air because they didn't think Elmer Fudd should be blasting rabbits and ducks. She came right back at me by pretentiously quoting a research study to support her views, took a triumphant breath, and awaited what she thought would be my feeble response.

Fifteen minutes into what I thought was a mugging—I had wanted to talk about bunnies and tweety birds—I fired back. "I'm well aware of that study," I snipped, and then cited other studies that revealed either a slightly negative correlation or no correlation at all between cartoon violence and human action. I was content with my response, anxiously awaiting what I knew would be her feeble response.

"Let's go to the phones," she said. For the most part, the audience asked interesting questions, with the host usually spending more time in presenting her views than I did in answering audience questions. Then, abruptly, she mellowed. "You certainly have a wealth of knowledge," she cooed. "I was wondering, do you have a favorite cartoon show?" Apparently, since I didn't answer correctly the first time, I got another chance.

"Rocky and Bullwinkle," I replied, explaining that Jay Ward's creation probably had the sharpest satire of all television shows. I was going to elaborate when she again explained that the plotting done by Boris and Natasha to the Moose and Squirrel couldn't be very healthy for impressionable minds.

"I believe some studies show that cartoons may affect persons already prone to violence," I said, "but have no effect on persons who are not themselves violent." Commercials saved me from her response.

Back on air, she again introduced me and cited *Cartoon Monickers*, the book about animation history that I was huckstering. "Let's go to the phones," she said again, and again the audience was more interested in the origin of cartoons and how they're made. Five minutes before the hour, it was time to close it up, but not before one more question.

"By the way, one other thing before you leave," she asked, "what's your favorite cartoon show?"

This time I was determined to get it right. "Beany and Cecil?" I asked hesitantly. When she said nothing, I briefly discussed the 1950s cartoon show created by Bob Clampett who had been one of the Warner Bros. pioneer directors. "I loved all the puns and double entendres," I said, awaiting her response that cartoons were responsible for the moral breakdown of the American family, and that the world was at risk because of the conflict between Dishonest John and his targets Beany Boy and Cecil the Seasick Sea Serpent. But, she didn't. All she said was, "That's nice," thanked me for showing up, again mentioned the book, and went to another set of commercials.

I left the studio convinced I was yet another batch of chum for talk-show sharks—and wondering if I would ever get my favorite cartoon show right.

Blood on Their Lenses

"If it bleeds, it leads" is local TV's aphorism which dictates that violent crimes and traffic accidents lead off the nightly newscast. Focusing on broken body parts is more "visual" and easier to cover than the economy, Senate hearings, and the health care crisis. If it isn't violence that grabs the viewer, it can usually be something so soft that no self-respecting newspaper would run it any higher than the bottom of Page 17.

But, now and then, it's hard to find an assortment of accidents, fires, and murders. And so it was that KFAD-TV's pan-

People are drawn to violence in the news

234

icked station manager met with his news director late one afternoon to go over the final line-up for the "6 O'Clock Aren't-We-All-Happy?" news.

The station manager wasn't happy.

"What do you mean leading off the news with a report that some jokers at the Public Health Service found the cure for AIDS! Weren't there any accidents? Fires? Murders?"

"Sorry, Boss, there's nothing out there."

"Nothing!? Is that 'nothing' as in 'no accidents,' or 'nothing' as in 'I'm close to finding another job?!'"

"Boss, we really tried. I've got five camera crews running around right now."

"Think you can get two of them to run into each other? We'd pay the hospital bills."

"Boss, don't you remember? The union made us agree to a six month moratorium on stories that involve us maiming our crews just for the sake of ratings."

"Some union," the station manager huffed. "Doesn't even want its members to get more air time."

"It's only for six months," said the news director. "After that, maybe we could cut the brake linings on Unit 3 and have Unit 4 cover it. But for now, the news scanner is dead."

"What happened to that fatality on Mulberry?"

"By the time we scrambled the chopper, the drivers had exchanged insurance numbers and left."

"Left?!" thundered the station manager. "No one leaves when there's a camera crew on the way!"

"Best we could figure out, it was just a few paint scratches."

"Any of the cars red? You guys get there faster and maybe it'd look like blood. Check the cops again."

"Sorry, Boss. Even Philly's not reporting any murders in the past 24 hours."

"Then go out and shoot someone!"

"Sorry, Boss, I can't do that."

"Yeah, you're right. Tell Susie Sweetwater to do it. Her ratings are down. This oughta help."

"Susie's in the middle of her reading class right now, and you know how she hates to be disturbed when she's learning new words."

"Then Heartthrob! He's got the highest personality rating of any local anchor in the country. Audiences salivate whenever he's on. The public would back him even if he had assault weapons and made welsh rarebit out of the Easter Bunny."

"It's an hour until air," the news director reminded the station manager. "Heartthrob's already in Makeup. They're darkening his hair tonight."

"Roseanne!" shouted the station manager. "She's always good for something. Think we can get her to kill someone?"

"We have two crews on her," said the news director, "but all she's doing is threatening a couple of writers and a producer or two. Besides, we've done that story 23 times this month."

"Check with the crew you have permanently assigned to Madonna. She's been quiet lately."

"Out of the country."

"Get me a fire! Forest. Trailer. Stove. I don't care what kind!" the station manager demanded, smashing his coffee mug against his desk, and cutting his wrist. "Blood!" he shouted. "We have blood!"

"It's only a scratch," said the news director.

"It's blood! And it's good for a grabber. Grab a producer. Come in with an extreme close-up full-frame, then pull back to a medium shot. Dissolve to some of the file footage of the O.J. crime scene. Here's your lead: 'Violence in California leads to national bloodletting.'" He paused a moment. "Make sure you run teasers on this every five minutes."

OBSCENITY

Labels of Indecency

Throughout history, whenever there is a rise in the creative arts, reflecting a newer, more liberal, culture, there is an increase in calls for censorship of what some believe to be immorality. It was no different during America's post-war era known as the "Jazz Age" and "The Roaring '20s." This time, America's emerging film industry was the target.

Reacting against the scandals of Hollywood's movie stars, against the town that became known as "Sin City," and against films that often mixed alcohol, forbidden by the 18th Amendment, sexual suggestiveness, and crime, came hundreds of local and state censorship boards that had the authority to ban films. Thus, a film that might be acceptable to a local board in Cincinnati could be banned by a state board in Mississippi. The

236

authority for censorship came from a Supreme Court decision in 1915 [*Mutual Film Corp. v. Ohio Industrial Commission*] that determined studios were businesses and their products were not protected by the First Amendment.

Partially to avoid governmental interference, the movie industry in 1922 created an umbrella organization, Motion Picture Producers and Distributors of America, and hired Will Hays, a conservative former Postmaster General, as its president. Its purpose was to establish a positive image for the film industry.

In 1927, the year the first "talkie" was released, the film industry came under even more attacks. "Silent smut had been bad, vocal smut cried to the censors for vengeance," wrote the Rev. Daniel Lord, a Catholic priest who led a legion of Catholic religious leaders who demanded a prohibition against what they believed was rampant immorality in the film industry.

In response to increased attacks by organized religion and even more fearful of governmental regulation, the industry created a self-censorship code, primarily written by Lord.

The Motion Picture Production Code itemized restrictions in the areas of language, sexual suggestiveness, and crime. Among its 36 points, it also prohibited any attacks upon religion or depiction of mixed-race relations. Will Hays convinced the studios that acceptance of a self-regulating code would be the best way to avoid governmental interference and a ban on films by religious leaders. The industry adopted the code in 1930, but, there was little enforcement. Three years later, the Catholic Legion of Decency (later renamed the National Legion of Decency) imposed its set of standards, a rating system onto every film produced in Hollywood. (A= Morally unobjectionable; B =Morally objectionable in part; C = Condemned. The "A" ratings were subdivided into four categories, with A-IV being suitable only for adults, but with reservations.)

In 1934, the studios, having come under increased attack, hired Joe Breen, which PBS later called "a strict Catholic moralist from Philadelphia," to oversee the movie industry's Production Code Administration (PCA). "The vulgar, the cheap, and the tawdry is out," declared Breen, emphasizing, "There is no room on the screen at any time for pictures which offend against common decency." The new code required that no film ever "lower the moral standards of those who see it." The PCA had authority not only to force script changes, but to fine any theater up to $25,000 if it showed a film without the PCA approval.

The threat of governmental incursion into film content ended in 1952 when the Supreme Court essentially reversed itself and ruled that films were protected by the First Amendment. [*Burstyn v. Wilson*]. However, that decision, which should have given broader First Amendment rights to the film industry, had little immediate effect. The nation was embroiled by a witch hunt by politicians, businesses, and Americans who claimed they were the true patriots, to root out and destroy all perceived Communistic influence in the entertainment industry. In their rabid quest to label any dissident as a "Communist," and to achieve what they mistakenly believed was for purity in Hollywood, the harpies of the House Un-American Activities Committee (HUAC), destroyed careers of some of the nation's leading citizens, as well as more than 300 of the best writers, actors, directors, and producers, most of whom had little or no connection to the Communist party, all of whom were subjected to unconstitutional attacks upon their rights of free speech and free assembly.

In 1954, on the top-rated "See It Now," journalist Edward R. Murrow and producer Fred Friendly used film footage of Sen. Joseph McCarthy's own tactics and words to allow Americans see how vicious and unconstitutional the attacks had been. An overwhelming public reaction against HUAC and the McCarthy tactics led to a partial collapse of what became known as the McCarthy Witch Hunts. Although Congress continued HUAC until 1975, by 1955 the attacks upon the entertainment industry had begun to wane, and the *Burstyn v. Wilson* decision three years earlier finally led to disintegration of religious-based film censorship, and an increase in artistic freedom. In 1959, former president Harry Truman called the committee and its continued tactics, the "most un-American thing in the country today."

In November 1968, with politicians and numerous consumer groups increasing their attacks about violence, sexual content, and excessive use of what they called "filthy language," the Motion Picture Association of America (MPAA) and the National Association of Theater Owners (NATO) established a voluntary ratings system. Unlike the Motion Picture Production Code, the new ratings system wasn't prescriptive—it didn't establish standards and rules of what producers couldn't do. This newer, more liberal, code was descriptive—each film

238

would be submitted to a ratings board, which would determine to which public group the film was intended. The Legion of Decency ratings of A-1, A-II, A-III, and A-IV, B, and C, were modified to G (suitable for all audiences), M (mature), R (restricted to those under 17 who were accompanied by an adult), and X (forbidden to all except adults). The rating of M eventually became PG (parental guidance), X became NC-17, and PG-13 (restricted to persons over 13 years old) was added. No film was condemned. In 1978, the Legion of Decency combined its own B and C ratings to O (objectionable.)

The purpose of the newer code, said Jack Valenti, MPAA president, was to give "advance cautionary warnings to parents so that parents could make the decision about the movie-going of their young children." The reason for the newer code, said Valenti, was because:

> It was plain that the old system of self-regulation, begun with the formation of the MPAA in 1922, had broken down. What few threads there were holding together the structure created by Will Hays, one of my two predecessors, had now snapped. From the very first day of my own succession to the MPAA President's office [in May 1966], I had sniffed the Production Code constructed by the Hays Office. There was about this stern, forbidding catalogue of "Dos and Don'ts" the odious smell of censorship. I determined to junk it at the first opportune moment.
>
> By summer of 1966, the national scene was marked by insurrection on the campus, riots in the streets, rise in women's liberation, protest of the young, doubts about the institution of marriage, abandonment of old guiding slogans, and the crumbling of social traditions. It would have been foolish to believe that movies, that most creative of art forms, could have remained unaffected by the change and torment in our society.
>
> The result of all this was the emergence of a "new kind" of American movie—frank and open, and made by filmmakers subject to very few self-imposed restraints.

With several minor modifications, the movie code became a model that led to ratings codes for television, DVDs, and CDs. A few years after the movie code, producers of direct-to-video films and films intended only for adults established the Film Advisory Board with six separate ratings.

By the late 1990s, the television networks and the newly-emerging video games market figured out if they didn't do anything about gratuitous sex, violence, and obscene language, then Congress would. Justification for government interference was the reality that because the airwaves are public, a base for the formation of what became the Federal Communications Commission, the FCC could regulate content to meet the "public interest convenience, and necessity." Thus, the First Amendment, seen as an absolute right by the print media and by the film industry, was not seen as absolute when applied to radio or television, The solution, the television industry believed, to additional governmental regulation were labels and a chip.

In 1997, the TV networks, spurred by Congress and the FCC, established a system of labels, with specific labeling of age maturity, sexual content, graphic violence, and profanity. Exempt from labels are sports and news. The ratings icon appears in the upper left corner of the TV screen for the first 15 seconds of every half-hour program; for programs longer than a half-hour, the icon appears for 15 seconds at the beginning of each half-hour of that program.

The "V-chip," placed into every television set manufactured after 2000 allows individuals to block certain programs. However, the FCC says the TV networks inconsistent in their voluntary ratings and often "underlabel" a show, and the V-chips are rarely used by parents to block programs.

Of course, we are carefully assured by the networks—whose cash crop on Saturday mornings is toy companies—that all the current TV shows are so peaceful and respectful of human life that none qualify for the label that dictates "violence ahead."

Mary Elizabeth ("Tipper") Gore, the wife of future vice-president Al Gore Jr., with three other prominent wives of politicians, formed the Parents Music Resource Center in May 1985. By August, their high profile and intense lobbying activities got 19 record producers to put labels on albums. A month later, Congress held hearings. In November, all members of the Recording Industry Association of America (RIAA) agreed to put advisory labels on CDs and records. Like the labels established by the film industry, these labels were merely descriptive. However, several chain stoeres (including Walmart) refused to carry any record or CD with a warning label.

Even with labels, the entertainment industry figured out

how to attract younger audiences while pretending to care about their "psychological" development.

The Federal Trade Commission, in a July 2004 report, pointed out:

> The studios continue to advertise violent, R-rated films and DVDs on TV programs with large teen viewership. . . . In addition, some studios have conducted promotions for R-rated films in venues likely to attract significant numbers of young teens, an apparent resurgence of a practice that previously had decreased. . . . [DVD retailers] sold R-rated DVDs to 81% of teen shoppers seeking to buy them.

The FTC also found that most of the major artist CDs that carried warning labels about explicit content, including violence, targeted those under 17. Of 118 electronic games the FTC reviewed that carried a "Mature" label, about 70 percent put those under 17 in their sights, with marketing plans for about half of the games specifically directed to those under 17.

The music industry, reported the FTC in 2004, "has substantially curtailed advertising in print media popular with teens but continues to place ads on television shows with substantial teen audiences." The labels, whether on music, video games, or films, are like light to moths; R-rated movies are the ones with the gratuitous sex scenes, filthy language, and excessive violence. Because they are "forbidden," they are the ones to be heard, played, or viewed by pubescent teens.

Pornography in Congress

I'm guilty. I did it. I'm not sorry. And, under no condition do I intend to apologize.

In 1996, I was a co-conspirator in a plot to subvert the federal government, including Congress and the President. Joe Shea, editor of the *American Reporter*, of which I was corresponding editor, decided that the Communications Decency Act (CDA) was both immoral and unconstitutional. In trying to stop pornography, Congress had written an act that would have also blocked on the Internet discussion of significant political and social issues, including AIDS, abortion, and teenage pregnancy. It would have also restricted discussions among support groups for victims of rape and sexual abuse; even dozens of classics of literature would have been banned from the Internet if they included language the government didn't think "appropriate."

Shea decided to challenge the proposed Act by publishing a fiery polemic about the issues of free speech—you know, the concept that Jefferson and the Founding Fathers believed to be the backbone of our new country, but which almost everyone has tried to tear pieces from at one time or another. He secured Steve Russell, professor of constitutional law at the University of Texas, and former presiding judge of the Austin, Texas, Municipal court, to write the expletive-included article richly laced with dozens of obscene four-letter words aimed at the Congress.

"We deliberately used indecent language to argue a political case," says Shea. "I was kinda scared," he adds, "I was violating a law endorsed by 86 members of the Senate and almost all of the House, and which had most law enforcement agencies behind it." He says he knew he and his editors could have been arrested the moment he hit the "SEND" button. Penalties could be two years in prison and a $100,000 fine. None of us withdrew our names from the masthead.

Judge Russell's story ran on Feb. 9, 1996, the day President Bill Clinton signed the legislation. Three months later, *Harper's Magazine* ran a condensed version of Judge Russell's article. Harper's was safe from prosecution; it was a print medium; the law applied only to publication on the Internet, something that would have been impossible to enforce anyhow. By now, *Shea v. Reno* and companion suits filed by the American Civil Liberties Union had begun their paths to the Supreme Court. On a rare 9–0 vote, the Supreme Court in 1997 affirmed lower court decisions that the CDA was unconstitutional.

Slightly more than two years after haughtily declaring it knew what was best for the people—and that violating the First Amendment was in our best interest—Congress, always with its finger in the air, put onto the Internet the voyeuristic and vindictive Starr Report that told America in explicit detail the sexual affairs of President Clinton. Without question, the Starr Report was "arguably indecent," as the Federal District Court in New York once termed Judge Russell's article. (Hipocrisy)

Not defeated, Congress tried another tactic. Its intent, other than to pander to public sensibilities, was to protect children from harmful content, including pornographic pictures and, possibly, the lures of pedophiles. The Children's Internet Protection Act (CIPA) required libraries to install filters on all pub-

242

lic computers in order to receive federal funding. But, the Act was too broad and unconstitutional, according to a federal appeals court in May 2002. The court ruled that the filters not only blocked Constitutionally-protected speech, but weren't effective in restricting pornography, which is not protected by the First Amendment. The Court determined there were far better and more effective ways to restrict obscene and pornographic content than the use of filters on Internet-connected public computers. "Filters provide a false sense of security that children are protected when they are not," said John W. Berry, president of the American Library Association. "The issue of protecting children online is complex," said Berry in response to the Court's ruling, "and it requires complex solutions with parents, librarians, and community members working together."

As hypocritical as is the Congress, as loathsome as is the obscenity-filled Starr Report, both are protected under our libertarian philosophy. Because of a libertarian belief in free expression, and a unanimous Supreme Court ruling, Congress could use the Internet to present to the people the Starr Report as well as the videotape of the President's supposedly-secret testimony to the Grand Jury; the White House could issue its rebuttals; and people throughout the world could participate in a vast and sometimes "indecent" public discussion.

Of Matrons and Movies

Three middle-aged women, inhibited but longing to find out what the new morality was all about, snuck out of their homes early one afternoon and went to a movie.

The movie was shot in Sweden, but the subtitles were in English. Not many in the audience, other than the three ladies and a small group of cinema students, really cared what the subtitles said.

"They didn't tell us it was a foreign film," protested the first lady.

"I think they're talking Danish. You know how the Danes are," explained the second lady.

The third lady just giggled.

The movie was about a young girl who believed she was frigid. A rather frightening experience for a 14-year-old. So, she went to a psychologist for help. Soon, the psychologist and the

243

girl were in bed together.

"Horrible!" cried out the first woman.

"Disgusting!" protested the second woman.

The third woman just giggled.

The girl, "searching to find herself," traveled to Germany where she met a young student. The two of them did a lot of studying together.

"It's the Supreme Court and its radical rules!" declared the first woman.

"It should have been banned!" declared the second woman.

The third woman didn't declare anything. She was too busy watching the action on the screen.

However, this was a well-filmed movie with good color and adequate acting. By Supreme Court standards, it was "socially redeeming."

In Italy, the young girl met a fisherman; in Spain, she met a poet and a prostitute.

"I won't let my family see this!" huffed the first woman loud enough to disturb the other 18 movie watchers.

"Totally shameful," huffed the second woman.

The third woman huffed nothing. It's hard to huff when you're giggling.

After Spain came France. By now, the young girl had an armful of books she had collected throughout the continent. She had collected the works of Heine, the *Story of Raphael,* and a libretto from *Faust.*

"See! She's adding to her collection of dirty books," snickered the first woman.

In France, there was a vulgar show in a respectable-looking nightclub. The young girl became ill when two women wrestlers began rolling around in the mud. But when the young girl left, she accidentally ran into the city's most notorious district. Frightened, she ran until she bumped into a well-dressed, respectable looking, well-mannered gentleman who offered to take her away from the sordid life. They left in his Rolls-Royce.

"He'll save her!" joyfully proclaimed the first woman.

"He's so respectable. Maybe that's the message," happily proclaimed the second woman.

The third woman was having trouble controlling her nervous giggles.

The man was a sadomasochist. Looks are deceiving.

"Shocking!" cried out the first woman.

"Disgusting!" cried out the second woman.

The third woman just—*yeah*—giggled.

But the first woman who said "Shocking!" and the second woman who said "Disgusting!" and the third woman who giggled stayed until the end of the film.

Later, the woman who giggled her way through the girl's European adventures led a citizen's protest against what she thought were pornographic videos at a store in Waterloo, Iowa.

An Obscene Story

Throughout the country, people are creating barriers to what they believe is obscene, trying to ban everything from rap records and music videos to works of literature, newspaper columns, and museum art. Even the courts have become involved, changing definitions as quickly as chorus girls change costumes.

By the time the recent flurry in I-am-so-*shocked* legislation and prosecution slowed down, Sidney Thornacre, a mild-mannered stock clerk from Driven Snow, Iowa, was President of the United States, elected without opposition and on a 1–0 vote. It was 1–0 in the popular vote and 1–0 in the electoral college, the first time that anyone was elected president unanimously. How President Thornacre was elected is an inspiration.

It all began when the Driven Snow city council decided there had to be laws against obscenity. But the Supreme Court had long ago determined that for laws to be fair, they had to be spelled out in painstakingly exact detail. The Supreme Court ruled it wasn't good enough just to say that obscenity was bad, the laws had to specify just what was bad.

So, the City Council read the appropriate books and magazines, watched the appropriate television shows and movies, looked into the Internet, and spelled out a series of ordinances so explicit they even made Hugh Hefner blush.

Naturally, the laws themselves were obscene and all members of the city council were sent to jail for having written them. After all, whoever is a part of obscenity must be punished. And that's how the district attorney and his entire staff, who first read the ordinances to determine what it was they were prosecuting, were themselves then prosecuted and sent to jail.

One after another, the prosecutors became the prosecuted. Although many recognized what would ultimately happen, they had a duty to perform. After prosecuting the guilty for reading the obscenity statutes, they and the jurors willingly accepted their own prosecution. America's sense of family values had to be preserved. Soon, the entire population of Driven Snow was in jail, victims of rampant obscenity.

From Driven Snow, it spread to every village, town, city, state, and into the nation's capital. The president of the United States, hoping to stop the problem, read the ordinance, admitted guilt, and then resigned, leaving the country without a president or government—the Congress had been among the first ones to read the ordinance.

And that's how Sidney Thornacre—the only person in the country who never voted; never read a newspaper, magazine, or book; never watched TV, went to the movies, or used his computer for anything other than to play games; or read any obscene ordinances—on Election Day blundered into the White House to apply for an open position as a custodian—and found himself in charge of a mansion and a country. On that fateful day, he alone drove back to his home and to his precinct polling place where he was precinct captain, judge, poll watcher, and election counter—and cast his lone vote. Then, he made that vote official by going back to the nation's capital. As the country's only member of the Electoral College who had not read the ordinance, he cast a unanimous vote for himself for president.

On a wall in the Oval Office, Sidney Thornacre—president of the United States, commander-in-chief of the Armed Forces, secretary and staff of all the cabinet departments, chief justice of the United States, lone member of Congress and White House janitor—has a framed copy of the anti-obscenity ordinance—with appropriate sections blacked out.

"R"ating the Movies

The most hyped film of the summer of 1999 was Stanley Kubrick's 13th and last film, *Eyes Wide Shut*. It may have been a brilliant film, but we'll never know because most of the audience was lured to the theater not to see great writing, directing, or acting, but Tom Cruise and Nicole Kidman naked.

Eyes Wide Shut originally received an NC-17 rating because there was, said the visually-enraptured raters of the Motion Picture Academy of America, too much nudity. To earn an "R" rating, Kubrick digitally inserted actors and props to block certain actions in the much-reported orgy scene.

The hypocrisy of Hollywood's Suits-for-Brains, few of whom were ever part of the creative process, has decreed that most movies should have some sexual suggestion. Many films have nude scenes, even when there's no logical reason. The illogical reason, of course, is to lure teenagers, who comprise the largest segment of the box office, into "R"-rated films. But, there can't be too much nudity, otherwise people will think it's pandering, something Hollywood does with every blink of an eye, but never admits.

In prudish America, nudity is regulated. In England and most of Europe, nudity is accepted on stage and screen. In those countries, however, the depiction of violence is censored.

The opening scenes of the violence-drenched *The Wild Wild West* (1999), which opened about the same time as *Eyes Wide Shut*, showed a high-tech flying decapitation device, its victim, and what happens when the two meet. The rest of the $100 million bomb was a tribute not to acting, directing, or story, but to banal sexual innuendo and high-tech special effects. For 107 tedious minutes, we were exposed to a variety of digitally-enhanced shootings, hangings, and stabbings, and a hero who is aptly described as someone whose philosophy is to "shoot first, shoot later, shoot some more, and when everyone's dead, ask a few questions." The best actor was an 80-foot tall mechanical tarantula that spit flame balls into towns as wooden as the actors' lines. But, for all its violence, the movie was rated only PG-13 for audiences in a country in which violence is the leading cash crop.

The Summer surprise hit of 1999 wasn't a $100 million film with $10 million stars, washed by a $20 million publicity package, but an 87-minute mockumentary psycho-horror film shot on an initial $60,000 budget. *The Blair Witch Project* was a brilliantly-conceived film by 30-year-old Eduardo Sanchez, a Cuban refugee, and 35-year-old Daniel Myrick. Both were novice filmmakers from Florida. Relatively unknown actors Heather Donahue, Joshua Leonard, and Michael Williams doubled as cinematographers to add authenticity to the fake documentary. As the great writers and directors know, and which was in evidence throughout *The Blair Witch Project*, but which most filmmakers and studio executives fail to understand, is that terror is more effective when it isn't graphically portrayed with blood and guts on screen. *The Blair Witch Project*, which doesn't have digital animation, works because of good storytelling and acting. The movie swept the Sundance and Cannes film festivals, got heavy discussion on the Internet, attracted a major distributor, and was booked nationwide, fueled by something unique in the film industry—raw talent.

There is no nudity, sexual suggestion, or graphic depiction of violence in *The Blair Witch Project*. However, it was rated "R" because of the use of a four-letter word and its variations realistically spread throughout the "documentarians'" language.

Let's imagine two scenes. At the end of a dark alley is a Rambo-like demented skinhead with Nazi symbols and "White Pride" carved onto his arms, a MAK-10 assault rifle in one hand, a TEC-9 held in the other, a foot-long knife sheathed onto his belt, extra clips stuffed into oversized pockets, and a dozen grenades and a few hundred more rounds of ammo in a duffel bag slung across his shoulder. Same scene. Different movie. A naked woman in that same darkened alley yells, "Fuck you!" Our movie raters want us to believe we need to fear nudity and "dirty words" more than violent psychos.

A Scary Movie

At the Bloomsburg, Pa., Cinema Center, a family of four—mother, father, and two elementary school children—decided to see *Scary Movie*, an 88-minute hilarious spoof of teen-slasher sexploitation horror films. The family could have chosen any of 11 other films, including four that were rated "G" or "PG" or even three PG-13 films, but they chose the raunchy R-rated *Scary Movie* on its first evening of general release in the Summer of 2000.

On the front door of the 12-screen multiplex are one-paragraph typeset summaries of the films. This one warned customers that the *Scary Movie* rating was based upon "strong crude sexual humor, language, drug use, and violence."

Rick Wenner, senior projectionist, said he also warned the family the film wasn't suitable for children. But they decided to see it anyhow. Ratings are only "suggestions," enforcement voluntary.

Directed by Keenan Ivory Wayans, whose cutting-edge comedy, "In Living Color," broke numerous TV conventions, *Scary Movie* satirizes *Scream, Halloween, The Blair Witch Project, The*

Matrix, innumerable sexploitation slasher films, teenage sex comedies, and tosses in frequent bursts at society's establishment conventions.

Set at B.A. Corpse High School, where the students all appear to be in their 20s and 30s, the movie opened with a combination of bathroom humor (the future victim passes gas), racial stereotypes (actress Carmen Electra, once married to basketball superstar Dennis Rodman, tells the wanna-be psycho killer, "My boyfriend's Black and he's gonna kick your ass."), nudity (the victim, in a skimpy nothing-there bra and panties, flees slo-mo through sprinklers) and violence mixed with a double-take joke (the wanna-be killer stabs his victim in the breast, only to pull out a silicone implant.) The rest of the movie was a series of grossed-out scenes connected by the thinnest of plot lines—not unlike the movies it parodied.

During the past century, Hollywood has changed its target audiences several times. The current *object d'greed* are teens, who are less than 20 percent of the nation's population, but spent more than half of the $9.8 billion ticket revenue theaters collected in 2008.

When most theaters were in downtowns, America's children could hang out with friends, shop, and see a movie. Today, with most of the nation's 39,000 screens at the air conditioned and tiled downtowns known as shopping malls, America's children still hang out with friends, shop for clothes and CDs, and watch a movie. It's just as convenient now, as then, for parents to drop off their children, and get four or five hours of freedom. But now, there's as many as 24 screens in one place. The bubble-gum-and-skateboard crowd, their pants hung low and caps turned backward, may say they plan to watch the PG or PG-13 film, but sneak into the R-rated films faster than the flicker of a celluloid frame going past the projection lamp.

At the Bloomsburg multiplex, the family of four watched every titillating scene that mocked and exaggerated the studios' need to include violence, sex-and-toilet humor, crude language, and nudity to arouse the "we are cool" cookie-crumbler generation. Before she left the theater, the mother told the senior projectionist, "You were right, it was pretty vulgar," but then offhandedly noted, "Well, they see worse than that on Home Box."

This wasn't an isolated case. Hundreds of teens and pre-teens saw the movie in rural Bloomsburg. Millions more watched it at more than 2,900 screens nationwide. *Scary Movie,* shot for about $20 million, brought in $42.5 million in its opening week, well ahead of *The Perfect Storm* in its second week, *The Patriot* in its third week, and Disney's PG-rated *The Kid*, which also opened that week, but at only $12.7 million. The numbers placed *Scary Movie* as the highest opening gross of any R-rated film in Hollywood history, second largest of any comedy (behind *Austin Powers 2*), and 16th largest overall. The movie topped out at about $100–$110 million, with most of its sales to the 13–21 year-old audience. The movie probably should have carried an NC-17 rating. Rated R suggests that not even the most imaginative producer will easily find content to qualify for an NC-17. So successful was *Scary Movie* that there were two sequels.

Watching nudity, seeing violence, and listening to coarse language will be something all children will be exposed to as they grow up, and which Hollywood studios are more than willing to provide. Watching *Scary Movie* before they're 17 won't emotionally cripple any child. It just removes yet another thin layer of a person's childhood, a layer that is needed so children have the time to be children. And that may be the scariest part of the movie.

Janet Jackson and Nos. 523 and 524: There Are No Half-Time Shows in War

On the day that Justin Timberlake ripped open Janet Jackson's blouse during the half-time of the Super Bowl to reveal part of a bejeweled breast, which created a national firestorm of protest in February 2004, American Soldiers 523 and 524 died in Iraq. Along with the two American soldiers, 14 were wounded. Also that day, two suicide bombers killed more than 100 Kurds and wounded more than 200.

Back in the United States, CBS, which broadcast the game, MTV which produced the half-time show, and Viacom, which owns both CBS and MTV, said they were shocked and outraged that Timberlake and Jackson would do such a despicable act. The NFL said it was "embarrassed." The two singers claimed the blouse-ripping was the result of a "wardrobe malfunction." The network, of course, said little about the crotch-grabbing rump-slapping other parts of the show.

During the week after the Super Bowl, Americans sent more than 200,000 complaints to the FCC; it was almost as many as all the complaints for all alleged violations the previous year. FCC Chair Michael Powell, calling the half-time spectacle "deplorable," quickly launched the full resources of the FCC to investigate Jackson's breast, which had been exposed on network television for exactly nine-sixteenths of a second. Congressmen and senators groped prime time audiences to express their outrage against indecency on television, and demanded higher fines for flashing. The nation's newspapers gave the story its front page, ran sidebars inside, and continued the story for days. TV news, talk, and entertainment shows constantly rebroadcast the offending salacious breast-baring, the flesh now pixilated or blurred. The half-time story became the most popular search topic on the internet; the clip, often bootlegged, became the most downloaded one in the internet's history.

On TV network news and in fictionalized prime-time series, we see violence and body parts on the street. On the afternoon soaps are every violation of the Ten Commandments, and a few violations that not even the residents of Sodom and Gomorrah knew about. But, this didn't draw the ire of the sanctimonious "family values" public. A nipple-covered bare breast did.

Ratings draw advertising, which is what runs the nation's media. With 90 million Super Bowl viewers, CBS could command $2.3 million per 30-second commercial, many of which pre-pubescent teens would say was a combination of "cool" and "gross." But, there isn't much return on investment for stories of substance. Let's take a look at some other stories that don't cause much public outrage or get even a fraction of the media coverage.

The nation's unemployment rate the month of the Super Bowl was 5.6 percent, with most of the 8.3 million unemployed having been laid off or outsourced. Even the 8.3 million figure presented by the Department of Labor was much lower than the reality. By government standards, anyone working at least one hour a week is considered to be employed. The statistics also don't consider that thousands of companies hire workers for only 30–35 hours a week in order to avoid having to pay benefits, or that hundreds of thousands of jobs are filled by persons who once worked at other companies for better benefits and higher pay before being laid off, or that about 300,000 Ameri-

251

cans, after months of unemployment, have just given up and, thus, aren't counted. Where is the massive national outrage?

More than 46 million Americans don't have health coverage; about 250,000 persons are chronically homeless, another three million are homeless at any one time; the huge national deficit may force a cut-back in social security benefits. Those stories never received the news coverage that Janet Jackson's bare breast received.

Per-pupil spending in the public schools declined by more than four percent in the two years before the Bare Breast Halftime. But the news media didn't focus on that, and 200,000 people didn't write the government to protest. Nor did 200,000 persons protest war-profiteering by Halliburton, Dick Cheney's former company, which still pays him a six-figure annual income.

There is less spending for the environment, but the only ones who seem to care might be spotted owls, people whom are derisively call "tree huggers," and some "alarmists" who think hazardous materials in the water and air may not be the latest fad diet. But, the media, if they even noticed, ran only small stories in their "B" sections.

The deaths of the Americans and Kurds were blocked from the front page banner headlines by the scandal of a semi-naked nipple at a football game. Because of the media exploitation, because politicians saw a chance to rant against indecency while mounting their own adulterous affairs, and because 200,000 Americans protested one second on network television, there was a crisis, and the full resources of the federal government were mobilized to handle it. In May 2006, the FCC declared it wouldn't reduce the $550,000 fine against CBS—$27,500 for each of the 20 network owned-and-operated (O+O) stations. The following month, President Bush signed into law a Congressional bill increasing the maximum fine for on-air obscenity to $325,000 per incident. Had that law been in place during the Super Bowl nipple-bare, CBS could have been fined $6.5 million. Arguably, since the FCC could have fined each CBS station, not just those owned and operated by the network but also affiliates as well, under the new law CBS could have been fined as much as $73.8 million for a one-second "wardrobe malfunction." In July 2008, a federal appeals court overturned the FCC fine, citing it as arbitrary and capricious. The FCC four months later appealed that decision to the Supreme Court, which vacated the decision in May 2009 and ordered the 3rd

Circuit Court of Appeals in Philadelphia to give the issue "further consideration."

Almost every American knows who Justin Timberlake and Janet Jackson are. Because of the media, and a vast ubiquitous publicity machine, we know the names and lives of the "American Idol," the "Apprentice," and dozens of celebrities, wannabe's, and the "stars" of 60 hours of "reality TV" each week. Only a few know the names of PFC Armando Soriano and Staff Sgt. Roger C. Turner Jr., the two Americans killed in Iraq the same afternoon as a half-time show.

LABOR, BUSINESS, AND ECONOMICS

'We're Management; We Don't Have to Tell You Anything'

Shirley Collins sat in a nondescript office, facing the editor of the *Globe-Times* of Bethlehem, Pa. Nearby sat an outside consultant and an attorney from Chicago. We're re-structuring the newspaper, said the editor, reading from a prepared script; your work is unsatisfactory, he claimed; you're being terminated, he emphasized.

In the seven years she had been at the newspaper as feature news editor, Shirley Collins had never received a formal evaluation from any of her supervisors, although she did receive several awards, the most recent being second place for lifestyle sections in the annual Keystone awards contest of the Pennsylvania Newspaper Publishers Association.

But, the well-rehearsed script the company provided its participants April 5, 1988, didn't allow the editor to give individual evaluations the day of her firing. Nor was it likely they would.

On the day she was fired, Shirley Collins sat there and listened to an editor claim that her work was "unsatisfactory." We have an agreement, the editor read, explaining that if she signed the eight-page agreement and resigned rather than be fired, she would receive "extra benefits," including about one week of severance pay for each year worked, continuation of health and life insurance benefits for a limited time and, if eligible, be able to collect all pension benefits due.

Of course, there were a few "tradeoffs" in order for Collins to receive all these "extra benefits"—she would have to agree to

253

give up many of her rights. For one year, she would be forbidden, without *Globe-Times* consent, to associate in any way with any newspaper or magazine publishing company or any radio or television station that broadcast news programs within 25 miles of the *Globe-Times;* for two years, she would not be allowed to associate with the Times Mirror Co., publisher of the competing Allentown *Morning Call,* or Thomson Newspapers, Inc., publisher of the nearby *Easton Express.* Not only couldn't she work for those organizations, she couldn't even deliver newspapers for them or rent an apartment if the owner was one of the forbidden companies.

Among other rights she would have lost had she signed the agreement, she would have had to agree to never disclose the contents of the termination agreement, except to immediate family and her attorney; she would have had to "cooperate with and assist the *Globe-Times* in any investigations, proceedings, or actions" relating to her employment or "to any matter in which I was involved or of which I had knowledge of while an employee of, or a consultant for, the *Globe-Times";* she would have had to pay all costs and expenses incurred by the company should it bring any charges against her for violation of the agreement, or should she bring any charges against the company "relative [to] any such action, proceeding, claim or charge."

And then there was Paragraph 6 which deleted her statutory and Constitutional rights, including the right to bring charges against the company for violations of Title VII of the Civil Rights Act, the Age Discrimination in Employment Act of 1967, the Fair Labor Standards Act, the National Labor Relations Act, and the Pennsylvania Human Relations Act.

Shirley Collins refused to sign the agreement. She was again urged to consider the many "extra benefits" she would get from signing, and was told that Management was sorry that she chose not to take advantage of those fine benefits. She didn't know why she was being fired. She was a 55-year-old woman, with a master's degree in library science, and another master's degree in journalism from Columbia University, which she had earned shortly before she was hired at the *Globe-Times*—and now she was unemployed.

By the end of the day, more than two-dozen employees would be fired, including more than 40 percent of the editorial staff. By the end of the year, there would be several resignations, and more than 50 would have been fired; about two-thirds of the editorial staff would have been fired or left voluntarily as Management shuffled personnel, trying to find what it believed was the right combination to bring the newspaper out of a financial tailspin brought about when circulation plummeted from 39,572 in March 1981 to 21,702 in March 1988.

In an industry of one-newspaper towns, the *Globe-Times,* at one point one of the nation's better smaller newspapers, should have had its own comfortable monopoly. But in the 1980s, like most newspapers, it hadn't effectively planned how to compete with a regional daily, alternative sources of advertising, a recession, a population shift to morning newspapers, a reduction in the reading habits of most Americans, and a demographic time bomb that exploded when the advertising industry increased its emphasis on quality numbers rather than mere quantity.

The *Globe-Times* solution was a massive restructuring, focusing on image and a misguided effort to promote what it thought was "community journalism" at the expense of the hard news stories readers needed. Two months before the purge, the newspaper had fired Mary Wagner, a 21-year employee who was one of the better police reporters in America. Management later claimed she was fired because she was a poor writer who committed errors and wasn't a "team player," charges completely unsubstantiated. When the staff, shaken by her firing, asked the editor why Wagner was fired, he coldly replied to two of their representatives, "We're Management. We don't have to tell you anything." Later, Management admitted it had fired Wagner because she spoke out against what she, and most of the editorial staff, saw as a deterioration in quality, and because Wagner had begun to figure out what Management was planning.

But the problems Wagner pointed out, and typical of what was happening to newspapers during the last two decades of the 20th century and the first decade of the 21st century, became apparent with the one-day purge. Many of those fired were in their 40s and 50s, had worked at the newspaper two or more decades, and were arguably among the better workers in the industry. The purge left the newsroom decimated, stories uncovered, "happy news" filling the front page, and the readers wondering why they should even subscribe anymore.

Most of the staff who remained were uncertain of the direction the newspaper was taking—or even if they would have jobs the next week. By the end of 1989, even the editor who had fired Mary Wagner, Shirley Collins, and more than a dozen other reporters was gone.

Less than two years later, on November 4, 1991, the *Globe-Times*—its circulation below 19,000, its credibility shot—was merged into the competing *Easton Express.*

Pennsylvania law, like that of most states, gives private-sector employers in non-union operations the right to hire and fire "at will." The "employment at will doctrine," with very few exceptions, essentially states that private sector non-unionized employees are at the mercy of the employer. The concept is that the Management may fire an employee "for good cause, for no cause, or even for cause morally wrong." [*Payne v. Western & Atlantic RR,* Tennessee, 1884.] The United States is the only major industrial democracy that does not have federal legislation prohibiting unfair discharge. About 16.1 million Americans work under collective bargaining agreements; 112 million do not, according to data from the Bureau of Labor Statistics.

Most employees believe employers have a right to hire and fire "at will," not knowing that employment in much of the public sector and on unionized newspapers, magazines, radio, or television stations and networks gives the worker innumerable benefits and rights, including the right to be fired only for "just cause."

If the story of the *Globe-Times* had applied only to one newspaper at only one particular time in history, it could easily be dismissed as unique in American journalism. Journalists and the public could look over the events, argue about them, perhaps sympathize with the workers who were fired or with Management that said it needed to make changes to regain financial stability. Perhaps many might even think that some of the employees deserved to be fired; perhaps some would think that Management was morally and ethically wrong in how and why it fired many of the staff.

However, the issues aren't of personalities or events, or even in Management's decisions that led to the crisis or its efforts to recover. The issues are universal in American labor and in the newspaper industry, but more so when members of the editorial staff must carry the burden of loyalty to their profession and the community against loyalty to the corporation that pays their salaries, knowing they could be reprimanded, demoted, or fired at any time for any reason.

Had there been a union at the *Globe-Times,* the employees

would have been able to take advantage of well-established multi-step grievance procedures detailed in the collective bargaining agreement, including the right to go to binding arbitration in the case of termination or arbitrary job changes. In the United States, about one half the union-protected workers whose cases go to binding arbitration are restored to their jobs, often with back pay. The collective bargaining agreement would also have detailed specific agreements with respect to promotion, termination, restructuring, or a layoff. Further, the employees would have been protected by state and federal labor codes.

Without union representation, the workers had yielded equity to Management which has the money and resources to bring in consultants and attorneys to keep former employees, most of whom can't afford $150–$400 an hour lawyer fees, from mounting a significant legal challenge.

But there is still a "stigma" within the journalism profession about being a union member. "It's OK for blue-collar workers," goes the refrain, "but we're professionals." Perhaps one day, the professionals will realize that in the United States, the division by traditional class—lower, middle, upper—is no longer viable, and there truly has been a division along lines of the under-class, the workers, and the management; journalists must again recognize that they have far more in common with the coal miner than they have with the CEO.

The tragedy that is partially shared by the *Globe-Times* is not only the failure of newspapers to understand their audiences and the principles of journalism, but also of society to adequately protect all its workers.

An Hour a Day

It's dark and lonely at 5 a.m. on the 51 miles of roads between Bloomsburg and McAdoo in rural northeastern Pennsylvania. But, Bloomsburg is home, and McAdoo is where the Consolidated Cigar Corp. is, and that's where Jack W. Smith works. From 6:45 a.m. to 3:45 p.m. Almost every day, Mondays through Fridays, and occasionally Saturdays.

He says he'd move closer to his job, but he's hoping he won't have to work there much longer. He would like something better, but it's a job, and in this economy it's the only thing he can get. The job calls for him to take 300-pound rolls of paper and slit them into sizes to wrap tobacco. It was tough at first. His back and arms ached, and he suffered innumerable cuts. It's not easy when you're 54 years old and have never worked so hard in your life at physical labor.

"I'm one of the hardest working people they have," Smith proudly says, pauses a moment, and then says, with equal pride, "I'm just so happy to have a job."

For most of his adult life, he was employed. For four years, he was a cook in the Navy's submarine service. After that, he spent a year selling men's clothing. Then, in 1960, he got a job as a reporter with his hometown newspaper, the *Berwick* (Pa.) *Enterprise,* an 11,000 circulation afternoon daily that merged into a sister publication in the early 1980s.

Jack Smith had never taken a journalism course, hadn't even gone to college, but the editor was willing to try an enthusiastic cub who said he learned quickly and could "find all the news."

During the next 12 years, he proved his words, covering everything from PTA meetings to the police beat, digging out stories that reporters with years of experience and two college degrees couldn't find. And when the editor retired, Jack Smith was the natural replacement, a job he held for six years.

But, after 18 years as a journalist, he was 40 years old, not making a lot of money and had minimal benefits. He also had a wife and three sons. It was time for a new job, one that gave him the freedom he never had.

Taking a second mortgage on his house and everything in savings, he and his wife, Gail, opened a gift store in 1979. In the next few years, they made the business one of the more successful ones in nearby Bloomsburg. So, he did what many businessmen did—he expanded, opening stores in Berwick, about 10 miles away, and in Williamsport, about 40 miles away. It was 1987, the end of the prosperity phase of the Reagan–Bush era and the beginning of a recession. In 1989, he was forced to declare bankruptcy. He lost his house, most of his possessions and, more important, his self-respect. He was 52 years old.

He says he begged his former publisher for a job, but was curtly told there wasn't anything available. Not as a copyboy; not even as a janitor. He took state civil service tests, scoring in the 90s, but was never hired, even for entry-level public information jobs, something even 21-year-olds with a fraction of Smith's knowledge and experience could do. He was the highest scorer in a five-county area for a state social service job, but was never hired. He applied for other jobs, but says in most cases he "never got past the receptionists."

He thought that maybe one of his poker buddies could help him out. After all, they had been friends for several years. But the one who was an executive at a lingerie factory and the one who was partial owner of a carpet mill said there wasn't anything. And the longer Smith was unemployed, the farther they strayed from friendship, and Smith never knew why.

He had no job, his savings was gone, and he had no health insurance. Not many unemployed people can afford almost $5,000 a year for health insurance.

For a few months in 1990, he worked for the Census Bureau, eventually becoming a field supervisor in a five-county area. He got the Bureau's highest evaluations, but the job ended, and he was again unemployed. He was even desperate enough to consider several minimum wage jobs, knowing that an income of $8,840 a year wasn't enough to support one person, let alone a family. Alas, he didn't even get the minimum wage jobs.

Once, he even applied for a job to clean wards in the VA Hospital in Wilkes-Barre, but never got an interview. But that's how he got the job at the cigar factory. The owner of the plant, a friend who thought it would be demeaning to offer a job as a laborer to someone who had been a Navy vet, newspaper editor, and successful businessman, told Smith's wife, "If he's going to wash walls, have him come see me."

So, Jack Smith became the oldest slitter in a cigar company. In six months, he lost 30 pounds as his body wearied under the physical demands of his new job. Yet, he stayed with it, taking all the overtime he could, often working 12-hour days. "When I don't take the overtime," he says, "my check doesn't stretch as it should."

It stretches even less now since his rent was increased 30 percent. "The landlord said she had trouble meeting expenses," Smith says.

The month the rent went up, he began repaying a college loan. He had begun taking college classes, one or two at a time, shortly before his business failed. He had earned 47 credits when he ran out of money.

His wife took part-time jobs and stood by him, although she cried a lot. "My biggest joy is my family," says Smith, himself shedding a small tear when he says "we've become more cohesive the past few years. We're hanging tough together."

259

It's been almost two years now since Jack Smith was first hired as a slitter. It's been four years since his business failed, and society remembers his failure, not his success. He keeps applying for jobs. He keeps getting rejected. He's optimistic about the job he's doing, about his own life, but has lost some of his faith in the country that says it values opportunity, age, experience, and ability. It is something he thinks about five mornings a week as he drives an hour in the dark to get to work as a laborer.

[ADDENDUM—In 1994, Jack Smith began working as a bartender in a Berwick restaurant. Almost two years later, he and Gail opened a small co-op crafts store in a converted church. Then, in 1997, after passing several state examinations, he became an insurance salesman for Prudential, finally retiring in August 2002 as a supervisor. He retired in 2005.]

An Unequal Competition

And so there they were. The two of them. Locked into a professional struggle that neither of them knew about. He was a veteran writer. She was a young college graduate. Both wished to become teachers.

But she had one thing he didn't have. A state credential. She had taken almost two years of education courses. He hadn't.

Normally, he would have been one of the first to be weeded out, but somehow the clerks didn't notice he lacked the state credential. So there he sat. Facing the deputy superintendent of instruction, a man who had state credentials.

"I like your writing," he said, "but I'm afraid that without a general secondary credential we can't hire you. You need several courses. History of Education. The Philosophy of Education. Educational Methods. Thirteen, fourteen in all. Plus student teaching."

"But I want to teach writing, not education," he replied.

"I understand that," said the deputy superintendent, "but we require that every teacher have a mastery of the concepts of education."

"I have a master's in journalism and professional experience," said the applicant. In one long breath-drenched sentence he explained that in addition to having written for newspapers, magazines, and even television, he had a number of awards.

"Isn't that enough?"

"I'm sorry, it isn't enough."

"But I taught creative writing part-time at the university level for the past five years," he protested, pulling from his attaché case summaries of relatively high student evaluations. The deputy superintendent quickly scanned them, then put them aside.

"That doesn't eliminate the requirements. You can't teach in public schools until you learn *how* to teach."

"But I taught!" the writer argued.

"But you haven't taken education courses," said a most petulant deputy superintendent.

"I took two courses," said the writer, "and didn't see anything challenging in either of them." A little steamed, he went so far as to declare that most education courses seemed to be wastes of time. This insolence, of course, upset the deputy superintendent whose mission now was just to get rid of this pest.

"I can't hire you because—"

"Because I don't have a credential! What about the other applicants? Do they have my experience? Or, do they only have your license?"

"The state requires," said the deputy superintendent, his attitude bound by a set of conventional regulations, "that a person have a number of courses in education. As I mentioned earlier, it's important to know *how* to work with students of this age group."

"Doesn't knowledge or ability count?" the writer demanded. But before the deputy superintendent could answer, the writer continued, "In one of your district schools, a guy with a degree in psychology is advising the school newspaper. He doesn't have experience in journalism or creative writing, but he's teaching journalism."

The deputy superintendent coughed and hastily answered, "In that situation I believe he was already on the faculty, but due to a reduction in enrollment in psychology courses, the district either had to lay him off or find him another position."

"So you threw him into journalism."

"We didn't *throw* him anywhere!" snapped the deputy superintendent. "His credential includes teaching English, and he expressed an interest in teaching journalism."

"I have an interest in nuclear physics," the writer said sarcastically. "Of course, I don't know anything about it, but I'm inter-

261

ested in teaching it. I'll even take courses in education so I'll know nuclear physics better. And judging from what I've seen of your students, I could probably teach nuclear physics better than some of your English teachers are teaching writing!"

There was nothing anyone could have done.

And so the young lady with a degree in English who took all the education courses and completed student teaching but never wrote anything that was published, earned a position teaching creative writing and advising the school newspaper, yearbook, and literary magazine.

Occasionally, she mentioned something she learned from a class she took in college. But she never knew that the competition for her job had been her former teacher.

Traded for Two Rookies, an Editorial Clerk, and a Future Draft Choice

Finstermeister was furious. He stomped up to the desk of the city editor and shoved the afternoon edition of the newspaper in his face.

"How dare you!" Finstermeister demanded, his rage filling the news room.

The city editor peered over his stack of press releases, and with embarrassed compassion in his voice said, "Sorry."

"Sorry? Is that all you have to say!?"

"You know how reporters are," said the city editor. "They're a zealous bunch, and sometimes there's no stopping them when they sniff out a story. I was hoping to tell you before it hit the street edition, but . . . well, with all these press releases, I just didn't have time."

"You had time to trade me!" thundered Finstermeister, upset that after 15 years on the *Daily Tribune* he was being traded to the *Morning Bugle* for two rookie reporters, an editorial clerk, and a future draft choice.

"It was in the best interests of journalism," said the city editor.

"The contract requires that with that much seniority, I must be allowed to approve the trade," Finstermeister said smugly. "And, I don't like Maine!"

The city editor reminded him that he waived that right three years earlier in order to get only a six-day week? "It was just after your third child was born and your wife had two cops drag you home so you could also meet your first two children."

"But, Boss, I'm a darned good reporter."

The city editor shook his head sadly. "We don't need an environmental reporter any more. The readers want gossip about the stars. Fashion stories. More about investments and jobs and where to find good meals. Important things like that. We'll just add an occasional assignment to Smogbound's beat."

"But Smogbound covers business, and he's on every lobbyist's freebie list."

"Business. Environment. It's all reporting."

"I can do more than just cover the environment," Finstermeister begged. "My rookie year I led the league in rewrites, obits written under deadline pressure, fire alarms, and garden club parties. Five years later, I was a Pulitzer finalist for that series on hazardous waste dumping!"

"I admit you had some good years with us," said the city editor, "but you're not as young and as aggressive as you once were."

"Two years ago," shouted Finstermeister, "I took the Pulitzer for the series on design flaws and construction blunders on the Bellevane Nuke." Finstermeister was now inches from the city editor's face. "Oil! I did that series that proved Magnum Oil was price-fixing. I wrote about acid rain, the utilities' rate-gouging schemes, sewer run-offs, cloud seeding—"

The city editor cut him off. "Don't you understand? No one cares about the environment anymore."

"I'll learn to make color charts and graphs!" Finstermeister cried out. He paused a moment, and then desperately suggested, "I'll go back to editing the home improvement tabloids."

"You're a star, Fin, and we need to get rid of you while you still have some value. Those 14-hour days are breaking you down. Besides, we're in a recession, and we need to cut expenses."

"I'll take a cut. I don't need $27,000 a year. That's too much for a reporter anyhow."

"That's generous, Fin, but for your salary, we can get a cub reporter, save a few thousand, and still have enough left over for the publisher to reduce the mortgage on his vacation house in the Barbados. Besides, you fit the *Bugle's* needs, and the reporter it's sending us fits ours."

"I was president of the state's Press Club!" Finstermeister blurted out. "Didn't that bring a lot of prestige to the paper?"

"It's the system, Fin. You knew it when you came here."

Finstermeister looked around the newsroom, searching for understanding faces, but all the other eyes were buried in newspapers, hiding from reality. There would be no help from his colleagues today. "What about the readers?" asked Finstermeister. "A lot of people bought the paper because of my reporting."

"A month from now, they'll forget your name. They'll find other heroes. Heck, the way newspapers are going, in a few months they'll even forget we exist."

Sadly, Finstermeister shuffled his feet, resigned to his fate. "When do I report?"

"Take a vacation first and report in three days. The *Bugle* likes its reporters fresh." He paused a moment. "One other thing, turn in your style manual before you leave."

The $6 Million Journalist

The New York Yankees had just bought a first baseman for $180 million. For the next eight years, Mark Teixeira would earn about $22.5 million a season. The week before, the Yankees bought seven years of pitcher CC Sabathia's life for $161 million, about $23 million a season—and five years of A.J. Burnett for $82.5 million, about $16.5 million for each season, according to the Associated Press. None of the salaries included incentive pay or outside endorsements, which add millions to each salary.

The three new pinstriped multimillionaires joined third baseman Alex Rodriguez, who had a 10-year $275 million contract, and shortstop Derek Jeter, whose 10-year $189 million contract ends in 2010. First baseman Jason Giambi, who wasn't with the Yankees in the 2009 season, picked up about $23.4 million during the 2008 season. Although the Bronx Bombers bombed in 2008 and didn't even make the playoffs, they were on the fast track to the World Series of Obscene Salaries. They aren't the only ones in contention.

America pays major league professional athletes far more than even the most efficient long-term factory worker. For the National Football League the minimum wage is $225,000 a year; for Major League Baseball, it's $390,000; for the National

Basketball Association, it's $442,000. Almost every athlete earns far more than the minimum, with most earning seven-figure incomes, plus endorsements worth another 6- or 7-figure income. Leading all athletes is Tiger Woods, whose team of accountants and business managers had to figure out where to put his $128 million earned in 2008. "Only" $23 million was from playing golf; the rest was from endorsements and business deals.

Although about 70 percent of the 120,000 members of the Screen Actors Guild make less than $5,000 a year, A-list movie stars command at least $10 million a picture. Their worth is based not upon acting ability but upon their B.O.—box office, that is. Prime-time network TV stars grab at least $2 million a year. Charlie Sheen leads the list, with a salary of about $825,000 for each 30-minute episode, about $19 million for the 2008–2009 season, according to *TV Guide.*

Super models, whose main talent is to be anorexic and have high cheekbones, are pulling in million dollar salaries, with Giselle Bundchen netting a very gross $33 million in 2009. Kate Moss, Heidi Klum, Alessandra Ambrosio, and Adriana Lima each earned $6–9 million in 2008, just for modeling. Supermodels average about $70,000 a day. That's well above the average annual salary of teachers, social workers, firefighters, and police officers.

Miley Cyrus, who's just 16, raked in $25 million in 2008, about double what the *High School Musical* stars each earned in that year.

If you're a rapper, it's hard to be a part of the 'hood if like 50-Cent you earned $150 million in 2008. Jay-Z, who led the list in 2007, trailed with $82 million. The top 20 rappers each earned at least $10 million, and that's a lot of scrillah fo'shizzle.

Radio talk-mouth Rush Limbaugh has a $400 million eight-year contract that will carry his voice on 600 stations through 2016. Far behind are factually-challenged Sean Hannity with a five-year $100 million contract, and Bill O'Reilly, the bloviator-in-chief, who is cashing a measly $10 million a year.

Oprah Winfrey leads the list of celebrity income—she got about $385 million in 2008. Every TV celebrity judge makes more than the $208,000 that a Supreme Court justice makes. Leading the pack is Judge Judy, whose screechy shouting on TV earns her about $25 million each year.

The president of the United States, even the most incompetent one, earns $400,000. Compare that to the average salary for each of the Fortune 500 CEOs who earns about $13 million a year, about 400 times more than that of the average worker.

But, it's the average worker who is the one who produces America's goods, who helps other Americans. If life was fair, and people were paid what they were worth, there would be only a very small pay gap between bosses and workers. Here's some news I think should be published in the new year, but probably won't be . . .

In an exclusive to KBAD-TV, Avarice K. Toadstool, president of Amalgamated Conglomerate Industries, said he will increase the pay of all line workers to at least $175,000 a year. Toadstool also said his company not only will provide full health coverage and educational expenses, but will assist the workers to unionize. To pay for the increase, Amalgamated will cut executive salaries, quarterly "retreats," and stock dividends.

The federal government today approved the salary cap for all social workers. Although no social worker may now make more than $7.3 million a year, the base for entry-level social workers was raised to $450,000. Not included in the cap are signing bonuses and work-performance incentives. "We believe in the American philosophy of paying employees by what they're worth to the advancement of society," said Hull House director Jane Addams IV, who received a $2.5 million bonus last year for performance in suicide prevention assists, catastrophic disaster relief, and employment reclamation.

The Humane Society today signed Polly Pureheart to a 10-year $104 million contract, largest in history. "Polly's a triple-threat terror, and worth every penny we pay her," said general manager Wolf Greycoat. During a 22-year all-star career, Pureheart is the all-time leader in animal rescue/rehabilitation, arrests for felonious animal cruelty, and lobby influence. Pureheart is personally credited with 1,087 unassisted tackles of recalcitrant legislators.

The *West Wattabago Daily Blab* today signed investigative reporter David Bergman to a three-year $17.4 million contract, plus a $6 million signing bonus. Bergman, who had been the clean-up hitter with the *East Pacoima Tribune* the past four years, was granted free agency status in November. During 2008, Bergman led the league in school board meetings coverage and uncovering local political scandals. For each of the past five years, he was a consistent .300 hitter, averaging at least three successes for every 10 news stories he reported.

In a related story, Phillies pitcher Harry Horsehide became the highest paid player in sports when he signed a three-year contract for $108,000 a year. The new contract will mean general admission ticket prices will rise to about $10, with premium seating at $30, according to Phillies management.

Patriotic Unemployment

I had gone into the Unemployment Office to mine data for a story about the effects of the Recession upon middle-class Americans when Robinson came out, smiling and holding what seemed to be an unemployment check. It was the same Robinson who had worked more than 30 years in one job. Never late to work, never sick. Never promoted or demoted. Never stole; never argued; never complained. Loyal as a puppy.

"Robinson?" I asked cautiously. "Recession hit you, too? Been laid off?"

"You still working?" he asked.

"With circulation and ad revenue dropping, I don't know how much longer," I replied, "but for right now, there's still news to gather, stories to—"

I didn't finish. He grabbed my arm, looked around, and then dragged me into a corner away from traffic and peering eyes. I figured he had a choice piece of whistle-blowing, maybe something about CEOs collecting huge bonuses while laying off the workers." That wasn't what was on his mind.

"Don't say anything," he cautioned. "I'll get you out of this."

"Out of *what?*" I asked nervously.

"Out of employment. Quit now before they get you."

"*Who'll* get me?"

"The feds."

"The *FBI* is after me?" I asked frightened at the thought of being chased by an agency whose director once smoked cigars and wore dresses.

"FBI. CIA. VFW. Save yourself. Quit now and turn yourself in for unemployment compensation."

"You're a nut!" I proclaimed.

"Patriot!" he proudly corrected me. "I'm defending God, Mother, apple pie, and the flag. If it weren't for me, the country would collapse."

267

"Being unemployed is patriotic?" I asked suspiciously.

Robinson checked for feds, shoved a crumpled news article at me, and ordered me to read it. A record unemployment meant that corporations, with fewer workers and significantly fewer expenses, might survive the Recession.

The longer a worker stays on the job, the higher the salary; higher salaries force employers to raise rates and prices to the consumers who then demand higher wages to survive both the inflation and the Recession. By ranting against increasing minimum wage, downsizing the work force, shipping work overseas, and performing smoke-and-mirrors accounting practices, corporations could survive the Recession and assure every executive the right to an annual golf club membership. Laying off workers was true American patriotism.

"You're a journalist!" Robinson proclaimed. "You're already suspect as being unpatriotic. Save yourself. Quit now."

"But, Robinson, I *like* my job."

"Think you'd like a few years in Leavenworth? Treason isn't taken lightly in this country."

"But I'm still earning a salary, and you're unemployed."

"And a *patriot!*" he reminded me.

"That may be true," I agreed, "but you're still only receiving unemployment—"

"—welfare, food stamps, and AFDC!"

"AFDC?! Your wife left you six years ago. Both your children are out of college. How did you get Aid to Families with Dependent Children?"

"I adopted two orphans from Afghanistan. Mumbled something about keeping them safe from terrorism. It was a patriotic responsibility. Did I ever tell you about Vocational Rehabilitation? They pay me to learn a new job. All I have to do is go to school a couple of hours a day and collect a pay check."

Since there are mounting shortages of welders, nurses, and plumbers, even during these bad times, I figured Robinson would enroll in one of those programs.

"Journalism," he said matter-of-factly.

"Journalism?" I asked incredulously. "Reporters are some of the most underpaid, overworked people in the country. Even with poor pay and benefits, thousands are trying to get into the field, but there aren't openings!"

"Exactly!" said Robinson, smiling. "Exactly."

Productive Unemployment

Once a year, I and several hundred other reporters and columnists, write a Labor Day story.

A few of us may write about the personalities of the labor movement. About Mother Jones (1830–1930), the militant "angel of the coal fields" for more than six decades. Or, perhaps, we'll write about "Big Bill" Haywood (1869–1928) who organized the Industrial Workers of the World, a universal coalition, to fight for the rights of all labor. Maybe, we'll write about Sidney Hillman (1887–1946) who led strikes in 1916 to reduce the work week to 48 hours, from the standard 54–60 hours, and then helped found the Amalgamated Clothing Workers of America and the Congress of Industrial Organizations (CIO) before becoming a major political force for workers during the labor-friendly Roosevelt administration.

There may be stories about cigar-chomping Samuel Gompers (1850–1924), the first president of the American Federation of Labor, a job he held for 38 years. We might remember Saul Alinsky (1909–1972), whose concept of grassroots organzing became a base for Barack Obama's successful campaign for the presidency in 2008.

We might write about Eugene Debs (1855–1926), Joe Hill (1879–1915), and thousands of others who went to prison defending the rights of the workers to organize and demand better working conditions. But we won't become involved in the struggle, risk our jobs and futures. That's someone else's responsibility. We'll just follow inane rules and complain privately.

Hardly any of us remember Heywood Broun (1888–1939), one of the nation's best-paid columnists who risked his own financial stability to found The Newspaper Guild in 1935 to help those reporters making one-hundredth of his salary. We may believe that unions are acceptable for factory line workers, but we're "professionals," and mistakenly believe we don't need unions. We probably won't report that for years, six of the seven major newspaper chains had 20–30 percent profit margins, highest of any group. Nor will we report that newspapers to maximize profits through layoffs increased staff workloads that lead to errors and a failure to adequately cover our communities, a refusal to provide professional training and support budgets, and that compared to most college graduates, reporters are severely underpaid. And so we'll just continue to work unpaid overtime, split shifts, with minimal benefits and without an acceptable recourse for our grievances.

Some of us may interview current labor leaders, all of whom will say organized labor is having a tough time, but is still strong and vital, the only recourse against poor working conditions and unfair labor practices. But, we'll coldly report that only about 12.4 percent of all workers are now in unions, down from a peak of 35 percent in 1954.

We may interview the workers. An elderly man's remembrance of his life in the coal mines or breakers, and what Black Lung did not only to his own health, but to his family and friends. We might chat with an elderly woman who worked 12-hour days for a couple of dollars an hour in the heat and humidity of a garment factory. We may talk with a few current workers who, on the record will tell us they don't have it great, but it could be worse and overall, on the record of course, they work hard and are pleased with their jobs.

We won't remember that the Knights of Labor created the first Labor Day in 1882 and that the Congress made it a national holiday in 1894. But, we might interview a few readers to find out what Labor Day means to them. And, we won't be too shocked when most seem to say it means not a remembrance of the struggles for respect, dignity, and acceptable wages and working conditions, but of self-serving political speeches, hot dogs, burgers, and a pool party.

Some of us may write about the statistics of labor. We'll quote the Bureau of Labor Statistics that "non-farm payroll employment continued to decline," and that "payroll employment was down." We'll note that the Department of Labor reports there are so-many million Americans who are "not on temporary layoff." We'll quote the cold reality that "job losses continued in manufacturing," that "unemployment increased," and no one expects it to level off anytime soon.

Business euphemistically claims it is "downsizing" or "rightsizing." The "bottom line" is improved; corporate investors are being "optimally compensated." But, the reality is that American workers are being fired and "laid off," while corporate management, opening factories in Mexico, Thailand, and almost everywhere but the United States, are taking bonuses even during a recession. Even if executive management makes a few mistakes

270

along the way, and the "return on investment" isn't what the Board of Directors expects, almost all CEOs and their immediate underlings have the "golden parachute" that allows a soft drop from employment, yielding termination packages that can total millions of dollars and considerable benefits that no working class person will ever receive.

Of course, there are some industries that have gained in the downward economy. Retail sales, which the Department of Labor reports as having the lowest average wages, is gaining workers. But, that's because the average number of hours per week in that industry is about 29.6, reflecting the reality that it's just "good business sense" to hire 75 low-paid part-timers and save the benefits costs than to hire 50 full-time clerks.

If we dig, we might learn that although average pay for all labor has increased to $16.34 an hour, but that in terms of inflation the workers lost 45 cents an hour over the past 30 years. We might even report that although the cost of living rises each year, the minimum wage stayed at $5.15 an hour for more than a decade until, against significant opposition by the business community and Republicans in Congress, it rose to $7.25 an hour in July 2009. We might even report that a person earning minimum wage, and working 40 hours a week every week of the year, earns $15,080 a year, only about $3,880 higher than the federal poverty level.

But those are just numbers. To the 50-year-old who worked for one company half of his life, showed up for work on time, left on time, and tolerated the company's banal preaching about everyone is "part of our happy family," and then is laid off as an "economy measure," the numbers don't matter. To the worker who put in 20 years in one job, and then is fired for reasons that would be questionable under any circumstance, the numbers don't matter. To the $25,000-a-year worker who is told that for the third year she won't receive a raise because "we're having a bad year," but sees upper management not only get raises and stock options, but also hire other managers, all of them making five times or more than her salary, the other numbers don't matter.

Recent Department of Labor studies report that American workers are "the most productive" ever. That's because not only are they doing so much more to compensate for their fellow workers having been laid off, but because they live with the fear if they don't work even harder they, too, may be laid off, or lose promotions, in an economy that is going as far South as our manufacturing plants.

This year, I'm writing a Labor Day column. Next year, with all the layoffs and unemployment, and the blatant anti-labor biases of a large part of the workforce, there may not be much American labor to write about.

Synergizing America

Saturday night in the middle of Winter in rural Pennsylvania.

About the only social life were myriad Bingo games and fat-laden church dinner socials.

There was nothing exciting in the local theater that I hadn't already seen, and TV was spewing re-runs.' Time to tune in The Nashville Network. But, on this cold Saturday night, even TNN was unfriendly. No Statler Brothers. No Grand Ole Opry. Not even a luke-warm "Dukes of Hazzard." Just pro-fake wrestling. TNN had been "Viacomized."

Media conglomerate Viacom had exorcised the soul of the once-independent Gaylor-owned TNN, renamed it The National Network, and had stripped its country roots. In June 2003, targeting the 18–49 year old male, it renamed itself Spike TV.

The Nashville Network had begun in March 1983 with Ralph Emery hosting "Nashville Now," a variety-talk show that would anchor the new network. A decade later, "Music City Tonight," with hosts Charlie Chase and Lorianne Crooks, replaced "Nashville Now" when Emery retired. In 1997, Westinghouse, which had bought out CBS in 1995, added TNN and sister cable network CMT to its acquisitions. Just a business deal. Nothing more.

But, two years later, Westinghouse/CBS decided it was good business to shift from country to "country lifestyle," and cancelled several prime time series, including "Prime Time Country," "This Week in Country Music," and the re-named "Crooks & Chase." At the end of 2000, Viacom bought out Westinghouse/CBS for $50 billion, placed TNN under Viacom's MTV division, dumped long-time employees, and shifted most of the administration from Nashville to New York City. "Country lifestyle" was now replaced by "general entertainment." The intent was "to be as diverse as the nation itself and break out of a regionalism," said Herb Scannell, president of Viacom cable networks Nickelodeon and TV Land who now notched TNN on his résumé.

So long Waltons, the Real McCoys, and Boss Hogg. Bring on the apparently non-regional World Wrestling Federation's forms of fake-blood-and-head-banger entertainment, and mix it with numerous "Star Trek" reruns and other Paramount films since Viacom—which also owned CBS, Nickolodeon, TV Land, MTV, VH1, and Black Entertainment Television—also owned Paramount Pictures. Viacom, which recorded about $24.6 billion in revenue in 2002, also owned cable networks Showtime and The Movie Channel, the UPN-TV network, Spelling Entertainment ("Beverly Hills 90210" among other shows), Blockbuster, several theme parks including Kings Dominion and Kings Island, movie theater chains, radio and TV stations, and Simon & Schuster book publishers, the largest educational publisher in the country.

On December 31, 2005, after a merger six years earlier, Viacom split into a new Viacom and CBS Corp. CBS took UPN and the WB networks, which became the CW network in September 2006, the Paramount theme parks, Simon & Schuster publishing, Viacom Outdoor advertising, Showtime, and Westinghouse, among other properties. Viacom kept MTV, BET, Nickelodeon, Comedy Central, VH1, CMT, Spike TV, Paramount movie and home entertainment divisions, DreamWorks, Sega, and other properties.

Among other multi-billion dollar megamedia conglomerates are Disney, GE/NBC Universal AOL Time Warner, German-owned Bertelsmann, French-owned Vivendi, Australian-owned News Corporation, British-owned Thomson, and the Japanese-owned Sony. Through an intricate series of intertangling alliances, directors of one conglomerate often sit on the boards of others, while the conglomerates themselves own parts of each other. The trend of corporations swallowing other corporations, and conglomerates merging with other conglomerates could mean that the universe may one day be ruled by a squeaky-voiced black mouse with giant round ears.

The conglomerate advocates claim that in largeness is more efficiency, cost-cutting, and the development and use of greater resources to improve the product. They're right. But, also right are the opponents who see even more layers of management, layoffs and "downsizing" in the name of "streamlining," and the gradual development of a conglomerate with innumerable divisions, each with its own identity and target audience, but all of which reflect the ownership's values and mind-sets.

273

The six major conglomerate-owned film companies (American-owned Warner Brothers, MGM/UA, and Disney; and foreign-owned Universal, Columbia, and Fox) and five "mini-major" corporations bring in about 90 percent of all box office revenue, and essentially control distribution, even of independent films.

Only four major recording companies control nearly 90 percent of the recorded music in the U.S. All four are foreign-owned: Sony BMG (co-owned by Germany's Bertelsmann and Japan's Sony, and which own the RCA, Columbia, Epic, and Arista labels), Universal (owned by France's Vivendi, which also owns MCA), EMI (an English corporation, which also owns BMI, Capitol, and the Def Jam labels), and Warner Music (primarily owned by Canadian Edgar Bronfman, which owns the Atlanta and Electra labels).

Even during the Recession, with chains selling off newspaper holdings, chain ownership is the prevalent model for daily newspapers; only about 300 of the nation's 1,408 dailies are not parts of group ownership. Tied into all this is the lack of local competition. In 1923, 502 cities had competing daily newspapers; by the end of 2008, fewer than 10 cities had competing newspapers, and the probability that no city would have competing dailies by the end of 2012 is high.

Most book sales in brick-and-mortar stores are in Barnes & Noble, Borders, and Books-A-Million chains. During the mid-1990s, independent booksellers accounted for about one-third of the market; now they sell about 15 percent. However, of all book sales, about 43 percent are online, 32 percent through the stores, nine percent in independent stores, and 16 percent are miscellaneous sales, according to a Random House/Zogby poll of June 2009.

Seven megamedia conglomerates account for more than 80 percent of all book publishing in America. The publishers usually sell to wholesalers Ingram and Baker & Taylor or to a handful of large distributors. Barnes & Noble buys almost half of its titles from only 10 publishers. Combined, the major book-selling chains account for more than one-fourth of all sales, and about 40 percent of all adult hardcover trade sales, compared to the independent book stores that account for less than 15 percent of the sales of all books. Interestingly, grocery stores, which purchase almost all of their books from major distributors, account for about 10 percent of all book sales in America.

The conglomeratization of American media, with corresponding elimination of independent newspapers, magazines, book
publishers, and bookstores, leads to a more obvious pre-deter-
mination of what gets published. Charles McGrath, editor of
The New York Times book review—the *Times* and Barnes &
Noble have an "affiliate" relationship—says he often checks to
see if a book he might review is on the trade book shelves. Thus,
writers won't produce certain books that are well-written and
important if they don't believe publishers will buy them, but
may produce easily-promoted fluff to earn a decent pay check;
publishers may not sign worthy titles if they can't turn an
immediate profit and if they don't believe the major chains will
buy it in sufficient quantity to justify a large print run; and the
major media may not review books unless the chains put the
title on their shelves. It's not a conspiracy, just a reality of semi-
conscious interlocking entanglements among the media and
booksellers. "Insatiable greed has created more and more con-
solidation," says Margo Hammond.

The conglomerates "want a profit and want it now,"
Hammond said in a May 2003 column for Poynter.org. She
noted, the larger publishers "are no longer content to let a few
profitable titles subsidize the rest. Now every title has to pull
its weight." In 1960, William Jovanovich, chairman of publishing giant Harcourt Brace Jovanovich, said, "The day it gets to
be a choice between manuscripts and the balance sheet, I'll get
out of publishing." He was forced out in 1990 in a hostile
takeover.

Book publishing, says Hammond, "has become a popularity
contest." The break-even point for most smaller or independent
publishers is about 3,000–5,000 copies; the megaconglomerate
New York publishers are now looking at books that can have
sales of 20,000–30,000 copies within a few weeks of publication.
Because of the conglomeratization of the media, with innumerable intertangling alliances, about 15 highly-promoted novel-
ists account for about one-third of all fiction sales; the five
major New York City conglomerate publishers account for
about 85 percent of all best-sellers. Add the next five largest
publishers—all of which have extensive ties into the national
news media—and you have 95 percent of all best-sellers in any
year. With corporate business models replacing literary adventure, what seems to matter most is the bottom line. Editors ask,
"Can it sell?" Booksellers ask, "What's the promotion budget?"

The emphasis is upon names rather than writers, which is why presidential daughter Jenna Bush received a $300,000 advance for a children's book.

Good writing is often rejected in favor of probable spin-offs. It's not even necessary for films to show a profit in theaters. Book publishers now look for manuscripts that can be turned into film properties and sold to a sister company. Film companies, buying books even before they're published, can make their profits not in theaters but by selling videos to chain video stores, and air rights to television and cable networks which the parent conglomerate owns.

The Martha Stewart media empire is a series of interlocking enterprises. Her syndicated TV, cable, and radio shows, books, magazines, newspaper column, and internet commerce businesses promote each other; her exclusive association with Kmart to sell hundreds of Martha Stewart branded products has made millions for both of them; for more than a decade, Kmart also owned the bookstore megachain Borders Group, assuring almost omnipresent placement of Stewart's publications. The American media have become so incestuous that few people even thought it unusual that Warner Books paid former General Electric chairman Jack Welch a $7.1 million advance for his rules-laced business-guide autobiography, then announced a $1 million marketing campaign that included two days of interviews on the "Today Show" which is produced by NBC, part of the G.E. conglomerate. It's all called "synergy."

And it's synergy that downsizes staffs while calling it "streamlining," and has helped exclude worthy projects, while promoting a corporate climate that rejects the "regionalism" of The Nashville Network in favor of mass audiences that will raise the profits while dissolving America's literary and cultural diversity into reams of bookkeeping records.

Downsizing the News
and Pretending to Increase Quality

In July 2008, the *East Valley Tribune* of Mesa, Ariz, published a five part series that investigated illegal and unconstitutional actions by the Sheriff of Maricopa County, a 9,200 square mile, 3.9 million population county, which includes

Phoenix and Mesa. Written by Paul Giblin and Ryan Gabrie son, "Reasonable Doubt" looked at a popular sheriff who prides himself on how tough he is, but who had used that popularity to illegally enforce U.S. immigration law and mount an assault upon civil liberties. The series also looked not only at the hidden costs of the Sheriff's campaign against Hispanics, but also at how the Sheriff's obsession jeopardized the investigation of violent crime, including slower than optimal response time because his resources were often tired up with finding illegal immigrants.

In April 2009, Giblin and Gabrielson were awarded the Pulitzer Prize for local reporting. Gabrielson was in the newsroom when the announcement was made; Giblin was not; he and about 140 other newspaper employees, including Patti Epler, the metro editor who oversaw the series, had been laid off in January.

Trying to "maximize profits," Freedom Communications, owner of the *Tribune* and about four dozen other newspapers and eight TV stations, killed all local coverage for the 240,000-population Scottsdale and the 174,000-population Tempe editions, and transformed the newspaper from a seven-day a week publication to a four-day publication; a few months later, the newspaper, became a free circulation three-day publication.

In nearby Phoenix, the *Republic*, the state's largest newspaper and the tenth largest in the nation by circulation, eliminated 10 percent of its workforce at the end of 2008, after having shed newsroom staff during the previous two years. Those who remained were forced to take a one week unpaid leave.

The *Los Angeles Times* in 2008 laid off about 225 persons in its editorial staff, folded the local news section into the front section, eliminated 15 percent of its news hole, and significantly reduced national and international coverage. The *Times* had 1,200 on the editorial staff in 2001; it now was putting out the nation's fourth largest circulation newspaper in the nation's third largest metropolitan area with only 700 journalists, about 40 percent fewer than in 2001.

Responding to decreased circulation and advertising revenue, the *San Francisco Chronicle* eliminated about 300 of 575 in its Editorial staff; the *Miami Herald* cut 33, the *Atlanta Journal-Constitution* cut about 100 of its editorial staff, about 30 percent.

The *Detroit News* and the *Detroit Free Press*, like the *East*

Valley Tribune and dozens of other newspapers, went to a three-day a week (Thursday, Friday, and Sunday) home delivery schedule; the *Washington Times* killed its Saturday edition. Several metropolitan newspapers (among them the *Philadelphia Inquirer, Chicago Tribune,* and *Baltimore Sun*) filed for bankruptcy protection while they tried to reorganize.

Many newspapers couldn't reorganize. In February 2009, Denver's 200,000-circulation *Rocky Mountain News* closed after 150 years. The following month, the 127,000-circulation *Seattle Post–Intelligencer* after 143 years as a print newspaper became an online-only newspaper, putting 145 of its 165 journalists out of work. The *Christian Science Monitor,* one of the nation's most respected newspapers, killed its daily print edition in April 2009, announced a $3.50 an issue weekly edition, and expanded its online presence. In May, the *Tucson Citizen,* Arizona's oldest continuously published newspaper, closed. More than 120 daily newspapers closed in 2008 and the first quarter of 2009, according to Paper Cuts, which tracks the newspaper industry.

In Kirkwood, Mo., Todd Smith was laid off in April 2009 from *Suburban Journals.* A year earlier, he was shot while covering a city council meeting; the other six who were shot died before police killed the assailant. "I thought getting shot for the company might be looked at as something important, but I guess not," Smith told the *New York Times.*

The individual stories of journalists laid off since 2006 are powerful reflections of an industry struggling to remain relevant; the numbers are staggering, reflecting a combination of problems from the Recession, the encroachment of online journalism, reduced reading by the American public, journalistic bumbling, and owner greed.

During the second half of 2007, newspaper owners cut about 2,900 in the editorial departments. During 2008, newspapers laid off or froze more than 14,500 newspaper jobs, according to Paper Cuts. The layoffs in 2008 was the biggest loss in three decades, according to the American Society of Newspaper Editors. By the end of 2009, more than 20,000 jobs were expected to be lost.

About 85 percent of all dailies with more than 100,000 circulation, and about half of all dailies with circulations under 100,000, have cut the number of reporters, photographers, graphics specialists, and editors, according to a survey conducted by the Pew Research Center for the People and the Press.

With the layoffs, news quality has suffered. Reporters who remain are being forced to churn out more stories under deadline pressures. Almost no newspapers have proofreaders. About 40 percent of all newspapers report they have fewer copyeditors today than just two years ago. No proofreaders means more typos. Fewer copyeditors means sloppier copy, more factual error, and a lot more stories that are incomplete. There is less coverage of local news, more space being filled by press releases, and a significant decrease in investigative reporting and in-depth features. A newsroom filled with younger reporters—they aren't paid as much as the senior reporters who were laid off—leaves a newspaper vulnerable to a newsroom with less knowledge of the community and how to gather, report, and write news.

Newspapers have been in a freefall decline for most of the past three decades. There were more than 2,100 daily newspapers at the beginning of the twentieth century; by 1946, there were 1,763 daily newspapers; by the end of 2008, there were only 1,408 dailies. Community weekly newspapers dropped from 8,174 in 1960 to only 6,600 by the end of 2005.

Although the population increased from 237 million in 1985 to about 304 million by the end of 2008, newspaper circulation, which peaked at 62.8 million subscribers in 1985, dropped to 48.4 million by the end of 2008, according to the Pew Project for Excellence in Journalism. Even alternative weeklies dropped five percent in 2008, to 7.1 million. Trying to put a positive spin to the decline, the Newspaper Association of America tried to claim there were really 104 million Americans who read a newspaper every day (about 2.14 per subscription) and the readers numbered more than those who watched the Super Bowl (94 million) and local TV news (65 million).

Daily newspapers aren't the only medium to have downsized. Between 2003 and 2009, television networks cut their news operations and dumped hundreds of news staff. One station, WYOU-TV in northeastern Pennsylvania, eliminated its entire local news operation, saving about $900,000 a year but ceding its community responsibility to two rival stations. But the death of the news division hadn't begun with the Recession, but with management decisions over a period of more than a decade. Revenue for local TV stations dropped from $18.7 billion in 2006 to $16.5 billion in 2008, and is expected to be down 21.5 percent in 2009, according to *TV Guide*.

About 70 percent of all radio stations have only one reporter, with 97 percent having five or fewer full-time staff, according to the Radio and Television News Directors Association. Magazine and book publishing companies now assign much of their work to independent contractors. Of the nation's eight major news magazines, circulation at the end of 2008 was down about 4.8 percent, according to the Audit Bureau of Circulation. Ad pages were down 16 percent, according to the Publishers Information Bureau. Newspapers, TV and radio stations have increased the use of "stringers," part-time reporters who often work almost a full-time load, but are paid significantly less than full-time staff, and have no benefits.

The owners rightly blame reading habits of Americans. Readership dropped from 77.6 percent of all adults who had read newspapers daily in 1970 to 64.2 percent in 1995, according to Simmons Marketing. By 2008, only 48.4 percent of the American adult population were readers, according to the Pew Center. Less than one-third of all 13-year-olds are daily readers, according to a survey conducted by the National Center for Education Statistics.

The owners rightly blame the Recession. Subscribers are questioning their annual $150–250 investments, Businesses are folding, and the ones remaining are reducing newspaper advertising budgets. Classified advertising, a major indicator of the health of not only newspapers but also the economy, was down 20 percent in two years; there were fewer employment ads or classified display ads for real estate and autos, both industries hit hard by the Recession. Also affecting classified ad revenue is Craig's List, a national online classified ad operation that is the ninth largest website in the United States. Overall, advertising for print newspapers fell to $37.8 billion in 2008, a 24 percent drop from two years earlier.

The owners rightly blame the Internet for drawing readers and income. Online revenue for all sites was about $23.8 billion in 2008, about 10 percent higher than the year before, according to the Interactive Advertising Bureau. The Newspaper Association of America, however, counters the impact of online advertising by claiming, "56 percent of consumers researched or purchased products they saw in a newspaper," according to a Google analysis, and that "newspaper advertising reinforces online ads."

What the owners don't blame is themselves. They don't blame

themselves for coming late to the Internet, and then in a panic creating websites that essentially gave away the news from the daily edition.

They don't blame themselves for their greed. During the past few years, newspaper owners demanded and were getting 20–40 percent profit, the highest for any industry—and that includes Big Oil. With newsrooms and the news product already lean, the owners kept taking, but failed to properly upgrade the quality of news or the equipment. In a mistaken believe they could "maximize profits" and still give bonuses to executives but not the workers, they also failed to keep an adequate margin in reserve for the down cycles that are always a part of a nation's economic picture. Nevertheless, in an interesting twist of logic, the Newspaper Association of America, in a full-page ad published in dozens of newspapers in May 2009, claimed that newspapers "by and large remain profitable enterprises with operating margins that Wall Street analysts estimate will generally average in the low to mid teens during 2009." If that is true, then the massive layoffs and cuts to the editorial product were nothing more than panic attacks to continue to maximize profits at the expense of the quality of journalism.

Go to any journalism conference, and you'll see a lot of hand-wringing. Reporters and editors from all media are whining about how bad it is. They rightly blame owners and publishers. They also blame readers for accepting abbreviated news drops from TV and myriad cable networks. They whine about the Blogosphere and Internet domination. They complain about the short attention span of their readers. It's this and it's that. And so, with the help of $500 an hour consultants who eruditely harrumph their grandeur of divine guesses, they make cosmetic changes, giving the readers flashier graphics and shorter articles. They follow the 24/7 cable networks and increase entertainment and gossip. They spew syrupy "feel good" news. They say they want to be "relevant." Editors are placing light features and how-to columns higher than hard news. Some changes improve the product, most don't. A decade ago, the American Society of Newspaper Editors published a study that revealed Americans wanted less not more sensationalism, gossip, and celebrity news. Apparently, no one listened to the people.

The industry has already "maximized profits" by giving reporters and other staff low salaries and minimal benefits; it has downsized the news staff, and forced the remaining workers to take pay cuts and mandatory unpaid leaves. It has significantly reduced employee education programs, cut the number of pages, reduced the page size, and increased the use of material provided by syndicates and PR news releases rather than original copy produced by the local news staff. These latest cuts are deep into the muscle. Newspaper owners apparently believe that reducing quality improves profits. They need a course in Basic Journalism 101:

A quality news product will increase circulation.
Increased circulation will bring more advertising.
More advertising brings better profits and allows even
more news quality.

Even in a recession, news-starved masses, with myriad distractions and alternate ways to get news, will reduce the fall in print circulation if they are given a quality product worth reading. Eliminating reporters, and cutting benefits, employee training, and news coverage, which results in a destruction of employee morale and productivity, is not the way to save newspapers.

TECHNOLOGY AND PERSONAL MEDIA

Curbing the Paperless Explosion

It seemed like such a good idea at the time. A computer program that not only lets you fill in crossword puzzles, but also gives you hints, scores your results, and even lets you create your own puzzles. It was the perfect gift for my wife who lets several cups of coffee and the morning newspaper awaken her, and then leisurely spends 15 or 20 minutes filling out the crossword as dessert.

But, a week after I gave her the super puzzles disk, she still hadn't installed it in the computer. Finally, she admitted that doing crosswords on a computer screen just wouldn't be the same as relaxing at the dining room table.

For most of us, newspapers, which have been around in one form or another for most of recorded history, just "feel" right. We can read them all at once or let them lie around, reading an article now and then whenever we have time. Unlike radio, TV, or the movies which manipulate the audience into a predetermined time frame, the print media allow audiences to read at their own pace, and on their own schedule.

We can cut out a picture, an article, or column, stick it on the Fridge or put a Post-It note on it and send to a friend. We can tear out an ad or coupon and use it later in the week. We can make printer's hats for our children, or take the day's news to the beach. When we're through reading it, we can put the newspaper over our faces to block out the sun. It's possible to take a laptop to the beach, but when you put it over your face, you get real bad tan lines, and an even worse headache.

But, the Generation X-cess electronic whizzes and "mass communicologists"—who profoundly state that newspapers aren't even good enough to wrap fish or line bird cages anymore—claim the future is online. They believe all knowledge can be byte-encapsulated, and then dished out at the user's preference. .

The alarms have already been sounded. Newspaper circulation is in a freefall decline. The "chicken-littles" cackle out that online news and special interest computer programs will spell the decline not only of newspapers, but also all television and print media since more than half of all homes had PCs by 2001, the 20th year after the development of PCs. About one-third of all newspaper executives believe that the Internet is the "top reason" why the print media won't be as strong in five years, according to a survey by the Hearst corporation. Executives of the Knight-Ridder chain even claimed that print newspapers will be dead by the middle of the 21st century, victims of computer technology.

Interested only in the latest news about your favorite heavy metal band? Just type it in, and then let the computer do the searching. Want only information about gardening? Bring up the right menu, spend another five minutes to select the appropriate sub-menu, and then scroll through a list of titles until you find something interesting. Everything is available, and no self-serving gatekeeping editor is there to filter out 95 percent of the day's news.

But editors *are* needed. They help reduce the information overload that leaves most of us unable or unwilling to sort through piles of gigabytes to find what's important and what's fluff, what's accurate and verifiable, what's internet innuendo and polemic fiction disguised as news. But, owners of the mass media aren't stupid, and most newspapers and magazines have gone online with stories and videos, figuring it'd be easier to make a buck off people who just want to read about the latest sex scandals than to understand all the news.

Actually, since large masses of the nonreading public buy Sunday newspapers for the coupons anyway, it may be more logical to computerize everything. That way, readers can search for the right coupon—avoiding local, state, and international news—send an electronic signal to their grocery store, and then pick up their discounted food whenever it is convenient.

But, even in the assault upon their future, the local print newspaper is a necessity. Its format allows the reader to see many things at once, subconsciously noting the size of headlines and the placement of stories; we get a "feel" for what is important, and how stories relate to each other. Even if we flip through each section to get to the horoscope and comics, we absorb some news along the way.

But, America's Chip-for-Brains have a response. With "pagination," they claim they can turn a screen into a miniature newspaper, complete with headlines, pictures, and graphics. All we have to do is try to read that full page on screen that's the same dimensions as a junk mail letter, move our mouses over what looks interesting, magnify the story, then scroll through it a few lines at a time until we need new glasses. Most Americans have trouble programming a VCR, and these geniuses really believe we'll become technologically sophisticated enough to nimbly wander through a maze of electronics and menus and actually "find" all the news that's fit to scroll.

Embedded within the computer age, the "futurologists" further argue that the death of print media is predetermined in an environmentally-friendly paperless world. At first, it seems as if the 25,000 60-foot trees we need to kill to produce *The Sunday New York Times* could be better used. But, almost all newsprint is now recyclable, and the Newspaper Association of America points out that forests are being grown specifically for newsprint production, significantly reducing the erosion of our existing forests and timberlands—and possibly stabilizing the rising cost of newsprint.

The reality is that newspapers will be around as long as advertisers determine it's profitable for them to continue to buy space on a piece of pulp paper 15 inches by 22-1/2 inches. When they get better results from handing out flyers in malls or running 30-second spots on "Gilligan's Island" reruns, then newspapers in print will no longer exist. Hopefully, advertisers will continue to recognize the reality of why newspapers are important. We may complain about the local paper, but we still read it, each in our own way.

So, whenever someone tells me that in a decade or two newspapers will join the other dinosaurs of history, I tell them about my wife, her coffee, her voracious appetite to learn a little more about our world, her ad-clipping scissors—and her daily newspaper puzzles.

Scanning an American Life

I'm so excited!

I've just been accepted as a member of Sam's Club.

Because there are only about 720 clubs in the country, serving an exclusive list of only 47 million members, I had to drive 45 minutes to the closest one, and then sweat 20 minutes in line, wondering whether the Walmart board of directors would accept my $40 annual dues. Like exclusive country clubs, whose membership criteria is based upon social class and the ability to pay outrageous dues, Sam's Club once had numerous restrictions. It had demanded that members work for local, county, state, or federal governments; a school or college; a hospital or financial institution; an insurance, transportation, or utility company; or are a real estate agent, nurse, other professional, or are either on active duty or retired from the military. Persons who held membership in the 35 million member American Association of Retired Persons were also eligible.

Others accepted into the club included Walmart and Sam's Club vendors and associates, persons who owned or managed a business or who had purchasing authority for businesses, and anyone who was self-employed. Finally, Sam's accepted any of the 50 million persons who had a Discover Card, or were part of what Sam called an "affiliated" group, defined as "a selected credit union or association, company, or customer of selected financial institution 'Depositor Clubs.'" There was even a category for "additional qualifying group." The only ones excluded seemed to be members of the press, unless they could meet the rigid requirements of being at least 50 years old, owned a Discover Card, or could find a bank that would take their paltry paychecks. But, Sam's has become more democratic—pay $40, in person or online—and you have met its exclusive requirements.

Armed with a photo-laminated bar-coded blue card, I was ready to wheel my oversized shopping cart through the 120,000 square foot warehouse in search of one-gallon drums of pickles, five-pound cans of corn, and a skid of soft drinks.

Checkout time.

At Sam's, pimply-faced high school students and housewives needing extra income are paid slightly more than minimum wage to scan UPC-coded food and bar-coded membership card which alerts a computer to record and analyze inventory, and track each purchase a customer makes. At its best, it may mean special coupons from manufacturers. At its worst, it means Sam's eventually sells the data to a health insurance company that raises my rates because it determines I bought too many bags of junk food. It's no different at supermarkets and discount stores, most of which now have special cards to lure customers to believe they are getting special deals in exchange for giving up their privacy.

During the past few years, RFID chips have been implanted into myriad parts of Americans' lives to track them and their possessions. Chips can be implanted beneath the skin and carry a person's entire medical histroy; they can be included on prescription drug bottles to track illegal sale and counterfeit drugs, "At least 30 million people carry an RFID tag on them every day in their car keys or in their access control card to get into their office building or to buy gas or to pay a toll," wrote Mark Roberti, editor of RFID Journal. He pointed out "Everywhere RFID has been rolled out in the consumer environment, consumers have overwhelmingly embraced it. However, computer security expert Bruce Schneider disagrees. "When RFID chips are embedded in your ID cards, your clothes, your possessions, you are effectively broadcasting who you are to anyone within range," Schneider told CNN in October 2006. The information stored on an RFID chip can be read at a range up to 50 feet. "The level of surveillance possible, not only by the government but by corporations and criminals as well, will be unprecedented. There simply will be no place to hide," he said.

Tracking individuals has also become easier because of the vast use of cell phones. Most have GPS tracking devices that allow anyone—relative, police officer, or criminal—to track any of the more than one billion people who own cell phones.

Legally, anyone can obtain voluminous data about anyone who has ever registered to vote, owned property, sued, been sued, arrested, served in the military, been married or divorced, licensed by any governmental agency, or even attended a public school. The databases are what help reporters develop stories, some exposing corrupt governmental and business practices. The databases are also what allows sales people to find specific groups of people to add to direct mail and telemarketing campaigns.

The *illegal* trade in information gathering and surveillance—does anyone think it's impossible to learn how much money you have in your savings account or the latest reason why you had to go to the hospital?—is a multi-billion dollar a year business.

In 1996, Sen. Alan Simpson (R-Wyo.) proposed a national photo ID card, not unlike the one that Sam's issues for $40 a year or which almost every supermarket chain issues at no cost to the shopper. With multi-layered paperwork in a bureaucratic hierarchy, figure at least $10 billion to implement this scheme. The intent may be to assure us no illegal immigrants are allowed to buy bulk food at Sam's. But, the reality is that it was another way for the government to track its citizens, somewhat similar to the universal IDs issued by the former USSR, the Republic of South Africa, and most dictatorships. The proposal eventually wilted, but is revived every now and then when politicians believe their constituents would sacrifice privacy for security.

We already have nearly universal driver's licenses and state-issued photo ID cards, as well as universal red-white-and-blue cards of patriotic social security numbers issued to babies. The intent seven decades ago was simply to record every working individual for social security purposes; any other use is illegal. However, almost every agency and business from the IRS to colleges to the local video store now tracks taxpayers, students, potential employees, and customers by social security numbers.

What we don't need is another way for government or private business to track our lives.

A Technologically Perfect Imperfect Society

AIBO walked, sat up, and lied down. Talk nice to him or pet him behind his ears, and he wiggled his ears and wagged his tail. Scold him, and his eyes turned red. He played with a bone and ball, understood about 200 words and phrases, recognized shapes and patterns, and could dance to the beat of 30 different rhythms. AIBO didn't need to be spayed or neutered, and never needed to go outdoors. He could even play with you for up to 90 minutes—until you had to recharge his lithium-ion battery.

AIBO, a Japanese word for "pal" but which is also an acronym for Artificial Intelligence Robot, was a 3-1/2 pound furless 18-joint metal-molded dog-doll, with a 64-bit processor, 256 megabytes of memory, and a 350,000-pixel miniature color video camera as its eyes. Sony claimed AIBO "expresses its emotions, and can change its own behavior patterns by learning and maturing through contact with people."

Sony sold the first 3,000 models, each one at $2,500, within 20 minutes of placing them onto the internet in June 1999, the next 2,000 models within four days, and then all of a 10,000 model run "upgrade" shortly after it was introduced in November, turning away about 125,000 buyers. An 11-day "window" in late February 2000, with everyone guaranteed an AIBO, brought several thousand more orders. The third generation AIBO, released in time for the Christmas season 2003, sold for only $1,500–$2,000. That artificial dog even recognized its owner's face. Before Sony pulled the plug on AIBO production in March 2006, not only had more than 150,000 units been sold, but there were fan clubs throughout the world.

AIBO's ancestors were Tamagotchis and Furbys; in the mid-1970s, it was the pet rock. Not long after AIBO was machined, Matsushita spawned an artificial cat, and Honda announced it was also working on a human-looking robot, apparently for families in apartments that don't allow pets. Tiger Electronics and Sega Toys gave birth to Poo-Chi, a seven-inch long 13-ounce metallic mutt that is more like Furby than R2-D2. Tiger says the market for the $28 sorta-dog is women in their 20s who can cuddle Poo-Chi in their hands. More than a million units are expected to be sold. By Fall 2000, emotionally-deprived non-pet lovers could also buy Spike for $69.95, and i-cybie, including his 16 motors, for $125. Tiger says the three dogs "will be the must-have pets on everyone's lists."

For less than $50, including spaying or neutering and a vet's checkup, we can own a live dog, rescued from a humane shelter. But, that would mean a lot more work, a lot more care and compassion, and so we settle for artificial love in an artificial world we have created that isolates us from others.

At checkout lines, we take merchandise or groceries from our cart, put them onto a conveyer belt, silently watch while a mute minimum-wage employee swipes barcodes across a scanner. Often, a three-minute order results only in a half-dozen words. At some grocery stores, even employees aren't necessary since systems have been developed so customers can scan and bag their own merchandise.

We once chose our gas stations on the basis of service. Attendants checked our water, oil, fan belts, and tires. While cheerfully filling our tanks, they chatted amiably about everything from the weather to whether our car needed some special care. Now we check solely for the lowest price, pull next to a pump, hear a disembodied voice tell us, "Pump 5 is ready," fill our own tanks, and lay the money in front of a clerk who is also selling cookies, hoagies, and Lotto tickets. At many gas stations, we don't even need to talk to a clerk—at the pump, we slide a credit card, and get a receipt.

Banks and credit unions penalize us a couple of dollars to withdraw our own money if we stand in line to talk with a teller. So, we go to the ATM where we pay a couple of dollars to a machine that dispenses crisp 10s and 20s.

We can take thousands of courses by correspondence, and even earn college degrees without ever having to participate in a class discussion, talking with a professor, or even playing bridge in the student union.

We sit in front of our TV sets an average of seven hours a day, breaking only to go to the bathroom or refrigerator.

For those hours we can't find anything on the dozen broadcast or 100 cable stations, we hook up to the Internet, a cell phone, iPod, and BlackBerry holstered to our hips. We have become so efficient that we can e-mail our friends, acquaintances, and business associates so we don't waste precious moments by "idle chatter."

If we want "head-to-head" games competition, we can go online for someone a thousand miles away whom we'll never see, call, nor write. If we want a love-match, we enter a chat room.

We don't have to go to a newsstand or bookstore, browse the aisles, and chat with other customers and the clerks. We can get snippets of news from any of a couple of thousand newspapers and magazines that have condensed the news for us online. We order books from online companies with large warehouses and low overhead. We can even download e-books into portable micro-computers about the size of a fat 5x8 card.

With artificial insemination, we can produce babies in a sterile environment, hire nannies to raise them, and buy houses that give us "space" not neighbors.

We have become a health-obsessed, greed-induced society with sedentary minds. In our isolation, we jog around the problems of the poor and homeless, worrying about unemployment, workplace exploitation, and age discrimination only if they affect us personally. In the artificial world we created, we buy robotics to imitate life, not understanding the joy of life, not willing to help others ease the pain of their own lives.

We can upgrade our computers, and buy a robotic dog on the Internet. But we won't be upgrading our lives.

Windows Not of the Mind

I just wanted to buy a portable typewriter. A portable *manual* typewriter. The kind I could throw into the car, and take anywhere. I knew typewriters were obsolete in a world of laptops, iPods and BlackBerries; an entire generation of Americans have never used a typewriter. I didn't need a portable with a screen, hard disk drive, and a $2,000 price tag. I didn't want to add a $600 printer, nor a $500 word processing program that would allow me to create multi-colored Christmas cards. I just wanted something that didn't run out of battery power every four hours.

I went to three discount stores and one of the larger chain stationery stores where sales people gleefully showed me a choice of a dozen discounted models of computers, but no typewriters.

Smith Corona, the last American company to manufacture typewriters, had learned it could exploit Mexicans as easily as Americans, and took its business out of the country in 1992. Two years later, it stopped making typewriters.

I first learned to type when I was 11 years old. I had broken my right wrist, lamely tried to write with my left hand, and figured I could put words onto paper by using the fingers of my left hand to punch out keys of a stand-alone upright Royal manual typewriter. My handwriting never improved; my typing did. Using a two-finger hunt-and-strike system, I eventually surfed the keyboard at 60–65 words per minute. I wasn't as fast as my father who typed 80 words a minute, but he had to use all ten fingers.

All through college and my first newspaper jobs, I used manual typewriters, ripping, cutting, and pasting together sentences and paragraphs into comprehensive 600-word stories. It wasn't until after I completed doctoral studies in the mid-1970s that I finally bought an electric typewriter.

So I wouldn't be swallowed by the impending technological revolution, in 1982 I bought a "state-of-the-art" computer with one disk drive and 16K of memory, quickly produced "perfect" copy, and wondered how I could ever have written anything that couldn't be inserted or deleted by a couple of keystrokes.

During the next decade, I progressed through two other computers, and then to a Pentium with 3,000 times the memory of my first computer and 50 times the hard drive storage capacity. That computer had two floppy disk drives, a CD-ROM that held three disks, and a speaker system that rivaled anything high school kids put into their Camaros. Eventually, I yielded to saturation marketing campaigns, and "upgraded" to a Pentium 4 with enough memory to become a "Jeopardy" champion and enough hard drive storage to house a small library. Its operating system was now Windows XP Professional. The Microsoft brains will continue to upgrade and improve the operating system software as long as there's billions to be made from people who believe all the ads.

A few years ago, the university where I teach cancelled its courses in Typewriting (I, II, III, and Workshop), apparently sensitive to giving college credit for something that probably should never have been college courses in the first place. But, like matter, nothing is ever lost in an academic universe. So, the College of Business added Keyboarding. It was a more rigorous course. Not only did students learn how to "keyboard," they also had to master the 200 or so commands that would allow them to flawlessly print out their resumes, and then breathlessly wait for corporate America to throw multi-benefit contracts at their feet. But, just in case anyone thought "word processing" was too simple and the future wouldn't be paved with clauses of comfort for its graduates, the college created oh-so-'90s upper division courses, Electronic Document Preparation and Business Document Generation.

Both the College of Business and the College of Education

now teach desktop publishing, and one of our graduate programs teaches students in a dozen courses to produce interactive videos and instructional CDs. However, none teach the writing and editing skills necessary to wrap up the pretty packages within the 32 megabytes of memory.

In our journalism classes, 19-year-olds quickly learn that computerized spell checks, grammar checks, thesauruses, and style books can reduce their stress levels. Aided by programs that lay out templates and don't require them to know how to figure ratios and conversions, they soon design ads and full pages that rival anything *USA Today* produces. Sadly, if they master computerized graphics and page design, they will earn at least $5,000 a year more in the media than their fellow students who master writing and editing. It probably doesn't matter. Editors now spend less time editing than they did a decade ago, forced to do not only their own jobs but those of the backshop composing staff who were laid off or fired when publishers upgraded their plants' technology.

Today, first graders are taught to use computers. During their 12 years of basic education, they'll learn most of their skills from software programs loaded onto machines that resemble TV sets. Hopefully, they'll learn that good writing is not dsetermined by how good your computer is, that it's not the technology but the mind that advances society.

Some day, in our technologically perfect society, the power will go out and we'll be forced to confront our own illiteracy.

The Impersonal Society

Some of my favorite people are the ladies at the Bloomsburg, Pa., branch of the Philadelphia Federal Credit Union. Over the past two decades, they have put up with a lot from me, with hardly an audible sigh, although I am sure there was a lot of cheering when my wife took over balancing the checkbook a couple of years ago.

The Credit Union ladies know my account numbers and status better than I do, have bailed me out of numerous problems, and have even gotten used to the reality that I know my accounts not as numbers but by colors. ("Could you please check my balance in Red savings, then transfer fifty bucks into Red checking, thirty into Blue checking, and a hundred to pay Blue loan?")

Even when they've had a long and tiring day, the ladies smile, joke, and ask questions about how my family and I are doing. The only thing they get from my "small potatoes" accounts is the satisfaction they're doing a good job and an occasional box of candy, a green plant, and relatively-inexpensive Christmas gifts, which don't even begin to add up to the personal attention they provide to keep my financial affairs in order.

But, because of a conspiracy within the urban corporate office whose executives are into things like "time-management studies," the ladies have been slyly trying to convince me to use the push-button telephone to call an 800-number of a central computer where a digitized disembodied voice not only will tell me the status of my accounts, but will also transfer funds from one account to another and even pay bills. My human tellers even sweetly point out that it's easy to do telephone-to-computer transactions which are efficient and save me the $2 fee for almost every transaction a human teller has to do. I, of course, have just as sweetly explained that I have no ability to comprehend laborious written instructions that require me to push 132 different buttons just to hear a computerized voice tell me my account is overdrawn.

With MAC drive-ups, direct deposit, and the phone, I don't ever need to talk to a human again. The reality is that I am willing to pay a penalty just so I *can* talk to a friendly voice in a rapidly increasing technologically imperfect impersonal society in this, the Communications Age.

At one time, all telephone calls had to be made through a local operator who knew as much about you, your family, and the community as you did. Then, technology let us bypass a human, and we could do our own calling.

Call the average business and you now are greeted by a digitized voice giving you a menu. Listen to all the choices, push another button, and hear another menu. Some companies have four or five levels of menus, all so you can finally push a series of buttons and hear, "I'm sorry, I won't be in for the next six months. If you wish to leave a message, press 1; if you wish . . ."

We don't go to seamstresses anymore because we can now order by menu-driven iPods and Blackberries the same clothes everyone else is wearing. From vending machines, we can now buy not only candy bars and soft drinks but also insurance, VCR tapes, and even aspirin and condoms—and never have to talk to anyone. We speak into a clown squawkbox to order fast food which we eat in the car on the way to an aerobics class that treats us to a recorded cadence.

Although most clerks at supermarkets and department stores, who are usually paid minimum wage and receive no benefits, make at least an attempt to be friendly, an increasing number barely make eye contact while they languidly push items past an electronic scanner.

With the computerization of America, you can now have your computer talk to other computers and make airline and hotel reservations, order furniture, get information from databases instead of the library, and even hire a nanny, while never talking to a human.

On newspapers, we have replaced the wise older proofreaders and typesetters with dispassionate computers that have a passing knowledge of grammar and no knowledge of the community. Reporters are already researching and writing stories by calling up databases, transmitting the finished product electronically to editors who edit and send it electronically to the press; no one has to talk with anyone else.

In California, neighbors stand next to each other before their fire-torn houses. For many, it's the first time they have talked to each other in weeks.

Even the lines sound as if we care about each other—"I know where you're coming from," "I understand your hurt," and "Thank you for sharing that"— so we can pretend we are communicating while we plan our next sentence.

It seems the only time we talk with each other is when we unite at sports events to shout "kill the umpire!" Most other communication seem to be flipping fingers and calling lawyers. Indeed, the Communications Age has now become the Age of Un-communication.

The Beeper Cacophony

Barack Obama was determined that the only way anyone was going to take away his BlackBerry was if they pried it from his cold dead hands. Or, something to that effect.

In grocery store aisles, shoppers text message home to find out how many kumquats to buy. Others push a shopping cart, their ear attached to a cell phone so they can chat with one of their 287 best friends about anything from their daughter's dance recital to the latest neighborhood scandal.

At one time, only business executives had car phones. But, car phones are oh-so-'90s. Now, everyone seems to have a cell and a need to sideswipe parked cars and cut in front of other cars two lanes away. Using the latest technology, cell phone drivers can now drive, text message, take photos of that gorgeous brunette in the next car, read a snippet from the morning sports page, and check out the latest quotes from the decaying stock market.

In Halloween parades, two-year-old costumed girls in buggies are being pushed by mothers wearing a cell phone in their ears. On benches in front of hospitals, mothers idly blather into a cell phone while their pre-pubescent children text message their playmates about nothing in particular. In conference rooms and legislatures, American business executives and politicians are secretly twittering and tweeting.

In a nation of conspicuous consumption, Americans have spent more on minutes and I-net charges than on charities. Their cells have 3G technology, with Bluetooth, WiFi, GPS, PDA, MP3, MP4, 6 gig cameras, and packet switching. Hooked onto their hips are a pager, FAX, laptop computer, and portable satellite dish. For all I know, some good buddy may also be running a transistor-sized CB rig.

Americans spend more time than any civilization in front of screens, whether a 2-inch square mini-PDA or a 54-inch flat screen plasma. For exercise, they jog on a treadmill, seeing nothing, going nowhere, an iPod cord in their ears, and a Palm Treo perched on the handlebars so they can exercise their thumbs.

President Obama justifiably relies upon his BlackBerry, but many rely upon electronic communications as a status symbol or as a crutch so they don't have to make decisions or engage in face-to-face conversations. Such was the case at a party I thought I might have attended. . . .

It might have been an enjoyable party, but I didn't experience much of it since pagers, cell phones, BlackBerries, Palm Treos, and were going off all evening, and all I heard were excuses of why used car salesmen, real estate agents, and grocery store clerks had to break off conversations to answer the calls of nature.

"So, what's your sign?" a striking brunette asked me, only to excuse herself when one of her cell phones chimed some hip-hop music. Apparently her sign was Ice-T, with AT&T rising.

The knock-out redhead and I talked for three minutes before she got an urgent text message to alert her to call her service which relayed a poke from her boss who wanted to know what color dress she was wearing to work the next day so he'd be able to color coordinate his staff. At least that's what I think she said, but I wasn't sure because she was text-messaged 13 words into our conversation and spent much of the evening exercising not her mind but her thumbs.

The junior high school English teacher was paged, unleashed his cell phone, checked something he called an "app," and told his friend that his Treo just informed him that the temperature in Phoenix was 86.

An attractive blonde in the corner lusciously smiled at me, teasing me with a come-hither look. I was about to come, but she got tweeted. I had no idea whether that's sensual or not, but it compelled her to rush off into a dark corner and twitter back. I think she kept twittering until a failed whale shut down her system.

While waiting for a movie usher and waitress who simultaneously excused themselves when they were tagged by a Facebook request, I overhead three people by the bar ask each other what our hostess must have been thinking to have actually invited someone so low on the prestige scale that he wasn't wearing any electronic devices.

"Could be a diversity thing," said one politically correct matron. "You know, we invite a Black and a luddite columnist to our party."

Feeling alone and needing a drink, I asked the bartender for a virgin piña colada, but before she could crush the ice, she received a text message from Starbutt across the room who needed two whiskey sours with a twist of lemon. When Starbutt, Bartender Jo, and 832 of their closest friends finished texting each other, I got a glass of diluted pineapple juice with a trace of coconut.

After an hour of watching the Information Age, I noticed another soul all by himself.

"Interesting party," I said opening the conversation.

"Yeah," he mumbled. "I just hope I get some action tonight."

"Since everyone's poking everyone else," I said. "I doubt there's much action anyway, especially when everyone seems to be so Linked-in that they have blurred the lines between business and personal lives."

"That's what I mean," he said. "It's now been 27 minutes, and no one has called or IM'd me. It's so humiliating."

Not having done my good deed for the day, I sighed, and shuffled off to find the only landline telephone in two counties. He answered his cell phone and chatted with me about the price of kumquats. He was most thankful, especially when I didn't try to talk to him again so he could carry on simultaneous conversations with the striking brunette, the knock-out redhead, and some guy who was selling life insurance.

About the time I was ready to leave, the hostess told me I had a telephone call. It was Marshbaum wanting to know if I needed him to come in early the next day. "How'd you find me?" I asked.

"I was driving along the interstate finding dumb things for you to write when I thought I should check in. So I called Horsehide who paged Littany who text messaged Bullnose who poked Chartbound who said you were at some muck-a-muck's party, so I called Ringtone."

"You have a car phone?" I asked.

"Car phone? Don't be ridiculous. That's so '90s. Got a 3G cell with Bluetooth, WiFi, GPS, PDA, MP3, MP4, 6 gig Mpx, and packet switching. Also a pager, FAX, laptop computer, and portable satellite dish. Also running a CB, good buddy. Gotta be on top of things in case you need a really dumb statement at a moment's notice."

"When's the last time I needed you moments from deadline?" I asked.

"Makes no difference," he said. "Sometime you may, and you'll be happy you could get to me."

"That's all well and good, but I don't have any of those communications devices."

"Check your office in the morning, Boss. Got some nice units for you, too. It'll only cost you a thousand or so a month to find me."

"Marshbaum!" shouted, "I don't have an extra thousand a month to pay for cellular phones, paging equipment—"

"No problem, Boss. Got a great two-year plan, and it's all deductible."

A Nation of Polls and Predictions

The national TV networks, with the print media drooling in their shadows, began "predicting" the presidential winner in each state nanoseconds after the polls closed in the 2008 general election. They based their pretend-scientific analyses upon exit polls, directed by consulting companies populated by statisticians, mathematicians, and academicians of all types.

We have become a nation of polls and predictions. During the past decade, the news media have changed their role of presenting, analyzing, and interpreting information to guessing what may or may not happen in an insatiable rush to be first. Reporters who voted in only their second general election now write detailed analyses and predictions of upcoming elections, based upon "scientific polling procedures." Polls dominate news coverage, and politicians read them as religiously as churches have Bingo games, afraid to make decisions without being told what to think. The news is no longer what the candidates are doing, but what other people think of the candidates and the candidates' reactions to the polls. Naturally, our follow-the-sheep nation supports those ahead in the polls. In a convoluted Mobius strip of logic, the media then devote more of their news coverage to people who are ahead in the polls. Unless you're a celebrity, if you have a brilliant and workable plan for the future of America but are a "third party" candidate or an independent, you get minimal coverage. After all, the polls proved you don't have a chance of winning, so why should the media waste time and space?

The media also have their "secret" polls, designed just for election night. In a race for ratings, the media, especially the TV networks, once tried to be first to predict a winner, based upon what they believe is a "scientific analysis" of the vote—"With 3 percent of the vote counted, WPOL-TV predicts . . ." When voters, politicians, and advertisers said the early predictions, even before the polls closed, weren't fair—people might change their vote to match predictions—the national networks decided to wait until the polls closed in the East before predicting winners, leaving about 100 million disenfranchised Americans in the other time zones.

But, "scientific polls" are occasionally wrong, no matter how many statisticians are involved. Almost every poll in 1948 predicted that Tom Dewey, the Repuiblican governor from New York, would be elected president. So sure was the *Chicago Tribune* that its election night newspaper declared Dewey the winner. Harry Truman had to wait until all the votes were counted until he could continue his presidency.

Polls and predictions now dominate far more than political coverage, having seeped into weather, sports, and general news.

The three network-affiliated TV stations in northeastern Pennsylvania once told their viewers they were only at the fringes of a blizzard, and probably wouldn't be hit. The next day, their viewers shoveled 18 inches of snow. A couple of weeks after the blizzard, the forecasters told the viewers to prepare for four to 12 inches of snow the next day. The next day, a few lonely snowflakes drifted aimlessly, and then evaporated. Some TV stations give us seven-day forecasts, as if they think we place any credibility in a seven-day forecast when the 12-hour forecasts aren't accurate.

We expect weather people to be wrong. They can't help it. In weather school, their professors give them a 60 percent chance of getting an "A," and they end up with a "C," accompanied by a discussion of the highs and lows for that grading period.

Most sportswriters are happy being right at least half of the time. In our newspapers, we are subjected to thumbnail pictures of the sportswriters, a couple of community residents and 15 column inches of their predictions for several of the weekend high school, college, and pro games. It's even worse on TV. The sportscasters think they should tell us not only their predictions, but also the Las Vegas odds. The reality, however, is they even bungle the scores after the game is played.

Newspaper editors with nothing better to do with their lives send out a reporter and photographer to do "Person on the Street" interviews. The question of the day to a half dozen people who can't even balance their own checkbooks, is, "Do you agree with the President's Stimulus Bill?" These polls are unscientific and useless, but, circulation increases another dozen or so that day as relatives of those polled buy an extra copy of the paper.

Routine TV polls are even more insidious. For a buck—split between the phone company and the station—you can call a 900 number during the 6 O'Clock newscast, answer a yes/no question, and hear the results at 11. However, we don't know how many fools wasted a buck, if most of them were rich dowagers with the time and money to call in a dozen times, friends or enemies of a particular candidate or issue, or 13-year-old pubescents who thought by calling the 900 number they'd hear a TV anchor talk dirty to them. Maybe it's time for the rest of us to talk dirty to the media.

The Fine Art of University Grantsmanship

You're probably not going to believe this, but a scientific foundation once awarded a $5,000 research grant to a behavioral scientist to study the television viewing habits of cats. The reasoning behind the grant, said the society's spokesman, with not even a chuckle, is that animals, especially cats, react to voice and picture patterns on the television screen, although they don't comprehend what is taking place. The spokesman even went so far as to suggest that cats prefer to watch only good television programs and shun the poor ones.

While the officers of the Society aren't going to have many problems—all they have to do is wait patiently for the report and try to act serious about the whole thing—the poor media researcher, eager for tenure and promotion, is likely to be burdened with uncountable problems.

At the home of Freddy Feline, the researcher, a portable laptop computer loaded with statistical programs strapped around his shoulder, timidly approaches the cat.

"Hey, Man, what are you doing in my sandbox?"

"Oops. Sorry. Ahem, well, I'm your average ordinary university media behavioral research scientist, and I've come to interview you about what television programs you watch."

"You feeling all right? Humidity not too high?"

"Look, Cat, I've really come to find out what you like on TV. I bet you watch cartoons. Felix the Cat, Krazy Kat, and Fritz the Cat!" The cat yawned, so the researcher tried another direction. "You scout the opposition! Lassie? Rin-Tin-Tin?"

By now, the cat was convinced the researcher was a few numbers short of a full equation, but the researcher was persistent. "How about comedies? *Everyone* loves SitComs!"

"Cats aren't everyone."

"It's *adventure* you like!" beamed the professor. "Maybe a jungle show with lions?"

"Only if the diet is media researchers."

"Reality! 'American Idol'? 'Real World'?' The Cat just yawned.

"Drama? Science Fiction? 'Star Trek' is all over the tube. Surely, you've seen at least one episode!"

"You're spaced out," said the cat unsheathing his claws.

"I know!" shouted the professor, "you're a socially-aware cat. You watch '60 Minutes,' '20/20,' and 'Nightline'"!

"You're loony," the cat replied, waiting for a chance to dial 911 to ask the Media Researcher Unit at the state hospital to make a house call. "I don't watch TV."

"But you've just *got* to watch television. It's the American way!"

"Look, Man, like I've been trying to tell you, n*one* of us cats watch television!"

"*None* of you?" came the startled reply of the media researcher, his Ph.D. dripping with an unused grant. "Then what's the TV doing by the couch?"

"Oh, *that*," grinned the cat, "I like to sharpen my nails; that's the only good piece of wood I can find. It's about all that it's good for."

"Look, Cat," the researcher pleaded, "I've got this really neat grant—$5,000 from the Society—and it's to find out what cats watch on television. And besides, I can get a publication credit and—"

The researcher didn't even finish his sentence before the cat's bright green eyes flickered. "You mean some nuts gave an even bigger nut five thousand bucks to interview cats to find out what we watch on the scratching post?" And then, the cat began to think. "He gets $5,000 to interview cats. And, after all, I *am* the most important part of the study." He decided it was only right for him to help. "Look, Prof, like I said, none of us cats watch television. But, I'll tell you what I'll do. You keep asking questions. I keep denying them. You're bound to miss at least one or two shows. If I can't deny I don't watch what you don't ask me, who'll be the wiser?"

The media researcher was once again happy. There would be a publication credit, tenure and promotion.

In an exclusive section of some American city, there walks a very, very happy professor . . . and a cat with a $5,000 bankroll.

301

Cellular Research

People who drive and use cellular phones at the same time have a greater risk of running red lights, stop signs, and getting into accidents than do people who concentrate on their driving, according to a professor at the Rochester Institute of Technology. His research reveals that drivers with a cell phone run a 34 percent higher risk of being in an accident. If they use the phone, light a cigarette, and read the morning paper on the way to work, they . . . well, actually, along most of the nation's roads they'd probably fall into a pothole before running into another car.

In rebuttal to the professor, the Cellular Telecommunications Industry Association (CTIA)—which for all I know is a clandestine branch of government—claimed that not only was the study flawed, but that fully-charged cell phones don't cause accidents, people cause accidents.

I'm no research genius, but it doesn't take too many brain cells to figure out driving and talking don't mix, a view shared by 13 countries which ban drivers from using hand-held cellular phones.

Nevertheless, I began to wonder what else is out there we might not know if grant-governed researchers didn't uncover the facts of life about the media, both personal and mass. For instance . . .

—Two researchers at the University of Wisconsin, armed with a grant, determined that telephones are used to get gossip and news, as well as for relaxation and entertainment. That, of course, is a step above the "media behavioral" research scientist who got a grant to watch the television viewing habits of cats.

—During the past three decades, psychologists, sociologists, psychiatrists, educators, and "mass communicologists" secured about $100 million in funding to conduct more than 8,000 studies to determine the effects of violence upon children. The results seem to indicate that violent children who watch violent cartoons tend to become violent, whereas non-violent children who watch non-violent cartoons tend to fall asleep a lot. Possibly the latest research might prove that violent criminals who get V-chips implanted within their brains by second year medical residents tend to have more headaches than those who take aspirin.

—Somewhere at this very moment, a team of "mass communicologists" is probably conducting a content analysis of the newspapers of western Montana between 1931 and 1945. From three tons of statistical analysis, they'll conclude that there is a correlation between the number of ads in a newspaper and the number of pages. They'll condense it into 15 hack academic pages which will be presented at a "professional meeting," rewritten, then published in an "academic" journal, thus giving credibility to the researchers who add another notch onto their quest for tenure and promotion, rather than knowledge and understanding.

Now, I must admit that it's true that I have also done some research in the past few years. Among my startling conclusions have been . . .

—Most people who wear glasses don't have 20/20 vision. Neither do most Washington beltway columnists who not only think they can see into our lives and tell us what we're thinking, but can predict who we'll vote for—and why.

—People who listen to Rush Limbaugh have a higher proportion of radios than homes in which the entire family is deaf. However, the deaf people are happier with not being able to hear people tell them about Rush.

—People who watch reality TV shows also watch *The Wizard of Oz* and cheer for the scarecrow who's searching for a brain.

—And speaking of people with no brains . . . Preliminary research indicates that the only case of a CEO getting fired for incompetence was one who told the stockholders they would have to take a smaller profit next year since he was increasing worker salaries and benefits, and then hiring more workers to improve the quality of the product. Come to think of it, this may be the only case of finding a CEO *with* a brain.

—Larger media conglomerates have a tendency to swallow up smaller media conglomerates which had previously swallowed individual media companies.

—Most politicians (and quite a number of high-salaried journalists) proclaim they're for the working class. Then, after the TV cameras are gone, they go to their country club and agree with their upper-management dinner companions that the biggest problem in America is the demands from the working class.

303

ENTERTAINMENT

TELEVISION

Reality Blights

Doc. about MJ aired on ABC to combat Joe Millionaire videos.

NBC aired MJ interview after Fear Factor

ABC-TV had a great idea. To counter-program FOX-TV's two-hour season finale of "Joe Millionaire" in February 2003 during a ratings "sweeps week," it would re-run a two-hour interview-documentary about pop star Michael Jackson it had previously run only 10 days earlier. The documentary, based upon an eight-month investigation by journalist Martin Bashir and with Jackson's full cooperation, first aired on England's ITV. It revealed more than most stories over the past three decades about one of music's most innovative pioneers, as well as his plastic surgeries, his "social weirdness," and his alleged but never proven pedophilia.

NBC-TV also had an idea of how to counter-program "Joe Millionaire." At 8 p.m., it ran the reality show, "Fear Factor," in which seemingly normal people jump from trucks, eat roaches, and are covered by snakes. Afterward, it would air a two-hour documentary about Jackson—and discuss surgeries, weirdness, and alleged pedophilia.

VH1 the previous weekend had aired the ITV interview five times. Dozens of TV shows, including network morning news-entertainment shows, the major networks' evening news shows, and all of the Hollywood "news-and-puff" ones, had done mini-features about Jackson following his ITV interview.

The "sweeps week" counter-programming on Feb. 17, 2003, by ABC and NBC—CBS ran two half-hour sitcoms—didn't work. ABC drew 9.4 million, less than a third of the audience the first time it ran the interview; NBC drew 14.6 million. "Joe Million-aire" drew 42.6 million viewers, largest in FOX's 17-year history that also included pop culture hits "The Simpsons" and "Married: With Children."

The "reality" mini-series had taken Evan Marriott, an average intelligence pumped-up "hunk" who claimed he had made only $19,000 a year as a construction worker, put him and 20 women into a chalet in France, claimed he was heir to a $50 million fortune, and titillated a voyeuristic American public who salivated at the thought that when the seven week competition was over, "Joe" would select one of the breathless candidates to be his wife. It was a Cinderella story with gold-diggers, nubile nymphs, and several doses of malevolence coated by deceit among the would-be brides.

Reams of promotion by FOX led to thousands of newspaper and magazine articles, and uncounted hours of TV and radio chatter. *The New York Times* mentioned the "reality" show 29 times in the six weeks before the season finale. The *Philadelphia Inquirer* ran a dozen articles and included the show's continuing soap opera details in at least three dozen more. The *Los Angeles Times* ran 17 stories; the *Chicago Tribune* ran seven. Cover stories and multi-page spreads appeared in *People* and several other national magazines.

So popular had Reality TV become that ABC's "The Bachelor" and "The Bachelorette," similar to "Joe Millionaire," but with fewer lies, helped tear 20 percent off of the audience of NBC's "The West Wing," which had earned Emmys as Outstanding Drama in each of its first three seasons. But, NBC didn't have to worry much about gross income. It still had 10 Reality shows

With heavy media play and millions each week logging onto internet message boards and chat rooms, Reality TV has spun into the preferred way for millions to escape from a declining economy, a barrage of stories about political and corporate greed and corruption, and the war on terrorism.

During the 2008–2009 season, Reality TV shows grabbed more than one-fourth of all prime time scheduling for the six major on-air networks. Conceding the power of unscripted TV, the Television Academy of Arts and Sciences added an "Emmy" in 2008 for Outstanding Host of a Reality Show.

Reality TV primarily appeals to 21–49 year olds with upper middle class lifestyles and income, advertisers' prime target. The genre, which includes game shows, talent shows, and "day in a life" shows, had its origins almost with the birth of commercial television following World War II. "Candid Camera," in which Allen Funt and his crew set up outrageous acts to record the reactions and embarrassments of the unsuspecting and naive public, was probably the first. Unlike many of today's shows, it wasn't vicious or mean. Chuck Barris would later create "The Dating Game" in 1966, "The Newlywed Game" a year later, and several others which combined game shows and double entendre but family-acceptable sleaze that became the base of today's Reality TV.

"Talent Shows" had their origin in "Major Bowes Amateur Hour" on radio in the 1930s, "Arthur Godfrey's Talent Search" and "Ted Mack's Amateur Hour" on TV in the 1950s, before being vectored into a new direction by Chuck Barris' comedic farce, "The Gong Show" (1976–1980) that spawned the megasmash hits, "American Idol," "America's Got Talent," and "Dancing With the Stars." Requiring less talent are "Project Runway" and "America's Next Top Model," both of which take pre-selected model wannabes and process them.

"Day in the life shows" probably began with "Nightwatch" (1954–1955), a CBS radio series that followed police in Culver City, Calif., a Los Angeles suburb. The 48-episode series became the base 35 years later for FOX's "COPS," which allowed viewers to see police as they hunted and seized everyone from speeders to killers. By its 21st season in 2009, the show had become a staple of the network's entertainment line-up.

MTV's "The Real World," beginning in 1992, had cameras recording the second-by-second lives of seven 20-somethings put together into a house with a hot-tub, all of it to excite an ogling public. Amidst the voyeurism, critical social issues emerged to let teen viewers realize that a "real world" includes more than just all-night partying. Among continuing themes through all seasons, with each season in a different city, were prejudices and biases. For "The Real World: Key West" (2006), the housemates and producers faced the problem of a 24-year-old college graduate who was anorexic and also unable to stay away from an abusive boyfriend, against whom she had filed a protection from abuse order. It was in that season the cast also had to deal with a hurricane evacuation. Between January and April 2009, "The Real World" was set in Brooklyn for what producers called a "grittier" world; later that year, Cancun, essentially an American resort in Mexico, was the featured site. By the end of April, when the World Health Organization classified the Swine Flu (H1N1) pandemic as a Stage 5 alert, with probable origins in Mexico, the taping had been completed.

The "fly-on-the-wall" concept expanded year by year and network by network until MTV twisted the genre into an outrageous comedy by casting the Ozzy Osbourne family in a 30-minute Tuesday night series that drew 7.7 million viewers at its peak in 2002. "E!" Network became a player when it created the "Anna Nicole Show," featuring a former stripper and *Playboy* bunny of questionable intellect who became a household name after marrying an 89-year-old oil billionaire who died 14 months after the marriage. Other celebrity-reality series followed the families of KISS bass player Gene Simmons, pro wrestler Hulk Hogan, pop singer Paula Abdul, and Mötley Crüe drummer Tommy Lee who spent six episodes at the University of Nebraska.

Other popular "day in the life" shows included "Blind Date," "Elimidate," and "Shipmates," all of which set up hard-body and bodacious contestants on blind dates. "Temptation Island," which placed several couples on an island and "tempted" each with "hot" singles, was a ratings hit in its first season in 2001. However, viewers were titillated enough the first time; the second season fared poorly in the ratings. A "revival" a year later also failed to deliver high enough ratings for FOX to keep it on air. TV Land, which airs popular shows that are no longer being produced, entered Reality TV in 2009 with "The Cougar," a 40-year-old mother of four who, over a mini-season of eight shows, had to choose a boyfriend from 20 men, all of them in their 20s.

"Fear" shows place the cast into situations that lead viewers to experience both panic and revulsion. Based upon a show from the Netherlands, "Fear Factor," beginning in 2001, became an NBC-TV hit, and then dropped off the air after six seasons when viewers got their fill of the stunts and turned to other Reality TV shows.

"Survivor" rescued CBS-TV's sagging ratings in 2000 to reveal a world in which several people placed into two "tribes" on a remote part of the world would willingly undergo mind and body humiliation, vote off others for practical, personal, and political reasons, and arouse viewers to "see" all the human traits and emotions—as well as a few barely-clad lithe bodies.

ABC-TV learned a lesson when it became giddy and greedy with "Who Wants to be a Millionaire?" and increased its expo-

307

sure from weekly to three or four times a week, seeing "top 10" ratings for each night it aired before it fell off the charts from overexposure in 2002. The show, originally based upon a British version—its title was from a song in the film, *High Society* (1956)—returned as a successful syndicated daytime quiz show in 2002, with Meredith Vieira as host.

Reality TV is defined as "unscripted TV," but these "writers" are a combination of the producers who establish the framework and the video editors who take several hours of rather boring video footage and squeeze it into an hour of stimulating enticement to lure millions of younger viewers into a breathless frenzy.

For the TV networks, which are now paying a minimum of $2 million per episode for scripted shows—"ER" (1994–2009), once cost about $13 million an episode during its peak, and "Friends" cost about $10 million in 2003–2004, its last season—it means having to pay significantly less money for the no-name "stars," comparatively far less for the sets, and significantly less for those who are dubbed "writers" of unscripted game shows. Unlike scripted TV shows, which earn their producers and studios profits in re-runs and syndication, Reality TV shows are usually a one-time exposure; after the world knows who selects whom, or which fool is the most willing to be publicly humiliated and embarrassed, the public loses interest—at least in that show. But, like any addict, the public and their networks need a "fix," which is why more than 100 different series aired by the end of 2009.

Like all fads, Reality TV, which isn't an accurate depiction of reality, will also wither from overexposure as other fads come into the marketplace. But, for the decade it has dominated TV viewership, it brought an enjoyable few hours to the people and profits to the networks. It just hasn't come close to what the medium's pioneers had envisioned.

The Monday Night Football Game

The minuscule cocktail tables, red cloths draping their round tops, threaten to tip when pushed; nevertheless, they serve their dual functions as repositories for drinks and cigarettes, and as excuses to cluster chairs.

The semi-stuffed chairs that surround the tables, however,

are sturdy, made with a wood-like veneer for the back and base, and covered with a synthetic something-or-the-other that is supposed to look like leather. At the beginning of every afternoon, four chairs surround each table, making for intimate experiences; but the chairs roll, and during the evening will roll back and forth from table to table.

Along one wall, with its fake fireplace motif, are recently-manufactured Victorian-style couches and high-backed chairs. On the walls are photomurals—one of deer grazing in the field, the other of geese in flight. Near the geese are fake-wood bookshelves supporting *Reader's Digest* condensed books and plants that will never die.

A 60-foot U-shaped bar edged in Naugahyde softness guarded by 25 or 30 fake-oak bar stools is on the opposite side. Against another wall, not far from wood-paneled restrooms, six mics and four speakers quietly frame a Lilliputian bandstand that supports a set of drums and an electronic organ programmed so that anyone who can count to 4 can play it. On Thursdays, Fridays, and Saturdays, three singer-musicians will have their sounds amplified to the threshold of possibly wilting the plastic flowers.

Wood beams and amber chandeliers above, red and black patterned carpeting below. The lights are forever dim. Dim for effect; dim for illusion.

It's now 6 p.m., Monday. There are a few people here, most in their 20s and 30s. At the bar sits a lady, perhaps 25 or 30, maybe more, flanked by two men. The lady could be a secretary or junior executive. Her golden highlighted hair is gelled, curling-iron permed and blow-dried to give her a perfectly natural look. She wears makeup and lipstick; Max Factor on her face, Revlon on her lips. Her fashionably low-heeled pumps add an inch to her height. Her pink silk blouse and tan wool skirt could not have been bought more than a month ago. The two men, also in their late 20s or early 30s, could be lawyers or junior executives or ad salesmen. Suits of blue, ties of red. Modishly-long razor-cut blown-dry hair as painfully attained as the lady's covers half their ears. A slight fashion statement but nothing too extreme. Clean-shaven with a gentle splash of Bijam. Expensive-looking watches and 10-karat gold college rings.

First one, then another, talks to the lady. Then both talk to her. For part of the evening, she'll delight in being in the middle. They'll talk to her and with her; maybe later, about her.

But right now, they're both talking with her. About nothing really. They had earlier identified themselves by their occupations; she had identified herself by her astrological sign. Of course, this had meant that the two men had to identify their own signs. Compatibility is important in a place like this.

A man sits nearby, a touch of talcum and after-shave hinting the air, a V-neck casual synthetic drip-dry shirt hugging what probably was a washboard abdomen, drip-dry 501s hugging his waist and thighs, leather shoes caressing feet that undoubtedly have been adequately powdered. A few moments later, another man, almost a copy, but with a golden chain dangling in his "V"—few men will be bare-necked—sits down. There's now one immaculate lady surrounded by four *GQ*-approved men. To others, it appears they're close friends—buddies—pals. Singularly, they talk with her. About cars. About careers. They talk about this. And they talk about that. About promotions and job security, racquetball, jogging, or time-sharing. About something each of them read in *Maxim* or *Penthouse*, but which they remember as having read in *The Wall Street Journal*, or *Esquire*, or *Business Week*. The high cost of apartments and condos is a major problem. Finding a good stereo system or cellular phone for the BMW or Lexus is a major problem. Every now and then, there might be a discussion, but never controversy, about the Middle East, affirmative action, or the environment, the mouths parroting *TIME* and *Newsweek*, their concern as deep as cocktail glasses, as lasting as cocktail napkins.

Cocktail waitresses—costumed in black high heels, black-net hose, micro-mini fluffy skirts, push-up bras disguised beneath titillating-cut blouses—hustle the drinks while the customers hustle each other. No glass will be allowed to be empty more than moments. There's always another drink to be served, another tip to be earned.

At a table, a young man orders a Vodka-7; at another table, a young lady orders a Vodka-7. They have something in common. They glance at each other, and away from each other. She gets up, goes to the *hors d'oeuvre* table, and delicately places small carrot sticks and shrimp puffs on a small paper plate. It's just enough, but not too much. Must watch that waist. She turns, and almost falls over the gentleman who exchanged glances with her. She apologizes. He apologizes. They apologize. They giggle over their embarrassment of almost falling into each other, begin some small talk, then wander to a table at a neutral site. It's all so superficial, but no one cares. They need to be with someone. So they'll keep searching . . . reflecting . . . being conversationally attractive.

A pair of "barely-21s," a few months into the work force, enter and sit at a table. She's carded, her ID discretely checked by a waitress. This is too lucrative a business to be jeopardized by a Liquor Board violation. Her companion, blowing smoke rings from a Marlboro positioned beneath an anemic brown-blonde mustache, is accepted without ID. They order piña coladas and think they're in love.

Two 30ish ladies sit near one of the bookshelves. They talk what must seem to be "girl talk." Two 30ish guys sit near another bookshelf, talking "man talk." It isn't long before there are four people at one of the tables and no one at the other, and God-only-knows what they have to talk about.

The regulars greet each other; the infrequents settle in—watching—waiting. Four more razor-cut, blown-dry junior somethings enter, survey the swingles scene, find everyone attached to someone else, order Heinekins and Millers, talk, joke, make polite noises, and imagine they're successfully cool.

It's now 8:30. More than a hundred people are here. Talking. Chatting. Discussing. Talking about jobs and vacations, cars and condos. Every day it's the same. Every day the people are the same. And they all talk about never—*ever*—planning to get into a rut like Jim or Karen or Roger or Maureen. They all reaffirm that although they love their jobs and are more than amply rewarded, soon they'll be promoted or move to something better. There's always something better, whether people or jobs. And they're so busy hearing themselves that they don't know that no one's listening, but they'll be sure to "thank you for sharing that," or letting us know that they "can relate to that."

For the last time this evening, the *hors d'oeuvre* table is replenished, and the price of drinks goes up another fifty cents; Cokes and beer are now a buck-fifty, mixed drinks as much as $4.50. The sandwich-and-salad special is $7.95—chips and pickle slices included.

Nine O'clock. The bartender finally pushes buttons on a remote control, and from a large-screen television, Rams and Eagles appear. There's noise from the television and noise from the lounge. People are chatting and watching, hustling, munching, and drinking; in their confusion of who they are, and what

311

they want, they'll settle for instant friendships made in front of a cathode ray tube that changes pictures 30 times a second. The Monday Night Football Game is about to begin.

Re-running America— and Other Concerns

Like all mass media, television informs, entertains, and persuades. Often, it does all three exceedingly well. Sometimes, there are significant concerns, and quite a few questions.

—At one time, television was divided into 13-week blocks. This allowed news directors to fire anchors whose personality quotient and hair style withered, and network programming chiefs to dump a series whose ratings dropped faster than a politician's ethics. There were three 13-week blocks a year for entertainment shows; the fourth block was for Summer reruns.

However, the Suits-with-Gold-Chains figured it was not only less expensive to rerun a prime-time show, but that the public will tolerate anything as long as it's a hundred variations of the same thing. The result is that there are only about 22 new episodes of each show a year; the rest of the time is spent on reruns, "specials," or one-time pilots that were ordered by the nephew of the senior vice-president's second cousin. Of course, this means less money for writers, directors, and actors who are paid on a per-episode basis, and more for executives who are paid no matter how insignificant their brains.

—With the cost to produce a one hour prime-time TV show averaging about $3 million an episode, and figuring 22 shows a year, that's at least a $66 million outlay by the network, which brings in $100,000–$500,000 per 30-second ad. Being the producers, we do what every other producer does—we skim the profits, tell the cast and crew there's barely enough to cover costs, and take our rightful $10 million a year. At that rate, and assuming we can keep the $11 trillion national debt from increasing more than $13,000 a second, if producers donated even half of their profits before creative accounting changed the numbers, we should be debt free by the time the TV networks get an original idea.

—Whenever TV devotes more than 90 seconds to any story, it hires "expert" commentators. During the two Gulf Wars, the networks provided employment to retired generals. For most celebrity arrests and trials, it's the lawyers. The commentators, like most TV anchors, are White, college-educated, TV-quality clean-shaven-handsome, makeup-beautiful, and upper middle-class or upper-class. A typical day's TV news coverage includes lengthy snippets from the trial, reporters' comments, reporters talking to each other for their reactions, and reporters talking to lawyers who believe it's their sacred duty to uncover every mole on the face of the trial; yet, they still miss the greater body of criminal justice issues.

The media's failure to recognize and hire others who would have knowledge about crime in America is symptomatic of their fetish with what they believe are the "experts." It's no different when two people come into a newsroom—a well-groomed Suit with a press release about some owner's nephew getting a promotion, and a bag lady with information about police abuse of the homeless. Does anyone doubt which one the reporters will talk to first—assuming Security hasn't already thrown out the bag lady?

—Why do TV interviews always have cut-away shots of the reporter pretending to pay attention to what the news source is saying? Do we really need to see the reporter silently emoting three times in a 90 second interview?

—Several years ago, the late night talk shows booked authors for the last segment. Now, they book mounds of noise disguised as alternative rock groups. Does this indicate a change in American culture and values, or only that associate producers no longer can read?

—Every time I turn on a TV set, some actor or actress is pumping the charity-of-the-moment. There's perennial favorite Jerry Lewis and Muscular Dystrophy. For the homeless, we have Billy Crystal, Whoopie Goldberg, and Robin Williams. There's outlaw country singer Willie Nelson for Farm Aid, and squeaky-clean Osmonds for the Miracle network. Even Sally Struthers gets into the picture by pumping for some starving foreign children who need our fifteen bucks a month so they can take correspondence courses and become brain surgeons. Most believe in their causes; a few do it because of a publicist's suggestion. With all the good charities taken up, I wonder if some aspiring actress was denied an audition because her agent couldn't find her a suitable charity.

—Why does almost every starlet who's taken three acting les-

313

sons believe she has been given innate wisdom to "feel" her character and rewrite Arthur Miller's script?

MOVIES

Title Inflation

It took two directors, two executive producers, three producers, four writers, and very bad acting to ruin *Down to Earth* (2001), starring Chris Rock as a Harlem comic who dies before his time, and then is sent back to earth in a different body. In Hollywood's share-the-blame standards, this film is a Paramount release of a Village Roadshow Pictures presentation in association with NPV Entertainment of an Alphaville 3 Arts Entertainment production.

More telling than the cauldron of producers and companies was that this particular "bomb" was the fourth version of a late 1930s Broadway hit, written by Harry Seagall. The first movie version, *Here Comes Mr. Jordan*, had only one director, one producer, and one production company. Starring Robert Montgomery as a boxer, with all-star actors Edward Everett Horton and Claude Raines, the film became a critical success. In 1947, Columbia remade the film as *Down to Earth*, with Rita Hayworth as a muse sent to help a struggling Broadway musical. Like its predecessor, there was only one director, one producer, and one production company. And, like the 1941 version, it too was a box-office critical hit. Three decades later, Warren Beatty starred as a quarterback in *Heaven Can Wait*, with a screenplay by Beatty and Elaine May. This time, there were three producers, including Beatty—and seven Academy Award nominations.

It took a director, four producers, an executive producer, a co-producer, an associate producer, and a couple of writers to create *Sweet November (2001)*, another bomb, this one starring Keanu Reeves as an uptight ad exec and Charlize Theron as a free spirit with a terminal secret who entices and enchants men, forces them to explore their lives and values, and then leaves them a month later. The 1968 version, a far superior production written by Herman Raucher and starring Sandy Dennis and Anthony Newley, had only two producers. More important, it easily had twice the charm of the remake which showcases the Hollywood new age reality that cameras and editing can make even mediocre actors appear on screen as multi-million dollar properties. *Gone With the Wind* and *Citizen Kane,* unarguably Hollywood's top two films, each had only one producer.

See Spot Run (2001), with a mastiff outacting David Arquette and almost everyone else, required eight writers, three executive producers, three producers, and two co-executive producers.

The Break-Up (2006), about two characters who had broken off a relationship, ironically starred Jennifer Aniston, who had recently broken up with Brad Pitt amid almost unprecedented media exposure. To explain the fictional break-up, the movie required five writers, two executive producers, two producers, two co-producers, and two associate producers.

Sex and the City (2008), based upon the hit TV series, credits two executive producers, five producers, one line producer, and two associate producers for a 145 minute film that grossed over $150 million but received mixed reviews.

Action-adventure stories often carry several people with "producer" somewhere in their title. *Spider-Man 3* (2007), with gross revenue of about $340 million, had three executive producers and three producers. *The Dark Knight* (2008), like *Spider- Man* a critically-acclaimed blockbuster film, required four executive producers, three producers, one line producer, and one associate producer. However, Batman himself required only boy wonder Robin and faithful butler Alfred Pennyworth to produce his adventures. *The Incredible Hulk* (2008) required four executive producers, three producers, and three associate producers to bulk him up.

Stoner movies have always been popular, especially since the target audience of movies is teenagers. *Up in Smoke* (1978), Cheech and Chong's first movie, had a paltry list of only two producers and one associate producer. However, the genre itself spawned more producers than smoke. *Harold and Kumar Go to White Castle* (2004) had six executive producers, two producers, one co-producer and one associate producer. The second in the series, *Harold and Kumar Escape from Guantanamo Bay* (2008) had three executive producers, two prouducers, five co-producers, one line producer, and one consulting producer.

For television productions, to the mix of producers, executive producers, line producers, co-producers, and co-executive producers, add in a few supervising producers. It isn't uncommon for one TV series to have a dozen or more persons with "producer" in their titles. For talk shows, add at least a half dozen associate producers, most of whom are responsible for making phone calls.

Broadway is no better than Hollywood when it comes to title inflation. The *Norman Conquests*, which received the Tony in 2009 for best revival of a play had 22 persons and organizations listed as producers; *Hair*, the best musical revival, had 20 producers. *Billy Elliot*, the best musical, had four separate organizations as producers; *God of Carnage*, the best play, listed six individuals and two organizations as producers.

Newspaper reporters who rewrite press releases might be the one-person automotive editor/real estate editor/air transportation editor. Her boss—who also supervises the books editor/films editor/fashion editor—might be the associate managing editor for features who reports to a managing editor for features, supposedly a separate but equal title to the managing editor for news, the managing editor for sports, and the administrative managing editor.

In the corporate structure of the larger book publishing companies are a plethora of editorial assistants, assistant editors, associate editors, editors, senior editors, executive editors, and a mix of various levels of vice-presidents, some of whom may even be literate.

Banks hand out titles with as much regularity as they create new fees. Wells Fargo Bank has four senior executive vice-presidents, three executive vice-presidents, one group executive vice-president, and dozens of vice-presidents and assistant vice-presidents. Wachovia had 12 executive vice-presidents before its acquisition by Wells Fargo in 2009. Even the friendly neighborhood community bank that prides itself on smiley $8–10 an hour tellers, employ a wad of persons with "vice-president" somewhere in their titles.

The American auto industry, deep in bankruptcy and reorganization, has several dozen vice-presidents. Academics has also succumbed to Title Inflation. At most colleges are several vice-presidents, each with at least one assistant and associate vice-president.

If corporate America, which already owns the government, could figure out a way to amend the Constitution, we might now return to a structure of electing an elite board of directors, which we'll call the Senate, which will then elect a chairman of the board and CEO who will oversee thousands of vice-presidents, instead of just thousands of politically-appointed special assistants, deputy special assistants, cabinet secretaries, undersecretaries, deputy undersecretaries, and assistant secretaries.

The Hustle

The hustle had begun less than six hours after they buried the producer when the production manager on a 30-minute "infomercial" decided he wanted four times more money since he figured it was now more difficult without the producer.

The widow, who had been in "The Industry" for 17 years, said there wasn't that much money, especially since the production manager had taken it upon himself that evening to hire not only another production assistant, but also a script clerk whose only talent seemed to be that she smiled a lot at the production manager.

But the production manager knew there was now no way production could be completed without him—and his friend. The friend was a salesman who somehow had become the star's agent, and then decided to become a producer. After all, with his gold-color Cadillac, $150 shoes, open shirt, and three golden chains strung around his neck, he looked Hollywood.

In his best macho voice, the salesman-producer proclaimed to cast and crew, "We'll do whatever is fair." He decided it was "fair" for everyone, including him, to get more money. Naturally, the additional expense would come from the widow's pocket—and from the "star" who was convinced that "good" production needed even more money. Well, thought the widow, at least she could count on the Russians not doing anything stupid. She was wrong.

The "Russians" were two Russian immigrants who had been neophyte film makers in the Soviet Union, but who had defected because they were denied "artistic freedom." Neither was political; they just wanted a chance to get more work.

The now-deceased American producer-director had been the only one who had given the Russians film work in more than three years. When the producer-director died, the Russian first assistant director became the director at twice his original salary. Within hours, he claimed the American director of photography didn't know what he was doing, and gave control to the other Russian who had originally been hired as a production assistant.

The day after the producer was buried, the Russians demanded even more money. Naturally, the salesman-agent agreed; it was, as he proudly proclaimed, "only fair." Then, a young assistant cameraman decided that twice his contract rate was "only fair." And someone else submitted an expense voucher for eight hours driving time for a hundred mile trip.

Next, the salesman-agent who thought he was a producer decided the script needed changing, so he changed it without consulting the writer or director, and set back production two more days and several thousand more dollars. Then, he decided it was time to tell the film editor and sound engineer they weren't competent and to dismiss both of them, although the film editor had taken numerous productions through final edit during his three decade career.

When the unions started questioning some work rule violations, the salesman-agent tried "sweet talking" them—he called it PR—and handed out some "gifts." Only because the now-deceased director-producer had such a good working relationship with the unions, and because of concern for the widow, did the union return the gifts and decide not to shut down the production and bring the amateurs up on numerous charges, including stupidity.

So now, "The Magnificent Four"—the salesman-agent, production manager, the director, and the cinematographer—were going to edit the film—if they could just get it out of the lab.

"The film won't cut," the widow had been saying all along, knowing that the way it was shot after her husband's death was so scattered that scenes didn't match, and that an editor would have an impossible time putting it all together.

"You're crazy!" they told her, and kept shooting fill-in scenes, raising the budget but not the possibility that the 30-minute infomercial would look like anything but a quilt of scenes.

"You don't have a film," she now firmly told them to their sarcasm. But, when they tried to get the negative out of the film lab, they were told that, indeed, they didn't have a film. By law, the widow was the only one who could release the negative; after all, she was the one who had previously paid for it.

For the next six months, the four would-be film makers, their lawyers and cronies, tried every trick they could to get the film. None succeeded.

"Buy me out," she said cooly. They had no other choice. But at least they were now "Hollywood," and could use their production credit to convince other companies to invest in making infomercials, even if the production quality relegated it to late night television.

A Classical Case of Dis-honor

It was early morning when Marshbaum burst into the office, and breathlessly asked for my agent's phone number.

"He only represents published writers," I reminded my occasionally able assistant.

"But this is a best-seller!" he proclaimed.

"He doesn't handle historical romances, celebrity know-nothing tell-alls, and diet books."

Marshbaum was offended. "You think I'd write trash? I'm going to write a classic."

"Marshbaum," I tried to explain, "you don't set out to write a classic. It becomes one afterwards."

"Not a problem. I'm going to call it *Gone With the Wind*."

"You can't steal a title," I said astonished at his new level of stupidity.

He looked at me as if I had once again failed Comp 101. "Titles can't be copyrighted," he reminded me. "I can call my chart-topper anything I want. I'd-a-thought you big-shot columnists would know something other than when Happy Hour is!"

"I doubt anyone will buy your book," I retorted.

"That's the beauty of it," he said. "Not only am I going to use Margaret Mitchell's title, I'm also going to use all of her words. Same book. Exact same words. New book jacket. Big sales."

Although I function well in the early morning, I knew Marshbaum was a late night person. Apparently, his brain was fermented by watching too many Jerry Springer sex-and-hate-fests. "That's plagiarism," I said.

"That's marketing," he responded. "I'll write every word, just as Maggie did. Maybe change the time frame a bit here or there. Add some updated words. I mean, 'fiddle-dee-dee' is bound to have some four-letter replacement."

"It's insane!" I told him.

"It's *Psycho*," he told me. "Gus Van Sant just did it with Alfred Hitchcock's classic. Frame by frame. New actors; same shooting script."

The original *Psycho*, with the shower scene and Bates Motel—where Marion Crane checked in, but didn't check out—was filmed in six weeks during 1960. Written by Joseph Stefano, and based upon Robert Bloch's novel, the movie became one of the 100 best films of the century, according to the American Film

Institute. And, by anyone's standards, the way it was filmed made it the most compelling work of suspense and horror ever produced. Van Sant, who directed the Oscar-nominated *Good Will Hunting* (1997), says he was paying a tribute to Hitchcock by copying the original classic. The big difference was that the new *Psycho,* released in 1998, was in color, and you got a voyeuristic glimpse of Anne Heche nude. "I was planning to put Scarlett and Rhett into a hot tub," said Marshbaum. I patiently explained the difference between film and a novel. "There's very little original in films, anyway," I said.

"Have you been to the bookstore lately," he asked with a smirk. "Wanna see shelves of the same formula, packaged with four-color covers that entice you to part with three hours of your gross income?"

"It may be true that publishers may be putting out the same tired clap," I admitted, "but you can't just take a classic, retype it, and sell it as a tribute to Margaret Mitchell!"

"They did a *Gone With the Wind* sequel," he said. "Piece of drivel. All those historical romances are the same thing, only with a different title, and some phony woman's name as an—" he almost spit it out—"author!" I was about to interrupt, when he continued. "They did three sequels and one "pre-sequel" to *Psycho,* four *Lethal Weapon*s, six *Rocky*s, seven *Nightmare on Elm Street*s, nine *Halloween*s, 11 *Friday the Thirteenth*s, and 11 *Star Trek*s. What better way to honor excellence than by re-doing the original?" He paused a moment, looked into my eyes, and proclaimed, "At least you know it'll be good."

Kernels of Truth

It was an important news day. The massacre in Rwanda, which followed a period of stability following a three-year civil war, continued with no hope for peace, and would claim 200,000–400,000 more lives. In Somalia, warlords were still fighting small battles for political control. In Haiti, soldiers murdered two dozen fishermen. Serbian artillery was still hammering targets in Bosnia. South African politicians were campaigning for office in the country's first election in which all citizens could vote. In America, thousands still were not receiving adequate health care, President Bill Clinton had called for Social Security to be taken out of the Department of Health and

Human Services and become an independent agency, and Americans were planning to go to Yorba Linda, Calif., to pay tribute to former President Richard Nixon who had died a few days earlier.

But, the most important news story, the one CNN and the networks pumped all day long, the one that was splashed in inch-high type across six columns on newspaper front pages, told a shocked America that theater popcorn was dangerous.

The Center for Science in the Public Interest told reporters that a medium bag of popcorn, popped in coconut butter, had more fat than a day's high fat menu of a bacon-and-eggs breakfast, a Big Mac and large fries lunch, and a steak dinner with baked potato and a mound of sour cream. Add a few wisps of butter, and you need a rotorouter to clean your arteries. The Council claimed that theater owners use coconut oil because it gives popcorn a unique theatrical flavor that the almost-healthy corn oil or air popping can't.

After learning that cigarette smoke is dangerous, thousands of Americans stopped smoking after sex. But, because of AIDS and other venereal diseases, they also decided to abstain entirely. So, they went to R-rated movies, but now we learn they can't even munch popcorn, and must now practice Safe Kernel.

Because about 90 percent of all movie house revenue is from food sales, the impact could force theaters out of business. If attendance at movies drops because of a drop in popcorn sales, then thousands of actors, costumers, and film projectionists will be thrown into the unemployment lines. There's nothing more pathetic than seeing Clint Eastwood whimpering to an unemployment clerk about how hard he tried that week to get a decent minimum-wage job.

Those addicted to popcorn might be able to smuggle in a bag or two. Naturally, theaters, to preserve their dwindling profits, would have to hire popcorn police to make sure that didn't happen. Since there's no ban on assault weapons, the Kernel Kops could spray a few thousand rounds of 9 mm. shells against popcorn smugglers.

Somewhere, a governmental body will soon prescribe there must be separate sections of the theater for those who eat popcorn and those who don't. After all, secondary popcorn smell can be almost as devastating as drinking a gallon of coconut oil. At the very least, there would have to be warnings on popcorn bags, like, "Eating too much popcorn can make you go blind" or

"Making noise while eating popcorn can injure your eardrums and annoy that spike-helmeted biker nearby."

More than a decade after the popcorn "revelation," Congress still hasn't convened a special select subcommittee to analyze the impact of popcorn upon society. Apparently, the Popcorn Lobby was too influential.

A cigarette company executive, with a straight face, once told a Congressional Committee that cigarette smoking was no worse than eating Twinkies. If he had said that cigarette smoking wasn't as bad as munching theater popcorn, he'd probably be a hero of the industry by now.

Of course, producers will continue to churn out R-rated movies with 62,000 violent acts per hour, and feel rather safe about their Constitutional license to practice freedom of celluloid. And the news media will still miss significant and important stories to go for the fluff and puff.

Mega-Mouths, Squawkers, and the 'Hollyweird'

The talk show squawkers call them the "Hollyweirds" and "Left Coast Hollywood Kooks." Makes no difference if they're writers, actors, directors, producers, or grips and gaffers. Makes no difference if they're poets, artists, sculptors, dancers, cartoonists, musicians, or singers. It makes no difference if they live in Southern California or Iowa. As long as they're in the creative arts, they're "Hollyweird."

No one knows when the term was first used, but it first became popular on radio talk shows during the first Clinton presidential campaign of 1992. The Righteous Ranters had increased their screeching in 1999 when numerous celebrities spoke out against the presidential candidacy of George W. Bush. And, then, having seen Al Gore lose the election in 2000, the creative community not only had the audacity to oppose President Bush's let-the-oil flow domestic policies but they, like millions of others, spoke out against the President's one-note chorus to go to war in Iraq on claims we now know (and many knew then) were stirred in a cauldron of lies.

Although callers to talk shows say that although Americans have the right of free speech, celebrities should "keep their pie-holes shut," since they not only aren't knowledgeable enough to be in politics, but that they unabashedly use their fame to lure the naïve media into reporting their views. The celebrities "are abusing their stature [and] need to be put back in their place [and] need to understand where they are in the great food chain of life," said John Kobylt, talk-show host at radio powerhouse KFI-AM in Los Angeles.

Of course, none of the hosts understand that they are also celebrities who use the media to pound their views into the public. Rather than challenge their ideas, the talk-show hosts and many of their audience often resort to name-calling, spitting out venom that classifies celebrities as "whackos" and "looney-tunes." During the War in Iraq, the talk-show addicts falsely and maliciously claimed that anyone—celebrity or laborer—who disagreed with President Bush's call for war not only supported world-wide terrorism, but didn't support the troops; they were branded unpatriotic traitors. The talk-show hosts and their callers don't even need to identify these "traitors." Americans know they're the Dixie Chicks, who told the world they were ashamed of George W. Bush and were soon southern fried in the media. In October 2006, the Weinstein Co. released Barbara Kopple's documentary, *Shut Up and Sing*, the story of the nation's response to the Dixie Chicks' comments against the War in Iraq and of President Bush. Both NBC and the CW networks refused to air commercials for the film; they claimed the commercials were disrespectful of the President.

Others who were targetted as unAmerican because they spoke out against government policies were Ed Asner, Kevin Bacon, Alec Baldwin, Cher, George Clooney, Matt Damon, Mike Farrell, Norman Lear, Paul Newman, Sarah Jessica Parker, Robert Redford, Rob Reiner, Tim Robbins, Julia Roberts, Susan Sarandon, Martin Sheen, Aaron Sorkin, Meryl Streep, Barbara Streisand, Lily Tomlin, Robin Williams, and thousands of others who have spoken out against the war in Iraq or the political philosophy of those who place themselves as the nation's "only true patriots."

Joe Scarborough, a former congressman from Florida, declared Danny Glover was "un-American" for speaking against President Bush. To make America whole again, Scarborough posted the phone number for MCI and told his MSNBC viewers to call the telephone giant to dump Glover as a spokesperson. Thousands did just as they were told.

So powerful is the backlash against celebrities that Lori Bardsley, a housewife in North Carolina, collected more than 100,000 online signatures in a little more than one month on her petition that claimed celebrities were "using their celebrity [status] to interfere with the defense of our country."

Patriotic Americans Boycotting Anti-American Hollywood (PABAAH) went even further. It not only called actors Sean Penn and Janeane Garofalo traitors, it demanded the Attorney General to charge writer/film maker Michael Moore with treason. PABAAH's mission was to get Americans to boycott movies that featured actors who opposed the Bush–Cheney Administration. They wanted people to boycott *Sky Captain and the World of Tomorrow* (2004) because Gwyneth Paltrow said she worried about "a weird, over-patriotic atmosphere" in the United States.

Advertising pitches are acceptable; social and political opinions by celebrities aren't. "The media created us, puts us on the air, and then says, 'How dare you use your rights as a celebrity?'" TV producer Robert Greenwald told the Reuters news agency.

Although opposed to the creative community, the talk-show crowd had no hesitation when it brought out multi-Grammy winner Travis Tritt who majestically declared, "to be a good American . . . you have to get behind President Bush." The Bush–Cheney campaign of 2004 didn't reject the endorsements of Jessica Simpson, Bo Derek, and Britney Spears. It didn't reject the support of Drew Carey, Dixie Carter, Charlie Daniels, Larry Gatlin, Kelsey Grammer, Ricky Schroeder, James Woods, the entire NASCAR starting lineup, and Shirley Jones who, like Tritt, said she found it "astonishing to see how many of these Hollywood big-wigs are trying to undermine President Bush."

Charlie Daniels called anti-war celebrities "the most disgusting examples of a waste of protoplasm I've ever had the displeasure to hear about," and said he wouldn't go to any of their movies. "Barbara Streisand has opened her alligator-sized mouth wide before her humming bird brain has had a chance to catch up," ranted R. Lee Ermey, whose best-known role was as a drill sergeant in *Full Metal Jacket* (1987). His argument, reported in London's *Sunday Telegraph*, was that Streisand used the "'bully pulpit', helped by her fame, and people think she's talking for Hollywood."

Long before he became a two-term Republican governor and

then a two-term president, Ronald Reagan was a staunch Democrat and president of the Screen Actors Guild. At a time when super-patriots were sloshing the epithets of "Commie" and "pinko" upon everyone who had an opinion different from their own, Ronald Reagan initially stood with his membership of actors, looked Congress in the eye and declared he wasn't about to play into their hands and name names during the witch hunts of the early 1950s. The nation has also been represented by actors Sen. George Murphy (R-Calif.); Sen. Fred Thompson (R-Tenn.); Harvard-educated but forever "Love Boat gopher" Rep. Fred Grandy (R-Iowa); and singer Rep. Sonny Bono (R-Calif.), who appeared several times on "Love Boat,"and whose fourth wife, Mary, followed him into the Congress where she has served six terms.

No Republican screamed in agony when moderate Republican Gov. Arnold Schwarzenegger told a prime-time TV audience during the Republican National Convention in September 2004 that he was there to help terminate the "girlie-man" Democratic opposition. Schwarzenegger had used his celebrity status to announce his candidacy to more than seven million viewers on the "Tonight Show Starring Jay Leno." The announcement was so important that it blew off the nation's front pages stories about Marines landing in Liberia and soldiers being killed in Iraq. Schwarzenegger's appearance with Jay Leno was featured on the morning news/entertainment shows, and led evening network news reports. The next day, Schwarzenegger appeared on almost all major TV entertainment programs. Dozens of satellite trucks left the Kobe Bryant circus they created in Colorado to report the rape trial of an NBA superstar in order to carry the Arnold Juggernaut to millions of Californians and hundreds of million Americans.

Schwarzenegger's successful campaign that led to his inauguration in November 2003, after having received 48.6 percent of the vote, caused talk-show addicts to twist into knots. They supported him, but were conflicted because he's liberal on numerous social issues. He's pro-choice, believes in limited gun control, and is strong in both affirmative action and educational reform.

In campaign rallies in 2004, President George W. Bush castigated those whom he claimed believed the "heart and soul of America can be found in Hollywood." To large raucous preselected audiences which roundly booed the "Holly-weirds," the

President then jerked them into a cheering throng of super-patriots—the equivalent of TV and film extras—when he declared, "The heart and soul of America is right here in——." Just fill in the blank with whatever community the campaign descended upon.

Like every celebrity, this President—like other presidents before him, like other presidents after him—had his own body-guards, publicists, and posse. Before every public speech, he rehearsed his lines, sat for several minutes of makeup, hair dressing, and primping, and from a stage backed by profession-ally-crafted scenery read his speech from a teleprompter. The resemblance to a Hollywood set was lost upon those who spit out celebrities' names as if they were a wedge of spoiled cheese. Also lost is the irony that for nine years Bush was on the board of directors of Silver Screen Management, a film production company that once had a lucrative distribution deal with Walt Disney, which had dumped *Fahrenheit 911*, the Michael Moore film critical of—who else?—George W. Bush.

Every politician—from presidential aspirant to candidate for the local village council—Democrat, Republican, Libertarian, Socialist, or Green Party—liberal or conservative—meek or over-the-top—becomes a celebrity, the reality reflected not by their own views, but by how the media perceive them and report their campaigns.

Applauding Hollywood's Patriots

Sandra Bullock and Leonardo DiCaprio each donated $1 million for disaster relief following the December 2004 Sumatra–Andaman earthquake/tsunami in Southeast Asia. The Steven Spielberg family donated $1.5 million. Jet Li donated more than $125,000; Jackie Chan added at least $64,000. Among several dozen rock bands which donated proceeds of their concerts or made outright donations, U-2 and Linkin Park each donated $100,000; Ozzie and Sharon Osbourne donated $200,000. At the Laugh Factory in both Los Angeles and New York, major comedians donated their time, with proceeds benefiting the victims. The Red Cross says innumerable celebrities made anony-mous donations.

Dozens of "A"-list celebrities, many with Oscars, Grammys, Emmys, Tonys, and Obies became part of a live broadcast fundraiser for the tsunami victims—and worked the phones to take pledges from Americans whose names were unknown outside their own communities. George Clooney, who had helped organize the creative community for the 9/11 telethon that raised more than $130 million three years earlier, again rounded up his friends and their friends for "Tsunami Aid: A Concert of Hope."

Clooney and the creative community were again there for the victims of Hurricanes Katrina and Rita in Fall 2005; he donated an additonal $1 million. Also donating $1 million each were Nicolas Cage, Celine Dion, and rappers Jay-Z and Diddy. Steven Spielberg donated $750,000. Hillary Duff donated $250,000. John Grisham, whose best-selling books have been turned into box-office smash movies, donated $5 million.

Several stars set up foundations specifically to assure that funds were sent directly to those most affected by the tragedy. Michael Jackson recorded "From the Bottom of My Heart," with all proceeds going to hurricane victims. More important, the stars donated their time. Hundreds volunteered their talents at telethons and charity auctions; hundreds went into the storm-ravaged Gulf Coast to personally work with the victims. Harry Anderson, Harry Connick Jr., Ellen DeGeneres, and Wynton Marsalis, all originally from New Orleans, were there to help the people. Montel Williams not only provided food and juice for hurricane victims, he worked with them; Jamie Foxx, Samuel L. Jackson, Julia Roberts, John Travolta, and numerous others working with relief agencies, brought food; Gloria Estefan, Andy Garcia, and Jimmy Smits took toys to the children; Rapper David Banner grabbed what he could from his closets and delivered clothing to victims in his native Mississippi; Rosie O'Donnell's For All Kids Foundation donated $3 million. Sean Penn, vilified for several years by the talk shows, spent days in the New Orleans area helping people. When talk show hosts questioned his motives, claiming he was doing it just for the publicity, Penn fired back: "I'm a 45-year-old man with two kids, and I've had plenty of attention in my life. I don't need to dive into toxic waste for that."

Rush Limbaugh and his Dittoheads call most of the creative community "the Hollyweird" and "Left Coast Hollywood Kooks," traitors who should be exiled. But it is these "kooks" who are among the first to respond to humanitarian needs.

In 1985, Bob Geldof organized Live Aid. From Black Sabbath and Judas Priest to B.B. King, Joan Baez, and the Beach Boys, dozens of the best pop singers and musicians came together for 16 hours that led to more than $100 million in contributions for the people of Ethiopia who were dying in a famine that had been flamed by the world's neglect.

Shortly after Live Aid, acting on Bob Dylan's suggestion, Willie Nelson, Neil Young, and John Mellencamp organized Farm Aid to help struggling farmers who were being forced into poverty and bankruptcy by corporate farming.

Following 9/11, Madonna and Julia Roberts each donated $2 million for victims and their families. They were only two of thousands from the creative community, most earning less than $50,000 a year, to contribute.

The "Left Coast Liberals" have been the face of almost every charity in America. It's Danny Kaye and Audrey Hepburn who spent innumerable days every year working with UNICEF in places Americans seldom want to tour. It's Jerry Lewis, who has worked tirelessly for the Muscular Dystrophy Association for more than 40 years, and it's Paul Simon who's an active contributor for the Children's Health Fund, It's Michael J. Fox whose foundation has raised more than $50 million for research into Parkinson's disease. It's Marlo Thomas who has continued the work of her father, actor/comedian Danny Thomas, at St. Jude Hospital. It's Elizabeth Taylor who helped Americans develop a conscience about AIDS at a time when many Americans, if they even had heard about the fatal disease, believed it was "God's revenge" for people being gay, a belief that unfortunately still remains among the ignorant. It's Sting who campaigns to save the rain forests, Robert Redford who is active in environmental issues, and Bono whose work with Amnesty International is as important as his music. It's Angelina Jolie, who unselfishly works with Third World poverty and who donated $1 million for Afghan refugees and $5 million for an animal sanctuary in Cambodia. It's Bradley Whitford and Jane Kaczmarek who organized Clothes Off Our Backs, a continuing auction of stars' clothes that provides funds for not only tsunami victims but also for other humanitarian charities. It's conservatives Donnie and Marie Osmond, lumped into the "celebrity" swatch, who pitch for the Children's Miracle Network. And it's Paul Newman whose company, Newman's Own, donated more than $250 million to charities, and provides millions of dollars a year to help children with cancer and blood diseases. After Newman died in 2008, the company he founded continues to donate its entire profits to help people. Name a charity, and a celebrity is out front donating funds and time.

In Internet chat rooms, and on blogs and call-in radio shows, the vitriolic right wing babble that the "left-wing" donated millions to try to defeat George W. Bush for a second term in 2004 and John McCain in his 2008 presidential campaign, but failed to contribute like amounts for disaster relief. When confronted with the facts, which seldom happens on radio talk-shows, they blathered that the celebrities donated only so they could get their names in the papers. There is no medication for the verbal diarrhea that gushes from their loose minds that celebrities should be contributing to American causes, not those of "them furriners" who didn't provide money for disasters in the U.S. There's no salve that will heal the viciousness of the rabid-mouths who castigated the Heinz Endowment for donating "only" $450,000 for tsunami relief, or who believe Alan Alda, Kirk Douglas, Martin Sheen, Rob Reiner, Tim Robbins, Susan Sarandon, and Barbra Streisand, who donate millions to humanitarian causes, are self-promoting unpatriotic scum who should donate even more.

If the "Left-Wing Kooks" responded in similar fashion as the "Right-Wing Nuts" they would flood the Internet, the radio talk shows, and the newspapers' letters columns. But they don't. They just keep giving, some using their media-induced fame to generate even more donations for humanitarian needs, many of them making large donations of time and money anonymously. The creative community continues to give, even while being viciously attacked for using their self-endowed rights of dissent that Jefferson, Madison, and the Founding Fathers demanded of all citizens. And that's what true patriotism is all about.

MUSIC

Three Nights a Week

This is the true story of a better-than-average musician and a slick out-of-town entertainer.

It all began one afternoon when the struggling musician lined up a paying audition at a local nightclub. One hour—$50. If the audience liked what it heard, there would be a contract. Four hours a night; three nights a week; $50 per person per night. Not much, but it was work, and recently the musician's bass was in the pawn shop more than it was on stage.

Hopefully, this gig would last a few weeks, giving him spending money so he could cut back the hours on his day job as a carpenter. He called up a better-than-average drummer who was working at a drive-through car wash, and began searching for a lead singer.

Enter the slick out-of-town entertainer.

At one time, Slick was an opening act lounge entertainer. For years, he had made the rounds of clubs in Reno, Tahoe, and Vegas. But it had been awhile since Slick was on stage, and now he was broke. The musician knew Slick needed money, and Slick knew that the musician needed him in the trio.

Four hours before the audition, Slick showed up for rehearsal, and almost as soon as he unpacked his guitar began whining. The songs weren't right. The arrangements weren't right. The harmonies weren't right. The only thing right, of course, was Slick. Later that evening, the trio went to the club, two of them hoping that Slick wouldn't desert them, and Slick planning to desert faster than crowds leaving a free bar when the booze runs out.

For $60 an hour, the trio gave the audience what it wanted. When the set was over, the club manager agreed to hire the impromptu trio. Four hours a night; three nights a week; $60 per night per person. If the trio could "bring in a clientele," there would be more nights, more pay. But it wasn't going to happen.

"I'm not going to do it," Slick told a mutual friend of the bass player and expected the friend to tell the musician. "These guys aren't any good," Slick proclaimed.

"They're tired. They had to work day jobs. They'll get better. A week of rehearsal and—"

"Place is a dive. Look at the crowd. Bunch of drunks. Tell them I'm out."

"You tell them," said the friend curtly.

The following Thursday night, the musician and the drummer, with a replacement lead singer/guitarist, opened at the club to an appreciative audience. They danced; they drank more beer; they left nice tips. Everything seemed to be going well. But two weeks after that, the club manager said he couldn't afford the trio—who were getting $60 per person per night. "I'm sorry," he apologized. "You guys were good, but I just can't afford it." It was just a matter of finances. It happens all the time.

The next week, the trio was replaced by . . . *Slick* who, the night before the audition almost a month earlier, had left his home phone number with the manager. And, said Slick, he would work three nights a week for $125 a night—as a solo— thus saving the club about $175 a week.

Goodbye Trio; Hello Slick.

In a couple of weeks, many of the faithful customers, the ones who drank buck-a-mug beer and wanted dance music not ballads and folk music, began to leave, and a lot of new customers, who didn't come to dance, began sitting at the tables, buying three-buck mixed drinks and four-buck no-frills sandwiches. They didn't care how Slick got his job, or that he wasn't reporting his wages to the union. Slick was happy; the new audience was happy; the club manager was happy, and even raised the wage another $75 a week.

But, revenues began slipping. Although the customers were buying more expensive drinks, they were nursing them longer, just sitting and talking and not leaving as much for the waitresses as the beer crowd had. Soon, even this audience slowly began to leave. People can dance to the same music night after night, but they won't listen to the same tunes night after night.

Now, Slick may be ethically-challenged but he's no fool, so he had asked another club manager to drop by the club one evening, while there were still a lot of customers. Four months after his first set, after Saturday evening's last set, moments after he packed up his guitar and collected his pay, Slick gave notice. Five days later, he was at a new club. The original club no longer had a Slick, and the revenues fell even further as the new faithful crowd went somewhere else, and the old faithful crowd had long ago deserted, and Slick was somewhere else, making money on an endless journey to capture what once might have been.

Spearing a Tax Deduction

On a bright Monday morning, I bumped into my ersatz friend Marshbaum who was placing a change container at the Gas-High Mini-mart on Low Octane and Greed avenues.

"March of Dimes?" I asked.

"Dimes. Quarters. Ten-dollar bills. Whatever."

Since he misunderstood my question, I tried it another way.

"What charity? Humane Society? MS? Veterans Relief?"

"Even better. A museum."

"Science museum for kids? Art museum?"

"Not even close."

"I'm not playing 20 Questions. Put the danged label on your change can." I was sorry I asked. From a tattered vinyl briefcase, Marshbaum took out a peelable label proclaiming donations for the "Marshbaum Museum of American Culture."

"You can drop your spare change into it now," he told me.

"What's the scam?" I asked suspiciously.

"No scam. Legitimate museum. Just like the Historic Voodoo Museum, the International Toaster Museum, and the one that Britney Spears created."

"Britney Spears has a museum?"

"The roar of newspaper presses deafen you? Of course Britney has a museum. She built one in her hometown of Kentwood, Louisiana."

"She's barely old enough to drink beer legally."

"I'm sure she'll eventually put her can in the museum. It's certainly everywhere else!"

"Just because she can dance and lip sync at the same time doesn't warrant a museum. And in your case, even if you do build a monument, it will remain as empty as your own life."

"I shall build it, and they will come."

"They will come and be taken."

"Hey, I got credibility. I took first place in Air Guitar at the county fair. If I had a gaggle of marketing geniuses and choreographers, I'd be bumping and grinding before every 13-year-old, making millions, and planning a designer label."

"You don't even have enough to go into your museum."

"I think I'll have three sections. Just like the Queen of Bubblegum Pop. Teething years. Mouseketeer years. Pop star—"

"Marshbaum! You weren't ever a Mouseketeer."

"I *watched* them. I'm donating my TV set. It's the same age as Britney. Maybe I'll even throw in the *TV Guide* covers and 62,000 newspaper pictures that feature Britney's navel."

"And how do you justify your pop star section?" I asked sarcastically.

"I eat Pop Tarts all the time. I should have a used box somewhere."

"Mold has no value outside a lab."

"IRS doesn't think so."

"The IRS may be moldy, but I doubt—" I didn't even have to finish the sentence. Revelation and french horns played all at once. "It *is* a scam, isn't it! Most people have yard sales. You're donating junk to a bogus museum and taking tax deductions."

"And you think Miss Oops-I-Did-it-Again isn't? She's a publicist's nightmare, but she's got a museum. I figure she's taking a two grand deduction just for donating her court warrants. Another 20 or 30 grand for shoes. She has more costumes than an elementary school at Halloween. I mean where else would she put all that junk and get paid for it?"

"Are you really serious about this scam?"

"From the bottom of my broken heart."

Hard Rock on a Soft Platter

They put Bette Midler in the Easy Listening section at the chain music store.

Bette Midler! The Divine Miss M!

The bawdy comedian who aroused a nation with jokes, tales, and double entendres.

One of Disney's leading comedic actresses when it needed a little more edge in its films.

One of Johnny Carson's favorite guests.

The hard rocker whose on-stage sexuality and flash aroused a nation of everyone from pubescents salivating over raging hormones to the elderly who gasped—and then winked.

The actress who was nominated for an Oscar for her over-the-top performance in *The Rose*, a fictionalized look at the life of Janis Joplin, with a lot of Midler's own life threaded into the hard-driving script of Michael Cimino and Bo Goldman.

That Bette Midler. Sassy and brassy. Now shoved into the same section as Perry Como, Al Martino, and Bing Crosby, whose popularity ended long before the 1970s Disco era.

An aisle over in the chainsaw and blown amp sound of Heavy Metal were CDs of Metallica, the genre's signature band; its 1991 CD, "Metallica," praised by headbangers, rockers, and music critics, racked up more than seven million sales. Nearby were albums of Creed, an alternative '90s band, whose debut album, "My Own Prison," went quintuple platinum; its follow up, "Human Clay," topped out about 10 million, about eight million more than the sound track from *The Rose*.

In almost a full aisle, being fingered by several teens and a few just-former teens, were dozens of Hip-Hop and Rap CDs, all with lyrics that guaranteed not only wouldn't they be printed in community newspapers, they wouldn't receive airplay as well. But there they were, in the commercial marketplace, most of them laying down a beat of four-letter words, ranting against "bitches," "hoes," and "freaks," hedonistic and amoralistic, extolling drugs and violence, lashing out against society, authority, and commercialism, each CD commanding up to $26.99, with most about $19.99.

There were CDs of George Clinton who influenced Dr. Dre who influenced and produced dozens of the superstar rappers, including Snoop Doggy Dog and his hit on Dre's own 1992 debut album, "The Chronic: Nuthin' But a 'G' Thang," with its memorable chorus, "Bow wow wow, yippee yo yippee yay." There was DMX's three-million best-seller "oldies" hit from 1998, "It's Dark and Hell is Hot." Also in the section were recent CDs from Eminem who several CDs earlier, and still unapologetic, concluded the track "Kim," named for his wife, with the passionate lyrics, "Don't you get it bitch, no one can hear you? Now shut the fuck up and get what's coming to you. . . . Now bleed! Bitch bleed!"

Every quarter-generation—spurred by mass media megaconglomerate hype using radio, TV, print media, and the music recording industry—changes what they determine to be the "popular"—salable—music. And every generation faces its parents. The mothers of the early '50s rock generation smashed records and radio sets to protest the sneering rebelliousness and sexual wiggle of "The Devil's Music." But, their own parents had called the Be-Bop and Swing eras "cursed noise." Their children would later condemn acid rock.

During the past five decades, "The Devil's Music" was replaced by the "British Invasion," Surf, Soul, Disco, Funk, Acid Rock, Punk, Grunge, Heavy Metal, Ska, Techno, Gangsta Rap and Hip-Hop, and several styles that defy classification, each of which entered then exited, often replaced by something edgier, seemingly noisier and less musical.

Most rappers, as most bands over the past century, have evolved into a well-deserved oblivion. Each kind of music changes, setting a foundation for something to bounce off of it. Even in Hip-Hop, Dr. Dre's pioneering Gangsta Rap Compton Sound of the West Coast laid the foundation for the Bronx Sound of the East

Coast rappers, which evolved into the Atlanta, Philadelphia, and Phoenix sounds. Even the themes have changed, from the bitterness, violence, and revenge of the early raps to the more mellow looks at chronic and beans [marijuana and Ecstasy].

The music of Dr. Dre, Snoop Dogg, NWA, Public Enemy, Warren G, Jermaine Dupree, Ludacris, Kurupt, and D12 will endure. Within a decade, their CDs will be bumping up against those of murdered gangsta rappers Tupac Shakur and Biggie Smalls, of the ear-crushing heavy metal of Metallica, AC/DC, Mötley Crüe, Iron Maiden, Judas Priest, Megadeth, Twisted Sister, and Black Sabbath, of grunge bands Nirvana, Pearl Jam, and Alice in Chains, of rockers Aerosmith and Guns 'n' Roses, of The Who, KISS, and The Rolling Stones, of Bon Jovi and Van Halen—and of the Divine Miss M—in the Easy Listening section of the chain music stores.

Star-Spangled America

Jose Feliciano gave it a new beat.

Roseanne Barr shrilled it.

And thousands, of featured soloists have bobbled it or failed to hit the high-G.

"It" is the "Star-Spangled Banner."

However, according to a Harris Poll in February 2005, about two-thirds of Americans didn't know all of the words of the first stanza or even the origin of the song that became the National Anthem in 1931. Congress made that decision 117 years after Francis Scott Key wrote new words for "To Anacreon in Heaven," written in the late eighteenth century, and which was probably an English drinking song.

The National Anthem Project, partially based upon the Harris poll, is a multi-year project to try to make sure that all Americans learn the words and the historical origin of the song. It is sponsored by National Association for Music Education (known as MENC), with financial assistance from Chrysler/ Jeep. Among dozens of organizations that signed onto the project were the American Legion, the Girl Scouts, the National Endowment for the Arts, the National Association of School Psychologists, the National Lumber and Building Materials Dealers Association, and the Walt Disney Co.

The campaign began on Capitol Hill with singers from a high

school in South Carolina and an elementary school in Washington, D.C. More than six million children and teachers participated throughout the country in a concert carried by PBS and the Armed Forces Network. The campaign included "education initiatives in schools, special performances and alliances with professional sporting events, and an extensive mobile marketing tour," according to the Association.

Buried within the promotion, almost insignificant in the national PR spin, is a reality of what spurred the national campaign. "Recent budget cuts to school music programs have silenced our nation, cutting off students from access to learning about our country's historical traditions," said John Mahlmann, MENC executive director.

Because of cuts in arts funding, with increased budgets for sports and several other programs, about 28 million students were not receiving an adequate music education, according to a U. S. Department of Education study in 2000. One-fourth of all principals reported there was a decreased time spent on the arts in their schools, and one-third of all principals said there would be continued decreases in the arts, according to a study published in 2004 by the Council for Basic Education. Ironically, the decrease in music and the arts in schools might even be greater if not for sports—marching bands complement the football program; "rally bands," combos, and jazz bands complement basketball.

Nevertheless, fewer than half of all students receive music education at least three times a week, says Michael Blakeslee, MENC deputy executive director. Only about 40 percent of all public secondary schools require students to take even one credit in the arts to graduate, according to the latest figures from the Department of Education's Arts in the Schools survey—and that was conducted more than a decade ago. The requirements decreased since then.

Part of the problem, says Blakeslee, was implementation of the No Child Left Behind Act, which emphasizes basic skills. Rod Paige, former Department of Education secretary, says the program was never intended to reduce arts activities in schools, a claim Blakeslee agrees with. However, "interpretation and implementation of the Act by school districts has led to a significant erosion of music education, especially in the middle school," says Blakeslee. The extra time spent to meet the Act's criteria has reduced time spent in the arts. "If improving basic skills "doesn't work in how they're being taught in 30 minutes," asks Blakeslee, "why will they work at 90 minutes?" The increase in minutes in other areas at the expense of the arts is nothing less than "political expediency," says Blakeslee.

Although the way schools implement the No Child Left Behind Act may be a problem, American cultural values may be more of a problem. Extensive anecdotal evidence at all levels of education suggests that parents, guidance counselors, and others who have influence upon children and the educational system often encourage their children to "take classes that'll get you a job," while discouraging them from going into the arts. Mistakenly, they believe the arts, while "nice," may be frivolous in job placement opportunities.

Almost every country except the United States has a cabinet-level agency headed by a minister of culture to assist the creative arts. This may mean we either don't have any culture or that politicians may think culture is what's grown in petri dishes. Either way, the lack of such a department says a lot about American values.

Another problem is the Observational Society. Our children watch a limited range of music videos, listen to CDs their peers approve, and attend shrill overpriced concerts. TV and the movies have become not only ways for them to tolerate boredom, but have become the nation's babysitters. Like sports crowds, our children have become observers not participants. Like the previous MTV generation, they have become so accustomed to being entertained they have failed to become participants, whether in sports, cultural and arts activities, recreation—or in social justice or the political system.

Learning the words to the "Star Spangled Banner" is good. Participating in understanding the history of the music, and being able to sing it in groups is better. It plays to the patriotic urges of the nation. Nevertheless, if at the end of the music project, our children haven't become participants in society, haven't seen the necessity for the arts—whether dance, visual arts, music, theatre, or writing as just as important to society as plumbers, electricians, lawyers, and business executives— then all that would have happened is that Americans have learned words to a song and have gotten a warm, fuzzy feeling for the country, while still being ignorant of our heritage and still sitting on the sidelines of life.

337

Conventional Fund Spending

During the last week in January 2009, Joel Klein, chancellor of the New York City Department of Education, went to Albany to beg the legislature not to cut the school district budget.

Because of statewide budgetary problems during the Recession, Gov. David Patterson had proposed a $700 million state funding cut, with an additional $500 million cut in city funding. The result could lead to 15,000 layoffs, about 12 percent of the total employment, and a significant increase in class size for the one million students in the system. New York City already had the highest average size classes in the state. Although sympathetic to the nation's largest school district, legislators said there was little they could do because of revenue shortfall.

Less than three months after Klein pleaded for restoration of the budget, the New York Yankees and New York Mets opened their baseball seasons in new stadiums, partially funded by the taxpayers of the city and state of New York.

Citi Stadium in Queens replaced Shea Stadium as the Mets' new home. The $850 million 41,800 seat stadium and its surrounding areas were partially funded by about $190 million in various city and state subsidies, and a deal that would eliminate all property taxes. However, the most controversial part of the new stadium was its name. Citigroup, which had received about $45 billion in public subsidies in the 2008 bailout, paid $400 million over a 20 year period for naming rights. Nevertheless, public subsidies to Citi Stadium is small change compared to what the taxpayers were forced to provide to the Yankees.

To assist the Yankees, the City agreed not to charge any property taxes, paid about $150 million to demolish the existing stadium and built a park in its place, spent $70 million of the $320 million cost for a new parking garage, and built a train station near the park. Total public subsidy for the $1.5 billion 52,345 seat stadium, the second most expensive stadium in the world, was about $450 million, less than half of what Mayor Rudy Giuliani had proposed in 2001, and well above what Mayor Michael Blumberg thought advisable when he became mayor in 2002. The public subsidy, said Blumberg, was nothing more than "corporate welfare."

Both stadiums have dozens of restaurants, from fast food to

gourmet, and exclusive box seating. Individual ticket prices at Yankee stadium range from $5 in obstructed center field bleachers 500 feet from home plate during mid-week night games to about $2,600 for front row teak-armed seats and personal catering. The average price is more than $50 per seat. However, the vice on the taxpayers didn't end with the completed stadiums. About two-thirds of all revenue, including the cost of expensive seats and luxury boxes, comes from corporations, which use the expenses as tax deductions, according to a study by David Carter, professor of sports business at the University of Southern California.

New York taxpayers weren't the only ones to help subsidize privately-owned sports teams. The $1.1 billion Dallas Cowboys football stadium, also completed in 2009, received about $325 million in taxpayer funding. To help finance the stadium, the voters of Arlington, Texas, agreed with an increase in city sales taxes by one-half percent (to 8 percent), an increase in hotel occupancy tax by two percent (to 15 percent), and an increase in car rental taxes by five percent (to 10 percent). The privately-owned Cowboys is listed by *Forbes* magazine as the most valuable sports franchise in the United States.

In the U.S. are more than 600 convention centers, including more than 100 large centers built primarily with public tax money, almost all of which had support from the local business community and the media. At the same time Yankee Stadium and Citi Stadium were completed, work was continuing on a $1.3 billion expansion to the Jacob Javits Convention Center in Manhattan, originally built in 1986. The expansion had begun in October 2006 and was expected to be completed in 2010.

Trade shows and conventions were fewer following 9/11, but began increasing within five years, although still not to pre-9/11 levels, according to *Trade Show Week*. Nevertheless, even in a recession, cities have been building stadiums and convention centers. In 2005, there were 85.1 million square feet of exhibit space in convention centers in the United States and Canada, according to *Trade Show Week*. By the end of 2010, there will be about 92.7 million square feet of exhibit space, an almost 9 percent increase. But, there is a problem with the sudden increase of convention space. "When you look at the percent increase [in exhibit space demand] . . . a lot of it is taking place in about 60 percent of the buildings," Robert Canton of PriceWaterhouseCoopers told MeetingsNet.com. The other 40 percent, he said, "are struggling to fill their centers in a very competitive market that is flush with supply."

New Jersey in 1997 built a $268 million 500,000 square foot convention center, with a 500-room hotel on 31 acres in Atlantic City. But, the Center primarily helps corporations and organizations. As for the people, poverty and urban blight, marked by gutted stores and abandoned houses, stretches from Route 87 to the Boardwalk. Because of current tax laws, almost every expense for a person attending a convention for business purposes, and quite a lot of attendance at sports events, is deductible, thus reducing the individual or corporate tax burden. The benefit is to the middle- and upper-classes; few lower-income individuals attend conventions or sports events on business.

Across the continent from New Jersey, Seattle completed a $158 million convention center in 1988. Five years later, Boeing, the largest employer in the city, began laying off 38,000 workers, 25,000 of them in Seattle. An expansion in 2001 doubled its space to about 300,000 square feet; even in a bad economy, the taxpayers agreed to a second expansion, at a cost of about $766 million, to be completed in 2014.

In Phoenix, a $600 million expansion will triple its convention hall size to almost 900,000 square feet.

The cheerleaders for public financing, with most local news media supporting their claims, argue that the benefits far outweigh the expenses. They cite not only more public spending for local businesses but also increased employment. During the late 1990s and early part of the 2000 decade, with a strong economy, dozens of cities and counties began building convention centers, almost all of which were financed by taxpayer funds, almost all of which probably wouldn't have a profit for years, maybe never.

The $120 million Connecticut Convention Center in Hartford, opened in June 2005, requires about $3 million a year in subsidies. The $800 million Boston Convention Center, opened in 2004, requires about $15 million in annual subsidies, according to city officials.

The Los Angeles City Council in 2005 agreed to provide about $177 million in subsidies for a 55-story hotel next to the Staples Center. The purpose of the subsidy, according to the *Los Angeles Times*, was to bring "business to the Convention Center, which depends upon a $20-million city subsidy because it does not attract enough conventions." Because of the lack of conventions, the city pays the subsidy "from its general fund, which normally pays for police and fire services," according to the *Times*.

The taxpayers in Washington, D .C., are paying about $135 million for tax breaks for a $600 million privately-owned convention center hotel. Another $100 million is being provided by the convention center itself. "Convention Center boosters," according to the *Washington Post*, "argue that the monster 1,434-room hotel will finally attract all those promised medical and legal gatherings" that currently don't go to the nation's capital. Nearby, the city had already partially subsidized the privately-owned Verizon Center, home site for four sports teams and several entertainment events a year.

In Raleigh, N.C., a $221 million convention center, completed in 2008, has already become a money pit, forced to extend massive discounts to lure events and hotel patrons to its center. When the center was first proposed, the cheerleaders claimed a major economic benefit for the region. "We've already seen the convention center's economic impact estimates drop from $100 million a year to about $8 million," according to Dr. Michael Sanera, Research Director and Local Government Analyst at the John Locke Foundation.

A $1 billion expansion of Chicago's McCormick Place in 1997, and another $882 million expansion in 2007 will probably never repay the taxpayers' investments.

"Facilities rarely repay their construction costs," according to Ronald A. Wirtz, editor of the *FedGazette*, who argued, "the main arguments in favor of publicly financed stadiums, arenas and convention centers stress the economic activity created outside, rather than inside, the walls of these facilities. While such benefits are real and legitimate, they are often inflated and oversold."

About 46 million Americans don't have health care insurance; 37 million Americans live in poverty; 13 million Americans are unemployed; about 3.5 million people were homeless for at least a few days this past year, about one million were homeless for the full year.

Much of the money spent for convention centers could be spent to help improve the lives and programs for the elderly, disabled, and homeless, or for a massive jobs program that trains people not for service jobs that benefit the few, but for entry-level training in the health professions and environmen-

341

tal planning, social work, transportation, and labor education. It could also be used to reduce class sizes, develop stronger teacher education programs, and improve the quality of primary and secondary education. But we're using taxpayer funding to build convention centers and sports stadiums, and the media have become the biggest cheerleaders.

Swifter, Higher, Stronger . . . Greedier

Tabitha Matthews, a 15-year-old honors student, was one of 300 volunteers the Atlanta Committee for the Olympic Games (ACOG) selected to work at the softball competition in Columbus, Ga., in 1996. In exchange for two nights of training and 20 hours of work in the information booth, she was paid . . . nothing. She received no benefits, not even a pass to any of the games.

Each of the five days she worked, her mother drove her 30 minutes to Phenix City, Ala., where she caught the Olympics shuttle that took an hour to get to the stadium. The Olympics required their volunteers not only to take the shuttle but to pay $5, a fee the ACOG grudgingly rescinded only a couple of weeks before the games.

Not free were the mandatory uniforms. Like other volunteers, Tabitha was required to buy a pair of khaki shorts or skirt of her own choosing, and pay $10 for a T-shirt or $20 for a hunter green polo shirt, each with a swatch of flash red, a yellow star, and block white script that proclaimed, "Superstar." She and most of the other volunteers had no idea what "Superstar" meant. It wasn't even an official Olympics shirt. Official souvenir T-shirts sold for $18–$25, and baseball-style caps were priced at $15–$30.

The sweat and sacrifices of 10,500 athletes from 197 countries was nearly lost amid the commercialism and greed that threaded through the Olympian effort to create the 17-day competition. Just a few other items . . .

Each of the torch carriers who ran, biked, wheeled, or jogged a few minutes of the 84-day circuitous 15,000 mile trip from Los Angeles to Atlanta could buy their own torch for $275.

Tickets for the four-hour opening day ceremony were $636. However, having money didn't guarantee anyone a seat. Of more than 200,000 who wanted to attend, the ACOG selected only 15,000. The other 60,000 who vaulted past the fans were special Olympic friends, officials, and high-rollers, most of whose corporations paid for the ticket, and then deducted it from the taxpayers.

Synchronized scalpers reaped as much as ten times face value for single event tickets. Not to be left out of the dash for dollars, the ACOG added a $1 per ticket "fulfillment fee," a $10 one-time account set-up fee, and then tried a gold-medal scam.

A seasonal pass in a nice section of the stadium for all track-and-field events cost $1,779. But, the cost of individual tickets to all events would have been only $1,196. The official ACOG response was that a 50 percent surcharge wasn't unreasonable since the Committee was "entitled and empowered to offer ticket packages and price them as we see fit." However, after extensive media coverage, ACOG reconsidered the price, and refunded a lot of money to several hundred angry spectators when it became apparent it may have violated the state's two-year-old law against ticket scalping, a law the ACOG had vigorously supported.

Fortunately, there were other ways to make money.

Parking fees were about $25 a day, with the closest lots a mile or so from the stadiums.

The average temperature in Atlanta in late July is about 88 degrees, with humidity matching the temperature most days. Every few minutes, an announcer informed spectators in the 83,000-seat open air track-and-field stadium they should avoid dehydration by drinking a quart of water an hour. The only food and drink spectators were allowed to bring into the Olympics were plastic containers of water. Those who didn't wish to pay inflated prices at the local stores waited until they got to the stadium to buy a pint of Olympics-approved water for $2.75 from official sponsor Crystal Springs. If they hadn't already mortgaged their houses for water, fans dined on a junk food lunch of emaciated hamburger ($4.25), soggy fries ($3.25), and 50-cent peach pie, now priced at $2.25.

Fans who went all-out and had a Coke for that special sugar-kick spent $3.25, about twice the cost at professional sports stadiums, according to *Team Marketing Report*. But, Atlanta-based Coca-Cola needed to make money; it paid 40 million tax-deductible dollars to be an exclusive official sponsor.

Other enterprising Georgians—and quite a few carpet-baggers—hawked overpriced food and souvenirs from plywood stands that lined the roads leading to the stadiums.

343

Corporate tents, each bearing logos of official sponsors, covered Centennial Olympic Park, built over what once was a section of flophouses.

Official sponsors and ticket sales accounted for most of the $1.7 billion budget. The international radio and television media paid about $900 million for broadcast rights, but no one paid more than NBC which decided it could still rake in a profit after paying $456 million, and then budgeted $100 million for production costs.

Several dozen advertisers saw no problem in helping NBC recover its investment, knowing that 200 million Americans—and a world audience of over a billion—planned to watch at least one day of the coverage. Spread over 171-1/2 hours of the telecasts were about 1,500 advertising messages, each going for about $500,000 a minute.

Even "average" Americans made money off the Olympics.

Among major changes in the modern Olympics have been the addition of professional athletes and the domination of mass media sponsorships, including multi-million dollar broadcasting rights, neither of which were anticipated nor would have been acceptable when Baron Pierre de Coubertin revived the games in 1896 in Athens.

Some enterprising Georgians rented their houses and then left the area for three weeks. The average cost per night for a nice three-bedroom split-level was $750–$1,000, with two and three-week minimums. However, for only $100–$200 a night, visitors could rent a room in the house—refrigerator extra. Several regulations kept hotels and motels from price gouging, so they charged only about twice the normal July rate.

During the 1960s, the establishment freaked out when they spotted "hippies" wearing jeans patched by 3-by 5-inch American flags. During Olympics Fever, Americans were inundated by an overpriced collection of stars-and-striped dishrags, women's panties, shoes, blouses, ties, mugs, and watches, as well as several dozen official Olympic trinkets that included thimbles, playing cards, and sunglasses. There was even an official money clip for spectators who had any money left. About $5 billion in merchandise was sold by the end of summer.

Finally, the official underwear sponsor was Hanes whose Olympic slogan could have been the theme of all concessionaires—"Just wait 'till we get our Hanes on the Games."

The Day the Circus Came to Town

The circus came to town the other day, quietly and without fanfare. There was no mile-long parade with animals and bands, for the circus had snuck in on RVs and 18-wheel semis. No bare-foot boys, their faces sunburned from the summer, were idling by the gates hoping to be asked to water the elephants and camels in exchange for an admission. No one sold cotton candy or pink lemonade, for the menu was overpriced hot dogs, hamburgers, candy, heavily salted but unbuttered popcorn, and ice-laden carbonated soft drinks, all of them huckstered throughout the show.

No one tried sneaking in under the main tent, for there wasn't one, just an impersonal green-tinged concrete-domed auditorium that also hosted farm shows and rock music acts. People no longer flocked to the sideshow because this time even the sideshow wasn't there—perhaps a tribute to mankind's sensitivity to human concerns, perhaps because the circus could still sell tickets without having to display society's "freaks."

The ringmaster, a hired actor wearing a tux—not even shiny black hip boots and a scarlet red coat—stood just outside the center ring, commanded the attention of his appreciative audience, and with a flourish blew his whistle and called out the acts.

First into the show was a trainer and some lions. The trainer snapped his whip, and fired a pistol loaded with blanks and special effects smoke. The lions got up on stools, executed marching maneuvers—and yawned, undoubtedly wishing that the afternoon whistle would blow so they could quit work, go home, drink some beer and watch TV, or whatever it is that lions do when they're not working.

A couple of elephants and a half-dozen ponies ran around the center ring, stood up, bowed, and did tricks. All circus animals do tricks. Somehow, we believe that taking animals out of their natural environment, and then forcing them to conform to what humans think is cute, is something to be applauded.

It costs a lot to feed and care for circus animals and the people who perform with them, rent auditoriums, buy advertising, print tickets, hire a half-dozen local musicians, and pay the prodigious costs of liability insurance. In a wood-paneled board room in a steel-and-glass building far from the smell of sawdust, a group of directors—undoubtedly guided by a CEO advised by a gaggle of

MBAs and lawyers, none of whom have the talent to do anything more than pick up after the elephants—may have determined that to maintain the price-to-earnings ratio, and to continue to make quarterly dividend payments to its vaporous plethora of stockholders, this business had to cut a few animals from the show, maybe also cut back on some acts and support staff.

Far above the gray concrete floor sprinkled with sawdust, above the safety net held by a dozen hefty roustabouts, swung the aerialists, their split-second movements drawing appreciative gasps. After them, an illusionist made doves appear and a tiger disappear.

Between acts came the clowns, a half-dozen of them prancing, chasing, falling to the syncopated rataplan of their own drummer, now throwing a bucket of water, now a bucket of confetti, blowing whistles and honking horns, bobbing and weaving and ducking. Once the highest form of comedy, clown comedy is dying. Instead of wearing fright wigs and red-bulb noses, baggy pants, floppy shoes, and polka-dotted stuffed shirts, today's upwardly mobile comedians wear designer jeans and theatrical makeup; instead of perfecting pratfalls, their managers help them perfect stock portfolios.

The show ended 90 minutes after it began. The actors returned for a mini-revue, and then went to their RVs. The audience quietly walked out, past the entrance where they could still purchase circus T-shirts, programs, and recorded calliope music, assuming they didn't buy any during the couple of dozen or so times vendors walked the stands just to make sure everyone who paid the $8 admission didn't have anything left in their wallets or purses.

The acts that were seen only a couple of times in a lifetime now flood the television screens, and it's far easier for audiences at the end of a day just to stay home and push buttons on a remote control box.

But the circus is our reminder of a childhood when we didn't worry about mortgages and the languid economy, when our lives weren't complicated by problems with the environment, street crime, or if we could scrape up enough money for an overpriced prescription. As with all things, we matured, and the circus matured. Its freshness is left for the young who will have their memories, and for the elderly who have everything to remember and, maybe, for the dreamers who, like the clowns, will find their own drummers.

346

For Casinos, 'Six-Hour Visitors'
No Longer Make a Full House

Just about every month, Margo and Sam Marcus leave their home in Harrisburg, Pa., and go to Hollywood.

Not the Hollywood in California, home of the TV and film industry. And not the Hollywoods in Florida, Missouri, Maryland, or South Carolina. The Marcuses drive 15 minutes to the Hollywood Casino, one of nine in Pennsylvania. For more than 15 years, they had gone to the casinos of Atlantic City, about three hours and 170 miles to the southeast. But since Hollywood opened in February 2008, the Marcuses haven't been back to Atlantic City. They, several million Pennsylvanians, and the Recession are the primary reasons that gross revenue for the Atlantic City casinos dropped 7.6 percent in 2008, according to the New Jersey Casino Control Commission. Gross operating profits fell even further, from $1.25 billion in 2007 to $940.9 million in 2008, a 24.6 percent drop. All but one of the 11 casinos showed a loss in 2008. It wasn't any better in Las Vegas, which saw a drop of 10 percent revenue in 2008. In contrast, each of the Pennsylvania casinos showed a profit in 2008, with most showing double-digit profits.

Pennsylvania authorized casinos in 2004 to reinvigorate the horse racing industry and provide property tax relief. The first casino opened in November 2006. Casinos in Delaware, Maryland, Connecticut, and New York state also siphon income from Atlantic City.

Even with a nation in a recession, about $92.2 billion was spent on all forms of legalized gambling in the U.S. in 2008, about the same as the year before, according to the American Gaming Association. Las Vegas (both the strip and downtown) continued to lead, with revenue of about $7.38 billion in 2008; Atlantic City was second.

Forty-seven states have legalized slot machines, in casinos, hotels, riverboats, or racetracks. And, all of them make sure they have plans to take care of groups of senior citizens. About three-fourths of all revenue from Atlantic City casinos is from slots, and most of the slots players are at least 50 years old. Every day, 400–700 buses, each carrying 30–45 passengers, most of them women over 55 years old, pull into the casinos, stay six hours, and then leave. With travel time, combined with limited bus parking, the casinos figure that six hours is the "right" time for the "low-rollers." It's an "escape" for most senior citizens, the opportunity to be a part of the excitement of the noise-and-enter-tainment, to possibly win a few bucks—more important, to be in control of their own money, to know where it went, as opposed to the money the government takes from their retirement incomes.

Depending on which casino the bus goes to, and which day of the week it is, each bus rider could receive a $10–$30 bar-coded ticket for slot play at the casino, occasionally another $3–$5 good for the next trip and a $5–$10 meal credit. They can choose from any of more than 130 restaurants or 80 cocktail lounges.

However, with the Recession, fewer persons are taking the bus, even if the comps they receive when they arrive cover the cost of the bus trip. About 9.6 million bus passengers came to the Atlantic City casinos in 1997; by the end of 2008, partially-filled buses delivered 4.9 million visitors. In a slap to the Atlantic City casinos, buses now go from New Jersey cities to casinos in neighboring states.

On the casino floors, senior citizens scramble to their favorite slots—they have more than 35,000 to choose from in Atlantic City, and about 17,000 in Pennsylvania. Most won't leave for three or four hours, just shoving coin after coin into the machines, watching the dials spin, and hoping for a jackpot. They'll crowd the penny, two-cent, nickel, and quarter slots first; few ever try one of the $100 slots. Sometimes, even if there are people waiting, they will play two slots at once; if one doesn't pay, its neighbor will—at least that's what many figure. The casinos send provocatively-dressed waitresses around to provide free drinks for parched throats that yell encouragement to the machines. For those who have arthritis or don't have the energy to pull a lever, the slots have push buttons. The casinos want their victims to sit there, in one spot, and lose. If they could figure out a way to catheterize the players so they don't even have to go to the bathroom, they would.

By law, each slot machine in Pennsylvania must pay back at least 85 percent; the average is about 91–92 percent, according to the Pennsylvania Gaming Control Board. In Atlantic City, the minimum payback is 83 percent, with most paying up to 90 percent. The New Jersey Casino Control Commission even makes public which casinos have better payoffs and which groups of machines pay better than the others. Few study the numbers, and none of the casinos see any reason to post them.

Paper tickets, not coins, are now the currency of the casinos; players put in $5, $10, $20 bills; a digital pre-recorded sound of coins announces a win, even if the return is the equivalent of a three coin return on a five coin investment. When the player decides to "cash out," the push of a button releases the sounds of coins hitting a metal tray and the issuance of a paper ticket, which can be used at other machines or cashed in for real money.

For most slots players, the $10–$30 worth of "comps" is sufficient. But, for the late evening "high rollers," the ones who think nothing of dropping a few hundred every blackjack hand or roll of the craps dice, the casinos will provide free limousine or helicopter service, luxury suites, food, beverages, show tickets, myriad trinkets from key chains to suits, and just about anything a loser could want. Even during a Recession, the comps are still available, but the casinos spent about five percent less in 2008 than the year before.

"We always got comped," says Sam Marcus, but comps in Pennsylvania are fewer, usually coupons for discounts in restaurants or a few bucks of free gambling. Unlike other senior citizens—Sam is a retired political science professor and consultant for the Commonwealth of Pennsylvania, Margot is a retired social worker—they prefer blackjack.

Because Margot is a rated blackjack player, and because Sam also played the tables, they received at least one night free lodging, food, and a small allowance—"usually about $20"—when they drove to Atlantic City. "We never had to pay for anything," he says, "we just had to stay at the tables." The casinos don't care if a person wins or loses—they know many will win, most won't—as long as they stay at the tables. Pit bosses "clock" players' time at tables, not how much they won or lost. Sam played at the $5 and $10 minimum bet tables; Margot played the $25 minimum tables. It isn't unusual to see players bet $1,500 a hand—"they aren't at the tables long," says Sam, knowing the odds.

The slots are the most profitable part of a casino for the House; table games require at least one dealer per table, and a pit boss every three or four tables, 24 hours a day; the slots only require attendants to pay the big winnings and machinists to fix the occasional break-down. Blackjack in Pennsylvania is different from Atlantic City. Five players still sit at a curved table and make their wagers. The rules are still the same, but each player's game is separate from the others, and the deal is from one of five or six different buxom women on a video screen. At first there was a guy at the Hollywood Casino, says Sam Marcus, "but that didn't last long." Virtual reality, essentially a large video game, cuts the casino's expenses and significantly reduces any possibility of card counting. Margo and Sam Marcus say the convenience of virtual reality tables at a nearby casino outweighs the lure of the tables of Atlantic City.

As in Atlantic City, most players in the Pennsylvania casinos go home with less money than they came with. Bus company hosts often tell about passengers who keep playing, keep losing, and keep going to the convenient ATM. It's not unusual for a few senior citizens to drop most of their month's social security payments.

For their part, the casinos tell their players—in TV commercials, on all the printed literature, even in frequent announcements beamed from concealed loudspeakers—to "bet with your head, not over it." But then they put an acre of machines into an air-conditioned room that has no windows or clocks, and entice their victims to sign up for plastic card memberships that, when inserted into slots, record the number of times a coin was dropped, and lead to even more trinkets or coupons to entice them to return to the casino.

Each of the Pennsylvania casinos has a few stores, unlike their counterparts in Atlantic City. Visitors to Atlantic City can shop in dozens of stores within the casinos, at the 200,000 square foot Quarter at the Tropicana, or at the Piers Shops, a four-story mall attached to Cesar's Place by a covered skywalk that crosses the Boardwalk. The mall is on the location of the original Steel Pier amusement center. The Walk, a $76 million, 320,000 square foot shopping center in a four-block area between the convention center and the casinos, opened in late 2003. For those who want a break from gambling and PG-rated evening shows, the city that calls itself "America's Favorite Playground" boasts a large arts and cultural base, as well as numerous events not connected to the Boardwalk.

Atlantic City was incorporated in 1854, the year a railroad line was completed from Camden, across the Delaware River from Philadelphia, as a summer resort on a 3.9 mile long coastal barrier island. In 1870, the city built the boardwalk, primarily to keep sand off the front lobby carpeting of the hotels. The 10-foot wide boardwalk was taken down at the beginning of each Winter, and then replaced each Spring. At first, businesses were prohibited within 30 feet of the boardwalk; in 1883, with a new 14-foot wide boardwalk, private companies added businesses and amusements, including the Steel Pier, a ride-and-amusement park which was also the site of innumerable headline acts. To salt water taffy, dozens of small businesses, and rolling wicker chairs, the city rebuilt the 3.9 mile boardwalk, making it 24 feet wide, and lined it with even more private businesses.

The first modern Miss America contest was held in Atlantic City in 1921; the city built Convention Hall eight years later to lure conventions. In 2005, the Miss America pageant, looking for greater revenue to cover for its declining TV ratings, deserted the city for the glitzier Las Vegas.

During World War II, the military took over the beach-front hotels and turned the city into one of the nation's largest training camps and rest-and-rehabilitation (R & R) sites. However, the end of the war also brought an end to the prosperity. For the next three decades, Atlantic City declined as a resort; the rich moved onto other places; the poor remained. The city's population, infrastructure, and tax base declined. During the mid-1930s, the population peaked about 66,000; by the mid-1970s, it was about 46,000.

By the mid-1970s, Atlantic City had a deteriorating downtown, tenement housing, and the state's highest violent crime and poverty rates. And then came what the state called "a unique tool of urban development." The first of the Atlantic City casinos went into business in 1978 following a statewide referendum to allow gambling. Legalized gambling will save the city, proclaimed voters, legislators, and even businessmen who planned to mine the East Coast, smugly knowing that one-third of the nation's population live within six hours driving time of Atlantic City and could easily be lured to a gambling empire that promised instant wealth. Atlantic City, the investors believed, would become for the East Coast what Las Vegas was for the rest of the nation.

During the mid-1980s, speculators and the casinos had gobbled up all available land in Atlantic City, expecting as many as 35 casinos to rescue the city. Only when it appeared there would be a saturation of about a dozen casinos could the school district (which for the 1996-1997 school year received almost $37 million of its $73 million budget from the casinos) finally buy enough land to relocate its high school. But, the taxpayers of the $81 million 470,000 square foot high school still had to pay $9.7 million for 48.8 acres, a lot for a school district but less per acre than the $4.6 million the Showboat spent in 1995 for three acres so it could add 200 more hotel rooms.

Since 1975, the Atlantic City casinos have paid almost $8 billion in regulatory fees and revenue, property, corporate, local, state, and federal taxes. For its part, New Jersey has been so appreciative of receiving money that it built a 43-mile long expressway from the western part of the state directly to the Boardwalk. To lure even more middle and upper-class marks to the casinos, in 1997 the city and state completed a $268 million 1.2 million square foot convention center with a 500-room hotel, and then added a $100 million three block "corridor" to link the center with the Boardwalk. Between 1998 and 2001, the city and state combined to convert the deteriorating Convention Hall on the Boardwalk into a concert and sports arena, and then renamed it Boardwalk Hall. The Casino Reinvestment Development Authority provided $72 million of the $90 million renovation. Atlantic City also built a $12 million 6,000-seat minor league baseball stadium, financed primarily by casino taxes and $3 million worth of city bonds. By the end of 2003, Atlantic City had more than 16,000 hotel rooms, and a new $1.1 billion casino, the Borgata, with its 2,000 room hotel located on a 30-acre parcel in the Marina section, and the city's first two $1,000 slots.

Not benefiting from the taxes and handouts have been the city's permanent and transient residents. Beneath the Boardwalk, in cardboard shelters unseen by the "high rollers" who may lose more money in a craps throw than most people earn in a month, and not mentioned in any news or features from Atlantic City's public relations operation, are several dozen homeless. Almost one-fifth of all Atlantic City residents live below the poverty line, according to the 2000 U.S. census.

In 1996, the state's legislature authorized $175 million from casino taxes meant to aid the urban poor be directed back to the casinos to allow for their expansion. To make sure there's enough land for the casinos, the city and the Casino Reinvestment Development Authority used the power of the eminent domain to condemn and then seize homes, businesses, and land in the way of the casinos' expansion plans or in the route of improved streets going into the casinos. Most of the property condemned in the past few years, often against the will of the owners, isn't run-down or boarded-up; most are well-maintained, with a presence in Atlantic City several decades longer than the casinos.

Although city officials proudly proclaim a renaissance for the ocean front resort, they are also faced by the blemish that four of its past eight mayors were indicted on a variety of malfeasance and criminal charges, the downtown has deteriorated even further, there has been an increase in violent crimes and prostitution, and poverty is still the way of life for a large chunk of the 35,000 residents who live in a city with no theaters and only two supermarkets, one built as part of the $100 million strip mall for tourists. There is one advantage of the city's lower cost-of-living-more than three-fourths of the 47,000 casino employees, most of whom are in the service industry and making less than $15 an hour, live in Atlantic County.

Nevertheless, no matter what the city's problems are, no matter how deep the Recession, or how much business neighboring states have taken, the buses still come to Atlantic City, and senior citizens flood the casino floors by day, while the high-rollers take over by night. And the sound of recorded coins continues to lull Americans into believing the good dream belongs to them.

PERSUASION

Chicken Advertising

Kentucky Fried Chicken spent about $220 million in advertising in 2008; the U.S. Army spent at least three times that much. However, the chickens get better cluck for their buck.

No official record exists of the Pentagon's response to being beaten by the Chickens, but it's possible that Code Red alerts went throughout the 125 corridors of the world's largest office building. . . .

In a top-secret session in an underground bunker the secretary of the Army, several of his aides, a few assorted generals, a marketing specialist, a communication consultant, and a gold-chained advertising account executive met in a top secret session.

The marketing specialist, with 20 feet of computer paper spread across two tables, babbled endlessly about focus groups, synergy and convergence, chi-squares, gamma coefficients, and multivariant analyses. He thanked the generals for their time, dropped a four-figure bill in their laps, and then abruptly left for another meeting, probably with the Navy to keep them from falling further behind the Marineland budget.

The communication consultant suggested that sergeants should share their feelings in order to do a better job of "bonding" with their recruits. Moments later, he was recalled to active duty and sent to Iceland. It was now the adman's turn.

"Larger billboards?" the adman weakly suggested, hoping not to be sent to his former assignment in Baghdad, where he handled both the Shi'ite and Sunni accounts.

"What do the Chicken people have that we don't have?" asked the Secretary of the Army.

"Their Colonel?" he lamely suggested.

"Their *Colonel?*" thundered the Secretary. "We have colonels of our own. And generals! All those generals running around here are a menace!"

"I don't think you understand," explained the adman. "Their colonel is a nice grandfatherly type that people can relate to."

"What about *our* uncle?" scowled the Secretary.

"He was cool when we had the draft," said the adman, "but now that we have a volunteer army, I don't think Uncle Sam is the appropriate image. After all, he's got that beard and funky hat and—"

"Do we have any admen in Afghanistan, yet?" the Secretary asked an aide.

"No problem," said the adman wiping his brow. "How about

~~~~~~~~~

The Department of Defense awarded more than four million medals to Americans who participated in the Gulf War, which lasted about three months in 1991. A high-ranking Army officer, trying to justify the cost for what might have been a bad case of medal inflation, said that awarding the medals was not only good for morale but also good public relations for an Army that had severe morale problems following the Vietnam War.

increasing the choices a soldier has?" After the laughter died, the Secretary explained that soldiers don't have choices. "Chickens have choices," said the adman. "There's regular and crispy."

"Think!" the Secretary commanded. It wasn't something admen usually do, but if it would keep him from exchanging silk Gucci shorts for olive drab, he'd try thinking.

"Family plans?" the adman meekly suggested. When no one said anything, he brazenly continued. "We develop a real family plan. Mother. Father. Two kids. All in the Army. Remember, the family that shoots together is the family that dies for their country together."

"I'm not sure it'll fly," said the Secretary.

"It flies for the Chickens," said the adman. "Their family buckets are very popular."

"If we wanted to be popular, we'd have kept the communications guy," said the Secretary. "We're spending too much and getting too little. We're in a slump."

"When the Chicken has a slump," said the adman, "it has a sale. How about a 2-for-1 special? Maybe two guns for the price of one. Two pairs of combat boots or whatever."

"Sometimes one adman is twice what we need," moaned the Secretary who began signing travel orders.

"No biggie," said the adman. "I'll get a line on something. Lines! That's it! Soldiers are always complaining about lines. We claim that the Army doesn't have lines. No lines. Faster service."

"I'm sorry," said the Secretary, closing his note pad, "but lines are what makes this Army great."

"Sir," said the adman ominously, "there may be only one way to go on this." He paused for dramatic effect. "We declare the Chicken Place to be the site of terrorist activity. We go in, and nuke them back to the ice age. That eliminates the competition. Then, *we* get those pimply-faced high school kids who are working 20 hours a week to pay for gas, car insurance, and overpriced jeans. It'll be easy to convince them they're better off fighting a war we haven't declared against people we can't identify in lands we don't even have maps for in exchange for college tuition and a guarantee of a dozen wings every night."

The Secretary stood up, looked at all his aides and generals, and boldly announced that the misnamed Army Intelligence Corps will immediately begin surveillance on the Chicken Place. "And as far as this advertising account executive is concerned," said the Secretary, "give him the best suite in the Pentagon. He could very well be our secret weapon in this war against terrorism."

Cramping Up for Health

On bicycle paths and highways, on dirt roads and in parks, in heat, rain, and snow, people are darting in front of cars, chased by dogs and preppy muggers, in a never-ending quest for a faddish youth and the right to believe they match up to all the media models and their plethora of books and exercise videos.

And so it happened that one cool morning while walking in the park I was caught in the middle of the morning madness. From out of nowhere hundreds jogged past—sweating and straining, air cushions on their soles, earphones on their heads.

I was spun around several times. Dizzy, I tried to regain my composure, only to be hit again, as if the joggers were oblivious to everything else. At first frightened, but now angry, I tried to get up, only to be knocked down by another cluster of runners. Finally, I trapped one. Actually, he tripped over me.

"Confess!" I shouted. "Why do you run? What compels you?"

"Health," he said, panting and wheezing. "Makes your heart beat faster. By beating faster, it exercises it. Becomes stronger. You get a resting rate of 50, maybe 60. I read it in *Modern Maturity*."

"Why couldn't you just take a pill for it? Lots of pills will make your heart beat all over the place, and then stop on command."

"Must experience pain," he wheezed. "Article in *Maxim* said so."

"Do you experience a lot of pain?" I asked.

He took a series of small breaths, and told me that his feet hurt a lot more since he started running. He even blurted out that so did his ankles, thighs, knees, arms, neck, and even stomach. "We have to go through the pain to make us healthy," he said. "By staying healthy, I can work longer so I can buy more things."

"Like what?" I asked.

"Like these track shoes," he said, pulling one off a swollen foot while massaging a muscle cramp. "These shoes are made specifically for runners. They're completely cushioned with arch supports, a reinforced toe, and special color stripes to give it that extra special look of authenticity. Saw it advertised on TV. Six easy payments for only $19.95 plus shipping and handling."

"And they last for years," I said admiring the canvas.

"Oh, no! They last three, maybe four months. Even with these custom-made ten buck running sweat socks, all that sweat can really wear out a pair of shoes."

"I notice that you're wearing a floppy hat. Is that a runner's hat?"

"Sure is. Cost only $9.95, and worth every penny."

"The headband and wristbands?"

"Ten bucks on sale with a coupon from the local paper."

"The wrist wallet?"

"Only $14.95."

"The sweat suit?"

"If we don't have the proper suit, we'd be humiliated in front of our friends and neighbors. This one cost only $129 if you act now—and we'll throw in the shipping at no extra charge—but it'll last at least another five, maybe six months. Besides, these are specially made to allow us to perspire more. That way we lose more water. Five, ten pounds at a time."

"That's a lot to lose at one time, isn't it?"

"If it wasn't for the specially-coated salt pills available at your local health foods store, we'd lose even more."

"How much?"

"A buck a pill. You need two, three pills a day. Then, there's the mandatory stop at Duffy's."

"The tavern on Hydroponic Avenue?" I asked.

"You don't want to lose too much fluid. That isn't healthy. So, after we run, we all stop over at Duffy's to get a few drinks and buy some more pills."

"You drink beer after a healthy run?" I asked suspiciously.

"Beer. Whiskey sours. Carrot juice. Whatever keeps the machine going."

He paused a moment, his breathing down to only 80 puffs a minute, and then continued. "I'd sure like to talk with you longer, but I don't want to be too far behind. It's bad for the image. Besides, I've got to get to work. Make more money. Buy more running clothes."

"What do you do?!" I shouted after him.

"Advertising executive," he shouted back. "If you get a chance, stop by Duffy's for a drink. He'll also give you a good buy on track shoes, sweat socks, hats, sweatbands, wrist wallets, and running suits."

Tanness, Anyone?

Between a carpet of knee-deep snow and a nimbostratus ceiling, one of my friends is still sporting her summer tan. I know it's phony—and she knows that I know it's phony—but I have long ago stopped teasing her about it.

In her never-ending quest to appear to be magazine-ad beautiful and healthy, she has slathered skin tanning lotion into every pore of her body, laid out on roofs and beaches to catch whatever ray was passing by, and goes to a tanning salon at least once a week. I'm not sure she ever stepped into the surf.

For decades, I have endured the scorn of these fake-skin friends, their hair bleached to fireball yellow, their skin tanned to the color and consistency of obsidian, as they sweat their lives away, ruled by the nation's mass media which give them myriad examples of what editors and advertisers think are the "beautiful" people.

Nevertheless, I have always been content to know I had more genetic pigment than all of them, and don't need to cremate myself on a roof top to be healthy: A "natural 7," I reason, is far better than crapping out with a "phony 10."

Once, with the nation's magazines providing guidance, women desperately wanted to look pale. Ashen was admired. Pallid was wonderful! The lighter the skin, the healthier they believed they were, even if it meant hiding in a basement and fighting any attempt by Vitamin C to force its way into their lives. These women would read *Macbeth* and admire the ghost. Any darkness of the skin reflected that they weren't women of leisure, but (*horrors!*) working women—the kind who go outside and have to (*shudder!*) do things.

It changed in the early 1920s, not long after fashion designer Coco Chanel took a yachting vacation and came back tanned. The newspapers and magazines reported how beautiful and healthy she looked. Women, who longed for, but could not afford Coco Chanel creations, now decided they could try to become as tan as their favorite designer. Not just a little suntanned, but an I'm-darker-than-Whoopie-Goldberg-tan while they soak up those ultraviolets!

During the next few decades, when America couldn't find enough sun to char their skin and fry their brains, they bought sunlamps, reflectors, and gallons of "fake tan" lotion, guaranteed to make their friends believe they had just returned from a decade in Nigeria.

By the 1960s, physicians were delaring that suntans were unhealthy. Have you ever seen what a couple of hours a day in the sun can do to an unprotected body over a few years? If you don't have to chase away knife-wielding scouts from the Tandy Leather Co. from trying to skin you, then you have a chance to live until a ripe old age of at least 40. And if Tandy doesn't get you, there's a pile of melanoma waiting. Ever see what cancer of the eye or ear looks like? Ever see a jellyfish on a rotting log? Cancer scare? There's still sunblock. Just pick a number. Any low number. You'll "protect" yourself and darken up just like that Ban de Soleil model and look just as good. After all, would advertising agencies lie?

Advertising from "fake tan" companies guaranteed the world's fair-skinned population they could get all the tan they wanted without the harmful effects of the sun. However, the Food and Drug Administration said the companies weren't telling the truth; the Federal Trade Commission struck down almost all the advertising claims as phony.

Exit fake tan lotions, enter suntanning salons. In the semi-privacy of a casket, people could pay $20 for 15 minutes, slobber even more lotion on themselves, and look even healthier. The owners of the tanning parlors claim the harmful effects from the sun are UVB rays, not the "healthy" UVA rays of the caskets, and that "pre-tanning"—getting a base tan before going on Spring Break—was healthy. Not so, say the nation's dermatologists, who are no match for the UltraSun Turbo 20,000 tanning bed or the mountains of advertising that would fill all the nation's potholes and probably the Grand Canyon.

In 2008, Americans bought more than $600 million in sun tan lotions and oils, a 6.5 percent increase from the year before. The best way to avoid melanoma, they declared, was by slathering goo all over their bodies and getting just the right tan. After all, Coppertone's ads—in newspapers, magazines, and on billboards beginning in the 1950s—showed a playful puppy pulling down the bathing suit of a little tanned girl. Would Coppertone do anything to harm puppies or little girls?

Although many people desperately want to have the dark "healthy" skin that advertisers say they need, they aren't willing to appear to be "ethnic." So, just in case someone could confuse them with being Black, Hispanic, Jewish, Arabic, or any other genetically dark-skinned type, they strip their natural hair color, pour one of a hundred shades of blonde dye onto whatever is left, and become extras for what's left of the beach blanket surfer craze. Just as they believe the advertising agencies wouldn't deceive them, they believe blondes have more fun. Didn't that great American philosopher Lady Clairol say it? It must be so. And, of course, there are about 65,000 solutions on the market, each advertised as the greatest miracle since coconut oil, just designed to make you have fun while you lose every follicle in your genetic pattern.

Death by Healthy Doses

They buried Bouldergrass today. The cause of death was listed as "media-induced health."

Bouldergrass had begun his health crusade more than a decade ago when he began reading more than the sports pages of his local newspaper, subscribed to his first magazine, and decided TV news could be informative if it didn't mention anything about wars, famines, and poverty.

Based upon what he read and saw in the media, Bouldergrass moved from smog-bound Los Angeles to a rural community in scenic green Vermont, gave up alcohol and a two-pack-a-day cigarette habit, and was immediately hospitalized for having too much oxygen in his body. To burn off some of that oxygen, he joined two-thirds of America's "beautiful people" on the jogging paths where the media helped him to believe he was sweating out all the bad karma. In less than a year, the karma left his body which was now coexisting with leg cramps, fallen arches, and several compressed disks. But at least he was as healthy as all the ads told him he could be.

To make sure he didn't get skin cancer from being in the sun too long, he slathered four pounds of No. 35 sunblock on his body every time he ran, and went to suntan parlors twice a week to get that "healthy glow" advertisers told him he needed. He stopped blocking when he learned that suntan parlors weren't good for your health, and that the ingredients in the lotions could cause cancer. So, he wore a jogging suit that covered more skin than an Arab woman's black chador with veil— and developed a severe case of heat exhaustion.

From ultrathin models and billions of dollars in weight-reducing advertising that told him "thin was in," he began a series of crash diets. When he was down to 107 pounds, advertising told him he needed to "bulk up" to be a "real man." So, he began lifting weights and playing racquetball three hours a day. Four groin pulls and seven back injuries later, he had just 6 percent body fat, and a revolving charge account at the office of his local orthopedist.

Several years earlier, Bouldergrass had stopped eating veal as part of a protest of America's inhumane treatment of animals destined for supermarkets. Now, in an "enlightened" age of health, he gave up all meat, not because of mankind's cruelty to animals, but because a TV panel revealed that vascular surgeons owned stock in meat packing companies. Besides, it was the "healthy" thing to do.

He finally gave up pasta when he saw a TV report about the microscopic creepy crawlers that infest most dough. He gave up eggs because they contributed to his high cholesterol level, and then began eating them again when he learned they had protein and didn't cause major jumps in cholesterol. For more than five years, depending upon which magazine he read, he either did not eat eggs—or he did.

For a couple of years, lured by a multi-million dollar ad campaign and innumerable articles in the supermarket tabloids, Bouldergrass ate only oat bran muffins for breakfast and a diet of beta carotenes for lunch, until he found himself spending more time in the bathroom than at work. He eliminated the muffins entirely after reading an article that told him eating oatmeal, bran, and hood ornaments from Buick Roadsters were bad for your health.

Bouldergrass gave up milk when he learned that acid rain fell onto pastures and was eaten by cows. When he learned that industrial conglomerates had dumped everything from drinking water to radioactive waste into streams and rivers, he stopped eating fish. For awhile, based upon conflicting reports in the media, he juggled low-calorie, low-fat, and low-carbohydrate diets until his body systems dropped into the low end of inertia.

At the movies, he smuggled in packets of oleo to squeeze onto plain popcorn until he was bombarded by news stories that revealed oleo was as bad as butter and that most theatrical popcorn was worse than an all-day diet of sirloin.

When he learned that coffee and chocolate were unhealthy, he gave up an addiction to getting high from caffeine and sugar, and was now forced to work 12-hour days without any stimulants other than the fear of what his children were doing while he was at work.

Unfortunately, he soon had to give up decaffeinated coffee and sugarless candy with cyclamates since both caused laboratory mice to develop an incurable yen to listen to music from the Grand Funk Railroad.

Left with a diet of fruits and vegetables, he was lean and trim. Until he accidentally stumbled across a protest by an environmental group which complained that the use of pesticides on farm crops was a greater health hazard than the bugs the pesticides were supposed to kill. Even the city's polluted water couldn't clean off all the pesticides. That's also when he stopped taking showers, and merely poured a gallon of distilled water over his head every morning.

For weeks, he survived on buckets of vitamins because all the magazines told him that's what he should do. Then, after reading an article that artificial vitamins shaped like the Flintstones caused dinosaur rot, he also gave them up.

The last time I saw Bouldergrass, he was in a hospital room claiming to see visions of monster genetic tomatoes squishing their way toward him; he was mumbling something about cholesterol and high density lipoproteins. Tubes were sticking out of every opening in his emaciated body, as well as a couple of openings that hadn't been there when he first checked in.

Shortly before Bouldergrass died, he pulled me near him, asked that I write his obit, and in a throaty whisper begged, "Make sure you tell them that thanks to what I learned from the media, I died healthy."

Mixing a Bitter Pill for America's Drug Companies

The advertising copy for the front of packages of Legatrin and Q-Vel were once similar. The only major difference was that Ciba's Q-Vel used capitals; and Columbia's Legatrin used upper and lower case letters. Beneath their logos, in small type, both companies proclaimed the nonprescription drug was a "Muscle Relaxant/Pain Reliever." In bolder white letters, they also proclaimed each "Prevents and Relieves Night Leg Cramps."

Not so, said the U.S. Food and Drug Administration (FDA). Not only didn't the drugs prevent and relieve night leg cramps, but the quinine in the drugs could also cause severe medical problems, including spontaneous internal hemorrhages, visual, auditory, and gastrointestinal symptoms, as well as kidney failure, liver injuries, and severe dermatologic and blood damage. Hospitalization and deaths have occurred from reactions to the quinine, said the FDA, which ordered the companies in 1995 to stop manufacturing and shipping over-the-counter medicines containing quinine. Not affected was the use of quinine for treatment of malaria. Because of almost insignificant doses, the FDA order didn't apply to the use of quinine in beverages.

Columbia's Legatrin was the source of $4 million of its $9 million per year income; Ciba sold more than 1.3 billion cartons of Q-Vel between 1986 and its termination.

A century ago, Americans unknowingly took alcohol and opium-laced drugs that were advertised as curing every medical problem from "indiscretions of youth" to syphilis and cancer. The patent medicine quacks were making $100 million per year from drugs that not only didn't cure anyone, but could also lead to even more severe medical complications. Of that $100 million income, about $40 million went to bribe legislators to do nothing, and for newspapers and magazine editors to accept the ads and not investigate patent medicine claims.

In the U.S. Department of Agriculture, chemist Harvey Wiley spent 25 years trying to convince Congress that the patent "snake oil" medicines were harmful, only to be persecuted by his superiors. Finally, during the first five years of the 20th century, several national magazines, risking their own financial health, refused to accept patent medicine advertising, and launched major investigations that laid out the facts behind all the "wonder drugs." But, the states' legislatures and the Congress refused to do anything, their allegiances paid for by business, pharmaceutical manufacturers, and by the medical establishment itself.

Taking on the drug lobby, publisher William Randolph Hearst, then at the peak of his power, directed *Good Housekeeping* to establish a laboratory to investigate claims of all companies advertising in Hearst's publications, and to issue a "seal of approval" if the product did what it was meant to do without harming the public.

The Progressive administration of Theodore Roosevelt, spurred by the articles of several investigative journalists, had demanded the passage of legislation to protect consumers. But, lobbyists had bottled it up in a congressional committee.

Then, in 1905, journalist Upton Sinclair went undercover in Chicago's meat packing houses to document corruption within the U.S. Department of Agriculture that allowed companies to package diseased meat. After most newspaper and magazine publishers—themselves subject to bribes and lobbying by the meat packing and drug industries—rejected Sinclair's investigation, a socialist company published the first of several articles that eventually led to the book-length publication of *The Jungle,* now regarded as one of the nation's most brutal novels. The novel so inflamed the country—causing Americans to boycott packed meat and foreign countries to refuse to accept meat packed in America—that Congress had little choice except to pass the Pure Foods and Drug Act first proposed by Dr. Wiley and supported by the President.

A century later, Americans may become upset with the high cost of drugs, or of the plethora of ads which help drive up that cost, but because of America's muckraking journalists, a few courageous publishers, and a determined president, we aren't as suspicious of the advertising claims made by the pharmaceutical companies, nor are we as concerned about the safety of their product.

Overdosing on Drug Ads

One drug manufacturer wants us to "celebrate" relief from arthritis pain by taking its prescription drug. Its primary rival asks, "What's it like to look forward to the first few steps of the day?"

One company will help us stop burping and moaning, declaring, "For people with acid reflux disease, it's time to check your tummy out of the heartburn hotel." One of its competitors pushes purple pills upon us with a shattering question—"Did you know acid reflux could wear away the lining of your esophagus?"

Have high cholesterol? Four companies tell us we can live better by taking their prescription drugs. Depressed? Anxious? Tired? There's hope in pills. Forgetful? Repeating questions? Having trouble finding words? One company says it may not be "normal aging," but the onset of Alzheimer's Disease. Fortunately, there's hope in a 5 or 10 mg. a day dose.

In full-page color ads in national magazines and 30-second network TV commercials, combined with direct market flyers, and some newspaper and radio advertising, pharmaceutical manufacturers are spending aabout $5 billion a year in Direct-to-Consumer Advertising (DTCA).

About one-third "of all patients have asked their physicians for information on drugs they have seen in a DTCA ad," according to a 1997 study by the American Pharmaceutical Association. An independent *Prevention Magazine* survey in May 1998 determined that DTCA "allows people to be more involved with their health," and that such advertising "is an extremely effective means [not only] of promoting both the public health and prescription medicines [but] may play a very real role in enhancing the public health."

The FDA, which in the early 1980s had asked for a voluntary moratorium of drug advertising to assess its effects, then lifted the moratorium in 1985 following extensive studies, now supports advertising to consumers. FDA Commissioner Jane Haney, in November 2000, noted that "DTCA prescription drug promotion offers public health benefits that may outweigh the potential costs," and pointed out that such advertisements remind consumers "to get their medicines refilled and help them adhere to their regimens; advertisements also promote patients to ask their physicians about new medical conditions."

Opposition to DTCA has been heavy from physicians and some consumer organizations. The Committee on Bioethical Issues of the Medical Society of the State of New York claimed in October 1999 that direct drug advertising "provides no real benefit to patients," proposed that advertising to the public should be limited only to non-prescription drugs, and urged the FDA to reduce or eliminate DTCA. The New Jersey delegation to the 2001 meeting of the American Medical Association proposed a complete ban. In vigorous discussion, the AMA reaffirmed its 11-point position about what drug manufacturers should and should not include in ads to consumers, recommended that drug advertising include the disclaimer, "Your physician may recommend other appropriate treatments," but did not endorse an outright ban. Part of its reluctance may have been because the FDA and numerous media organizations have pointed out that a governmental ban treads upon First Amendment protections of freedom of speech.

For millennia, kings and the clergy had tried to keep the masses illiterate, believing mankind was incapable of rational thought. They believed the masses would misinterpret literature and the Scriptures; this, they believed, would not only bring about a chaos of the understanding of God's will, but also an erosion of the power of the state and clergy. It was an extension of this "divine right" of absolute rule that led the Royal College of Physicians in 1555 to declare, "No physician [shall] teach people about medicines or even tell them the names of medicines." The fear was that the people, not trained in medicine and incapable of rational thought, would be harmed by knowledge that only physicians were allowed to possess. That fear continued for more than four centuries.

Prior to 1984, American pharmaceutical companies advertised almost solely to health care professionals who acted as "learned intermediaries" between pharmaceutical companies and the public. But, with a rising consumer demand for information about their own heath care, and seeing a probable increase in income if consumers learned about certain medicines, the manufacturers decided the public could act as "learned intermediaries" to the medical profession. Direct-to-Consumer advertising increased significantly in 1997 after the FDA loosened restrictions on requirements to publish usage and side effects in all ads. The U.S. and New Zealand are the only two countries that allow DTCA.

Direct-to-consumer advertising peaked at $5.3 billion in 2007, significantly higher than the 1997 total of $1.1 billion, before dropping to $4.3 billion in 2008, according to Nielsen Media Research. The 18 percent drop was probably because of a combination of reduced advertising rates by the media, and less direct spending by the drug companies, both of them the result of the Recession.

Most avertising to the public is for about a dozen drugs for (in order) heartburn, insomnia, cholesterol, asthma and allergy, nail fungus, blood clots, and erectile dysfunction, according to a study published in 2007 by the *New England Journal of Medicine*.

The average American sees about 16 hours of drug advertising a year, according to a study published by the *Annals of Family Medicine* in 2007. That same year, IMSHealth, which specializes in health industry analysis, revealed that TV advertising is more effective the first two weeks after the launch of a new product, with diminished returns for about 36 weeks, while print advertising "has more has a longer, more gradual effect; it continued to draw new patients and increase thecumulative total of prescriptions at least through week 74 post-exposure." The combination of DTCA and sampling, says IMS Health, is a "one-two punch." IMS had previously reported that DTCA creates "awareness among consumers and sampling [ensures] that people can easily try the product." The pharmaceutical industry claims the cost of prescription drugs would be even higher if there were fewer ads and, thus, less volume.

The drug industry also spends more than $7 billion for gifts and special advertising to physicians including not only advertising in medical journals but also giving physicians everything from pens, mugs, and stethoscopes to free dinners, tickets to major sports events, and vacations that include discussions by pharmaceutical representatives. "There is clear evidence that doctors who accept drug-company gifts and money tend to prescribe the company's products," according to investigative journalists Jeff Gammage and Karl Stark, writing in the March 10, 2002, issue of *Inquirer Magazine.* In an attempt to counter a growing concern by consumers and regulators that the industry was experiencing out-of-control profits from setting out-of-control prices, and to pre-empt federal intervention, the nation's drug companies created a set of self-imposed guidelines to "benefit patients and enhance the practice of medicine." These guidelines, jointly created by the Pharmaceutical Research and Manufacturing Association (PHRMA) and the American Medical Association (AMA), limit the companies and their 81,000 sales representatives from giving physicians and other health care practitioners anything not directly related to health care. Some drug companies claim that physicians expected nonmedical "perks" for them and their families; some physicians claim drug companies were too intrusive. Cutting back on the "high-ticket freebies," however, has a side effect that should increase profits, while also allowing even more income to be spent on advertising to consumers.

About half of all physicians argue that not only does DTCA undermine their authority, it is deceptive. They are right. The purpose of advertising isn't to educate anyone but to manipulate them to buy something. Physicians who feel "compelled" to write prescriptions because they are "pushed" by patients who tear ads out of magazines can simply refuse to write the prescription, and then explain reasons to the patient why that drug may not be appropriate or another drug more suitable. Society still gives power to the health care provider, not the consumer.

Although many health care professionals now reject the myriad "freebies" pharmaceutical companies use to help "convince" physicians to prescribe certain drugs, most professionals still accept the gifts, and have almost no problem with the placement of about $500 million in journal advertising. What the professionals object to is that in a newer era in which consumers are better informed about health care issues, the physician may lose that "learned intermediary" power that was once inherent in medical care.

Physicians need not fear the consumer; they will still evaluate and possibly be misled by drug advertising just as they are now influenced, and often misled, by ads for cars, forthcoming movies, and suntan lotions. The solution to better health care is not the absence of information, but more.

Trading Rights for Dollars

The Food and Drug Administration (FDA) and the tobacco industry negotiated a $300 billion "settlement." In exchange for an immunity against being sued for wrongful deaths because of tobacco addiction, catastrophic illness, or death, the tobacco industry agreed to severe restrictions on advertising.

Among the restrictions are bans on outdoor advertising, the placement of ads in several thousand publications that "could" be directed to youth, all logo-oriented promotional items sent in exchange for coupons, and campaigns using symbolic humans, such as the Marlboro Man.

Although the federal government has every legal and Constitutional right to protect the health of the people, doesn't it seem odd that the tobacco industry is willing to give up many of its Constitutional First Amendment rights? And, doesn't it seem that this universal squeezing of advertising will benefit not only the larger companies, already well-positioned in the market, but also magazines with a substantial "adult" audience?

'Step Right Up and
Buy Into a Part of America!'

All across the nation, just about everything is up for sale. Golf and tennis tournaments now carry names of liquor and tobacco companies, auto manufacturers, regional phone companies, and quickie food restaurants. The end-of-the-season college football bowls are now named for insurance and oil companies, an orange juice processing company, a video rental conglomerate, and even a company that makes weed whackers. The PBS non-profit beg-a-thons easily match anything that advertisers can throw onto commercial television, and our nation's colleges long ago sold out to millionaire benefactors with the morals of junk bond dealers.

The sponsoring companies claim that without their money the nation's most hallowed institutions would collapse. While the nation spent anout $1 trillion to bail out failing major corporations, there are myriad opportunities for a governmental sell-out to bring in corporate revenue.

Overseeing all the buildings and clowns could be the Ringling Brothers Government Service Administration. It might be tacky for the President to greet ambassadors in the Reebok Rose Garden, and then invite them to dinner in the Burger King State Dining Room. However, the Oval(tine) Office does have a particularly nice ring to it.

The Chock Full O'Nuts Congress, of course, has been bought and sold more times than hog belly futures in the commodities market. But, for a few extra million to help pay off the national debt, Congress could formalize its long-standing practice of selling votes to corporations, associations, and lobbyists with unsavory reputations.

After being bought covertly for so long, the Department of Defense could acknowledge its indebtedness to the nation's war contractors and possibly rename itself the General Dynamics Department of Defense or the G-D D-O-D for short. For contractors without as much money to spend, perhaps the Department could sell off a base for only a few million.

Since members of the National Rifle Association believe Americans have a Constitutional right to blow apart anything with at least one cell, maybe they'd be willing to sponsor the NRA 2nd Amendment Armor Division. The 101st Screaming Eagles paratroopers might be renamed the H & R Block Juggling 1040th. The Navy could reap a bundle by selling rights to name newly constructed ships. The $500 million nuclear garbage scow could be named the U.S.S. Bernie Madoff, a tribute to the poster boy of Ponzi scheme corruption. To protect against enemy identification, the periscope of the nuclear submarine Michael Jackson could be disguised by a large sequined velvet glove.

The Hershey Chocolate Bureau of the Mint would be a sweet addition to the national menu, even if Hershey has outsourced much of its production to Mexico. The Sony Department of Commerce would help regulate foreign trade, and the Wite-out National Security Council would keep the nation in continual secrecy.

Donald Trump, whose name appears on anything made of concrete, could shell out a few million for the rights to the Trump Department of Housing and Urban Development. In case he needs additional financing, he might contact the CitiBank Department of the Treasury.

For a few million, Motown Records could buy the rights to the all-Black (robed) John Roberts and the Supremes whose record isn't gold but has been on the charts longer than anyone else's.

The Exxon Department of Environmental Clutter could team up with the Exxon Department of Interior to sell off what's left of our natural resources. They could then form a temporary partnership with the Halliburton Department of State to "protect" sand-infested oligarchies with vast oil reserves. Of course, since the American taxpayers have been in the hole so long, thanks to corporate and governmental greed, Interior might just want to throw a morsel our way and rename one of our national parks, the Taxpayer Grand Canyon.

Eyewitless Promotion

Once, when we were all naive, the media let the news speak for itself. However, several dozen consultants, aided by cowardly editors and news directors, believe the strength of a story isn't sufficient to carry audience interest. Newspapers explode with color, graphics, and multicolored sidebars. Making room for the hype leads to fewer and shorter stories. But, nowhere has news embellishment become more developed than in local TV news operations, trumpeted by pretentious graphics and full-orchestral fanfare, as seen on a typical newscast at KFAD.

"NEWS right NOW! *LIVE* from KFAD-TV, the all-news and entertainment station that's taking the lead in news and entertainment! This is the Eyewitless 15 Action News Team with all the news and information in River Valley! And now KFAD-TV, the Number 1 source of all news and entertainment in all of River Valley, proudly presents Eyewitless 15 Action News at 6.

The news starts RIGHT NOW!"

"Good evening. This is Harry Handsome."

"And I'm Susie Sweetwater. Tonight, we have TWO top stories. A fire in Potshot Township and the opening of a supermarket in East Rutabaga. But first, our BIG story. Harry."

"Thank you, Susie. Our BIG story concerns a family of six that's been wiped out in a hail of gunfire. And, here's the kicker—the cops went to the wrong house! We'll be back with that story and others, right after five minutes of these rapid-fire earth shattering messages." . . .

"We're back. But, first, this just in. *LIVE* on the Interstate is Eyewitless 15 Action News reporter Kiki Vertigo."

"Thanks, Harry. This is Kiki Vertigo *LIVE* with BREAKING NEWS on River Valley's premiere news and entertainment station. I'm *LIVE* on the Interstate, somewhere around Exit 35 or 36. Traffic is backed up almost a half-mile. Back to you, Harry."

"Kiki, do you know why traffic is backed up?"

"I didn't get any confirmation, but it appears the cause is more cars than the Interstate can handle at this time. This is Kiki Vertigo reporting for the Eyewitless 15 Action News Team."

"Thanks for that great *LIVE* report only on Eyewitless 15 Action News. At 11 tonight, Eyewitless 15 Action investigative reporter Polly Prattle tears open the previously untold story of the seamy underworld of Betsy Ross. And on Daybreak at 7 News tomorrow morning, Bob Covina begins his three-part indepth probe of the annual Miss Nude New England contest. On tonight's 11 p.m. Action Report, chief meteorologist Flake Sepulveda will ask some useless weather question, tell us the history of temperature, and then give the latest on the tornado that's heading east from Kansas and is expected to destroy Boston. ONLY on Eyewitless 15 Action News. KFAD-15. But first, let's break for some messages of critical social importance about where to buy your next used car." . . .

"We're back, and with sports for the Eyewitless 15 Action Sports Team is former minor league baseball reserve pitcher Boom-Boom Brannigan."

"Thanks, Harry. At the top of the sports news, a $5 million per year pro-basketball player has committed suicide. The National League announced plans to dissolve. And the Baltimore Orioles will move to Baghdad next season. But, first, a sports EXCLUSIVE on KFAD-15, your Eyewitless News Action

371

Team for all of River Valley. It's the second day of the season, and we have eight teams with identical 1-and-1 records. Now, how often do you think that happens? We'll be back with more sports right after these important messages." . . .

"We're back with more sports. At 11 tonight, we'll give you all the details about the suicide, the dissolution of the National League, and the Orioles flying off to Iraq. Back to you, Susie."

"Thanks, Boom-Boom. Straight ahead on Eyewitless 15 Action News KFAD is an EXCLUSIVE interview with Mayor Sammy Schmaltz who plans to announce a major building project for the Valley. Stay tuned to KFAD-TV 15, your Eyewitless 15 Action News Team. We'll be back and teasing you with even more stories right after these messages." . . .

"Finally, on the news station that has more promotion than any other station, we have this cute little featurette from the network. A Kansas-bred lion that was sunning itself near City Hall was thrown into the air by the tornado that's heading our way, and landed on its feet in Indianapolis where it qualified 15th for the Indianapolis 500 Mile Race. At 11, we'll have an exclusive interview with the lion. For the Eyewitless 15 Action News Team, the absolutely ultimate best news in River Valley, this is Susie Sweetwater."

"And this is Harry Handsome. Now to our disembodied baritone voiced narrator and his full orchestra."

"You've been watching Eyewitless 15 Action News on KFAD Live News 15, the all-news and entertainment station for River Valley viewers in the River Valley. KFAD, your eyewitness to life, liberty, and the pursuit of ratings. Good Night. And good news."

'And Now a Word From Your Local Sponsor'

In the *Police Academy* movies, Michael Winslow portrayed a cop who baffles and harasses the bad guys by imitating the sounds of helicopters, machine guns, and even the high-pitched sirens of police cars. Film goers know *Police Academy* is a comedic exaggeration. Unfortunately, the nation's military and paramilitary agencies haven't figured this out.

In 1990, the Army set up loudspeakers to blast rock music at opera-loving Panamanian dictator Manuel Noriega, figuring that no one could withstand "Voodoo Child" and "You're No Good" for long. During the first Gulf War, the Army set up speakers to transmit sounds of tanks to make Saddam Hussein believe an invasion was imminent. Although Saddam was captured almost 14 years later, before he was hanged he never revealed the truth behind the weapons of mass deafness, and we never learned if the deception worked or was just noise pollution.

In Waco, the Bureau of Alcohol, Tobacco, and Firearms and the FBI bungled their way into a two-month-long stand-off when they tried ousting wacko David Koresh and his Branch Davidians from their fortress by using psychological warfare. The Feds shined spotlights into the compound, and set up a ring of loudspeakers. They recorded a high-pitched screech from an off-the-hook telephone, cranked up the decibels, and beamed that noise into the compound. They also blasted Christmas carols, chants from Tibetan monks, military bugle calls, and rock music at the man who believed he was a prophet, a savior or, depending on the tide, the son of God. The spotlights and rock music didn't seem to affect the Davidians. The only ones affected by the psychological warfare were the Feds.

Although it didn't work in Panama, Iraq, and Texas, the use of media to force surrenders, whether from American criminals or international dictators, shouldn't be abandoned. For unlimited torture, the kind that Amnesty International would surely oppose, I'd set up large-screen TV sets. I believe I have the ultimate "surrender-at-any-price" programming.

I'd open the broadcast day with a sermonette by rocker David Lee Roth, followed by a 15-minute quick-cut montage of politicians and government officials saying, "Trust me." Next up would be two hours of clips from each of the 15,000 celebrity exercise videos currently on the market, followed by an hour of clips of "Stupid Funny Home Video Tricks" and two hours of afternoon soaps featuring actresses who can't act woodenly reciting words from writers who can't write.

Next would be a rerun of the deservedly-defunct musical TV series "Cop Rock" followed by classic music videos of Ratt, Twisted Sister, and Nine Inch Nails, and the adagios rapped by hip-hoppers Wu-Tang Clan and Obie Trice. Inbetween the programming, we'd beam endless commercials of Sally Struthers blathering about correspondence courses, some bald-headed guy telling how to restore hair, and Ed McMahon telling every known life form that it *could* be a winner.

About 6 p.m., bring on the local "Happy-Time News," with Susie Sweetwater's big exclusive of the winner of the Miss Rutabaga contest, Harry Handsome's biting feature about the county's largest cucumber, and Darla Dormant's questions to local residents—"How do you feel about having a lunatic fanatic murderer in your neighborhood?"

If that doesn't finish him off, bring on the Jerry Springer Trailer Trash Marathon, complete with locally produced TV commercials, followed by the Britney and her Navel Two-Hour Special. Sufficiently softened up and begging for redemption, finish him off with a six-hour shot of reality programming.

Jeanetics and the Cool 'Wannabe'

Just about everyone who wants to appear to be young, cool, and "with it," is wearing jeans. Students and teachers. Patients and doctors. Lawyers, cops, and criminals. In upscale Manhattan, the Yuppie crowd wears jeans and blue blazers; in middle America, reporters wear jeans with inexpensive shirts and ties. Wannabe rappers wear baggy jeans; and wannabe sex kittens wear low-cut form-fitting jeans with holes strategically placed.

Nuclear engineer and former president Jimmy Carter wears jeans since he was a peanut farmer and later became active in the Habitat for Humanity program of building houses for low-income families. Ronald Reagan wore jeans on his Santa Barbara, Calif., ranch; George W. Bush wore jeans when he was slicing through the underbrush on his mini-ranch in Crawford, Texas, while president. During their cross-country campaign of 1992, Bill Clinton and Al Gore wore jeans; George H. W. Bush wasn't re-elected, possibly because he didn't wear jeans on the campaign trail and, thus, appeared to be an un-American aging Yuppie out of tune with the economy and America's need to follow whatever advertising message was being beamed at the time. Barack Obama does wear jeans, but only occasionally. It was so unusual when he wore jeans on his campaign plane in May 2008, the media rushed stories into the news pipeline. Shortly before his inauration in January 2009, the Red Monkey Company produced a limited "Yes We Can" edition, informally known as Obama Jeans.

On labels as wide as barn doors, displayed on bodies nearly as wide, are free advertising for Calvin Klein, Gloria Vanderbilt, Liz Claiborne, Ralph Lauren, Sergio Valente, and Guess? The more affluent, or at least those who pretend to be, can purchase jeans from Armani, Versace, Gucci, and dozens of other companies for $200–$500. A few companies have even begun marketing custom-made premium jeans; APO sells a $4,000 version, complete with platinum rivets and diamond buttons. Even Levi's, which sells most of its jeans in department stores rather than boutiques, went upscale with a $501 price on a pair of 501s designed in a retro look. In Fall 2006, Levi's went high-tech, adding the RedWire DLX, which has a built-in iPod joystick in the front watch pocket, and a side pocket that allows an unseen iPod docking cradle. The jeans cost about $200.

Although jeans have now become a "boutique" item, their history is more than four centuries old. During the 16th century, India exported a heavy, coarse fabric known as dungaree, which was used by Portuguese and Italian navies to make sails. In Italy, merchants used serge cloth, another sturdy fabric, to make pants for sailors. The fabric was originally made in Nimes, France, and known as "serge de Nimes," or "denim." The name "blue jeans" is derived from "bleu de Genes," or "blue from Genoa." It would be a couple of centuries until blue jeans became part of a culture and a fashion.

The popularity of jeans is traced to the California Gold Rush during the early 1850s. Levi Strauss and his brother-in-law, David Stern, Bavarian-Jewish immigrants, had begun their careers in San Francisco, selling buttons, scissors, and strong brown canvas to to miners, who used it for tents and wagons. But, the miners told him what they needed was strong pants, not the cloth ones that tore easily. Strauss modified the cloth he had brought from Bavaria, and created "waist overalls." The pants were strong and durable. Miners, farmers, and the poor who couldn't afford the expensive wool slacks liked them. Strauss soon became rich from making and selling $1 pants.

By 1860 he switched to denim fabric with a back pocket. Jacob Davis, a tailor, added rivets to increase the strength. Other modifications to the original design included stitched patterns on the back pockets in 1873, a coin pocket in 1890 (it was labelled as "batch 501"), and a fifth pocket in 1905. Belt loops were added in 1922; rivet buttons were all miners needed for more than a half-century. Strauss never referred to his creation as "jeans"; he preferred "waist-high overalls." It wasn't until six decades after his death in 1902 that the company finally called the pants "jeans."

By the 1930s, with the popularity of film Westerns, Americans occasionally imitated the tough independent spirit of film cowboys who wore jeans. During the 1940s, workers in factories found jeans, now with zippers, to be comfortable and sturdy.

However, by the 1950s, the image of jeans had changed as two actors and a singer became the role models for rebellion. Marlon Brando wore jeans in *On the Waterfront* (1954), James Dean wore jeans in *Rebel Without a Cause* (1955), and Elvis Presley wore a pair of black denims in *Jailhouse Rock* (1957). The emerging rock and roll generation began demanding jeans. The older generation mounted its own rebellion—schools banned students from wearing jeans; restaurants and movie theaters refused to seat anyone wearing jeans, which were seen as a symbol of social protest and rebellion. A decade later, the hippies began wearing bell-bottom jeans. By 1982, with few hippies left, Donald Freeland of the Great Western Garment Co. came up with the idea of stone-washing; soon, customers had figured out they could put pumice stones in the wash cycle to make the jeans appear as if they had been worn several times while their owners lassoed maverick doggies on the range. Five years later, ripped and torn jeans, exposing flesh while leading people to believe their wearers have sexually active lives, became the nation's fashion statement. One of the first designers to have figured out how to con the public into believing there's nothing sexier than someone in hip-hugging tight jeans was Calvin Klein.

In 1980, 15-year-old starlet Brooke Shields seductively asked, "You know what comes between me and my Calvins?" She then cooed: "Nothing." A decade after introducing America to jeans and Brooke Shields, Calvin Klein spent $1 million just on advertising space to run an erotic 116-page ad mixture of naked men and women, jeans, Harleys, and tattoos in *Vanity Fair;* jeans soon became the aphrodisiac all America wanted. Calvin Klein is still selling sex and jeans, posing pliable and emaciated nude women draped over brawny men wearing nothing but— what else?—their Calvin Kleins. The company had concentrated on print advertising, but in 2009, almost three decades after it first introduced the Brooke Shields ad campaign, Calvin Klein created a soft-core porn ad, featuring four women and two men groping each other, wearing nothing but their jeans. The darkly-lit ad with spcial effects transitions appeared on the Internet and European television; American television and cable networks declined.

During the 1990s, it seemed as if every clothing manufacturer was rounding up the denim supply and painting it onto their models. Women who could pour themselves into a pair of designer jeans with nothing hanging over were to be admired; they apparently mastered the art of self-restraint to be thin enough to be uncomfortable. Size 14 women were trying to merge into size 8s, believing they'd look sexy being strangled in denim, while secretly gasping airfulls of oxygen from a portable tank that should have come with every pair of jeans.

Wranglers, originally targeted to blue-collar workers and the country music market, were once sold to the theme of "rodeo cowboys and the women who love them." For its media buys, Wrangler sent its advertising messages to country music radio stations, the Nashville Network, ESPN, *Western Horseman, Horse Illustrated, Quarter Horse Journal,* and *Field & Stream.* It sponsored the Professional Rodeo Cowboys Association, and took almost every available advertising space at rodeos, including the barrels in barrel races. For its model, it used country singer George Strait—"A western original wears a western original." During the 1980s, Wrangler, continuing to target a blue-collar middle-American market, sponsored Dale Earnhardt Sr. on the NASCAR circuit, and also used him in several ads. In 2004, Wrangler signed Dale Earnhardt Jr. and later football star Brett Favre as its spokesmen.

By the mid-1990s, a new kind of celebrity was emerging. After rapper Snoop Dogg wore a Tommy Hilfiger jeans outfit in 1994 on NBC's "Saturday Night Live," sales for the brand increased about $90 million. Snoop soon launched his own line, as did Outkast, Eminem, LL Cool J, Diddy, and dozens of hip-hop artists who tried to cash in on an urban baggy-pants style, possibly first introduced by JNCO Jeans, established in 1985 by Milo and Jaques Revah in Los Angeles.

Levi Strauss continued to push its straight-legged 501s, and then tried to pick up sales by backing off of the soft stone-washed jeans. In more than a century, Levi Strauss had sold more than 3.5 billion pairs of jeans, and once held a commanding 20 percent of the total share. The 501 advertising campaign for several styles is built around the "Original like you" focus. Levi's annual advertising budget solely for rivets-on-the-pockets, buttons-on-the-fly Levi's 501s, the tight-fitting straight-legged, narrow-ankle, rump-enhancing best-selling jeans in the world is about $20 million a year.

By 1996, its peak year, the company had sales of about $7.1 billion, before plunging to about $4.1 billion in 2002, a trend that had been industry wide. By the end of 2008, Levi Strauss had recovered only slightly, posting revenue of $4.4 billion. The company is the fifth largest apparent manufacturer, behind Nike, VF, Jones Apparel Group, and Liz Claiborne.

The emergence of the suggestive low-riding hip-huggers for women in the late 1990s led to a recovery of a half-decade of declining jeans sales. With Britney Spears and numerous other teeny-bop dancer-singers setting the style, hip-hugging jeans cut well below the navel, and designed for customers with no extra ounces of fat, became the choice of teenage girls. By 2000, Australia's Sass & Bide had begun selling the 2-1/2-inch zipper low-riders, setting some kind of a standard for how little denim it could take, and how tight they could be fit, to cover a teen's emaciated body. For men, Alexander McQueen designed the "bummer" jeans, cut to show rear cleavage.

Levi's, late to come into the low-slung market, joined the trend pushed by other companies by manufacturing low-riders and more expensive designer jeans for women. By the end of 2002, it even brought out a "cutesy" $45 pair of women's jeans that featured the outline of a man's hand on the rear pocket.

With sexual suggestiveness part of the pre-teen and teen culture, jeans manufacturers were using television to target teenage girls. A 30-second TV commercial for low-slung tight-fitting MUDD jeans, an inexpensive jeans targeted to teens, first aired in Summer 2003, showed a teen couple walking in a park. Suddenly, the sprinklers come on; the boyfriend runs, but the now-drenched teen girl, giggling and touching her MUDD-covered body, frolics in the water. The boyfriend, seeing the sexuality, returns to give her a passionate kiss, ending only with the MUDD logo which comes onto the screen, apparently stopping the jeans-wearing children from going too far. MUDD first aired the commercial on MTV, BET, and the ABC Family Channel, reaching about ten times the audience of *Seventeen*, the magazine that reports and helps set trends for the younger teen set. MUDD confined its $2.5 million 2003–2004 media campaign solely to television. A 2006 all-media campaign dropped any sexual allure, but focused upon commnity service. "MUDD Girls

Move The World" featured six teens who had performed significant community service.

Lee took advantage of customer discomfort during the 1990s, and marketed Easy Riders for the 25–44 year-old age group, sending out the message, "If you really want to relax, maybe it's your jeans that should loosen up." Other ads asked, "Need a little more room in your jeans? Try Easy Riders from Lee. The brand that fits." For its target market, it focused upon up-scale women's magazines *Elle*, *Mademoiselle*, *Vogue*, and *Sassy*. To target men, it went with *GQ*, *Esquire*, and *Rolling Stone*. By 2006, Lee had begun advertising itself as "Lee. The jeans that built America," and "Behind the scenes since 1889," putting it in direct competition to Levi's.

In Spring 2005, Levi Strauss, whose sales had been flat for three years, stunned the industry with Intellifit. Fully-clothed customers step into a transparent booth; in 10 seconds, a low-power radio wave scanner records exact body measurements. The customer then receives a list of all the styles and sizes that are appropriate. However, since comfort often takes a secondary position to sexual suggestiveness, customers often squeeze themselves into jeans one size and a few inches below the navel than appropriate.

By Fall 2006, the tight-fitting low-slung hip-huggers with the extra short zippers had begun to yield to jeans that allowed women to have a little more modesty. The newest trend was the "boy-cut" and "boyfriend style" jeans. But, within a couple of years, the "skinny jean," form-fitting and sexually emphasizing every woman's curve, made its comeback.

The top female models earn $15,000–$25,000 a day, while male models make about half of that. However, the major jeans companies are spending large chunks of their promotional budgets to grab every celebrity they can—and the celebrities fully understand that making money by wearing a company's product is not only financially lucrative but yet another way to get media exposure. Once, companies branded their product to a specific demographic; jeans companies—there are now more than 200 of them—are targetting a wide cultural diversity. Wrangler (like Levi's long before) recognized the growing and influential Hispanic market, and created "Viva La Tradición" (Live the Tradition) theme for that market, beginning in Texas in 1992 and then spreading into California five years later. Dickies, which made its name on work clothes, acknowledges cultural diversity by who it uses for its celebrity endorsements; Dickies uses Tim McGraw, Stacey Ferguson of the Black Eyed Peas, Jay-Z, and Avril Lavigne as its models, covering fans of country music, pop music, hip-hop, and rock 'n' roll. J Brand uses Jessica Alba, Kate Moss, and Nicole Richie. The celebrity list for True Religion includes Courteney Cox, Jennifer Garner, Heather Graham, Kate Hudson, Angelina Jolie, Donna Karan, Heidi Klum, Jennifer Lopez, Madonna, Gwyneth Paltrow, Jessica Simpson, Usher, Bruce Willis—and Brooke Shields. About 750 million pairs of jeans are sold worldwide each year; about 450 million are sold just in the United States. Jeans are continuing to dominate what America, and especially its youth market, is wearing.

Sex and the Single Beer Can

Car manufacturers paint two-door convertibles fire-engine red. Jeans manufacturers fleece the public to believe there's nothing sexier than someone in hip-hugging denim. And beer companies have spawned bikini-clad lithe spirits to con cigar-chomping overweight never-hunks in grease-stained sloppy T-shirts to swill one or two six-packs every Sunday afternoon in front of a football-filled television set, and believe they're the sex-machines all America is looking for.

Sex sells.

Throughout the country, we're exposed to Blondes in Bikinis. For variety, there's Blondes in Tank Tops, Blondes in Halters, Blondes in Unbuttoned Short Shorts, Blondes in Cowboy Hats, and Blondes in Paint-Them-on-My-Body jeans. When the beer companies decided they should show a little more "multi-culturalism" in their advertising, they added brunettes and redheads—and put them into bikinis, tank tops, halters, unbuttoned short shorts, cowboy hats, and jeans.

More than four decades after the beginning of the civil rights era, the breweries finally found white-looking size 2 Afro-American women to promote beer—and gave them the opportunity to stretch out on white sand and lure customers into an idyllic setting of sun, surf, sex, and beer. With the election of Barack Obama in 2008, ad agencies and their clients began increasing the presence of Afro-Americans in both print and TV ad campaigns.

During the holidays, in print campaigns, the models wear clinging dresses with hems somewhere about waist level—red and white for Valentine's Day; red, white, and blue for Independence Day; orange for Halloween; furry red and white for Christmas; and green for St. Patrick's Day. Michael Shea's once placed a blonde in a slinky green dress cut above mid-thigh, and then added a shamrock and a beer bottle to entice the public to try "a naturally pure golden lager." Also evoking an Irish theme, Mickey's featured a large-busted model in a body-hugging green swimsuit; between her spread legs was an obviously-phallic Mickey's wide-mouth bottle. Among Miller's specialized campaigns was to place three women in short green dresses and ask America's sex machines to "triple your Irish."

Miller Lite, which opened the light beer market in 1973, and eventually became the nation's second best-selling brand behind Bud Light, targeted would-be macho males. In numerous TV ads, Miller Lite used sports legends and celebrities to debate the eternal philosophical questions of hops—"Less Filling" vs. "Tastes Great." Soon, former jocks and millions of never-was jocks were soon debating the same question. The result was an increase within five years from sale of seven million barrels to 31 million barrels a year. But, the company's marketing executives—who once promoted the brand as "Made the American way"—also knew that although patriotism and humor could be used to introduce a new brand, it was sex that sold and established it among the young male target audience.

A Miller Lite television ad in 2003 took the "tastes great, less filling" debate from sports humor into sexual suggestiveness. The ad featured two voluptuous women at an outdoor café debating the question. Quickly, the discussion deteriorated into a hair-pulling catfight, with both women ripping off each other's clothes as they wrestled on the ground, into a pool, and then, wearing only panties and bras, into a wet concrete pit. The "tag" was that two male beer drinkers had imagined what the perfect beer ad would be. Heather Todd, associate editor of *Beverage World,* said the ad could have been a "humorous spoof of the sex-crazed male mentality and the beer ad genre [but] to others it was a degrading sexual exploitation of women." However, unlike the "tastes great" vs. "less filling" commercials, this one produced no increase in beer consumption.

One of Miller's more popular campaigns was to promote its genuine draft product by showing a dress and shirt on a clothesline. In case the consumers missed the subtlety, it also had posters of models in skin-tight swimsuits, one of whom caressed a Miller Genuine Draft beneath a waterfall.

Waterfalls or showers have been settings for almost every brand in the Anheuser–Busch, Miller, and Coors lines. Coors extols cool, clear water—and string bikinis, cleavage, and beer. Its slender D-cup women are often seductively stretched out on beaches, purring about "real beer satisfaction."

In case a few rugged he-men aren't into beaches, there are macho-man motorcycles. One Coors poster showed a lady in short shorts, a halter-top, and a leather jacket, standing next to a Harley–Davidson. For the sophisticated beer-guzzler, there was a poster of a model in black heels and short black cocktail dress about to straddle a Harley Softtail. Her fuel of choice? Coors Extra Gold. Possibly unwilling to pay a six-digit licensing fee to Harley–Davidson—or having already spent its budget on $10,000 a day models—Michelob Dry, an Anheuser–Busch product, had a model in black heels and black cocktail dress merely caressing a beer bottle. For "variety," Budweiser, also an Anheuser–Busch product, had a brunette in a short red dress sitting seductively on steps. Nevertheless, most of the nation's major breweries have copied each others' "sophisticated" look to promote their "premium" beers, hawking not-so-subliminal attempts to make people believe that beer and "class" are synonymous.

Not so sophisticated is Colt 45, a malt liquor, from G. Heilman, which in the mid-1990s promoted its product by having a seductive woman in a short silky blue dress down on her hands and knees, her cleavage and come-hither look telling men, "Everytime." The sexually-suggestive ads replaced more traditional ads of a decade earlier in which actor Billy Dee Williams told Americans that "Nothing is Smoother Than an Ice Cold Bottle of Colt 45" and "It Works Every Time."

The corporate spokesmen for the nation's largest breweries say their advertising isn't sexist. However, breweries have been using women as lures in beer advertising since the late 1800s. The first ads had featured pictures of the breweries, logos, and cartoony bartenders or families enjoying beer. However, by the early twentieth century, the companies were regularly using women in their advertising. Most ads featured merely the face, heavily made up. The more adventurous featured women from the waist up.

Most of the women had long flowing hair, possibly a subliminal message that the models had "let their hair down" for the male beer drinkers. Their images were lithographed onto beer trays, coasters, and posters, and etched into newspapers and magazine advertising. Often, breweries combined women, beer, and the latest autos, especially during the first two decades of mass production. During the "NASCAR dads" era of the late 1990s and 2000s, the major beer companies sponsored racing, somehow tying together "responsible driving" and drinking; their print advertising, however, is more sex-driven.

In 1907, the Miller's High Life brand introduced the "girl in the moon" as its logo not only for all print advertising but on the neck of the bottle as well. The girl, dressed in a red ethnic eastern European dress and wearing a wide-brimmed red hat, made a comeback in 2005, after several decades of semi-retirement.

For several decades before prohibition during the 1920s and early 1930s, Budweiser had featured the angelic-appearing "Budweiser Girls" embossed on trays and related advertising media. Marathon featured a "bobby-soxer" in a tight sweater and short skirt suggestively posed next to a bowling alley, with the slogan, "Strikes You Right."

Rieger & Gretz Brewing Co. of Philadelphia, like many other breweries, combined the "angelic" with the sexual, featuring women in translucent gowns for the company's annual calendars. During the 1950s and 1960s, TV ads for Carling Black Label featured a perky blonde bartender, Mabel, who said little but at the end of each commercial gave the viewers a sexy wink. Every commercial, which had someone asking, "Hey, Mabel— Black Label," gave Carling's a significant boost in sales. The commercials were rated as the "best liked" in the nation by the Audit Research Bureau. The model's wholesome girl-next-door likeness was soon imprinted on everything from print ads in national magazines to billboards, trays, and cigarette lighters.

Rheingold brought national attention to its product with the annual Miss Rheingold contest from 1940 to 1965. The contest ended when Rheingold officials decided that there was too much cultural diversity in America to market a contest that had focused on White women as winners.

With the "sex revolution" of the 1960s, and increased competition, the major breweries lost whatever was left of their ages of innocence, and combined suggestive slogans and nearly naked women with the "come hither" look. Nude Beer took sexual suggestiveness even further. Eastern Brewing brought out its multi-label pale ale in 1983; scratch off the model's almost-not-there bikini top to reveal her breasts. The beer name, in different formulas, was soon picked up by a brewery in Mexico, and then by several other American micro-breweries. After a few years of dormancy, the concept resurfaced in the mid-1990s, when Naked Brew, a small Southern California company, produced labels for its own version of Nude Beer that asked customers to "peel to reveal," and for retailers to "Get Nude." In Australia, the makers of Skinny Blonde also combined nudity with technology. However, the only thing the drinker had to do was to finish off a 12-ounce bottle. The label featured a 1950s-style artist's rendering of a pin-up girl. As the customer drinks the beer, the lady's bikini disappears. "We had the idea of a pin-up girl from the get go; we thought everyone uses women in their advertising campaigns so why not put it on a bottle?" Hamish Rossen, a professional musician, told the *Times* of London in March 2009. Rossen said he and two of his friends, an actor and an artist, "had this idea of the disappearing bikini and researched into disappearing ink." The coldness of the beer keeps the label intact; as the cold beer disappears, so does the model's bikini.

Stevens Point Brewery of Wisconsin in 2008 released Point Nude Beach Summer Wheat, available only during Summer, and targetted to America's nudists. The label and the six-pack carrier featured a group of happy nudists, with props covering certain areas. The company, appreciative of the 47,000-member American Association for Nude Recreation endorsement, donated 25 cases to the Association's national convention.

New Belgium beer of Fort Collins, Colo., managed to merge sexual suggestion with environmental concerns. Its video ad for Skinny Dip Beer in Summer 2008 showed activists skinny dipping in the White Salmon River Dam to celebrate the forthcoming removal of the Condit Hydroelectric Dam, and the probable restoration of salmon breeding in the watershed.

American breweries aren't the only ones using sexual suggestiveness to lure men to drink beer. Most Western countries have a more liberal attitude about nudity than does the relatively puritanical United States. This attitude is reflected in their commercials. A television commercial for Hahn Premium, an Australian beer, showed a woman suggestively disrobing and taking a bath; a man jumps into the tub, splashing water, and grabs a beer. In Russia, Tinkoff Beer brought itself controversy—and sales—with sexual suggestiveness. In a 2002–2003 TV ad, a man wearing boxer shorts had his arms around two naked women; his lust, of course, was for the beer. The following year, a Tinkoff TV ad had two women walk into a lingerie shop, go into a dressing room where it became apparent they were lesbian lovers; with music crescendoing, they touch, feel, and kiss. A Tinkoff beer bottle pops its cap, and beer foams up and over its sides.

Pete's Wicked Brew wasn't so blatant in its campaign. The San Antonio brewery ran contests combining luck, beer, and sex. The sweepstakes winners got a day at a major league baseball game and an evening at a party featuring a *Playboy* playmate. To make sure no one missed the chance to play ball, Pete's reproduced the playmate's image on massive amounts of point-of-purchase displays, including banners, posters, pennants, and coasters. Media placement was heavy on Internet sites and radio. The playmate was heavy on suggestion.

Stroh's, founded in 1850, by 1991 had become the nation's fourth largest brewery. That year, chasing the top three beer manufacturers, Stroh's tweaked the public with a campaign for its Old Milwaukee Brand that featured the Swedish Bikini Team, four platinum-blonde women who parachuted into a camp of men. The campaign was supposed to be a parody of the sex-based campaigns of the other breweries, but was killed after one season when several Stroh's employees protested the use of sexism to parody sexism.

Disregarding Stroh's experience, Coors unleashed the Artic Angels in 1993, three blonde women in thigh-high black boots and body-tight black body suits to promote Artic Ice. Janet Rowe, Coors manager of corporate communications, claimed her company hadn't used sexist advertising "for some time." Not even the Artic Angels? That's a "local promotion discretion," said Rowe in 1995. Almost in the same breath, she admitted the company "has not developed any formal new policy on women in bathing suits." Nevertheless, although Coors developed campaigns that focused upon the environment and the clear water of Colorado, by the end of 2002 the company unleashed the Coors Twins, two buxom blondes whose only purpose was to convince men they could double their fun by drinking beer. Four years later, Coors ran a 30-second commercial that featured a bikini-wearing blonde on a beach. In each hand was a Coors Light. At the end of the commercial, the girl cooed, "They're plastic. And they're spectacular." The original line— "They're real. And they're spectacular"—was from a *Seinfeld* TV episode, spoken by a woman who was the object of leering puzzlement by the cast. Viewers who didn't know the Seinfeld connection, certainly understood the commercial's double entendre. However, with breweries using less sexually-suggestive ads, in 2007 Coors, which had developed the tag line, "The world's most refreshing beer," again emphasized the "cool, clear waters" of the Rocky Mountains.

But, Coors hadn't pioneered the "cool, refreshing" approach. A black and white animated Hamm's Beer bear was seen in pastoral settings, identified in print and television as "the land of sky blue waters." The advertising campaign for the Minnesota-based brewer, with its easily-remembered jingle, ran for several decades until Miller Brewing, the parent company, decided that the cute animated bear, now seen on almost every product imaginable, could induce children to transcend fiction and enter a world where they might enjoy a Hamm's.

Since 1987, Anheuser–Busch has been the leading TV advertiser for the Super Bowl, eventually paying as much as $3 million for a 30-second spot in 2009. However, partially because of the Recession, Anheuser–Busch dropped to second, behind Pepsico, in the number of ads aired during 2009 Super Bowl, but still maintained its lead in overall dollars spent during the previous two decades. Most of its ads, like most ads for the Super Bowl, use humor not sex to sell the product. Both the "frog" and "Whassup?!" campaigns of the 1990s, first pitched to the largest TV audience of the year, cemented Bud and Bud Light as the two leading brands in America. For Super Bowl XXXIX in January 2005, Anehuser–Busch had a plan to titillate the public while maintaining a "clean" but sexual message. The previous year, pop singers Janet Jackson and Justin Timberlake had participated in a "wardrobe malfunction" that led to a Jackson nipple-covered breast accidentally being exposed for about one second on national TV. The resultant "shock" by the nation's pseudo-moralists led to an FCC fine of $550,000 against CBS. For the parody, a fully-clothed actor portraying a stagehand had a replica of Jackson's costume open a bottle of Bud Light. The costume "accidentally" tears, and the stagehand frantically tries to repair it. However, the company killed the ad after consultation with both the NFL and the FOX network, which was televising the game. "Why take the risk? All you need is one person to be offended," an Anheuser–Busch executive told the *Wall Street Journal*. However, the company got even more play for their advertising message when it slyly made sure the original ad appeared on the uncensorable Internet.

The average *per capita* consumption of beer is about 30.4 gallons a year for all persons over the age of 21, according to the Beer Institute. Women are now about 30 percent of all beer drinkers, almost half of all Light drinkers, and consume an average of about 14 gallons a year. The use of "beefcake" in ads became more noticeable in 2006. Miller ads featured all-pro NFL running back Jerome Bettis, wrestler Triple H, and actor Burt Reynolds; however, the appeal was still to men. For his 30-seconds, Reynolds suggested that men should toast each other by clinking their beer bottoms, not the necks. "No thanks, Hollywood, I ain't into that," a cowboy replies, a not-so-veiled reference to the recent boxoffice smash, *Brokeback Mountain*, the story of two gay cowboys.

In 1997, Coors produced a print ad that emphasized the company's special benefits—including full health benefits for same-sex partners—for its gay employees. By 2002, the politically conservative company, which had once been the target of a nationwide boycott for its extreme right-wing views that included an anti-union bias, was producing ads that exploited its liberal beliefs in human rights. An ad that year featured a half-dozen gay employees; in 2006, the company posed five men in swimsuits—from baggy to Speedo—all of them near a case of Coors Light on the deck of a swimming pool.

On billboards, posters, and banners, in all print and visual advertising, the message is clear. Drink beer and achieve great athletic and sexual satisfaction. Americans are buying more beer for home consumption and are going to parties and bars to deliberately get drunk, apparently believing they can do things while drunk they can't do while sober—like vomit all over their dates.

Most of the dates appear to be in their teens or 20s. During the 1970s and 1980s, when most states had not yet raised the age of consent to 21, beer companies frequently sent sales representatives onto campuses. Among the representatives were Anheuser–Busch's all-purpose mutt, Spuds MacKenzie, and the Bud Girls, sexually-alluring models whose job was to help drooling male college students rush off to the local beer store. The Bud Girls campaign was a throw-back to the Budweiser Girl campaign of the 1880s, a multi-year single-themed campaign, which had been the first one among American brewers.

All states now require persons to be 21 years old to drink, but the beer companies have found other ways to target the college-age population. Heineken sponsored a 46 city "alternative music" concert tour in 2001. Miller is paying San Diego State University $75,000 a year until 2012 to display Miller banners in the school's basketball arena and baseball stadium. Anheuser–Busch has a similar contract for the football stadium. However, about one-fourth of all colleges in the NCAA have signed pledges that they will not only ban alcohol advertising on sportscasts, but will work to eliminate all references to alcohol in all sports broadcasts of college teams.

In 2006, for what could be a temporary anomaly, beer was no longer the most "in" thing among college students, according to a survey conducted by *Student Monitor*. The most "in" thing was the Apple iPod; beer and Facebook.com, a social networking website, tied for second. The only other time in 18 years that beer fell from the top place among college students, according to the survey, was in 1997, when the Internet became the "in" thing among students. The beer companies weren't worried; they had all claimed they didn't target the "under-21" demographic; they also knew students wouldn't give up beer for bottled water.

Alcopop companies (also known as malternatives), producing drinks that are alcoholic sodas, have become a popular choice among teens. About 41 percent of 14- to 18-year-olds say they have tried alcopops, according to the Center for Science in the Public Interest. Almost 56 percent of all high school seniors in 2004 said they had tried alcopops. Among the leading alcopops are Smirnoff Ice, Mike's Hard Lemonade, Bacardi Silver, Skyy Blue, Bartles & James, Seagram's Coolers, and Zima.

The companies say they don't target those under 21 years of age, and require all persons wishing to enter their web sites to register their age. But, once that fiction has been established, the sites are a combination of teen-appealing music, graphics, games—and bikini-clad girls, the same combination that drives their television advertising. The major malt beverage companies spend their advertising budgets primarily on shows that have large teenage viewership. However, unlike other major companies, Anheuser–Busch doesn't advertise on MTV because, says the company, "MTV skews too young."

Anheuser–Busch, Miller, and Coors (which merged as MillerCoors in 2008) dominate the sale of beer. Competing with the Top 2 companies would be economic disaster for the nation's 1,500 breweries. The cost to produce one poster for distribution to beer stores and customers could be $100,000. For that reason, there aren't many point-of-purchase posters by smaller brewers. And, because of a major policy shift to spend well over 90 percent of advertising budget on TV ads, the Top 3 also are not producing as many posters. With few exceptions, almost all of the advertising budgets for breweries not in the Top 10 is directed less on image, more on product and substance. And, some of the brands from the Top 3 brewers have moved away from sexual suggestiveness.

Keystone Light, a Coors product, used blue-and-white striped one-piece swimsuits on its models to promote the brand's label color. However, it now focuses upon humor, often with good-looking women and klutzy men. Its "tag" is "Always smooth, even when you're not." During the 1990s, Killian's Irish Red, another Coors brand, used a tall redhead in a white bikini who exalted salivating men to "try a tall cool red one." It now focuses more on sports and a newer "Never Rushed" campaign that fuses a leisurly lifestyle with the brand's slow-roast process.

Genesee, distributed primarily in New York and Pennsylvania, no longer connects sex with beer. Even with a healthy advertising budget, the company moved away from sexually suggestive ads in 1991. At the time, Paul Silverman, executive vice-president and creative director for Genesee's ad agency, told *Modern Brewery* the new campaign was "reflective of the company's philosophy of focusing on product; Genesee is pouring its money into what counts—its beer."

Yuengling, the nation's oldest brewery, is still family-owned, having rejected sale to larger companies several times. Its annual two million barrel production in 2008, placing it second among all American-owned brewers, is available throughout its home state of Pennsylvania, and in 12 other East Coast and

Southeast states. Like Genesee, Yuengling also avoids sexist advertising. "We haven't had to resort to those tactics," according to Dave Casinelli, Yuengling's chief operating officer. He says Yuengling sells "on the basis of consistent qualities. We just can't compete with the majors."

Heineken, manufacturers of the second leading imported beer in America, behind Corona Extra, began moving away from scantily-clad babe advertising by 2000. Its campaign now targets males in their 20s—a significant change from its previous target of males in their 30s—but uses humor to let us know it's "All About the Beer." Nevertheless, Heineken marketing executives also know that 21-year-old men are sexually active, so sexually-suggestive women are still part of most 30-second TV ads. In one of the better ads, a young man brought cheap beer to a party, placed it in a refrigerator, and then grabbed two Heinekens to impress a woman.

Foster's, an Australian beer, took advantage of its culture rather than its sexual attractions during the 1990s to tease Americans with a $15 million a year radio and TV campaign on "How to Speak Australian." The 30-second ads were primarily placed on VH1, ESPN, and Comedy Central.

"We don't need sex to sell our beer," says Dan Straub, president of Straub Brewing, which sells about 38,000 barrels a year and promotes its all-natural beer on the basis of taste, quality, and being "honestly fresh." Word-of-mouth, posters, and "a lot of community service" make the Straub brand known in western Pennsylvania.

Stroh's, which had once produced the Swedish Bikini Team, in the mid- and late-1990s has reduced its sex and beer message, although one poster showed a model wearing a Chicago Bears jersey and biker shorts. "Our whole campaign now," said Burke Cueny, Stroh's marketing director in 1997, is "more taste, more character. We're interested in featuring our beer in everyday situations as opposed to a fantasy-setting agenda." It was a commendable marketing plan. Two years later, Stroh's, which had been the third leading brewer at one time, sold its brewing operation to Pabst, which licensed it to Miller's—which uses sex to sell beer.

Sex still sells. And Americans still are lured to myriad products solely on the suggestiveness that using that product will get you that seductive blonde.

Missing in Atlanta

It wasn't at opening ceremonies. It wasn't seen much around the athletes. And it certainly wasn't in the closing ceremonies.

Whatizit, the sneaker-wearing starry-eyed blue blob mascot of the 1996 Summer Olympics, was more of a Whereizit.

The Atlanta Committee for the Olympic Games (ACOG) said there was no place for a Whatizit in the ceremonies because the mascot is more for children than for the pageantry and sophisticated "ooh/ahhs" the Committee expected from about 75,000 stadium fans and a couple of billion TV viewers.

Whatizit was first revealed at the 1992 Summer games in Barcelona following a closing ceremony performance by opera tenors Jose Carreras, Placido Domingo, and Luciano Pavarotti. It was the first computer-generated tech-age mascot, described by some as a scrawny mutant of a giant blue raisin and an overstuffed tick, a protozoan in red Keds, or even a giant sperm in sneaks. Many even dubbed him Bubba the Blue Slug. But, the IOC president liked him, and so he stayed.

During the four years since the Barcelona Olympics, the ACOG, based upon innumerable interviews with children, redesigned him to be more cuddly. Several thousand children submitted names, and a committee of children in Atlanta decided Whatizit would be the species name for the blue blobs, and Izzy would be the user-friendly name for the Olympic's "official character."

The Ogilvy & Mather advertising agency created the official Izzy story, determining he is "a mischievous teenager who lives with friends, family and athletes—all called Whatizits—in a fantastic world inside the Olympic torch." Inside of that world, Izzy dreamed of being the first Whatizit to compete in the Games. ACOG paraded the redesigned Izzy before the world in myriad promotions leading up to the Olympics. Children loved it; adults thought of it as a blue Barney.

Robert Hollander, ACOG's director of marketing, told the media "We felt we had a chance, through a mascot, to bring messages that were everything from geography, history, cultures of the different countries, sports, language, in a medium that kids really understand, which is video."

At electronic kiosks in Atlanta, an animated Izzy answered questions—punch the button about equestrians, for example, and watch Izzy ride a horse and answer basic questions, including how to purchase tickets. On video games, Izzy led children through a quest for five Olympic rings. On QVC, a home shopping cable channel, 1,000 Izzy games sold out in 12 seconds. Izzy animated cartoons and plush toys brought the Olympic message to millions of pre-teens.

In print, Izzy was ubiquitous. On T-shirts, caps, water bottles, and even Hallmark cards, Izzy gave a face to a $1.7 billion show of pageantry and athletics.

Although the ACOG didn't want Izzy mingling in its celebration, it didn't object to collecting licensing fees for companies to use Izzy's image to bring the Olympic message to most of the world's five billion people. Izzy's picture on official merchandise accounted for 20–30 percent of the $2 billion in licensed Olympic merchandise, said Hollander.

Izzy is just one of a couple of dozen Olympic characters, most of whom were treated better by their sponsors at the actual games. The first Olympics mascot was a dog for the 1932 Olympics in Los Angeles. However, the next mascot didn't show up until 1968; the Winter Games in Grenoble featured Schuss, a skier; the Summer games in Mexico City featured an unnamed jaguar. Subsequent mascots were Waldi, a dachshund at the 1972 Summer Games in Munich; Avrik the Beaver for the Summer Montreal Summer games, and Olymoiamandl, a big-nosed red-capped snowman at the Innsbruck Winter games; Roni Raccoon (1980, Winter Lake Placid) and Misha the Bear (1980, Moscow, Summer); Sam, Walt Disney's eagle, for the 1984 L.A. Summer Olympics, and Vucko the wolf at the Sarajevo Winter Olympics that year; Hodori, a bowler-wearing tiger at the 1988 summer Olympics in Seoul, and Howdy and Hidy polar bears for the Winter Olympics in Calgary; Cobi, a strange-looking dog with sun glasses for the 1992 Barcelona Summer Olympics, and Magique, a mountain fairy that looked like a puffed balloon star and half-normal human for the Winter Olympics in Albertville, France; 13th century Norwegian twins Haakon and Kristin for the Lillehammer Winter Olympics in 1994; and four big-eyed plush snow owls for the 1998 Winter Olympics in Nagano, Japan. The 2000 Sydney Summer Olympics brought to the center stage Olly, a kookaburro; Syd, a platypus; and Millie, an echidna. The 2002 Winter Olympics in Salt Lake City featured Powder, a snowshoe hare; Copper, a coyote; and Coal, a black bear. The 2004 Summer Olympics in

Greece were modern versions of ancient Greek dolls Athena, the goddess of wisdom; and Phivos, god of light and music. The mascots of the 2006 winter Olympics in Turin were Neve, officially described as "a gentle, kind and elegant snowball"; and Gliz, "a lively playful ice cube." China was especially creative in developing its mascots for the 2008 Summer games in Beijing. The five Fuwa, children-like caricatures representing the five Olympic rings, were Beibei (the fish), Jingling (the Panda), Huanhuan (the Olympic flame), Yingying (the tibetan antelope), and Nini (the swallow). The first syllables of each name when put together (Bei Jing Huan Ying Ni) form a sentence that, loosely translated into English means, "Welcome to Beijing."

Mascots, more than any one athlete, help identify and promote a team, event, or company, giving what the owners and promoters hope are "warm fuzzy feelings" that lead to the purchase of tickets and merchandise.

Almost all sports teams have mascots, whether the more popular ones from the cat and dog families or the more unique furry green "phanatic" of the Philadelphia Phillies and the funky chicken of the San Diego Padres.

Several companies also have official mascots. There's Ronald McDonald for the world's biggest fast-food burger chain, and Charlie the Tuna who is never caught by Starkist.

States have official animals—whether it's California's grizzly bear or Texas's armadillo—as well as official flowers, birds, and insects, all of them representative of the state, and suitable for inclusion on innumerable marketing opportunities.

Mascots also identify the major political parties; Democrats have the donkey, although it once had the rooster; Republicans have the elephant. Uncle Sam is America's "official character," the bulldog is England's, and the dragon is China's. Even stamp conventions have mascots; China had an official mascot for the 1999 World Philately Exhibition.

The Olympics likes to proclaim that in its own way it's a metaphor of the human spirit. When the sugary hype is stripped away, it may be true. But, also true is that the Olympics used Izzy to bring recognition and income to itself, and then abandoned him for the run of the Olympics when his usefulness was over. The IOC actions may be a more accurate representation of the true "human spirit."

Premature Evaluation

On CBS-TV's "Early Edition" (1996–2000) bar owner Gary Hobson got the *Chicago Sun-Times* a day early. This gave him less than a day to save humanity. Sometimes his heroics prevented a drowning or a fatal auto accident; other times, he prevented a murder. Once, he saved the *Sun-Times* itself from a bomb when his cat didn't bring in the newspaper at 6:30 a.m. That's when he knew if the newspaper didn't have an edition, it was in trouble.

Metro newspapers usually have an "early edition," a newspaper put on the streets the night before, but which carry the next day's date. Unlike Hobson's special paper, these early editions don't give the news ahead of time. Buy one on the published date, and you'll be reading day-old accounts of who-shot-whom. Nevertheless, most of the nation's 48 million newspaper subscribers receive their newspapers the day it's published.

Unlike newspapers, magazines have a longer "shelf life." Thus, a magazine that appears in June might have an August publication date so readers could buy it two months after publication and still think it's current, even if the news and features have first been covered in a newspaper's "early edition" three months earlier. Even the major news-weeklies "fudge" the publication date by up to a week after distribution.

A book's publication date is also often a sham. Books published in the second half of the year will often carry copyright dates for the following year.

Movie studios have "sneak previews" before a general release to give themselves a chance to test audience reaction—and audiences the chance to think that they're getting something wonderful before anyone else.

Want super secret savings? Open your mail. Chances are at least once a month you have either been invited to a special "preview" sale at the local department store, "an offer not available to the general public!" In alternate months, you might even save "as much as 50 percent!" by cashing in a special rub-off card "not valid if rubbed off prior to purchase."

The Christmas season was once confined to December. However, retailers long ago convinced the American consumers that two weeks wasn't enough time to find all the bargains Jesus would have bought if he had the time. To counter that problem, retailers began their advertising and sales campaigns the Black Friday after Thanksgiving, and a grateful nation extended its appreciation by seizing more merchandise in one day than any other day of the year, except for Christmas Eve. But, even a month wasn't enough, and now Santa costumes are being rented the day after Halloween. "Christmas in July" sales are common. Perhaps this year, Santa could wave a flag and shoot off fireworks. If this trend continues, Christians will celebrate the birth of Jesus the day after Easter.

New cars once were revealed in the same year they were first manufactured. A few decades ago, manufacturers began showing their new cars in November, just in time for Dad to buy a 40-foot yellow bow and give Mom a Christmas gift. Of course, pre-feminist Mom would have preferred that Dad spent a little less on metal and glass, and more with vacuuming, dishwashing, and child care.

Then, in a spy-vs.-counterspy scenario probably suggested in *MAD Magazine,* marketing geniuses with dipstick minds that are constantly sucking up Detroit smog thought the gullible public would believe that a Wombat V-12, released two days before the competing Balderdash 3.8, was the superior vehicle to burn 12 miles a gallon on a super-charged race to the grocery store. Next year's models are being showcased during Spring of the year before. Somewhere in the bankrupt auto industry, mechanical engineers are probably working on the Silver Odyssey 2018, complete with space-age titanium technology and on-board revolving computer, to be revealed in 2015.

It's all a scam to make us believe that like Gary Hobson we are one of the chosen ones who are smart enough to get something before its time.

Spin Doctors in the Lincoln Room

I got a newspaper for Christmas.

Before you send condolences—"You may be a liberal, but you deserve better than *that*"—let me explain.

The newspaper is the August 25, 1862, edition of Horace Greeley's *New York Tribune.* In 1872, in the last year of his life, Greeley had won both the Liberal Republican and Democratic nominations for the Presidency, only to lose to a rather inept U. S. Grant running for his second term. Greeley, who grew up impoverished and ridiculed for his appearance, had become the most respected and influential journalist of the antebellum and Civil War eras. Unafraid of controversy, Greeley had founded the first newspaper union, gave his employees majority stock in the company, and advocated that women be allowed to vote. He was also a fierce abolitionist. In response to Greeley's published letter demanding emancipation, President Lincoln wrote:

> "My paramount object in this struggle is to save the Union, and is not either to save or destroy Slavery. If I could save the Union without freeing *any* slave, I would do it; and if I could save it by freeing *all* the slaves, I would do it; and if I could do it by freeing some and leaving others alone, I would also do that."

That statement was published in the *Tribune*—under a small one-column headline, on page 4 of an 8-page newspaper.

Greeley intended no disrespect to the President. Because of mechanical constraints, newspapers only had one-column headlines. His readers would find all of the news, even if it wasn't splashed across the front page, with multi-column screaming headlines, color splashes and charts, and a 4-column photo.

Had the Civil War occurred today, and Lincoln been president, the statement about abolition may have been quite different. . . .

In the Oval Office are the President and a "spin doctor," officially titled a "Senior Special Assistant."

"Mr. President," says the spinner, "there's nothing much to report. Just a few bags of mail." The President sifts through a couple of letters.

"Why, this one is from Mr. Greeley," says the President. "I wonder what he wants."

"Nothing important," says the Aide, snatching the letter. "Some nonsense about slavery. I already sent him a form letter stating we appreciate his comments, and hope he will donate to our next campaign."

"Maybe I should say we must defend the Union at all cost."

"Your obsession with keeping the union together is splitting this country apart! You could offend the Southerners."

"But they're the ones who are seceding! They won't even be voting in the next election."

"A statement like that could throw the election to a Southern

Democrat. If that happens, we could lose the Senate and the House. Worse yet, 5,000 Presidential assistants would be out of jobs and forced to find legitimate work."

"Maybe I could say we could free the slaves in conquered territory, like Mr. Greeley demands."

"Bad idea, Mr. President. The ones who are freed may not want to be free. The slaves who aren't freed might become upset you freed some and not them. The abolitionists would be upset if you freed only a few, and the Southerners would be upset if you freed any. You shouldn't say anything that could be misinterpreted or be controversial."

"But a President must have opinions and not be afraid to express them." When the Aide stopped laughing, he reminded the president that politicians aren't elected on what they say, but upon what they don't say, and that image was far more important than substance.

"Perhaps you're right," said the President. "Prepare me a suitable Presidential statement."

Two weeks later, after 49 presidential assistants discussed, debated, wrote and rewrote the text, President Lincoln responded to Horace Greeley's plea for abolition:

"My fellow Americans . . . and to those who don't wish to be Americans at this time. After considerable discussion with all parties, including my esteemed colleague Mr. Jefferson Davis, I am pleased to say that I think circumstances are such that while a united country has many good points, I can also see the advantages of two coexisting nations with mutual respect for each other, and separate but equal constitutions. But, it is the American people who will have to decide this issue. As President, I can only present my views, which are based upon whatever the polls and my myriad advisors say is politically expedient. Further, I believe this issue called slavery is a local issue, and should be solved by the states themselves, unless at least 51 percent of the voting public from each of the states think another decision should be made. The Presidential telemarketers will soon be calling you to find out what would be the popular thing to do."

The President then turned to his Chief of Staff and asked, "Know anything about this place called Gettysburg? I may soon need a few thousand words that makes the people think I care about something but won't hinder my re-election chances."

Crocodile Tears on a
Cash Register Patriotism

The news release was bold. "In view of the September 11 attack on the World Trade Center and the Pentagon," it stated, "this is the time for Corporate America and all government agencies to enhance the safety and security of the nation's high profile buildings." Not exactly a revelation. It took only one more sentence to underline the company's intent.

"Windows and doors are normally the weakest static construction elements in a building," continued the release, "and are therefore the first to fail during violent activities and brute forces of nature. . . .Your property needs protection!"

The next few hundred words explained how my readers could choose a security level—and color—of windows to provide that security—"from burglarproof to hurricane resistant and ultimately bullet and blast resistant." Thousands of businesses, like the window company, obtrusively are using the 9/11 tragedy to sell their product.

One investment company's news release informed the press that if we followed world events, "you probably know that the prices of commodities and stocks reflect international politics and tensions!" It explained that as the "U.S. prepares its response, tensions could escalate even further in the Middle East. This could have a DRAMATIC IMPACT on the supply of oil and gas therefore increasing worldwide prices. If this happens, oil and gas companies and THEIR SHAREHOLDERS could be poised to MAKE MONEY from any price increases." To make money from the tragedy, I just had to contact this company to learn which "undervalued" stocks I should buy.

A writer offered newspaper editors about 400 words detailing Osama bin Laden's aura, hoping to lure them into buying her weekly column, "Ask Your Aura." Not surprisingly, she determined that his spirituality is "connected to a preference for evil."

Most corporate America had pulled all advertising from the TV networks and national news magazines for up to a week following 9/11 while they re-evaluated their campaigns. When they returned, they had draped themselves into red, white, and blue bunting, and told us it's patriotic to spend money in a lagging economy.

A fairly large publicity firm, targeting book authors, ran a small American flag next to its logo, and told us the company "continues to offer our heartfelt thoughts and prayers to those touched by the events," that it salutes "the heroism of those who continue to work tirelessly in rescue and relief efforts," and will continue to work with the media "to provide our clients with the optimum level of exposure." In case we didn't understand the last sentence, it told us the time to pull back on advertising and promotion isn't now because "our experience has shown us that events like this, although very saddening, create unique opportunities that might not have presented themselves before." To take advantage of this "unique" opportunity, the company even developed a program that for only $750–$3,000 would target the media with our message.

One-shot magazines, full of color pictures, began coming off rotary presses within hours after the towers collapsed. Books about the tragedy were rushed to press; almost any book that had even the remotest tie-in was being hawked. Fueled by Internet rumor that 16th century French physician-clairvoyant Nostradamus predicted such a tragedy, thousands of Americans flocked to bookstores and online companies to buy copies of his books, edited by others. One book with a Sept. 27, 2001, publication date, quickly moved into the top 100 titles on Amazon.com.

On thousands of fiberglass and plastic highway signs, words of hope trumpeted words of advertising. Below "God Bless America," we saw "Chili Fries, $1.49." Below "United We Stand," we were told "Special Prices on Carpets."

During the 1960s, war protesters who wore clothes with the American flag design were beaten by "patriots"; for several years after 9/11, the fabric of America was "patriots" who wore just-manufactured high-priced T-shirts, pants, and bandannas, all with images of American flags and slogans.

One direct mail flyer combined the flag, a patriotic call, a message of sympathy—and my inviolate right to buy sofas on sale. General Motors, trying to sell cars, declared "in this time of terrible adversity, let's stand together. And let's keep America rolling." (In 2009, during the Recession, GM's Chevrolet division wanted us to put on our "rally caps" and buy cars.)

A laser eye surgical conglomerate tried to convince us getting clearer vision was somehow patriotic. Its newspaper images were of an exhausted firefighter, and of someone it claimed to be an FBI agent who praised the company's health plan for federal employees.

A Cleveland mayoral candidate ran TV ads, declaring "If tragedy strikes, who could lead?" On the screen were still photos of the towers and a woman holding a flag.

Perhaps these patriotic businesses all meant well. Perhaps they were saddened by the tragedy, and wanted to let us know they cared about the victims and our country. Perhaps, they were tortured by the magnitude of evil and the shards of the American fragment that will haunt us for a generation that they will realize the best way to celebrate the American spirit is to treat their own workers better, and to absorb a smaller profit rather than to lay off workers. But as long as businesses try to mix sentiment and hard sell advertising, there's no question our traditional red and green Christmas seasons will continue to be lathered in a red, white, and blue jingoism of fourth quarter crocodile tears pouring over a cash register patriotism.

'I Approve This Message' is More Than a Campaign Tag: Propaganda and the Government

There are a lot of ways to win a war. But, just in case the war is going badly, instead of increasing manpower and computer-driven weapons, call out the Pentagon's crack elite troops of the Joint Psychological Operations Support Element, PsyOps, more commonly known as the Pentagon's propaganda machine. The Pentagon, which has the world's largest PR operation, created a TV news operation, and a U.S-funded and controlled Iraqi radio and TV network. Its public affairs officers are better trained, and often more professional and ethical, than most civilian PR professionals. And that's where the war in Iraq was heading for more than five years.

The Department of Defense, according to an investigation first published in the *Los Angeles Times*, paid three PR agencies—SYColeman, Science Applications International, and the Lincoln Group—about $100 million each on five-year contracts "for media approach planning, prototype product development, commercial quality product development, product distribution and dissemination, and media effects analysis." The "communicologists" called the program "international perception management." The purpose of all that gobbledygook was to influence Iraqis not only to support American political philosophies, but also to make them believe that the occupying American military force was there to help Iraq realize its full potential as a part of a Western democracy. Included in this war to combat Iraqi insurgents was a wide array of sophisticated weapons, including web sites, T-shirts, and bumper stickers.

In 2004, the government had paid the Lincoln Group $6 million, specifically to use the media to influence public opinion in Iraq. Lincoln, paying $40–$2,000 an article, planted about 1,000 articles. Some of the recipients may have been Sunni religious scholars, according to the *New York Times*. Executive vice-president of the Lincoln Group is Christian Bailey, who was co-chair of the 2004 Republican National Convention in New York City.

The articles were written by American troops, translated into Arabic or Farsi, and placed by the Lincoln Group into Iraqi newspapers. Lincoln staffers also wrote articles for placement, without attribution of the source, and often sent copyrighted stories from other publications. But, just in case the writings of Americans weren't enough, Lincoln paid as much as $200 a month, dependent upon acceptable output, to a dozen Iraqi journalists to write stories favorable to the United States government. With their country in anarchy, with incomes sharply cut, and necessary resources unavailable, it wasn't difficult to understand why formerly-independent journalists could be persuaded to accept bribes. Also accepting bribes was the management of *al-Mutamar*, a newspaper with close ties to Ahmad Chalabi, who was influential in convincing President Bush that Iraq had weapons of mass destruction; for his "information," Chalabi and his anti-Saddam "rebels-in-exile" received several million dollars. During the years that Chalabi was Oil Minister and then Deputy Prime Minister, the U.S. apparently decided it was acceptable to pay him to reprint stories favorable to American interest and, thus, assure his continuing cooperation. However, Chalabi, now tainted by lies and deception, failed to win a seat in Parliament, and left office in May 2006.

David Isenberg, senior analyst with the Washington-based British American Security Information Council, an expert in foreign policy and national security issues, for the Dec. 3, 2005, issue of *Asia Times*, explained why the government's program was so insidious:

> It is worth emphasizing that because of the security situation, US correspondents in Iraq are rarely able to leave the Green Zone in Baghdad or other US military bases to engage in on-the-ground reporting, and thus must rely, in part, on reports by Iraqis in the Iraqi press to assess the situation on the ground.

Isenberg's analysis was also a subtle condemnation of the American media, which primarily used second-hand information, much of which was extremely unreliable. The American people whose taxes funded the program undoubtedly didn't receive their money's worth. The Iraqi people aren't stupid—they saw through the stories and discounted the propaganda, whether coming from the U.S., from the Iraqi provisional government, or the insurgents.

In the 1960s TV series, "Mission Impossible," agents were sent off to do clandestine activities, but if they were captured, the Secretary—we never knew which cabinet department—would "disavow any knowledge." By contracting the Lincoln Group, the Pentagon had "plausible deniability"—it wasn't the government but an independent contractor disseminating propaganda. The White House and the generals all claimed they didn't know what was happening in the field. Scott McClellan, President Bush's press secretary claimed in December 2005 that the *L.A. Times* investigation was the first time anyone in the White House learned about "the military using this Lincoln Group to plant stories in Iraqi newspapers," and pledged to find out more about the news disinformation operation created within the Department of Defense.

Overall, between 2003 and the end of 2005, the Bush–Cheney Administration spent about $1.6 billion for public relations and

~~~~~~~~

"[A despotic] government always [keeps] a kind of standing army of newswriters who, without any regard to truth or to what should be like truth, [invent] and put into the papers whatever might serve the ministers. This suffices with the mass of the people who have no means of distinguishing the false from the true paragraphs of a newspaper."   —Thomas Jefferson, 1785 advertising campaigns, both to promote the war overseas and for domestic programs, as well as to inflate the Administration's public perception, according to the Government Accountability Office. This was above payroll, expenses, and other costs of persons employed in public relations within the federal bureaucracy.

It's not illegal to use propaganda overseas. It is both illegal and unethical to use it against the American people.

In 1990, the Kuwaiti government, with some knowledge by the Bush–Quayle Administration, hired Hill & Knowlton, the world's largest PR agency, to represent Kuwait and convince Congress of the need to attack the occupying Iraqi army. Among the campaigns the PR agency undertook was to bring forth a Kuwaiti teenager who swore she saw Iraqi soldiers throw a baby from an incubator in a Kuwaiti hospital. It was that mini-campaign that led many members of Congress to vote for authorization to commit U.S. forces in what was first Desert Shield and then Desert Storm in 1991. The incident, alas, was manufactured; the teenager was a member of Kuwait's royal family, most of whom had taken their wealth and fled to the fleshpots and nightclubs of Cairo and London, leaving in their wake Kuwaiti's citizens to face the oncoming armies.

The Bush–Cheney Administration didn't just rely upon independent PR firms, it turned the White House into a PR agency, and used tactics that any reputable PR specialist would disavow. Stories in January 2005 by the *Los Angeles Times, USA Today,* and Salon.com revealed another part of the Administration's overall propaganda campaign.

During the 2003–2004 fiscal year, the Bush–Cheney Administration paid a private PR company to develop and execute a full program of propaganda in support of the "No Child Left Behind Act." As part of that contract, Ketchum Communications paid $241,000 to Armstrong Williams, a conservative columnist, to write columns and influence other journalists to promote the Act. The Tribune Co., which syndicated Williams' commentaries, later cancelled his contract for the breach of ethics. Ketchum also produced a series of pre-packaged video news releases to promote that law; the company's version were fake news stories, complete with a fake reporter. Many TV stations, without question, ran that news clip as part of their regular news programs.

The Department of Health and Human Services gave syndicated columnist Maggie Gallagher $21,500 in 2004 to push the Bush–Cheney Administration's marriage initiative, a $300 million campaign that promoted a socio-political agenda to create a Constitutional amendment barring same-sex marriages, to increase marriages as a way to strengthen family bonds, and to attack political leaders who disagreed. The previous two years, she received $20,000 to write a booklet, *Can Government Strengthen Marriage?*, published by a private organization but funded through a Department of Justice grant. Also taking federal money to promote the marriage initiative was Michael McManus, whose "Ethics & Religion" column appeared in 35 newspapers. McManus personally received $10,199.98 for speeches and travel; Marriage Savers Inc., of which he was president, received an additional $48,993. Paying ethically-challenged reporters and lobbying by the federal government are both illegal.

Not illegal, but certainly questionable, was how easily the White House staff allowed Jeff Gannon to obtain press credentials to cover the President. At daily press conferences, Gannon lobbed softball questions at the White House press staff, who called upon him frequently. Gannon also sent out, often with no changes, White House press releases as if they were hard news. However, as a few members of the media eventually learned, Gannon was really James Guckert, a $200 an hour gay escort. It was the perfect professional combination—the world's oldest profession merged with the Fourth Estate.

The purpose of political rhetoric, said George Orwell in 1946, is "to give an appearance of solidarity to pure wind."

The White House used Pat Tillman as its "poster boy" to spur Americans into supporting the war, and to increase enlistments. But it was his death in Afghanistan, not his life, which the White House commemorated.

Tillman was an All-American football player, a *summa cum laude* graduate of Arizona State University, and was in his fourth year as a safety with the NFL's Arizona Cardinals. Inspired to join the military after 9/11, Tillman turned down a three-year $3.6 million extension to become an Army Ranger. Against military "advice," he refused all media requests for interviews during his training and deployment. He believed he was a soldier, just like any other soldier.

Specialist Tillman and an Afghan soldier were killed in April

2004; two American soldiers were wounded. The Army claimed Tillman was killed in a 20-minute firefight after being ambushed by the enemy, and awarded him the Silver Star for bravery; the citation read, "While mortally wounded, his audacious leadership and courageous example under fire inspired his men to fight."

As the media began picking up the story, the military began spinning it harder, fabricating battle specifics. According to Army documents, a Ranger unit mistook Tillman and several other soldiers as the enemy, and began firing. One of the Rangers later told an Army investigator there was no attempt to identify Tillman's unit before firing upon it. Even after the military concluded that two allied forces had accidentally fired upon each other, the military and the White House continued to propagandize the death of a millionaire athlete who gave up fame and wealth to become a soldier in the War Against Terrorism—and to protect its own image. The military ordered troops not to talk about the incident, except to parrot the developing script of the events; members of Tillman's unit burned his body armor and uniform to hide the fact he was killed by "friendly fire."

In April 2007, Spc. Bryan O'Neal told a Congressional committee that he was ordered by the battalion commanding officer not to say anything to Tillman's brother, Kevin, an Army Ranger who was in a nearby convoy. Kevin Tillman later told a Congressional committee of at least four specific incidents where the military notified families that enemy fire not friendly fire or accidents were the causes of their sons' and husbands' deaths.

It wasn't until several weeks later that Tillman's family was finally told the truth. Even then, an initial report that condemned the tactics used by the attacking unit was later sanitized by a one star general. An Army investigation later called the attack gross negligence. Tillman's parents later said their son was killed by "a combination of shoddy leadership and clear violations of the Rules of Engagement as well as violations of the Law of Land Warfare." Pat Tillman Sr., more than a year after his son's death told the *Washington Post*:

> After it happened, all the people in positions of authority went out of their way to script this. They purposely interfered with the investigation, they covered it up. I think they thought they could control it, and they realized that their recruiting

405

efforts were going to go to hell in a handbasket if the truth about his death got out. They blew up their poster boy.

His mother, Mary Tillman, told the *Post*:

> The military let him down. The administration let him down. It was a sign of disrespect. The fact that he was the ultimate team player and he watched his own men kill him is absolutely heartbreaking and tragic. The fact that they lied about it afterward is disgusting. . . . The truth may be painful, but it's the truth. You start to contrive all these scenarios that could have taken place because they just kept lying. If you feel you're being lied to, you can never put it to rest.

Post reporter Josh White noted that Mary Tillman "was particularly offended when President Bush offered a taped memorial message to Tillman at a Cardinals football game [October 2004] shortly before the presidential election last fall." He reported, "She again felt as though her son was being used, something he never would have wanted."

In March 2006, the Pentagon initiated a criminal investigation into causes and cover-up of Spc. Tillman's death. One year later, the Inspector General of the Department of Defense said that nine officers, including four generals, should be held accountable for inappropriate conduct. Among the concerns were a failure to pursue all facts, a failure to properly and quickly inform Spc. Tillman's family, and failure to inform superior officers of the nature of the death from "friendly fire." None were court martialed. Seven enlisted soldiers had previously received relatively minor punishment for their part in the cover-up, but none were court martialed.

The Army later modified the wording on Tillman's Silver Star citation but didn't rescind it. "The award of the Silver Star," said Tillman's parents, "appears more than anything to be part of a cynical design to conceal the real events from family but most especially from the public while exploiting the death of our beloved Pat as a recruitment poster." They noted that "Emails discovered in the conduct of investigations refer to a 'Silver Star Game Plan.' This certainly at least suggests conspiracy."

The Tillman family issued an official statement that in "three years of struggling with the Pentagon's public relations apparatus, we have never been dealt with honestly." They accused the military of "a conspiracy to deceive." Included in that con-

406

spiracy were changes to an eyewitness's report. In April 2007, three years after Spc. Tillman was killed by "friendly fire," Pete Geren, acting secretary of the Army, acknowledged, "We as an Army failed in our duty to the Tillman family, the duty we owe to all the families of our fallen soldiers: Give them the truth, the best we know it, as fast as we can." It was only a partial apology, one directed to the family; the government never acknowledged that a deliberate campaign to spin the truth to meet political needs was also not acceptable.

In response to a bipartisan request by the House Oversight Committee in July 2007 for documents that could have revealed what happened, and why, and could have shown collusion between the White House and Pentagon to politicize Tillman's death and then to cover up their own actions, President Bush refused to turn over those documents. He cited "executive confidentiality" as his reason. White House counsel Fred Fielding said that the Department of Defense and staff in the White House had already turned over more than 10,000 pages. However, most of those documents were copies of press clippings. Committee Chair Henry Waxman (D-Calif.) and Ranking Member Tom Davis (R-Va.) wrote Fielding, "The document production from the White House sheds virtually no light on these matters." To certain documents Fielding did provide, extensive sections were blacked out, with Fielding claiming those portions reflected "purely internal e-mails between White House personnel." Both Waxman and Davis responded that the reasons Fielding cited "are not appropriate reasons for withholding the documents." The Department of Defense refused to provide any correspondence about Pat Tillman sent from or to Gen. John Abizaid, commander of Central Command at the time of Tillman's death.

The use of propaganda by the American government isn't new. Every president, to one extent or the other, has tried to modify public opinion; some even violated the Constitution by imposing select forms of censorship. In 1917, shortly after a razor-thin second term victory, Woodrow Wilson had considered taking the advice of his senior military staff to impose censorship upon the nation. World War I, at that time known as "The Great War," and confined to Europe, had been going on for three years; the nation was divided by those who wanted the United States to enter the war, and peace groups and isolation-ists who didn't. Mass rallies by both sides threatened the any kind of reasoned and peaceful discussion.

George Creel, a veteran investigative journalist and a friend of Wilson's, convinced the President not to listen to the military, but to try a new approach. "Expression not repression" was what Creel believed would unite the country and maintain the spirit of the First Amendment. The result of Creel's pleading was the creation of the Committee on Public Information (CPI). Its purpose was to influence public opinion to accept and then promote the entry of the United States into the war. The CPI created a multi-faceted operation that became the base of modern propaganda and public relations. During its two years of existence, the CPI wrote and spun news, established a nation-wide poster campaign, promoted the sale of war bonds, and created a speakers bureau with more than 75,000 persons who gave four-minute rallying speeches. Underlying the program was the creation of a nation of hate, a campaign to dehumanize and demonize Germans. Its tactics included persuading the young film industry to produce anti-German movies, some of which depicted Germans bayoneting children.

By World War II, all sides had become master propagandists. Once again, the U.S. set a base of speeches and posters to convince Americans why it was in their best interest for the nation to enter World War II. However, it was Nazi Germany, with Joseph Goebbels, whose title was the minister of public enlightenment and propaganda, who used the base established within the U.S. two decades earlier to establish what media professionals recognize as the greatest propaganda campaign in history. At the age of 24, Goebbels had earned a Ph.D. in literature from Heidelberg University. He became a reporter and playwright, but his reputation would be intertwined with Hitler, who considered the intellectual Goebbels one of his closest friends and advisors. As had the U.S. in World War I, Goebbels used rallies, speakers, newspapers, magazines, posters, and film to reach the masses, but now he also had the use of the newly-developed radio medium, which would unite a divided nation. That unity would be based upon a lesson he learned

~~~~~~~~~

The engineering of consent is the very essence of the democratic process, the freedom to persuade and suggest.
—Edward L. Bernays, *The Engineering of Consent*, 1947

from the Americans—just as the Americans had demonized Germans to rally public support, he needed those whom he could blame for Germany's economic problems. Nazi Germany's "final solution" to its problems would be to eliminate Jews. Ironically, Goebbel's two closest advisors while he was a student were Jews.

In the November 11, 1758, issue of England's *The Idler*, Samuel Johnson wrote: "Among the calamities of war, may be justly numbered the diminution of the love of truth, by the falsehoods which interest dictates, and credulity encourages." A more succinct version was stated in 1918. In the Senate of the United States, during the last year of World War I, and under Democrat Woodrow Wilson, Sen. Hiram Johnson (R-Calif.) lamented that "the first casualty when war comes is truth." There is nothing that has been done by any ruler, at any time in history, to have disputed the words of the two men named Johnson.

Creating a Best-Seller

Nothing is more pathetic than an author sitting at a card table surrounded by unsold copies of his latest book while watching humanity pass by in front of a book store in a crowded mall.

For several days every year, I'm pathetic.

Potential readers turn their eyes away, picking up their pace as they jog past the card table, avoiding me as if I were the lead locust in the upcoming 14-year plague. With humor, sarcasm, even pleading, I call to them. Most have innovative reasons why they don't stop. "Got other shopping to do," they mumble as they head to the Dollar Store. "I'll be back," they lie. But people do wander into bookstores.

In 2008, about 75,000 publishers brought out about 250,000 new titles and editions, according to the R. R. Bowker Co.; consumers spent about $34.6 billion for new books, including about $8.8 billion on general trade books, according to a survey conducted by the Book Industry Study Group (BISG). Americans also spent about $2.2 billion for 111 million used books, according to BISG. However, they also spent about $62 billion for every kind of cosmetic, $90 billion on liquor, and $300–500 billion on gambling in all forms.

About 26,000 places in America—including drug stores, grocery stores, and even bookstores—sell books. A mall store, such as B. Dalton or Waldenbooks, might stock 20,000–40,000 copies; a 25,000 square foot Barnes & Noble or Borders superstore, in its own building outside a mall, might not only have a coffee shop and music store, but also more than 100,000 copies of books. Among those copies, sometimes shelved spine-out, sometimes buried in unopened cartons with other titles, are some I have written. But, for book signings, the stores make sure there are flyers, posters, a card table and chair up front, and books on display. It usually doesn't cost them much; publishers help pay for the newspaper and radio ads to promote a signing. If the books don't sell after a few weeks, bookstores, which usually get a 40–50 percent discount—the distributors which sell the books to bookstores usually take another 10–20 percent—can return them to publishers for full credit.

But, first, the books have to be on the shelves. Food distributors pay for shelf space in supermarkets; book publishers don't have to pay for space on most shelves in bookstores, but if they want premium space—books at the end of an aisle, stand-up cardboard displays near the front of the store, mini-"dumps" on counters, floor space for a 50-copy display—they pay, sometimes as much as $10,000 a month for premium space in chain stores. The thinking, of course, is that people see a lot of books in a favorable spot and will buy because they think others are buying.

Publishers who don't pay for premium position can lure bookstores to carry their titles by offering contests and premiums—everything from free books and deep discounts to plush stuffed animals and vacation cruises. Random House didn't have to do much to have the nation's bookstores carry Tom Brokaw's *The Greatest Generation* (1998), interviews with Americans who lived through World War II. But, to make sure the book got decent exposure, the publisher created a contest—bookstores would compete for the best book displays. The winner would receive 200 free books, as well as a special guest appearance by Brokaw who was not touring the country to promote the book. He didn't have to; he was on almost every early morning and late night TV news, entertainment, and talk show, did radio satellite tours, and an AOL chat session. More than two million copies of *The Greatest Generation* were in print by the end of its second year of publication. Brokaw later wrote *Boom!: Voices of the Sixties Personal Reflections on the '60s and Today* (2007).

Daisy Maryles of *Publishers Weekly* said that "the operative word for non-fiction [best-sellers] is platform—authors need to be famous in another field; they need to be experts in the subject they are writing on; they need access to the media or, even better, to *be* the media." Increasing the possibility of a booking are the publicists who have innumerable personal and professional contacts with the shows. With the exception of columnists—publishers are reluctant to publish collections of columns, no matter how popular the writers are—a byline with one of the nation's top-circulation metro dailies can lead to a lucrative book contract. Better, being on television also helps assures publication and sales.

It's not hard to promote a book by a celebrity, especially one annointed by *People* or the *National Enquirer*. And, even the most novice book publicist can get promotion for Stephen King, Tom Clancy, and Nora Roberts. They can also get a warm, fuzzy feeling when their companies' books about sex, sin, and diets sell better than anything else on the list. With the industry spending seven-figure royalty advances and six-figure promotion budgets on just a few authors, most authors don't even get a chance to see their books published, no matter how well written and insightful. Those that are published are usually hidden in a promotion budget the size of a Wall Street stocks salesman's conscience. Book promotion is now author-driven as fewer publishers are putting the resources into pushing books. It's just not cost-effective to push all books, say the corporate minds. So, just as all America has had to learn to be part of a self-serve nation—they now pump their own gas, and scan and bag their own groceries—authors now have to do most of the promotion. Because of the lack of significant promotion for all but the "probable" best-sellers, midlist authors and non-celebrities have been forced to spend more time promoting their books than writing them. It's not unusual for authors to take their entire advance—few royalty advances top $10,000, and many are in the $1,000–$2,000 range—and go into credit card debt to hire publicists, or to develop their own publicity, hoping the resulting royalties justify the costs. They seldom do. The success of a book is often dependent upon the knowledge and ability of the author to generate promotional opportunities.

Authors use innumerable ways to get recognition. They buy thousands of inexpensive four-color bookmarks, postcards, one-sheet flyers, even refrigerator door magnets that are imprinted

411

with the cover of their book. I usually include a bookmark or postcard in every envelope I send, especially ones going to places that send me bills or which include self-addressed postage-paid envelopes to respond to pleas for money. J.A. Konrath, author of *Whiskey Sour* (2004), even bought 10,000 coasters, each imprinted with the cover of his book, to hand out to everyone he met who worked in a bookstore, was a reviewer, or could be a customer. Other authors buy imprinted keychains, note pads, and miniature flashlights—anything that could even remotely tie into their titles. One author pasted pages from her book onto her naked body; others have pasted their messages onto balloons, beer bottles, and blimps.

Authors will call any organization that might have any kind of connection to their title—a coffee table book about moose in America, for example, might lead to calls and letters to hundreds of Moose lodges. Authors have also hawked books in beauty salons, sports bars, and farmer's markets.

At least three to four months before publication, publishers send to the media advance review copies (sometimes known as uncorrected galleys or bound galleys, especially if it isn't a finished product for sale) and media kits, complete with hyperventilated "news" releases, trinkets, and solicited "blurbs" from a coterie of authors who are friends or bound by the informal expectations of being published by the same conglomerate.

Most of the major trade books for Fall distribution are previewed in May at a four-day BookExpo, attended by more than 25,000 booksellers, publishers, authors, vendors, and the major mass media. At this convention, with big-name celebrities, "publishers suck up to booksellers by seeming to include them in the glamorous, glitzy world of big-time publishing," wrote Sara Nelson in the *New York Observer*. She explained that publishers will invite the booksellers "to splashy cocktail parties with their star authors, schedule intimate private dinners and join them for nightcaps at tony hotels." During those few days in May, publishers pile on freebies of every kind to entice the booksellers. "It's not unusual to see a bookseller at 9:45 a.m. haul three tote bags full of galleys, buttons, T-shirts and other give-aways to his car [or storage area in the convention center] . . . then rush back inside to gather up more," wrote Nelson. For the other 51 weeks a year, according to Nelson, publishers would "sooner lunch and sup and party with each other—and, of course, complain that the business has become so repetitive, so insular that you see the same 20 people everywhere you go—than with mere merchants."

At the 2002 convention, an aerialist and a prostitute lured book buyers. Phillippe Petit walked a high wire to promote *To Reach the Clouds: My High Wire Walk Between the Twin Towers*. But his feat was overshadowed inside the convention center. Heidi Fleiss, whose client list included some of the more prominent celebrities and business people in Los Angeles, found out that a notorious reputation can lead to the best-sellers list. Fleiss introduced the concept of a book about her life as a society madam. Like more than 2,000 publishers and vendors, she rented space for a booth. But, unlike publishers and vendors, she created a faux-bordello in her space, and staffed it with college-age models to lure authors, journalists, booksellers, industry vendors, and publishing and distribution company personnel to her booth. "I'm a businesswomen. I know how to sell things, and I know sex sells," Fleiss told *Publishers Weekly*. Not long after the show ended, Fleiss had a major distributor for *Pandering* (2003), her $50 text-and-photo book that detailed more of her life than the lurid details of the who-was-doing-what-to-whom book that publishers and the public preferred. While hundreds of booksellers say they were shocked at Fleiss's display, some cynical journalists saw no problem with having a mock-brothel at a booksellers convention. After all, they reasoned, the industry had long ago prostituted itself to the dominance of marketing and promotion over substance.

Independent book reviews can help spur sales. It makes little difference if the review is positive, negative, or insipid since a basic dictum of promotion is that any ink is good ink as long as the name is spelled correctly. For most major publishers, primary targets are the major trade publications, among them *Publishers Weekly, Kirkus Reviews, Booklist*, and the *New York Review of Books*. However, getting the major book review media to consider a book is often based not upon book quality but whether the author or publisher is willing to put together a heavy financial package to push the book.

"What we choose to review or not is based on maybe the kind of buzz a book is getting pre-publication," Robert J. Hughes, *Wall Street Journal* senior book critic, told an Authors Guild meeting in January 2003.

Also affecting book sales, especially for midlist authors, are the cutbacks by daily newspapers in all areas, from reporters and copyeditors to news pages. Dropping or cutting back book review sections became an easy choice for many newspaper publishers when book publishers began trimming their own advertising budgets, and then budgeting the remainder on other forms of advertising and promotion.

Print ads are often placed more for the author's ego, and often to let the major chains and others in the publishing industry know that the publisher is supporting a specific title, than any significant sales benefit to the consumer. Because of the nature of the industry, publishers may often turn to online promotion in any of several hundred sites. Although the Internet now has a greater reach than any other medium, the effectiveness of book sales generated by internet advertising, except for specific target audiences, is questionable. There are hundreds of sites, both print and online, that specifically review books or which include book reviews for budget-challenged publishers and authors; the only payment necessary is a free copy of the book and a reasonably-produced media kit.

On a day when I was selling a couple of dozen books in Wilkes-Barre, Pa., radio shock jock Howard Stern was two hours away in Philadelphia deluged by 15,000 sales of *Miss America*. Stern's one-day sale was significantly ahead of Gen. Colin Powell, who had received a $6.5 million advance for his autobiography, and managed a one-day sale of almost 3,500 copies; and Speaker of the House Newt Gingrich whose best one-day sale was 1,800 copies, still about 50–100 times more than the average writer sells at a bookstore stop.

Unless the author is a celebrity, there's usually no one waiting in line. It's up to the author to generate the interest. On occasion, I have hired a struggling local musician, magician, or clown to attract small crowds. Often, a bowl of candy may attract potential customers, some of whom think it's mighty nice of the bookstore to provide them with a handful of miniature candy bars for lunch. Some authors bring in wine and cheese for more formal receptions. Many will wear special T-shirts with imprints of their book cover, sometimes a baseball cap or even a specially-made pin related to the book's theme. Sometimes, we bring in shills who, in exchange for pizza and beer, stand around the card table and pretend to be enchanted by whatever it is the author is saying, leave for a few minutes, and then return as a new *persona*; nothing attracts buyers like small crowds. Usually, it's just me and the mall walkers.

Holding whatever book I'm trying to sell, I pitch the passing parade with a steady patter of whatever I hope might work, drawing amused smiles and a few sales. I've suggested that my latest book *might* be the recipe for better physical fitness since hefting two copies of my book—one for them, one for a friend—*could* replace having to buy dumbbells. Once, I patiently explained to three women on a quest for an "all-you-can-eat-and-still-lose-weight" book that the store had sent all its diet books to the bindery since the dust made the books too fat to sell. "Do you know when they'll be back?" one of the ladies sweetly asked before she realized the hoax.

Personal contact is one of the best ways to generate individual sales; it's also not cost-effective for publishers. Thus, only the "biggest names" are supported by publishers. It took two good selling books by J.A. Konrath before his publisher agreed to pay for gas mileage and hotel accomodations for his Summer/Fall 2006 book tour for *Rusty Nail*. Konrath's plan was to stop at 500 bookstores during his cross-country tour, generating sales, goodwill with booksellers—and media publicity that would lead to additional sales.

On any given day, hundreds of writers, unsupported by their publishing houses, are on the road, using creative intelligence to find gimmicks to sell copies to everyone from gas station attendants to independent bookstore owners. They give dozens of speeches—to clubs, schools, and every kind of readers club. Most authors have websites and blogs; many even have their own fan clubs, even if the only members are relatives and friends.

Unlike celebrity authors who fly first class and stay in five-star hotels, mid-list authors tour in their vans or RVs, stay in campgrounds, inexpensive motels, or with friends and relatives, pay for most of their expenses, and personally hand out flyers, bookmarks, bumper stickers, or other trinkets to entice readers.

The modern book tour was probably the creation of Jacqueline Susann (1918–1974). She had been a B-list actress and advertising copywriter/producer before she began a writing career. Ronald Preston, assigned to edit Susann's manuscript, as quoted in *Lovely Me: The Life of Jacqueline Susann* (1996), by Barbara Seaman, said Susann was "a painfully dull, inept, clumsy, undisciplined, and thoroughly amateurish writer. . . . I really don't think there is a page of this [manuscript] that can stand in its present form. And after it is done, we will be left with a faster, slicker, more readable mediocrity."

But, what Susann had was the desire to hustle herself and her books—and the advice and direction of husband Irving Mansfield, one of the nation's better press agents, who stuck by her although she was abusive, demanding, and had innumerable affairs. To promote herself and her books, Susann brought coffee and doughnuts to drivers who were delivering her books, went on TV talk shows, and then went throughout the country, from bookstore to bookstore, largely unsupported by her publisher, to hype sales. *Valley of the Dolls* (1966), her second book, has sold about 30 million copies, making the fictionalized tell-all about sex, drugs and Hollywood the best-selling novel in history. A movie version the following year and an updated made-for-TV film in 1981 spurred book sales. Susann followed up *Valley of the Dolls* with *The Love Machine (1969), Once Is Not Enough (1973),* and *Dolores (1976),* each of which also was poorly-written, required extensive editing, was extensively hyped, and reached best-sellers lists.

One of the most effective forms of promotion is electronic media. Because author personality is often more important than substance, authors fine-tune a "spiel" and hit the radio and television book circuit. Appearances on major talk-shows, even if for only a few minutes, can generate sales of at least 2,000–10,000 copies.

It isn't unusual for an appearance on the nationally-syndicated "Oprah" to generate several hundred thousand sales. Authors and publicists with schmaltzy titles directed to the women's 25–55 year old age group, the primary demographic of book buyers, swamp the production staff with news releases, press kits, galleys, bound proofs, books, and uncountable trinkets to get the talk show host to consider the book for her book club—or at least mention it on air.

Radio interviews conducted by phone allow authors to sit at home or in the office and spout witticisms half a continent away. Authors don't even have to be present in TV studios. With satellite technology, authors can show up at their publishers' or publicists' offices, step before a camera in a mini-studio, and be seen instantly on any TV station in the country. Often, a best-selling author will spend an entire day in a studio being interviewed by one news host after another, each TV station claiming an "exclusive" interview. The host doesn't even need to be there. In a publicity studio, the author merely answers questions a publicist writes; the answers are electronically sent to the TV station where the reporter-anchor-host does the set-up, asks the prepared questions, receives the pre-recorded answers, and then closes the interview. Although most TV stations stop short of electronically putting the author and host into the same frame, most *will* establish the interview so it *appears* the station's on-air talent really is interviewing the author.

The easiest way to get radio and television promotion for a book is to be a nationally-known celebrity. TV producers, often in their 20s, want to meet celebrities; and the TV hosts themselves often think they are in the same social circles as other celebrities. Celebrities can afford personal publicists; most authors can't. The going rate for a publicist to set up just one city for an author tour is anywhere from $500 to $2,500. For that fee, the author usually gets a package that includes radio, TV, and bookstore appearances; it may also include a newspaper blurb or feature, depending upon how easy it is to influence journalists in that particular city. Although few producers from the major radio and TV infotainment shows seriously consider books not pitched by major publishers and publicists, non-celebrity authors who are persistent can often get producers from radio and TV stations in small and mid-size markets to book them for a few minutes of what is usually interesting and informative on-air discussion.

If you're a celebrity or pro athlete writing a memoir, inspirational book, or even a novel, the odds are good that success in one medium will be transferred to another—and then snapped up by radio/TV producers who see higher ratings dangling before them.

"These days, it's nearly impossible to make a splash on the paperback bestseller charts if the author isn't already a known entity, the book isn't part of an established brand and/or Oprah hasn't given the title a nod," executive editor Daisy Maryles wrote in the March 19, 2001, issue of *Publishers Weekly*. Flippantly, but accurately, she also pointed out, "Heck, it's hard to get any attention without these elements in hardcover, too, but you can sometimes get lucky on that list with a news hook or a great review."

During the 19th century, major American novels were first serialized in national magazines. It gave publishers the opportunity to judge reader reaction before committing to a major hard cover distribution; it gave readers a chance to look over new stories before buying the hardcover editions. Few books are serialized in the 21st century, but publicists and editors often try to get magazines to excerpt a few thousand words in one of the issues.

The development of the Internet, the ubiquitous presence of computers in homes and offices, and the development of lightweight e-readers with reader-friendly display screens, as well as technology that allows books to be downloaded to cell phones, iPods, and BlackBerries, have freed authors and publishers from the heavy costs of production of bound editions. For a small fee, readers can download books from e-publisher web sites; for a few dollars more, they can purchase paperback editions at prices significantly below those necessary for profitable bookstore distribution. Annual wholesale e-book revenue of the 15 larger e-book publishers in 2008 was about $52.4 million, about 10 times revenue in 2002, according to the International Digital Publishing Forum. Related to e-book publishing is the development of web-based promotion. Promotion on social network sites—among them Facebook, YouTube, MySpace, and Twitter—have resulted in more specific targets and lower promotion costs.

Publishers have learned that direct mail campaigns can be more effective and cost-efficient than heavy media placement and a briefcase of money to get books into stores and authors onto tours. Direct mail/print—known as "junk mail" by most Americans not in advertising—can cost as much as $1 per piece, with design, printing, labor, and postage figured into the cost. The response is usually 2–5 percent, even for a targeted audience; an effective campaign requires a large address database. Direct mail/electronic, known as "spam," costs only a penny or so a message. Brokers can provide specialized lists of just a couple of thousand names to general lists of several million recipients. Even if two-thirds of all recipients delete the message without opening it, there are still a few hundred thousand left who will get that message and, maybe, respond.

The proliferation of the available titles, the cut-backs in promotion for all but the top titles, and the necessity of all authors to promote a title has also changed the dynamics of their relationships with journalists. At one time, the critics and feature writers enjoyed talking with authors. Now they not only avoid authors—except, of course, for nationally known author-journalists and TV personalities and those whose front-list titles appear on the best-sellers lists—but often answer calls only from publicists. It seems only reasonable since the Marketing department, rather than Editorial, often decides what is publishable; bookstores usually buy on the basis of promotional campaigns. Bob Minzesheimer of *USA Today* says that having authors talk to him isn't appreciated. "If I'm hearing directly from an author, it's not a good sign," he told Salon.com in 2002. Jonathan Yardley of the *Washington Post* agrees. "I really, really, really don't like authors to contact me," Yardley sniffed, emphasizing that dealing with publicists is preferred because, he claimed, they're professionals and serve as a "sieve, a filter, to the process" of which books to review.

One author, whom most book critics would love to have contact them, however, is J. D. Salinger who went into a publicity exile after publication of *Catcher in the Rye* in 1951. It's possible that Salinger believed a work should stand on its own; it's also probable that had he sent in the manuscript during the past two decades, many publishers would have rejected it, especially if Salinger indicated he had no intention of doing author tours and TV appearances.

When William Faulkner won the Nobel Prize for Literature in 1948, every one of his novels, none of which had sold more than 2,000 copies, was out of print. In 1995, *Beavis and Butt-head's Ensucklopedia* sold more than 400,000 copies, more than books by critically-acclaimed authors Peter Benchley, E. L. Doctorow, Joseph Heller, Jack Higgins, John Irving, James Michener, and Herman Wouk.

Scarlett, by Alexandra Ripley, the officially authorized sequel to Margaret Mitchell's *Gone With the Wind*, supported by a $600,000 promotion budget from Warner Books, hit the best-sellers charts in 1991 despite almost universal condemnation by the critics. Molly Ivans in *The New York Times* called the book "seriously awful." The *New Orleans Times-Picayune* called it "dreadful." However, it was *TIME* that summarized what the book industry had become during the previous decade—"The deal came first, the writer came second, and then the publicity

419

machine passed them all." The book sold more than two million copies, and was turned into a six hour TV miniseries in 1994.

In contrast to Ripley and the sale of books that may not be well-written but hyped and sold by myriad promotion techniques and budgets as if a book was nothing more than "product," is John Updike, who earned two Pulitzer Prizes for fiction. In May 2006, at the annual BookExpo convention, Updike told booksellers he believed "the written word was supposed to speak for itself and sell itself" without massive author promotion.

About 80 percent of all Americans say they want to write a book, according to a study done in 2002 by the Jenkins Group. About one-fourth of all Americans believe they can write a novel. "We're in an information-oriented society," says Jerrold Jenkins, "and technology today allows people to share their ideas quickly with a wider audience than anyone could have imagined a year ago."

For those wanna-be writers, many of whom can boast only that they're excellent typists, appearances on the "Today Show" and a yacht docked at their private resort are only illusions. For most, even those who receive excellent critical acclaim for their books, keeping a day-job is a necessity. Of the 45,000– 60,000 works of fiction published each year, the average first novel sells 500–1,000 copies, not enough for either the author, who usually earns about 10 percent of the book's list price, or publisher to make any money.

Nothing I have ever written—and nothing I ever plan to write—is heading to a best-sellers list. With a few exceptions— such as Rachel Carson's *Silent Spring* (1962) and Ralph Nader's *Unsafe at Any Speed* (1966)—social issues journalism, even well-written and supported by aggressive marketing, just doesn't reach anywhere close to best-seller status. One time, I tried to explain to a 40ish woman overcome by peroxide and makeup that my book of short columns—"It's a perfect bathroom book!"—was a humorous look at some serious social issues; but she slapped me with reality—"Oh, no! I wouldn't be able to sleep if I read your book. Those kind make me so upset."

"Go ahead, try it!" I implored. "I've even read it twice myself." When there was only a blank look, I sent her into the section on Romances.

From mall-sitting, I realized that the peroxided, made-up 40ish lady who said she didn't read social issues book was right.

The public wants books about social issues about as much as the impoverished living in tenements want roaches. What the people want—and usually only if hyped on a TV show—are how-to, self-help, and celebrity tell-all books, as well as books about cooking, computers, diets and exercise, and sex and intimacy. And, they want it to be a "page-turner." None of that languid character build-up stuff for our fast-paced MTV Society/ Information Age worker. I'll soon be starting my next book, a guaranteed best-seller, *How to Quickly Be Your Own Best Friend on TV Talk Shows While Using Facebook to Learn the Sensual Intimate Secrets of Baking Diet Pornographic Cookies with Jennifer Aniston and Barack Obama.*

. . . Or, maybe, I'll just call it *Sex and the Single Beer Can.*

~~~~~~~~~

"The news media blew the coverage of the Iraq invasion, spoon-feeding us lies masquerading as fact-checked verities. They missed the past decade of corporate scandals. They cheered on the housing bubble and genuflected before the financial sector (and Gilded Age levels of wealth and inequality) as it blasted debt and speculation far beyond what the real economy could sustain. Today they do almost no investigation into where the trillions of public dollars being spent by the Federal Reserve and Treasury are going but spare not a moment to update us on the 'Octomom.' They trade in trivia and reduce everything to spin, even matters of life and death."

—John Nichols and Robert McChesney, "The Death and Life of Great American Newspapers," *The Nation* (March 31, 2009)

About the Author

Walter M. Brasch, Ph.D., a former newspaper reporter and editor, is a university professor of journalism and mass communications, and a syndicated newspaper columnist.

He is also the author of 16 other books, most of them focusing upon the fusion of historical and contemporary social issues, including *Black English and the Mass Media* (1981); *Forerunners of Revolution: Muckrakers and the American Social Conscience* (1991); *With Just Cause: The Unionization of the American Journalist* (1991); *Brer Rabbit, Uncle Remus, and the 'Cornfield Journalist': The Tale of Joel Chandler Harris* (2000), *The Joy of Sax: America During the Bill Clinton Era* (2001), *America's Unpatriotic Acts: The Federal Government's Violation of Constitutional and Civil Rights* (2005), *'Unacceptable': The Federal Response to Hurricane Katrina* (2006); and *Sinking the Ship of State: The Presidency of George W. Bush* (2008). He is also co-author of *The Press and the State* (1986), awarded Outstanding Academic Book distinction by *Choice* magazine, published by the American Library Association. He is also the author of the more than 200 magazine and journal articles, writer-producer of 25 multimedia productions, and was a copywriter and account executive, specializing in political, entertainment, and social issues. His community service includes work as a public information specialist for nonprofit disaster relief organizations. He is a founding board member of the Northeast Pennsylvania Homeless Alliance.

During the past two decades, he has won more than 150 regional and national media awards from the National Society of Newspaper Columnists, Society of Professional Journalists, National Federation of Press Women, Pennsylvania Press Club, Pennsylvania Women's Press Association, Pennwriters, and other organizations.

He is a co-recipient of the Civil Liberties Award of the American Civil Liberties Union, 1996; and was honored by San Diego

423

State University as a Points of Excellence winner in 1997. At Bloomsburg University, he earned the Creative Arts Award, the Creative Teaching Award, and was named an Outstanding Student Advisor. He was honored with the Martin Luther King Jr. Award for Humanitarian Service, and is the first recipient of the Dean's Award for Excellence, recognizing superior teaching and research/writing. For the Pennsylvania Humanities Council, he was a Commonwealth Speaker.

He is president of the Pennsylvania Press Club; previously, he was president of the Keystone State professional chapter and deputy regional director of the Society of Professional Journalists, from which he received the Director's Award and the National Freedom of Information Award. He is founding coordinator of Pennsylvania Journalism Educators, and is a member of the National Society of Newspaper Columnists, Author's Guild, National Writers Union (UAW/AFL-CIO), and The Newspaper Guild (CWA/AFL-CIO), as well as national scholarship honorary organizations Phi Kappa Phi (general scholarship), Kappa Tau Alpha (journalism), Alpha Kappa Delta (sociology), and Pi Gamma Mu (social sciences.)

Dr. Brasch is featured columnist for *Liberal Opinion Week*, consulting editor for the *American Reporter*, senior editor for *OpEdNews*, and a member of the editorial board of the *Journal of Media Law and Ethics*.

He is listed in *Who's Who in America, Contemporary Authors*, and *Who's Who in the Media*. Dr. Brasch earned an A.B. in sociology from San Diego State College, an M.A. in journalism from Ball State University, and a Ph.D. in mass communication/journalism, with cognate areas in American government and language and culture studies, from The Ohio University.

Visit Dr. Brasch's web site at
http://www.walterbrasch.com